From Concept to Customer:

Portfolio, Pipeline, and Strategic

Project Management

From Concept to Customer:

Portfolio, Pipeline, and Strategic

Project Management

By Michael J. Termini

Society of Manufacturing Engineers
Dearborn, Michigan

987654321

Library of Congress Catalog Card Number: 2009924030
International Standard Book Number: 0-87263-861-8
ISBN 13: 978-087263-861-7

Additional copies may be obtained by contacting:
Society of Manufacturing Engineers
Customer Service
One SME Drive, P.O. Box 930
Dearborn, Michigan 48121
1-800-733-4763
www.sme.org

SME staff who participated in producing this book:
Rosemary Csizmadia, Senior Production Editor
Jerome Cook, Cover Concept
Mark Moten, Cover Design
Frances Kania, Production Assistant

Printed in the United States of America

No one can undertake a project like this without the support of a loving and understanding family. It is no different for me. I want to dedicate this book to my wife, Susan, and our four children for their unwavering support throughout the project. And, as always, my appreciation to my parents for giving me the courage to constantly undertake new challenges, and for their love and support throughout my life.

My thanks, too, to all of the project managers I have worked with over the last many years for their dedication to the projects and the organizations that they serve. I wish you all much success in your careers.

Table of Contents

About the Author

Michael J. Termini is President & CEO of The Consulting Alliance Group, Inc. He has over 40 years of pragmatic industry experience, holding executive management positions with corporations like United Technologies, Hallmark Cards, Dresser Industries, PACCAR, Johnson & Johnson, and numerous government agencies around the world. Author of *The New Manufacturing Engineer* (SME 1997), *Strategic Project Management* (SME 1999), and *Walking the Talk: Moving Into Leadership* (SME 2007), Termini has also written over 100 articles and training programs in the fields of management and leadership, business process improvement, strategic planning, concurrent engineering, integrated product development, agile manufacturing, and organizational reengineering. Michael Termini holds an MBA in Marketing from the University of Missouri-Kansas City and a BS in Aerospace Engineering from the University of Missouri-Rolla. He is a frequent lecturer and management trainer at numerous universities and professional organizations, including the Society of Manufacturing Engineers. Termini also has been featured as a host and guest speaker for numerous live television broadcasts for PBS, NTU, and FTN.

Preface

Each year, in my capacity as president of The Consulting Alliance Group, I deal with literally thousands of project managers from all over the world who have never been given even rudimentary training for their assignments. For some odd reason, there is a misguided belief that anyone with the ability to perform well in his or her usual business environment can naturally slip into the role of a project manager, with little or no preparation. As a result, many a good individual contributor has seen his successful track record (or even career) go up in smoke from just one unsuccessful assignment as a project manager. That's what motivated me to write *Strategic Project Management: Tools and Techniques for Planning, Decision Making, and Implementation* (SME 1999), which was aimed at providing insight into various methodologies to help project managers effectively plan and execute projects, control risks, and make the right decisions. This new book is based upon the 1999 book and our work on a global scale with both novice and veteran project managers who have come to us seeking assistance. As a result, it incorporates a much broader, comprehensive perspective of project management, covering the entire concept-to-customer cycle of complex strategic projects.

As our projects have reached an international scope, it has become apparent that the problems plaguing our domestic projects are also reflected in the projects undertaken by our international counterparts. So to all of our associates around the globe, I hope you enjoy this new book and that it proves invaluable in your efforts to successfully plan and implement your projects.

Good luck and best wishes to you all!

Introduction

Project management in today's global markets requires an entirely new blend of management and technical skills. The project manager of the 21st Century can no longer be solely the technical or business expert in charge of a particular product, service, or functional activity. To successfully manage increasingly complex, broadly cross-functional projects, the project manager must possess numerous other attributes. For example:

- the ability to understand and develop strategic organizational objectives, along with the tactical skills to ensure their successful implementation;
- marketing skills to accurately assess the customers' explicit and implicit requirements, and then to effectively prioritize them;
- organizational skills to select, motivate and, when necessary, discipline personnel from diverse organizational and functional groups to ensure that they can work together to attain established project objectives;
- the ability to develop and implement proactive project management control processes to ensure that the project remains on schedule and on budget;
- acumen to manage time so that it works for, rather than against, the project team;
- follow-through to ensure that corrective actions are taken quickly and decisively, thus guaranteeing that the project objectives are never compromised; and
- courage and foresight to make decisions, in the face of politics, functional resistance, and/or confrontation.

Truly great project managers have learned how to ignite interest and excitement in members of their project teams while motivating them to succeed in even the most difficult project and business environments. They do so through their individual leadership skills, as they are rarely granted the formal position with which to influence changes in organizational cultures, policies, or procedures. These successful project managers have learned that while it is impossible to "manage" individuals who do not report directly to them, it is possible to achieve the required individual and collective results from their team members through effective leadership.

My intent in writing this book is to examine and document methods for developing and employing critical project management skills in an organization, irrespective of industry segment; to follow the project cycle from concept to customer including all aspects of planning and control. The emphasis is on providing novice and seasoned project managers alike with insight into real-world, practical applications from more than 40 years of hands-on experience with world-class multinational organizations. The techniques herein are proven, the approach sound, and the results measurable and significant.

Case studies have been taken directly from client files. They illustrate the application of various project management strategies, as well as strategic and tactical planning tools. Client names have been withheld to ensure confidentiality. Their stories are, nonetheless, critically important to demonstrate the effectiveness of the tools and techniques explained in this book, and to highlight the potential for results.

Among the topics included in this book are:

- portfolio and pipeline management techniques as the drivers of strategic projects;
- the development and application of comprehensive project planning tools;
- the development of proactive, quantitative risk management tools that are both forward and backward looking, identifying existing and potential failure modes throughout the life cycle of the project;

- traits of and leadership techniques used by successful project managers;
- the importance of alignment and balance in creating the project team—how to select, control, and motivate the diverse talents required for the project management team;
- the common and predictable mistakes made by project managers and their teams that lead to early failure of their projects;
- the importance of "under-committing and over-delivering" on project expectations—incorporating into the project scope the explicit and implicit project expectations established by senior management and customers;
- the importance of alignment assurance between project expectations and the project team's ability to deliver them;
- why establishing results-oriented project performance metrics guarantees measurable results;
- effective acquisition planning to minimize one of the largest single predictable failure modes in most projects;
- techniques in comprehensive budget planning and cost control;
- fundamental process control techniques that will help keep the project on budget and on schedule;
- avoidance of perception problems through effective communications planning;
- integrating quality management techniques into project compliance planning to ensure acceptance of the project results;
- tools to use in building an accurate and useful tactical project plan utilizing work breakdown structures (WBS), the critical path method (CPM), program evaluation and review technique (PERT), graphical evaluation and review technique (GERT), and Gantt charts;
- using cycle time management techniques to aid in achieving quantifiable results from the project while consuming less time and fewer corporate resources;
- employing concurrency to reduce project cycle time and its associated costs;

- accurately assessing project support systems and addressing deficiencies early;
- assessing risks to the project and controlling their impact through risk management techniques, contingency planning, and trade-off analyses; and
- importance of documentation throughout the project management cycle.

Project managers will find comprehensive explanations of how to:

- determine the project scope and deliverables;
- prepare an effective project proposal;
- identify the skill sets required on the project team to effectively cover all project requirements;
- understand the project environment and those factors that impact that environment;
- discern the problems and opportunities that the project team must address;
- identify the appropriate approach to deliver the project; and
- develop and implement the tactical project plans, budgets, communications plans, acquisition plans, compliance plans, and risk management plans.

This book follows a step-by-step approach, supported by tools, techniques, and examples to illustrate each important aspect of project management. As the reader becomes more familiar and comfortable with these methodologies, they can be employed in a more concurrent manner. But the project manager should be cautious. As with any other business or tactical skill, there is always a tendency to take shortcuts. Don't! Each step in the process is critical.

1
Project Management Overview—Past and Present

INTRODUCTION

Managing complex, multi-faceted, strategic projects is much like running any organization as a senior manager—but more difficult.

Senior executives are granted the authority with which to force change through the organization by dictate if necessary. Project managers, however, are rarely given that same level of authority. As a result, successful project managers have developed the skills enabling them to effectively "lead" rather than simply manage the change processes dictated by the project requirements. They work with and through employees at all levels within the organization to effect the required change, to launch new products or services, or to improve existing business processes. To do so, these successful project managers remain proactive, analytical, and visionary in both the planning and execution of their projects. They earn the respect, trust, and recognition of those around them, especially in the face of adversity because they walk the talk, make the tough decisions, and maintain the high degree of self-control required of a good leader. And, after all, isn't that exactly what business managers and executives are required to do every day? Time has shown that men and women who possess the ability and skills to successfully lead projects are also generally successful in leading business enterprises later in their careers.

PROJECT MANAGEMENT TODAY

Project management is far more than a simple fill-in activity for technical or business professionals to undertake in conjunction with their normal duties. Because of the strategic nature of many projects (discussed in more detail in Chapter 2), project management requires:

- a high degree of commitment to both operational and fiscal results,
- an acceptance of accountability for conformance to project and customer requirements, and
- people skills to forge a synergistic chemistry between diverse functional groups to achieve a common goal that rarely has a clearly defined approach.

Project management is a decidedly structured methodology for analyzing and managing complex assignments or problem-solving activities that are impacted by a multitude of internal and external variables, influences, and environmental factors. To be successful, the project manager breaks down each complex situation or assignment into a subset of manageable, well-defined activities that can be controlled and monitored to achieve established project objectives and expected deliverables. In other words, before the project manager takes any action or launches a project plan, he first understands clearly and accurately:

- the occurrences that will impact his project now and throughout the project's life cycle,
- why those things are happening, and
- the most cost-effective and risk-adverse approach to maximize expected project deliverables in the eyes of the project sponsor or customer.

There is no guessing or shooting from the hip. Decisions are based on fact. Actions are based upon a thorough understanding of those relevant facts. Bias and subjectivity are eliminated through analysis of the facts and an understanding of what those facts mean within the project environment. Nothing is taken at face value. Assumptions are always validated. Risks are identified, quantified, and incorporated into the project planning. Nothing is left to chance. Nothing.

If you do not know where you're going or have a map to show you the way, no road will get you there.

THE STRATEGIC PROJECT MANAGEMENT MODEL

Strategic project management combines comprehensive up-front planning and analysis with detailed downstream monitoring and controlled execution. This ensures that strategic and tactical issues are addressed early in the project where numerous options are available to the project manager. With time, many (if not most) of those available options evaporate, and with them the project manager's ability to influence the ultimate outcome of the project.

As illustrated in Figure 1-1, strategic project management contains a complex assortment of concurrent planning, execution, and control mechanisms, all designed to minimize risk and maximize the potential for successful project completion. Shortcuts are never an option. Effective project management requires attention to detail, the follow through to ensure appropriate actions are taken when required, and nothing is left to chance. Like running the business as a senior executive, all facets of the project are thoroughly planned and controlled to ensure success.

By combining the strategic and tactical elements of project management into the strategic project management model, all problems, issues, constraints, and opportunities are identified and resolved before they adversely impact the project. Control is enhanced and risk minimized throughout the project's life cycle. This "StraTactical" approach to project management incorporates the concept of concurrency to ensure that multiple planning and control modules are developed simultaneously, thereby reducing the overall project planning cycle. This is a logical approach based upon proven business practices that have been optimized over time in both government and industry sectors worldwide.

TRADITIONAL PROJECT MANAGEMENT TECHNIQUES

Project planning was traditionally done in a sequential, serial manner. Activities were performed in series, essentially passing from one functional group to another. Each functional group worked autonomously with little concern for the needs or requirements of the next in sequence. The results were frequent changes, false starts, and delays due to a lack of focus on the total

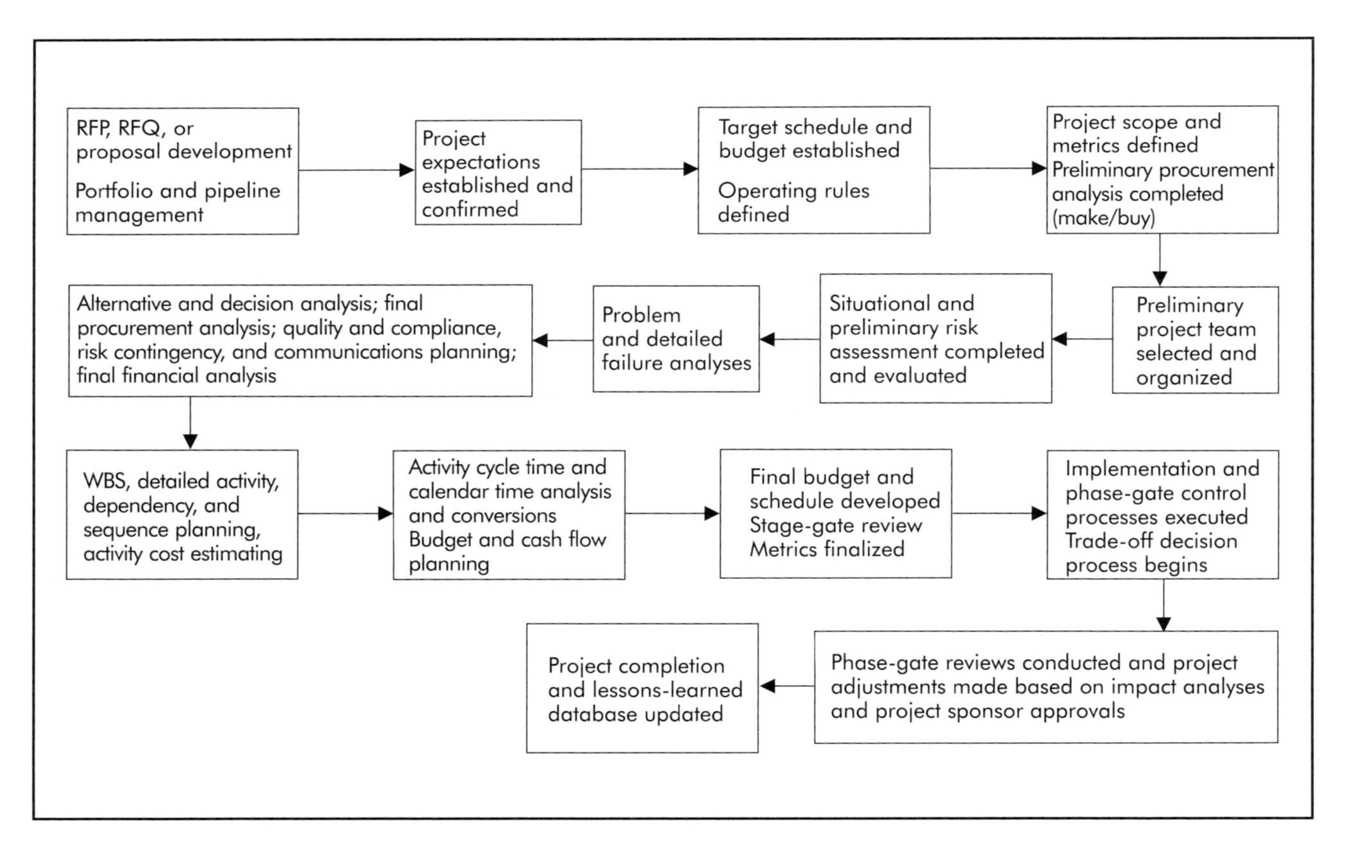

Figure 1-1. The strategic project management model.

project requirements and timing. Costs escalated and time was lost, throwing most projects into an early failure mode that usually went undetected until it was too late to recover. Information was "batched," awaiting completion by a particular discipline or functional group. Once completed, the information (and project) was "thrown over the wall" to the next functional group. Responsibility for the hand-off remained undefined, thus accountability was lost early in the project's life cycle.

With traditional project management, functional priorities constantly took precedent, leaving the project activities to be done at a later date. Little attention was paid to the assigned project activities until deadlines approached or, worse, were missed. As the delays mounted, communication and cooperation between functional groups deteriorated, giving rise to finger pointing. As the positioning deepened, less focus was placed on regaining control over the project and more emphasis was placed on fixing blame. The effectiveness of project management was compromised as functional silos were erected to protect individual departments and disciplines.

In the traditional approach, costs escalated as the time for completion of each activity grew. The longer it took to complete the project, the more resources were consumed, and thus the more costs incurred. That is why the traditional sequential approach was often costly and risk oriented.

With all project management techniques, the ability to influence the project's outcome is at its maximum early in the project cycle. As time goes on, however, the ability to impact the project outcome begins to decline until it becomes ultimately nonexistent. With the traditional project management approach, involvement in the project was at its minimum early in the project. As pressures began to build, involvement was increased as exposure became greater. In other words, people got serious about the project at a point when they had the least ability to influence the outcome. This is not exactly logical, but nonetheless true (see Figure 1-2).

Overlapping Project Management Methodologies

Because the traditional project management techniques continued to produce less than acceptable results, many organizations

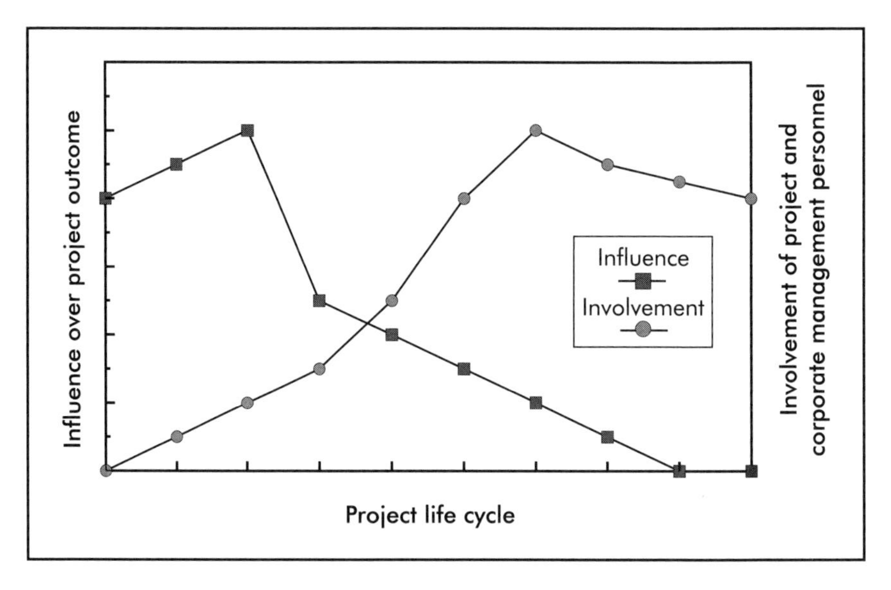

Figure 1-2. In traditional project management, people became more involved in a project when their ability to influence the project was at its weakest.

adopted alternative methodologies. One of the most commonly used techniques focused on overlapping several project activities in an effort to reduce the total project cycle time. The theory behind this approach was that some downstream activities could be safely started *before* the previous activity was completely finished. While the theory had merit, even with this approach most projects were compromised early in the project's life cycle because downstream focus was limited to the next activity or functional group rather than the entire project and all of its associated downstream activities. Communication, however, did improve but only slightly, and primarily between those functions immediately upstream and immediately downstream of the current activity. Information remained generally batched, then processed on a "need-to-know" basis. So, what was good for the project normally gave way to what was good for the functional group currently working on the upstream activity. Time was lost as functional priorities continually altered the effort and resources allocated to the project. Improvement was still needed.

CONCURRENT PROJECT MANAGEMENT THEORIES

As global competition began to intensify in the new millennium with a major focus on concept-to-customer timing, concurrent project management methodologies became more widely utilized. Today, success in the government, manufacturing, and service sectors requires the ability to consistently provide products and services of superior quality at competitive prices, often customized in batches as small as one unit, with minimum, if any, advanced notice from the customer. This "virtual" market requirement necessitates agility in all phases of project management. It is characterized by information sharing within the project management team, within and among all affected corporate functions, as well as with external support providers and customers. The information shared includes everything relative to:

- the product or service deliverables for which the project is chartered; their cost, compliance, and performance criteria, target pricing, and volumes;
- the processes that will generate the product or service, including suppliers of the raw materials or contracted services used within those processes; and
- the applications in which the product or service will be consumed, along with the metrics applied by the end users within those applications.

Concurrency in project management (known as left-side planning or fast tracking) has been found to be fundamental in reducing not only the total project cycle time but risk throughout the project. By definition, *concurrency* in project management is the creation of an environment in which all functional disciplines that contribute to the project perform their activities simultaneously versus sequentially whenever possible, thereby reducing the project schedule to its minimum.

Concurrent project management techniques gather critical input from all affected parties and disciplines in the early stages of the project where the impact of a change is less costly and has less of a detrimental impact on the total project schedule. The economic and budgetary feasibility of the project are confirmed early in the project where options are still possible, thereby eliminating 11th-hour surprises.

Because the team has a common purpose and focus, disciplines are maintained and follow-through is excellent. Problems surface early in the project life cycle and are resolved immediately, so significant implementation-side changes are few, and their impact on project costs, deliverables, and performance is minimal.

A study conducted in early 2008 by the Consulting Alliance Group (CAG) in cooperation with several major government and industry-sector organizations encompassing over 1,000 projects confirmed the benefits of using strategic project management techniques:

- 85% reduction in new product development cycle time in the controls industry;
- 60% reduction in new product launch cycle time in the electronics industry;
- 55% reduction in the launch cycle of new services in the financial services industry;
- 80% reduction in automatic teller machine (ATM) processing cycle time in the banking industry;
- software design changes reduced by over 70%;
- project completion times reduced by over 50% in the construction industry;
- manufacturing assembly times reduced from 7 weeks to less than 2 hours in the automotive industry;
- five-fold reductions in project costs in the telecommunications industry;
- ten-fold reduction in form and fit errors in the heavy equipment industry;
- 40% reduction in project cost and resource consumption in the aerospace industry;
- 30% savings in inventory costs in the computer/electronics industry;
- 80% reduction in project reschedules in the information technology/systems integration industry; and
- 70% reduction in total project expenses in the utility sector.

The Impact of Surprises

The value of strategic/concurrent project management methodologies is that they minimize late-term surprises. The reason why they are so devastating is simple . . . the projects are strategic (bottom line) in nature, not merely enhancement-type projects. As detailed in Chapter 2, when a project manager commits to a particular set of project deliverables, schedule, and budget, senior management builds those bottom-line enhancements into the business and financial plans of the organization. Senior management then incorporates those project-derived enhancements, products, or services into the strategic business plan for the following period, and notifies the customers of their intended availability. Senior management, thereafter, notifies the market makers that buy and sell the corporation's stocks and bonds of the benefits that will be derived from this project, driving up the expectations for the organization, and correspondingly its stock valuation.

The projects of today are strategic in nature. No longer are they just minor improvement issues or opportunities.

If the project fails to live up to the commitments made to and ultimately by senior management, the net result is often disastrous. It is no longer just a minor slip. Because the projects are strategic, their impact on the bottom line is demonstrative. Compounding the situation, the failure of a single project within the organization's portfolio of projects and key business initiatives directly compromises its strategic, business, financial, and operational plans for the period, leaving it exposed to competitive and market changes.

The New Metrics

To address the key variables in time-sensitive markets, world-class organizations have reengineered their project management methodologies to focus more heavily on earned value control metrics like:

- resource utilization;
- concept-to-completion project cycle time;

- total project cost and cash flow impacts;
- return on capital invested;
- risk management costs and controls;
- organizational impact;
- compliance costs and controls; and
- return on limited resources.

Resource utilization includes the consumption or deployment of capital, facilities, technologies, materials, capital equipment, tooling, and personnel. *Total project cycle time* includes every element in the new project life cycle, including:

- knowledge and data acquisition;
- concept investigation;
- project planning and definition;
- project execution;
- any and all restarts, reschedules, or reworks of the project plan;
- project closure and sale to management or the customer; and
- customer support and training.

Project cycle time includes the *total consumed time* from the start of the project until it is completed. This includes all value- and non-value-added time, queue time, wasted time, restarts, reworks, and reschedules. Obviously, the shorter the cycle time is, the better. Time is money. With extended project cycle time comes additional risk as well. The longer the project takes, the higher the probability that something will go wrong. As such, time and risk are always key elements in the project planning and execution processes. In general, the probability of project success remains relatively high through the first 8 to 12 months. Thereafter, the probability of success begins to decline rapidly as illustrated in Figure 1-3. The trick is to structure key project deliverables into 6–8-month intervals. Ultimately, the objective is to complete the entire project in less than 12 months. But when that cannot be reasonably accomplished, the structuring of key deliverables and milestones within the 6–8-month phase greatly enhances the probability of overall project success. It reinforces a tradition of success within the project team that comes from experiencing consistent

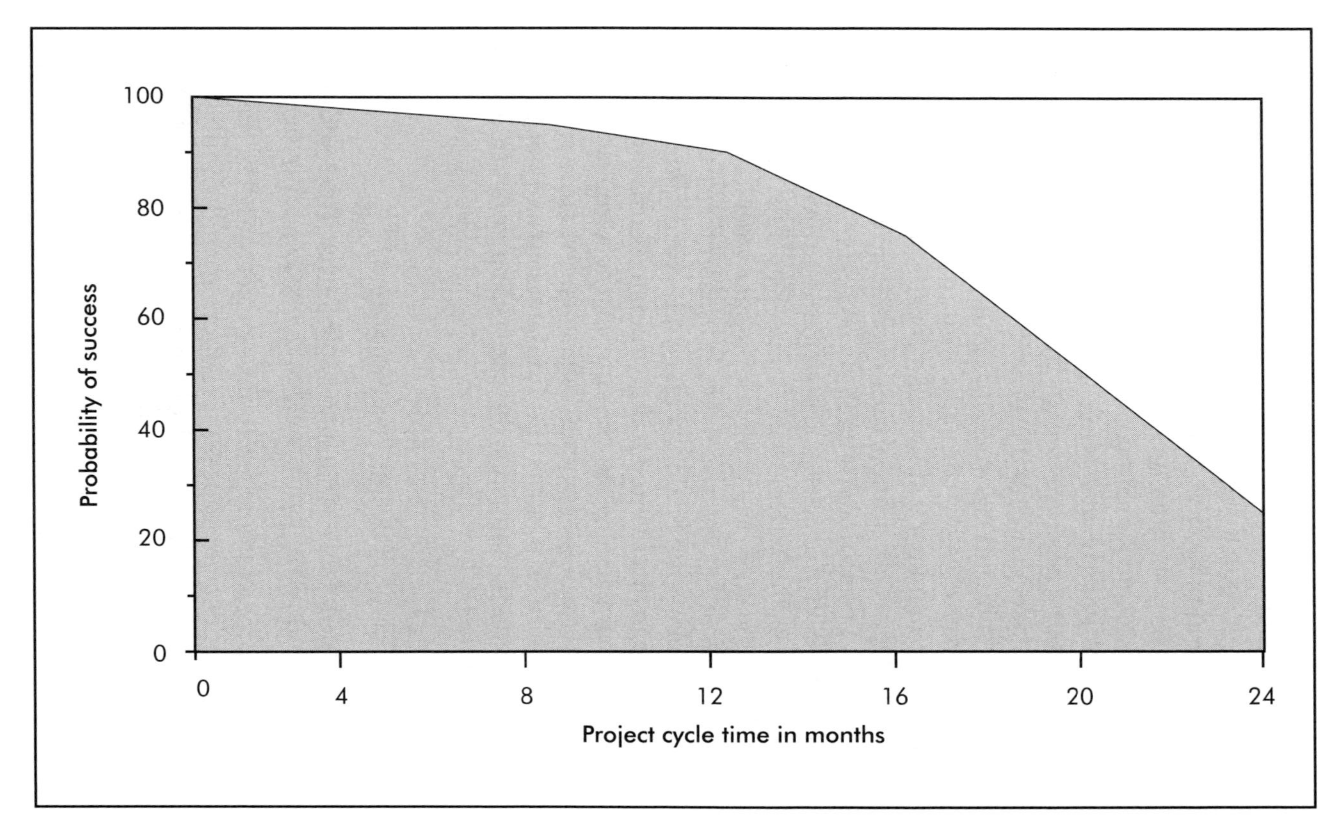

Figure 1-3. The probability of a project's success begins to plummet dramatically after the initial 12 months.

and predictable successes in executing project responsibilities and meeting project goals.

Why is the 12-month rule so applicable and predictable? Business and markets are dynamic. Over time, they change due to numerous factors, such as technological life cycles, economic changes in domestic and global markets, competitive issues, internal constraints, or just the attention span of senior management. Markets, thus businesses, are driven by 12-month performance metrics like dividends, yields, and profits. So once a project exceeds 12 months, everything starts working against it.

How project costs escalate throughout the project's life cycle, as well as the project manager's ability to alter the project's outcome over its life cycle, are also important considerations. As Figure 1-4 depicts, project costs understandably escalate throughout the project's life cycle. In contrast, however, the project manager's ability to influence the outcome of the project falls during that same time frame, leaving the project manager with little control when project costs are at their highest. It is therefore critical that effective project planning be done before a tactical plan is implemented. Once the project is underway, change is costly and risky. Project management should be thought of the same way as we think of total quality management (TQM)—prevention is always less costly than failure. That is the fundamental rule of quality and risk management, and thus the overriding rule of strategic project management.

Benefits of Strategic Project Management

Aside from the obvious savings in project cycle time and costs, strategic project management provides myriad other benefits.

1. It aids the project manager and the project team in identifying concept, design, process, production, and supply chain problems early in the project planning cycle where they can be addressed quickly, with minimum impact on the project's performance, budget, and schedule.
2. It promotes and enhances the development of cross-functional creativity within the project team that, in turn,

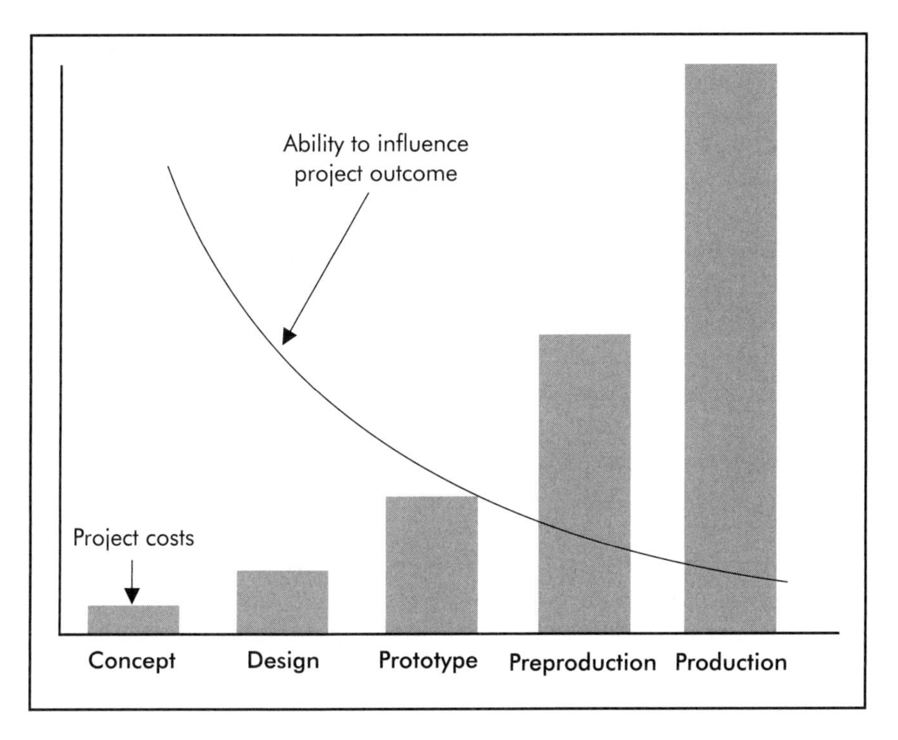

Figure 1-4. During a project's life cycle, costs tend to rise while the project manager's ability to control those costs diminishes.

promotes better and faster problem resolution, with a focus on customer versus functional priorities.

3. The concurrent methodologies improve company-wide communication and cooperation by effectively breaking down functional "silos" and parochial thinking.
4. It promotes true project team thinking and involvement by forcing interaction at all levels and at all times throughout the project.
5. It promotes early involvement by all outside contractors and suppliers to isolate any and all external factors, supply-base issues, and organizational constraints prior to tactical execution of the project.

6. Products, processes, and services can be designed for existing or planned automation, thereby maximizing the utilization and capabilities of available facilities, systems, equipment, and resources.
7. It reduces the number of downstream process, product, system, or service design changes (either customer or internally generated) and their associated costs by forcing problem identification and resolution into the early project planning stages. The up-front planning time may increase, but the downstream return-on-investment in time and total resource consumption is typically significant.
8. It forces the go/no-go decision point to the beginning of the project planning cycle where options are available, limiting the exposure and risk of project cost and schedule overruns.
9. It eliminates the "scope creep" that results from inadequate or incomplete up-front project specifications or requirements from the customer or project sponsor, giving the project manager the ability to accurately define the project scope, and thus plan the project correctly.
10. Effective planning frequently reduces total project resource consumption by as much as 50–60%. The result is the completion of the project in half the time and for less than half the cost of traditional project management approaches.

The objective of strategic project management is simple . . . *under-commit and over-deliver*.

Strategic Project Management at Work

Initiate the project, plan, execute, and complete it . . . before the customer can change his mind. By so doing, success can be ensured!

Following is an excellent example of strategic project management from the government sector . . . that's right, the government sector. It was extracted from an article carried in the *Dallas Morning News* on June 30, 1991, but remains a benchmark of best practices for project teams today. The example illustrates that effective project scoping, situational assessments, risk analyses, and process/cost controls will lead to exceptional results.

"The Bunker Bomb"

"Thirty-seven days after U.S. Air Force officials circulated a request for help in destroying reinforced underground Iraqi command bunkers that had survived direct hits from 2,000-pound bombs, GBU-28 eliminated Bunker No.1 at Al-Taji Air Base. A project team comprised of Texas Instruments (TI), Lockheed, and Eglin Air Force Base personnel created (in 37 days) a high-technology weapon of unprecedented power that would have ordinarily taken at least 18 months to develop.

"On January 21, 1991, the Air Force in effect gave TI, Lockheed, and its own project staff a free hand to get the job done as quickly as possible, and worry about the paper work and bureaucratic channels later. A Lockheed employee remembered reading about the stockpiling of old gun barrels. The barrels were located at the Letterkenny Arsenal in Pennsylvania. Within hours, Eglin personnel had a shipment of 8-inch howitzer barrels en route to the Watervliet Arsenal in New York without waiting for approval. By February 1, Army machinists at the arsenal were machining the barrels into what would become the bodies of the new bombs.

"Lockheed's assignment was the warhead; TI's, the guidance systems. On February 12, before the Air Force had settled on a final bomb design, let alone contract terms, TI officials took a chance and booked the only available productive time on the Dallas-based LTV Aerospace wind tunnel over the weekend of February 16 and 17. They had four days to build a quarter-scale model of the bomb, set it up to test body and fin configurations, and develop guidance software to achieve pinpoint accuracy with a bomb that existed only as a computer model.

"The TI engineers worked in concurrent engineering teams throughout the weekend, generating what they hoped would be successful data. Monday morning they began feeding that data into computer simulations. On Thursday, at the Air

> Force's insistence, two completed sets of guidance systems were shipped to Eglin before TI engineers had performed their own final tests. Two more sets were requested for Nellis Air Force Base in Nevada just as soon as those tests were completed. That turned out to be Saturday, February 22.
>
> "Sunday morning, one inert bomb was test dropped on the Tonopah Test Range, where it penetrated over 100 feet into the ground. On Tuesday, the second bomb penetrated more than 22 feet of concrete at a Holloman, New Mexico test. Hours before that test, however, Eglin personnel had filled the warheads of their two bombs with explosives. They were immediately flown to Saudi Arabia where, less than 8 hours after they arrived, they were on their way to a rendezvous with Bunker No.1. Their project was a success."

In reading through this example, consider the strategic actions the alliance deployed to dramatically reduce the total project cycle time without introducing an unacceptable level of project risk. Consider too, what would happen if your project management team was given a similar degree of freedom to plan and implement your projects, without the usual bureaucratic interference and oversight. The issue is trust. Every successful project manager has earned the trust of her management staff by consistently demonstrating the ability to make sound decisions through the effective planning and execution of the projects she has been assigned. The actions of the project manager and her team speak louder than mere words. Success is measured one project at a time by the results generated.

Articles in *Business Week, The Wall Street Journal, The Harvard Business Review, USA Today,* and other top business journals frequently document the successes that prominent companies have achieved in reducing project cycle time, costs, and risks through the use of strategic project management techniques. Successes like these are increasingly common and will certainly proliferate throughout all business and government sectors in the future. In all cases, it is the project managers who set the stage for

Trust is a commodity that must be earned, over and over again.

successes like these, mediocre results, or outright failure of their projects. The secret lies in accurately scoping the project, building a project plan based upon validated facts and proven methodologies, comprehensive risk assessments and contingency planning, dynamic controls and corrective action techniques, and detailed implementation planning and execution. There are simply no shortcuts to effective project management.

2
Portfolio and Pipeline Management

"WHERE DID THE PROJECT COME FROM?"

Most project managers have had these words cross their minds at least once. For the most part, it often appears as though many projects are a knee-jerk reaction to a business or organizational problem at the operating levels within the organization. While this certainly does happen from time to time, it is not the norm. The vast majority of the projects launched are a direct derivative of senior management's strategic planning processes. This linkage to the organization's vision and mission, as a consequence, makes each of these projects individually and collectively strategic in nature. As a result, financial, operational, and product plans are all predicated upon the successful completion of these strategic projects. Failure is thus not an option. If a project fails, it will impact most, if not all of the organization's strategic plans for the upcoming period, rendering the organization incapable of meeting its strategic directives.

Once or twice each year, senior management defines or redefines the organization's near-term and longer-term vision (*what* the organization is to become), mission (*how* the vision is to be accomplished), and strategic plan (specific initiatives set in place to meet organizational objectives). From this complex planning process, a series of strategic initiatives are developed and then analyzed to form the organization's strategic portfolio of actions that will be launched to align its resources with its vision. Utilizing portfolio and pipeline management techniques that will be explained in detail later in this chapter, these initiatives are prioritized and then decomposed into individual strategic projects that are handed down to individual project managers. Once received by the project managers, the projects are required to be successfully launched and completed within predefined timeframes and budgets to coincide with others in the pipeline so that each strategic initiative is accomplished, and thus the vision realized.

PORTFOLIO MANAGEMENT

As Figure 2-1 illustrates, portfolio management is a direct result of the strategic and business planning processes within the organization. It is utilized at the senior levels within the organization to assess, organize, and manage the initiatives that are important to meeting the organization's strategic and business plans. At this level, the focus is on organizational balance, effective resource utilization, and expected commercial value to the organization.

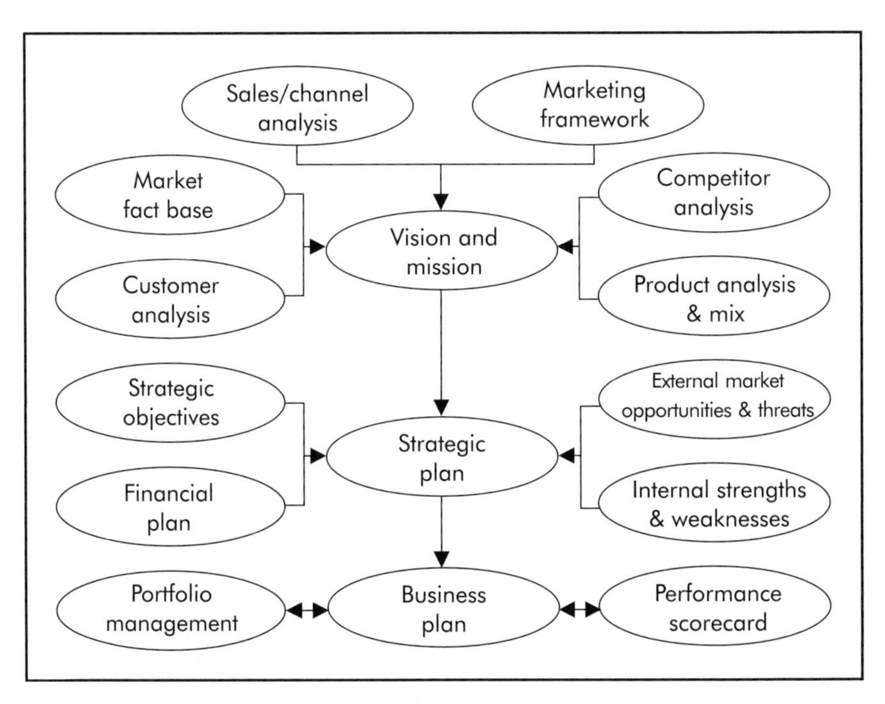

Figure 2-1. Organizational strategies.

Assessment, alignment, and prioritization are critical elements of portfolio management to ensure that corporate resources are allocated and deployed appropriately. Every opportunity is considered and every risk evaluated during the initial screening stages. All aspects of each opportunity or initiative under consideration are explored completely. The decision to pursue a particular opportunity or initiative is based upon a multifaceted series of analyses that consider incremental revenues, investment requirements, expected return on investment, organizational impact, and risk—just to name a few criteria. Optimization of the portfolio is a dynamic process that requires continuous evaluation of active and bullpen projects to ensure their close alignment with current business conditions and constraints.

This multifaceted approach incorporates several analytical tools. Figure 2-2, for example, considers the incremental revenues expected to be received from the portfolio. This criterion is typically used as a first-pass, "go or no-go" test for the portfolio. It factors in risk characterizations to arrive at revised expected returns over time. In other words, senior management factors into the returns calculation a probability factor, which is based upon the organization's history of success in achieving projected returns from similar initiatives.

In Figure 2-3, each initiative is assessed against its probability of success, as well as its impact on the portfolio if it should fail. This is done by utilizing a risk criticality index (explained in more detail in Chapter 11). In essence, any initiative with an unfavorable risk profile is either immediately eliminated from further consideration or reprioritized to a lower ranking in the portfolio.

Figure 2-4 illustrates a project segmentation analysis that categorizes projects or initiatives in the portfolio based upon the degree of process change/improvement versus the technological development required to support the project's implementation. The results of this analysis are factored against the operational and research capital available throughout the upcoming period and then filtered to ensure alignment with the corporate mission. Breakthrough projects, for example, are intended to establish a new core franchise, product family, or technological process base

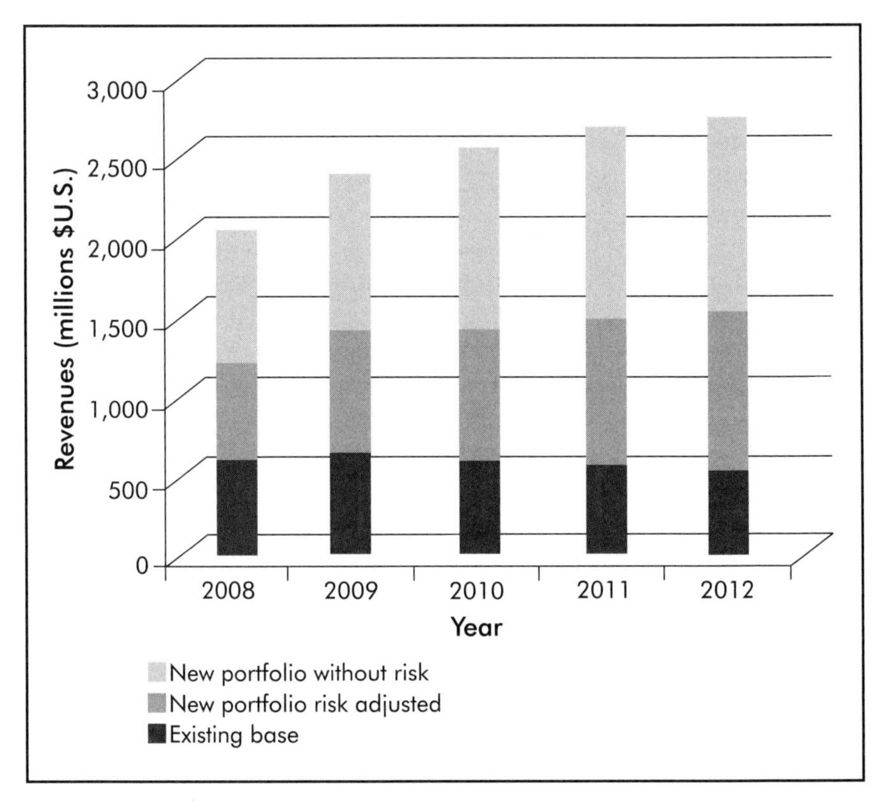

Figure 2-2. Incremental revenue analysis example.

for the organization. Platform projects, on the other hand, represent next-generation products with fundamental improvements in cost, quality, and/or performance leveraged from significant improvements to the existing process and technological baselines. Derivative projects are intended to introduce hybrids or enhancements to existing products and processes utilizing existing technological baselines. Finally, maintenance projects are intended to maintain the existing business, process, or product infrastructure.

The impact on organizational resources is also considered as part of the portfolio analysis to ensure that the hidden costs of productivity losses, employee retention and development, and business process overloads are adequately addressed. As Table 2-1 illustrates, each

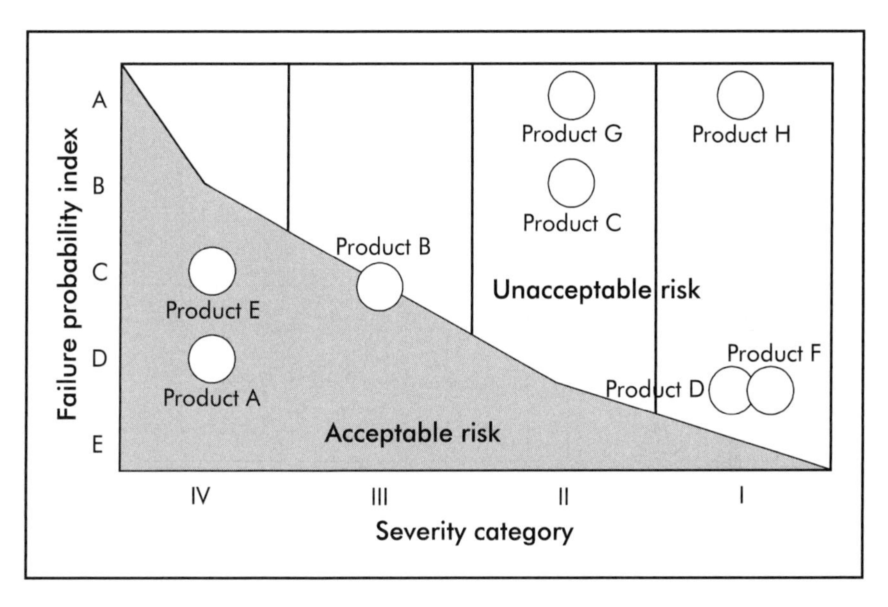

Figure 2-3. Portfolio risk criticality analysis.

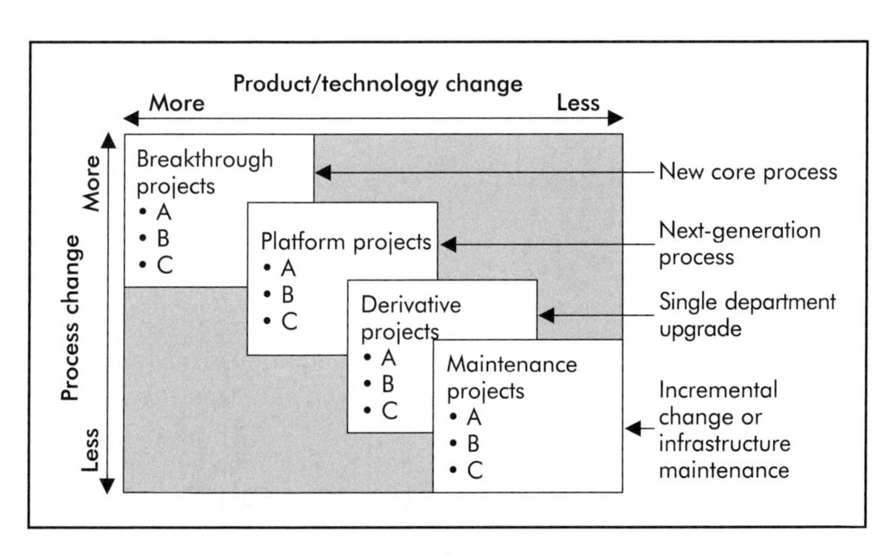

Figure 2-4. Project segmentation analysis.

Table 2-1. Effort-based portfolio analysis.

Category	Opportunity Assessment	Business Case	Marketing Plan	Operations Plan	Vendor Assessment/ Contracts	Training Plan	Project Plan
Products							
New markets, categories	X	X	X	X	X	X	X
New products		X	X	X	X	X	X
Sourcing		X	X	X	X	X	X
Line extensions				X	X		X
Programs							
Customer	X	X	X			X	X
Supplier	X	X	X			X	X
Customer technology solutions	X	X	X			X	X
Infrastructure							
Supply chain	X	X					
Infrastructure and systems	X	X					

project or initiative is measured against a baseline of the functional and organizational effort required to support it.

The final portfolio analysis tool utilized by senior management considers the investment and return from various combinations of projects and initiatives. Obviously, senior management seeks the combination that requires the lowest capital investment while providing the greatest expected return (risk based). As the example in Figure 2-5 illustrates, even when the investment requirements are the same between various portfolios, the expected returns can

Portfolio A

Invest $45M*

	Revenue	Cost	Probability
A	$500	$20	20%
B	$400	$15	80%
C	$300	$10	50%
Total	$1,200	$45	

Expected gross profit**
$570 – $45 = $525

*All dollar figures in millions
**Return based upon net income margin of 13%. Assume single-year cost and single-year return in year 3.

Portfolio B

Invest $45M*

	Revenue	Cost	Probability
B	$200	$15	90%
C	$200	$10	90%
X,Y,Z	$800	$20	90%
Total	$1,200	$45	

Expected gross profit**
$1,080 – $45 = $1,035

- Same investment as portfolio A
- Different portfolio composition
- For the same investment, portfolio B generates almost twice the expected return.

Figure 2-5. Revenue-based portfolio analysis.

be dramatically different. As this example illustrates, two alternative portfolios have the same gross revenue expectation, as well as investment cost. Yet the second portfolio yields over twice the expected return as the first when risks are factored in.

PIPELINE MANAGEMENT

Once senior management has completed the analysis, selected a final portfolio, and established the preliminary prioritization of the projects and initiatives therein, focus turns to getting the projects into the pipeline and ultimately into the hands of the project managers for implementation.

The project management office (PMO) staff or a senior management steering committee is typically responsible for pipeline management, which focuses organizational resources on optimizing the concept-to-completion cycle time. Many leading organizations have realized as much as a 50% reduction in this cycle through effective strategic project planning and control. Figure 2-6 illustrates a typical pipeline management process map. In essence, pipeline management techniques are designed to accelerate the entire portfolio of projects through the development process without introducing undue risk or cost. To accomplish this, standardized stage-gate control techniques are used.

Throughout the pipeline management process, portfolio priorities are constantly evaluated and adjusted. This is done to maximize the performance of the entire portfolio, as well as reduce the risk that one or more projects will fail to meet expected/committed performance levels and, by so doing, compromise the entire portfolio. Table 2-2 illustrates a typical portfolio analysis. In this example, the final project ranking reflects the current prioritization or sequencing in the portfolio (lowest score represents the project with the least risk in meeting all portfolio objectives). Corporate resources are redistributed as required to ensure maximum acceleration of all projects based upon the predetermined baselines of schedule completion and cost. Using this scorecarding methodology within the pipeline helps to maintain focus on the portfolio's priorities and organizational resource needs.

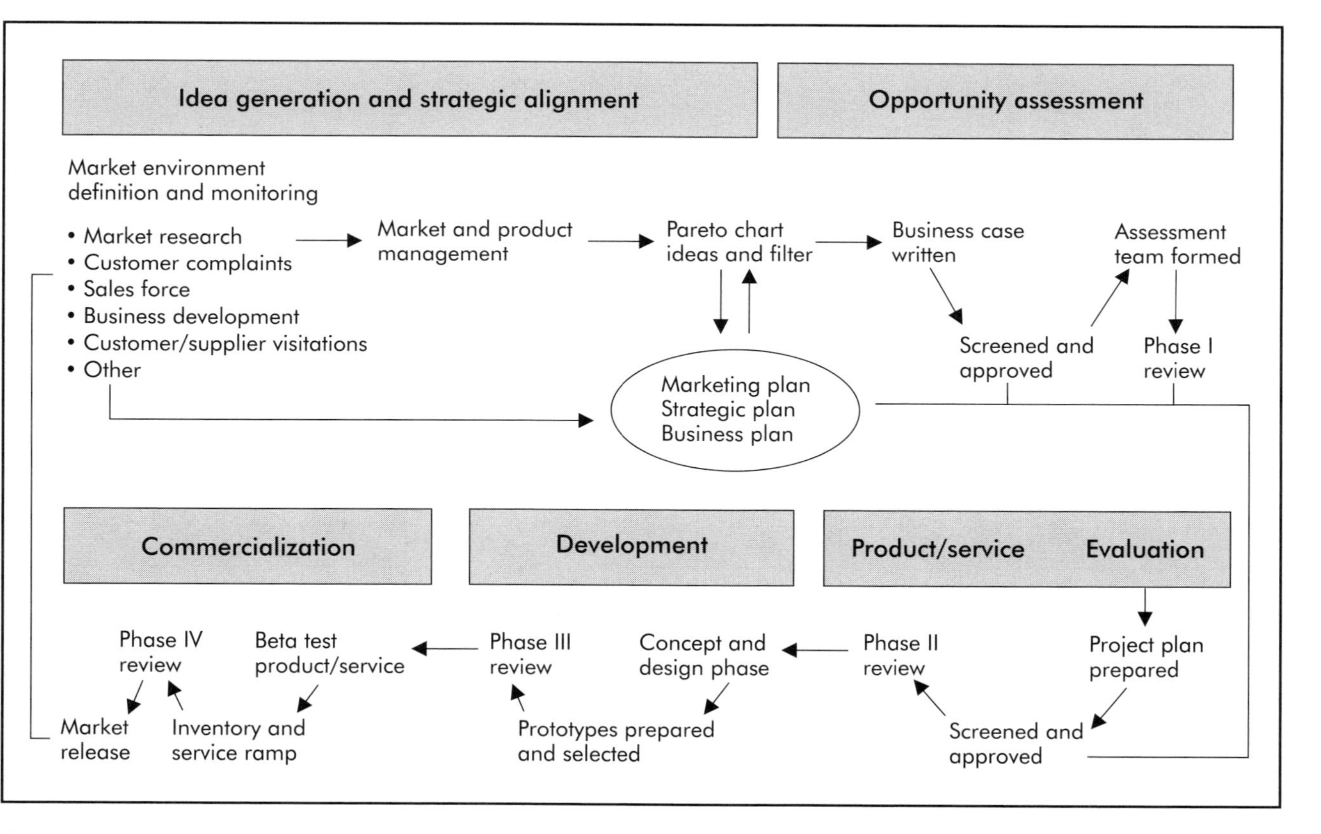

Figure 2-6. Pipeline management process map.

Table 2-2. Pipeline portfolio ranking analysis.

Category	Strategic Fit/ Importance	Competitive Advantage	Time to Launch	Cost/ Resources Required	Risk (Market/ Technology Risk)	Expected Benefit Potential	Final Project Ranking
Products							
Project A	1	3	4	4	2	1	2.5
Project B	5	4	1	1	1	5	2.8
Programs							
Project A	2	1	3	3	2	2	2.7
Project B	3	5	2	2	5	5	3.7
Infrastructure							
Project A	1	1	5	5	3	1	2.7
Project B	4	5	5	5	5	5	4.8

Note: Lower overall project score implies higher priority; scales would be assigned a range from high to low or weak to strong depending upon category being considered.

Stage-gate Assessment

At each stage-gate review, actual portfolio and project performance is compared against the master plan. The PMO staff or senior management steering committee then makes the decision to:

- move the project forward to the next stage of the project life or development cycle;
- re-direct the project through a change in scope, schedule, resources, or leadership; or
- cancel the project outright and move another bullpen project into the pipeline to compensate for the loss of the failed project.

The following questions are asked during a typical stage-gate assessment. While each organization will employ unique questions of their own design, the following provides a basis of understanding with which to illustrate how the actual process works.

Phase 0

Evaluate the product opportunity, how it fits within the overall strategy, and its priority.

- Is the market requirement and opportunity for this product significant enough to justify the cost and possible risks to the organization?
- Can the product achieve sufficient competitive advantage? (Why will this product win?)
- Does it look like the product can be successful (profitable) based on projected revenue and costs combined with existing and expected organizational constraints?
- Do the assumptions (financial, technical, market, and schedule) appear to be reasonable?
- Does the product have sufficient priority to justify the anticipated resource requirement?

Determine overall feasibility.

- Does the product look viable to develop?
- Are the major risks and contingencies acceptable?

- Can development be completed within the required market window?
- Are there major legal issues that would prohibit success?
- Are the installation and support requirements within the organization's current or achievable capabilities?

Determine Phase I readiness.

- Is the scope and general function of the proposed product sufficiently clear to move forward into Phase I?
- Is the proposed project team (core team) acceptable and does it include all the needed skill sets, commitments, and functional support?
- Can/will the required resources be assigned to complete the Phase I requirements?
- Are the Phase 1 scope, requirements, and expectations clearly defined?

Phase 1

Determine the potential for success. Clarify the product and its feasibility, verify estimates, assumptions, and plan development.

- Is there a clear understanding of the market and customer needs?
- Is the product expected to provide sufficient competitive advantage at the time of release?
- Do the product characteristics (functions, performance objectives, cost, etc.) reflect a thorough understanding of the market and any competitive advantage?

Determine product's business appeal.

- Is the financial analysis of the product opportunity sufficiently complete?
- Is the projected profitability and return on investment adequate to compensate for the risk and resources needed to successfully complete the project?
- Are all major risks understood and have appropriate contingency plans been made?
- Have the assumptions in Phase 0 been verified?

Determine Phase 2 readiness.

- Is the product clearly defined and technically feasible?
- Is the product development strategy reasonable?
- Does the plan include proper design controls?
- Has the team completed an initial design review? Do any of the known or anticipated corrective actions impact the project's direction or probability of success?
- Is the schedule based upon a comprehensive understanding of the work required and does it satisfy the window of opportunity?
- Can/will the required resources be assigned to complete Phase 2?
- Are the supporting plans (for example, quality, installation and support, market entry, etc.) acceptable?

Complete product design, coding, integration, and draft user documentation.

- Have the competitive environment, market requirements, or product specifications changed?
- Are all the product features completed and user interfaces finalized and frozen?
- Have the design and code reviews been held on all planned features?
- Is the product expected to provide sufficient competitive advantage at the time of release?
- Is the user documentation drafted?

Determine Phase 3 readiness.

- Has functional testing been completed on all planned features?
- Does the product meet criteria to begin the system/market test and is the test plan adequate?
- Is the code stable enough to have soft code/design freeze?
- Are defect arrivals on a downward trend? Is the defect backlog and first-pass yield under control and on a positive trend?
- Can/will the required resources be assigned to complete Phase 3?

Phase 3

Demonstrate the functionality and performance of the completed design. Complete the user documentation.

- Have the competitive environment, market requirements, or product specifications changed?
- Has the product satisfactorily passed system/final configuration testing?
- Is the user documentation ready for final production?
- Are product introduction tasks well underway?

Determine Phase 4 readiness.

- Can a product introduction date be set and met?
- Are there any major outstanding defects or design issues?
- Have the beta customer(s) been identified (if required)?
- Is the code/design stable enough to have hard code/design freeze and move to stabilization team support?
- Can the required resources be assigned to complete Phase 4?

Phase 4

Validate readiness of the product release and begin volume shipment. Transition the plan to the stabilization team.

- Is the product ready for release based upon the state of the product's introduction tasks, as well as the stability, quality, and production yields of the product?
- Are installation and training plans complete?
- What are the project's open issues and what are the resolution plans?
- Are the plans to transition support from development to the customer stabilization team in place?
- What did the project post-mortem review reveal?

SUMMARY

As Figure 2-7 depicts, portfolio management techniques are used by senior management to assess, address, and manage the collection of strategic initiatives and projects during the strategic

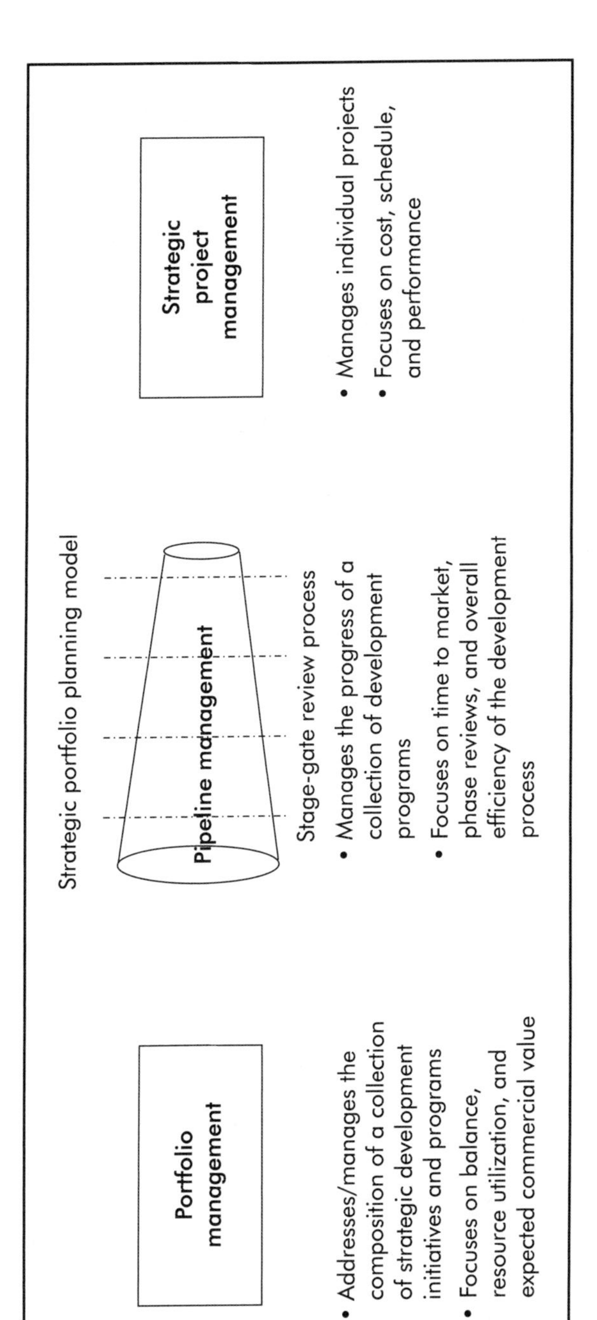

Figure 2-7. Portfolio, pipeline, and project management techniques.

planning process to ensure that the strategic objectives and corporate mission are achieved. The focus is on organizational balance and alignment, effective resource utilization, and generation of acceptable commercial value. Pipeline management techniques are then employed by either the PMO staff or a senior management steering committee to accelerate each project within the pipeline through to conclusion in the most cost-effective, time-sensitive, risk-adverse manner possible utilizing stage-gate review processes to maximize control. Ultimately, strategic project management techniques are utilized by the individual project managers to ensure that individual project goals and objectives are met. The balance of this book focuses on those techniques.

3
Project Proposal Development

OVERVIEW

In Chapter 1, the strategic project management process was illustrated (see Figure 1-1) to provide the reader with an understanding of the interrelationships that exist in the project planning and execution processes. In Chapter 2, the concepts of portfolio and pipeline management were detailed to demonstrate how projects are conceived, prioritized, and managed as an integral aspect of the strategic planning processes within a corporation. In this chapter, the process of proposal preparation is discussed. Readers will learn about the requirements for soliciting project work from external customers for integration into the portfolio planning process (see Figure 3-1).

External or contract project work is generally the result of a response to a customer's request for proposal (RFP) or request for quotation (RFQ)—a solicitation for project work. Proposals are also a result of an organization's sales and marketing processes in which new business with either existing or targeted customers (or targeted markets) is planned and executed utilizing proposals as the means to open doors.

But the generation of a proposal, in and of itself, is only the first step of the process. Should a customer deem an organization's proposal to be of interest or worthy of further consideration, the customer will "short list" the proposal for the second step of the process. This short-listing process is used to reduce the number of proposals under consideration, typically to three. Those three organizations will be invited to deliver a formal presentation to the customer where additional detail is provided and questions are

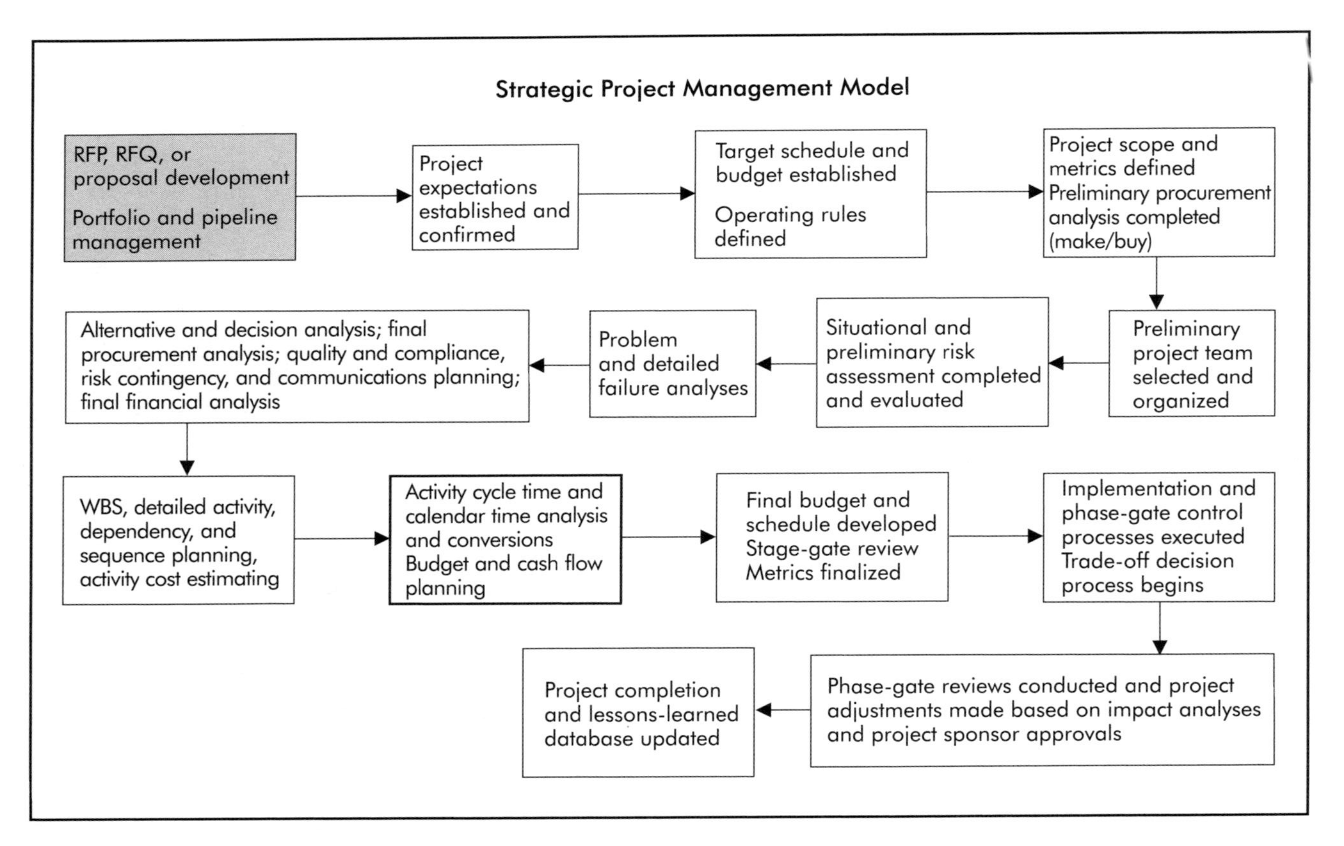

Figure 3-1. The project proposal's fit in the strategic project planning process.

addressed. From the presentations, a final proposal is selected. The winning organization then enters the customer's project into its portfolio and proceeds (as described in Chapter 2), prioritizing and managing the project until its completion.

Development of a successful proposal requires extensive planning, due diligence, and flawless execution. It also requires a significant degree of experience and skill to prepare a proposal that stands out from the competition. At the same time, the proposal must not commit the organization to deliver a project it is not capable of completing under the proposed terms and conditions (under-commit/over-deliver). In addition, there is a cost for preparing a proposal in both direct and indirect terms, which few organizations have quantified. In general, a small proposal will cost between $1,500 and $2,500 to prepare and deliver. Larger proposals will often cost more than $10,000 for their preparation and delivery. Of particular note, over 75% of the proposals submitted are not accepted by the potential customer. It is, therefore, not a sound business practice to arbitrarily generate proposals that have little probability of success in generating revenues for the company.

As Table 3-1 illustrates, proposal preparation is a multi-phased process that begins with preliminary research into project opportunities within selected target markets, followed by isolation of specific projects or business opportunities therein. Next, the project team assesses the applicability of the opportunity against internal business objectives, constraints, and capacities to ensure alignment with the mission established by senior management. From that assessment, a preliminary go/no-go decision is made regarding whether or not to proceed with proposal development.

If it is decided that the business opportunity merits further consideration, the potential customer is contacted to advise of the company's interest in submitting a proposal along with a corresponding request to be included in the customer's RFP/RFQ process. Once the RFP/RFQ is received, additional due diligence into the requirements of the customer and the project are completed, and a final go/no-go decision is made. If the project team determines it is in the best interests of the organization to invest

Table 3-1. Proposal preparation task list.

Task	Date Completed
Preliminary research into target customers	
Identification of specific customer projects of interest	
Assessment of project applicability	
Preliminary quote decision, go/no go	
Initial customer contact to advise of interest	
Receipt of customer RFP	
Final quote decision, go/no go	
Research customer requirements and drivers	
Define project objectives, goals, and scope	
Organize project proposal team	
Prepare proposal plan and work breakdown structure (WBS)	
Develop proposal budget	
Assign concurrent proposal tasks	
Monitor progress against milestones	
Review and revise as necessary	
Final proposal review and buy-off	
Delivery of proposal to customer	
Short-listed	
Prepare proposal presentation	

the necessary resources to submit a proposal, the customer's requirements, terms, and conditions are researched in detail. Specific goals, objectives, and expectations for the project are solidified from that research, as well as through discussions with the customer. The project scope is then established and the project/proposal team selected. As with the development of any other project plan, a work breakdown structure (WBS) is prepared to guide the proposal development process. A proposal budget is prepared and tasks assigned. Again, as with any other project planning process, milestones and controls are put into place to ensure compliance with targeted schedule and budgetary criteria. Once the final proposal is completed and reviewed, it is delivered to the customer for consideration and short-listing. If successful, preparation of a formal presentation is initiated.

One important point is in order: *the majority of problems encountered during the planning and execution of a project are the direct result of deficiencies or omissions in the proposal*. It must be done right. Once submitted, the organization and its project team are committed (legally and ethically) to deliver the project under the terms and conditions included in the proposal.

MAXIMIZING THE PROBABILITY OF SUCCESS

Most organizations have no idea why their proposals are rejected, much less why they are successful. As a result, their probability of success with future proposal submissions is never improved through experience. Much like the requirement for a lessons-learned database for project tracking (discussed in upcoming chapters), there is a similar requirement for an organization to monitor its proposal hit rate on an ongoing basis. This will help to identify the factors that led to success or failure in the past. As illustrated in Table 3-2, an organization's hit rate is generally directly proportional to the target markets it is pursuing. The more experience an organization has within a particular industry segment or with a particular customer, the higher its probability of being awarded the project. There are, however, never any guarantees. As a result, every proposal process is conducted with a high degree of professionalism and consideration of all of the factors required to win and successfully deliver the project. So as would be expected, focusing on customers and market segments in which the organization has a positive reputation and a broad base of experience greatly improves its chances of proposal acceptance.

As with any other business investment, senior management expects that an acceptable return will be generated. Consequently, the maximization of an organization's proposal hit rate is a vital consideration in its strategic planning and portfolio management processes.

Table 3-2. Proposal hit rate benchmarks.

Proposal Short-listed	Best in Class
Existing regional markets	80–90%
Existing domestic market	40–50%
Existing international markets	30–35%
New markets	15–20%
Awarded from short list	
Existing regional markets	35–40%
Existing domestic market	30–35%
Existing international markets	20–25%
New markets	15–20%

So how does a project manager ensure that his team's proposal will be accepted? It must be uniquely different from those submitted by the competition. While that may seem to be an obvious statement, it is often lost in the execution of proposal planning and development. If all of the proposals submitted for a given project look the same, contain the same approach, and promise the same results (and they typically do), how will the customer decide which to select? That answer, too, is obvious—price. Thus, if the company's strategy is being the low-price leader, then there is no issue. If, on the other hand, the company's strategy is to provide higher value versus lowest price, there is likely going to be a problem unless it effectively differentiates itself as such in the proposal. To do so, the project manager and his team first recognize that their organization has not only strengths, but also weaknesses that place real limitations on what the team can offer in its proposal. Working within those constraints is vital to their success in winning the contract and making an acceptable profit from it. Thus, the project manager selects project opportunities in which:

- the organization is capable of generating measurable value for its customer,

- it is difficult for others to compete because of the organization's core competencies, or
- the company is recognized as the industry leader.

As Table 3-3 illustrates, a simple evaluation tool provides the project manager with an objective assessment of each opportunity. Projects that are not consistent with the core requirements established by senior management, or the organization's core competencies, are simply not pursued. Contrary to most sales practices, not bidding on every opportunity offered by a customer is sometimes a sound business practice. It indicates that the organization is aware of its core competencies and works within them; the company is not in a financial position that forces it to accept any opportunity that comes along; and it is good at delivering on the projects it is awarded. All of these are positive indicators to a potential customer.

Table 3-3. Preliminary bid analysis tool.

Preliminary Bid Review	Yes	No	No Bid
Is this the type of project we want?			
Do we have the capability to handle this type of project?			
Is this project consistent with our business direction and mission?			
Is there sufficient time to respond?			
Is there sufficient data or information to respond?			
Are there sufficient personnel to handle this project if awarded?			
Is there sufficient funding to handle this project if awarded?			
Do we have a positive history with this customer?			
Is this project wired to another firm?			
Are the project expectations realistic?			

If the decision is made to pursue a given opportunity to the next stage, then the project team follows the proposal development process outlined herein. There are two underlying facts that drive the team's proposal preparation:

1. The best-written proposal will not succeed unless it satisfies the customer's hot buttons.
2. It isn't important what the project team wants to sell to the customer; it is what the customer wants to buy that is of prime importance.

PROPOSAL PROCESS

To reiterate, the objective of the proposal is not necessarily to win the project, but rather to get short-listed. Having this preferred status will allow the project manager to present the team's approach, controls, and credentials to the customer under the most favorable conditions. As Figure 3-2 illustrates, the process begins with due diligence into the customer's requirements, expectations, and hot buttons, as well as into the competencies and capacities of the project manager's own organization.

To ensure the maximum degree of success possible, the project manager's proposal is written with a focus on the customer's rating criteria. These are the metrics that will be used to compare one proposal against another based upon the customer's internally established project performance criteria. Typical criteria include:

- capability to manage a project of this scope, size, and complexity;
- reputation for success, reliability, and predictability;
- a customer-focused approach to project management and problem resolution;
- project-specific management experience of both the project manager and her team;
- support from the project manager's organization and senior management;
- competitive pricing versus expected value;
- innovation in approach and technologies employed for the project;

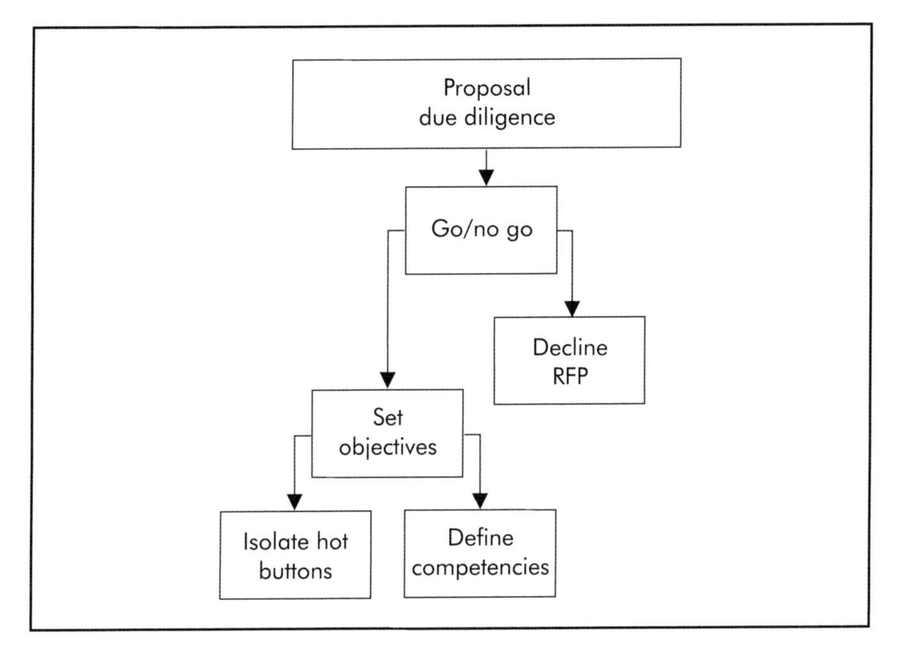

Figure 3-2. Proposal development process—second stage.

- technical expertise in disciplines required for the project;
- track record of fiscal responsibility;
- proposal content and format;
- references in the customer's field;
- history of minimal change orders and maximum change management efficiency;
- operating competencies, capacities, and process capabilities; and
- consistency in performance and compliance.

While certainly not a complete listing, the previous criteria represent many items that the customer will consider. Other hot buttons range from the size of the project manager's organization, current resource workloads, and project-specific experience, to indirect concerns driven by prior experience with the project manager, his team, or his organization; feedback from other industry peers; or the project manager's ability to work with customer representatives and management in a cooperative manner. In summary, the customer's hot buttons are varied and will change with time.

Next, the proposal is written in a way that differentiates the project manager's organization from others who will likely submit competing proposals. It is written in such a way as to:

- Look and read differently from others in both format and content.
- Compare and contrast the benefits (for the customer) to be derived from the methodology, experience, and/or technologies that will be applied in achieving the desired results versus those that are being proposed by the competition.
- Address those concerns of greatest importance to the customer including the hot buttons uncovered through the project team's due diligence.
- Illustrate expertise and competency in fulfilling all project expectations with the least degree of risk to, or impact on, the customer.
- Illustrate comprehensive knowledge of the customer's operations and industry.
- Establish a linkage between the customer's explicit and implicit requirements and the methodology or approach being proposed by the project manager.
- Focus on the benefits of working with the project manager, his team, and his organization.
- Leave no room for misunderstanding or misinterpretation.

In writing the proposal, the project manager focuses on the customer's needs and concerns by reinforcing in the terminology used for the proposal that it is the "*customer's*" project. This is a key point that will be discussed in more detail later. The project manager also demonstrates throughout the proposal a clear understanding of the customer's requirements with particular emphasis on "why" the customer's current needs or situation exist, as well as "how" the desired results will be achieved to address them. In other words, he demonstrates a clear linkage between the customer's evaluation criteria and the contents of the proposal.

The project manager also demonstrates within the proposal the individual and collective capacities and project-related experience of the project team members, along with how that team will effectively manage and control all aspects of the project for the benefit of the customer. His focus is to answer the question that is in the mind of his customer, "Why should I select you for my critical project?"

There are also several things that the project manager avoids when writing the proposal to clearly demonstrate his concern for the customer and the customer's project:

- He avoids a focus on what the project team has to offer or excessive emphasis on the project manager's organization and its focus, markets, or accomplishments, except as they relate directly to the customer's project.
- He avoids irrelevant data or information that has no bearing on the project or the customer's requirements.
- He avoids the inclusion of issues or actions not specifically requested by the customer or directly related to the project.
- He avoids the use of boilerplate terms and phrases in the preparation of the project proposal to ensure it gives the appearance of being uniquely prepared for the customer's project.
- He avoids incorporating solutions that every other bidder will use.
- He never challenges the customer's understanding of the issues or of their own operations, capacities, or competencies.
- He avoids inclusion of references to projects he or his team were not part of.
- He avoids incomplete thoughts that will cause misunderstandings or misinterpretation.
- He avoids grammatical or spelling errors (this should go without saying).

In writing the proposal, the project manager is always cognizant of the fact that the proposal must be easy to read (easy on the eyes), comprehensive without being repetitive or containing irrelevant data or information, and easy to understand to avoid misinterpretation. The proposal is also written to demonstrate the project manager's enthusiasm and excitement in managing the customer's project. The energy evident in the proposal is infectious; it sells the customer on the fact that the project manager and his team truly look forward to participating in the project.

To Bid or Not to Bid

Before the project manager commits the time and resources required to develop a proposal, a final reality check is in order. At this point, the project manager has spoken with the prospective customer and determined that there is mutual interest. The next step is a comprehensive and critical review of the RFP/RFQ to ascertain the team's probability of being short-listed. To aid the project manager in determining this, there are a number of indicators in the RFP/RFQ.

- Is the RFP/RFQ detailed, clear, and specific in all aspects of the project scope, deliverables, and expectations? If not, the customer may not yet have determined exactly what is required or if the project is of real value. In other cases, the customer may have intentionally left the requirements and specifications open-ended so that a pre-selected bidder will have the advantage of knowing exactly how to respond, giving them an obvious competitive edge. Yet another consideration is whether this is an indication that the customer is indecisive and will be difficult to pin down later for the specifics needed to plan and execute the project.
- Is the RFP/RFQ overly detailed or specific? If so, this may be an indication that the customer will be too demanding or unrealistic in his expectations for the project, or may simply be overly difficult to work with on a day-to-day basis. Yet another indication from this scenario is that because of the degree of specificity in the RFP/RFQ, the customer may believe that he has covered all options and is thus looking for the lowest price proposal to execute his plan. In this case, a bidding war is the obvious outcome. Another consideration is that there may be significant downside

penalties or contingent liabilities should the project not be completed as expected. Still another concern is that the customer will require redundant reporting and paperwork from the project team taking away resources and profits from the project.

- Is the RFP/RFQ already wired to a competitive firm? This happens. The project manager looks for an obvious relationship between the customer's proposal evaluation criteria and the project requirements. If the relationship is unclear or nonexistent, it is a strong indication that the business will be awarded to a preselected bidder. The same conclusion can be drawn if there are no defined proposal selection criteria, or if the customer is evasive in answering direct questions concerning the project. Other indicators that the project is already wired include the requirement for an unreasonably quick response to the RFP/RFQ, or if the project is linked to other projects already underway and managed by a competing firm.

With indicators such as these, the likelihood of success in getting short-listed, much less winning the project, is poor. The project manager is wise to seek other opportunities.

If, on the other hand, the initial assessment indicates that the RFP/RFQ is open to all bidders, the project manager compares the project scope, objectives, and requirements against his organization's mission, brand position, established or targeted markets, core competencies, current capacities, and financial capabilities. Still other questions the project manager seeks answers to include:

- Is the project funded?
- Is the scope well defined?
- Is the schedule reasonable given all known constraints?
- Are the required resources for the project available when and where needed?
- Have the risks been adequately assessed?
- Are there any hidden regulatory, quality, or compliance requirements that are unreasonable?

- Are the contract terms and conditions reasonable?
- Can a competitive proposal be developed that will differentiate the organization from others bidding on the same RFP/RFQ?
- Is the return on investment expected from the project reasonable?
- Are there other projects or opportunities available that will generate a higher return on investment or lower risk?
- Are all selection criteria defined and reasonable?
- Is the requested response time for the RFP/RFQ feasible given all internal considerations and resource loads?
- Is this a customer the team can and wants to work with?
- Does the project team have a positive history with this customer?
- Does the project team have demonstrable experience with this type of project?
- Will this be a prime/subcontractor situation? If so, who will be the prime contractor for the project?
- Will the resources, data, and information required from the customer for the project be readily available?
- Will the customer act as the project or program manager, or will the project manager be free to manage the project as he and his team deem most appropriate?

If the project will provide a reasonable expected profit, and if there are no hidden penalties that introduce unreasonable risk, then the decision is made to pursue it.

In assessing his team's probability of success in the bidding process, the project manager employs quantitative assessment tools like that illustrated in Tables 3-4 and 3-5 to minimize the degree of subjectivity in the decision of whether or not to pursue the project. Table 3-4, for example, is used to compare and contrast the project manager and his organization's capabilities against expected competitors. Whenever possible, data from the organization's "lessons-learned" database is used in the scoring of each criterion.

Table 3-5 illustrates yet another bid analysis worksheet that analyzes the project against a baseline of internal requirements or

Table 3-4. Final bid/no-bid worksheet.

Decision Criteria	Poor (0–3)	Fair (4–6)	Excellent (7–10)	Expected Rating	Competitor 1	Competitor 2
Experience						
Competency and capability						
Resource availability						
Funding availability						
Consistency with mission						
Profit potential						
Market potential						
Probability, short-listed						
Probability, award						
Competitive analysis						
Time to respond						
Information to respond						
Total score						

capabilities. A scoring mechanism like the following is commonly used for this type of analysis:

- Score of 59 or lower—low compatibility or probability, it is an extremely risky project. Even if you win it, you won't want it!

Table 3-5. Internal requirements bid analysis.

Bid Evaluation Criteria	Score
Existing favorable relationship with customer	
Experience level with projects of this type	
Success with projects of this type	
Compatibility with business direction	
Compatibility with core competencies	
Potential for success	
Potential for profitability	
Potential for future business with customer	
Potential for expanded business with customer	
Potential for expanded business in industry	
Financial stability/reliability of customer	
Ease of working with customer	
Requirement for minimal unpaid up-front work	
Requirement for minimal unpaid travel	
Availability of resources to support project	
Availability of funding to support project	
Availability of subsystems to support project	
Probability of senior management support	
Probability of being short-listed	
Probability of winning project	
Total score	

- Score of 60–69—fair compatibility or probability, it is a high-risk project and not worth the time and cost of proposal development under most situations.
- Score of 70–79—moderate compatibility or probability—a moderate risk, the project is pursued only if the risks and costs can be tightly controlled.

- Score of 80–89—good compatibility or probability—a low-risk project, it is pursued, but proposal costs and terms will need to be closely controlled.
- Score of 90–100—excellent compatibility or probability, the project is pursued.

If the Decision is to Decline

If, based upon the project manager's due diligence, the decision is made to decline the RFP/RFQ, doing so professionally will guarantee other opportunities in the future. The project manager prepares a formal response explaining that current business conditions prevent further consideration of the RFP/RFQ at this time. If the project manager has a sound basis for recommending that the customer consider a competitor, then the project manager makes the recommendation. He closes with a request to be considered for future project opportunities and extends best wishes to the customer for a successful project. Figure 3-3 is illustrative of a typical response letter.

Declining professionally is critical to ensure consideration for future projects. Typical mistakes made by inexperienced project managers guarantee just the opposite result. For example, raising the price to ensure the bid is not accepted by the customer is never a good practice. It only guarantees that future opportunities will not be forthcoming. Extending the schedule to ensure it exceeds the customer's needs is also a poor practice. It usually gives the impression that the project manager has poor project management skills. Again, in this case, future opportunities to bid will be limited at best. The best approach is to decline professionally and gracefully, letting the customer know that his business is of value and appreciated.

If the Decision is to Bid

If the decision is made to pursue the project, then winning is the expected outcome. To do so requires effective planning and execution of the proposal. Failure to do so guarantees the proposal will fail.

Example

Dear Mr. Smith:

Your consideration of XYZ, Inc. in the bidding process for your project was deemed a compliment that we greatly appreciate.

Unfortunately, due to current business constraints, we will be unable to submit a proposal at this time. The requirements and expectations outlined within your RFP would simply extend us beyond our current capacities given the commitments we currently have made to our other valued customers. Compromising the quality of our services to you or our other customers is inconsistent with our corporate values. So, in cases in which we cannot provide the level of quality service necessary to fulfill our customer's needs completely, we prefer to decline rather than to provide less than excellent service.

Although we are declining to bid on this RFP, please consider us on any upcoming projects that you may have in the future. We value our professional relationships with both new and existing customers and would certainly look forward to the opportunity to work with your organization in the future.

Figure 3-3. Declining an RFP/RFQ professionally in a letter.

Proposal development begins with establishment of a proposal budget to guide the team financially. As a general rule of thumb, the team should not spend more than 2–2.5% of the expected returns from the project to develop the proposal. Once the proposal budget is created, the project team assignments are made and a mini-project proposal plan is devised. A typical proposal development team consists of members from the project team, marketing and/or sales, technical writers, and legal counsel. As illustrated in Figure 3-4, each individual on the proposal team is assigned specific duties along with corresponding deliverables and their schedule.

To guide the proposal development process, the project manager utilizes a simple checklist tool as is illustrated in Table 3-6. The intent of the checklist is to identify all required steps

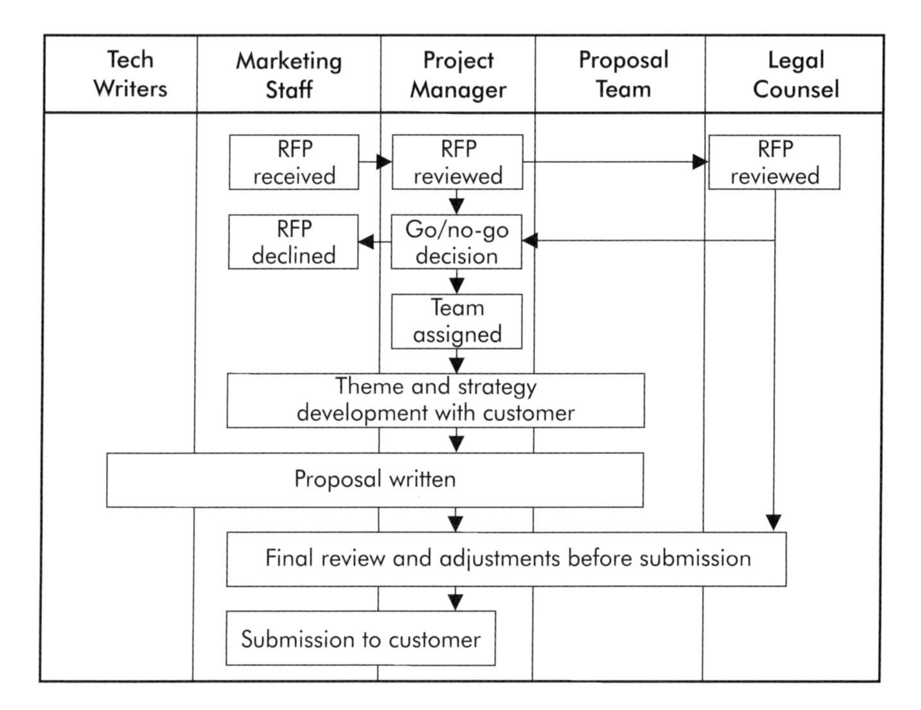

Figure 3-4. Proposal development team assignments.

in the proposal development process, specific assignments, and timing for the initial through the final drafts of the proposal. While this step may seem redundant, it is actually vital due to the scope of many complex project proposals. Any missing or incomplete element of the proposal will render it useless from the customer's perspective and thus a waste of resources of the bidding organization.

The next step in the proposal development process is to gather information and customer data to better understand the customer's expectations and hot buttons, as well as the project itself. To expedite this process, the project manager develops a series of guidelines for the project team to facilitate the information gathering, while at the same time placing as little burden on the customer as possible. Here is a typical set of guidelines:

Table 3-6. Proposal development checklist.

Proposal: ______________________ Date due: ____________

Proposal/project manager: ______________________

Section	Assigned to	First Draft Due	Second Draft Due	Final Draft Due	Complete
Cover letter					
Title page					
Table of contents					
Executive summary					
Introduction/statement of problem					
Statement of scope					
Statement of requirements					
Statement of approach					
Statement of methodologies					
Project control methodologies					
Quality control methodologies					
Project plan (schedule)					
Project budget/fee structure					
Expected savings or return on investment					

Project team's qualifications					
Contract consultant's qualifications					
Completed projects history					
Customer and professional references					
Awards and recognitions received					
Support materials: Project team profiles Graphics to be included Photographs to be included Videos to be included Brochures to be included					
Production activities: Proofreading Printing/copying Binding Tabs Shipping and handling					
Final review of proposal					

- Prepare a list of the information or data needed.
- Prepare questions that will yield the information needed.
- Target calls to specific individuals with the expertise to answer the required questions.
- Start with the general business issues and then work in the details.
- Saying, "I need your help" or "I don't know" is a perfectly good way to get the conversation started.
- Use what is learned with each call to lead to the next.
- Let the customer talk. Ask open-ended questions.
- Separate opinions from facts by asking for data sources.
- After each call, ask for other individuals that the team might talk with.
- When the conversation becomes repetitive, move on to the next call.

When gathering data for the project, the project manager and his team speak with customer personnel from as many levels within the customer's organization as possible to get an objective perspective of all available facts. A good practice in so doing is to match the organizational level of the interviewer with that of the customer representative. This will greatly improve the information-gathering process because individuals of the same level or discipline share a common bond that allows the information to be passed in a more informal manner.

During the information-gathering process, the project team is instructed to do no selling. The intent is simply to gather data with which to prepare the proposal. The team is instructed to ask open-ended questions, then to listen intently, taking copious notes. Often, it is important for team members to "read between the lines" to understand fully what is being said and why. Of particular importance for the team members is to:

- Determine if there is a strong sense of urgency in starting and completing the project.
- Determine if there is strong commitment to the project at all levels.
- Determine if there is a strong aversion to risk.

- Determine if there is sensitivity to the customer's own designs or concepts.
- Determine if there is sensitivity to bidders' litigation records.
- Determine if there is sensitivity to the bidder's size, financial capability, or resource availability.
- Determine if there is sensitivity to the bidder's primary industry, customers, or markets.
- Determine if there is sensitivity to the bidder's project success record or number of projects managed.
- Determine if there is sensitivity to the bidder's location.
- Determine if there is sensitivity to the bidder's fee structure.
- Determine if there are environmental and safety concerns.
- Determine if there are competitive concerns for the customer.
- Determine if there are funding concerns for the customer or bidders.
- Determine if there are political concerns among project stakeholders within or external to the customer's organization.

Information on the customer and her organization is also available from a multitude of external sources, including:

- industry trade groups;
- suppliers;
- customers;
- competitors;
- Dun & Bradstreet, Standard and Poor's, or Moody's reports;
- annual reports;
- stockbrokers, fund managers, or market makers;
- chambers of commerce;
- trade or business journals;
- bankers or creditors;
- board members;
- union representatives; and
- local politicians.

Depending upon the size, nature, and scope of the project under consideration, the data gathered is either general in nature or highly detailed. The following is a list of probing questions that can be considered in this process.

- Is the customer financially stable? (Can the fees be paid?)
- How large is the organization?
- Is the company growing, shrinking, or remaining unchanged in size?
- Who are the decision-makers for the project?
- What is the company's mission?
- What markets does the company serve?
- What does the company offer in the way of products and/or services?
- What is the company's reputation in the marketplace?
- What market share does the customer hold? (Is it growing, declining, or unchanged?)
- Who are the customer's main competitors?
- Is there a conflict of interest in working with them?
- What organizational, process, or personnel problems does the customer have?
- Does the customer currently work with any of our competitors?
- If so, is the relationship one that promotes competitive bidding?
- Have we worked with the customer in the past?
- What is the nature of our relationship with the customer?
- What other projects does the customer have underway or planned that we should consider?
- Do we know the customer's priorities relative to schedule, price, and deliverable?
- Is the project well defined?
- Are the evaluation criteria well defined?
- Are the evaluation criteria reasonable?
- What is the customer's track record on prior projects of this type?

- Is the customer's project manager knowledgeable of the technologies required?
- How well does the customer's project manager interface with contractors?

Knowing the competition is important. Consequently, the information-gathering process incorporates data on expected competitors along with an assessment of their probability of being short-listed and winning the project. The following are typical questions to ask relative to possible competitors.

- Who is our primary competition on this project?
- Who are the former and current customers of this competitor?
- What are the competitor's strengths and weaknesses?
- What are the competitor's normal fee structures?
- What is the competitor's track record?
- What is the competitor's hit rate?
- What is the competitor's quality of work?
- What is the competitor's reputation?
- What is the competitor's financial condition?
- What are the strengths of the competitor's key project personnel?
- Does the competitor hold any unique qualifications or advantages?
- How will the competitor likely structure and market his bid?

Table 3-7 illustrates a commonly used comparison technique. All expected competitors are baselined against a series of general criteria utilizing a comparative scale of:

- poor = 1–2 points;
- marginal = 3–5 points;
- good = 6–8 points
- excellent = 9–10 points

The competitor with the highest score represents the likely winner with all things being equal.

Table 3-7. Competitive comparison tool.

Selected Criteria	Our Organization	Competitor #1	Competitor #2	Competitor #3
Fees				
Experience				
Approach				
Guarantees				
Project team				
Track record				
Risk control				
Marketing				
Relationships				
Total				

PROPOSAL STRATEGY

A focused strategy for the proposal is essential to differentiating the project team's proposal from that of the competition. The strategy selected will demonstrate to the customer that the team clearly understands all aspects of the project along with the drivers behind them. It is important that the proposal demonstrates not only what deliverables the customer expects from the project, but also why those deliverables are desired. At the same time, the strategy is intended to be bold in addressing the customer's hot buttons and the project requirements. The strategy will ultimately be interwoven throughout the proposal in a subtle yet consistent manner, providing a common thread that links all of the sections together. In essence, the strategy is intended to provide irrefutable proof that the customer should select the project team's proposal over others submitted.

The strategy can take several forms, depending upon the results of the project team's due diligence into the customer and the competition. For example, the strategy selected can be competitive, responsive, or targeted.

Competitive:

- designed to expose the weaknesses of the competition;
- designed to showcase the strengths or advantages the project team has over its competitors; and
- designed to highlight the value or benefits the customer will derive from selecting the project team's proposal over those of its competitors.

Responsive:

- designed to address the customer's specifically stated expectations and requirements; and
- designed to address the drivers behind the customer's stated and implicit expectations and requirements.

Targeted:

- designed to illustrate why the project team is uniquely qualified, capable, and positioned to manage the project for the customer; and
- designed to highlight specific skills, processes, technologies, expertise, systems, or equipment the project team has at its disposal for the project that competitors do not.

As stated earlier in this chapter, the strategy selected by the team focuses on what the customer wants from the project versus what the project team wants to provide. *It is the customer's project.* The proposal and its intended strategy, therefore, always focus on and reinforce that fact throughout each section.

In developing the strategy, the team remains sensitive to political and regulatory requirements governing the customer, as well as to potential penalties and contingent liabilities that could be passed along from the customer to the team's own organization. At all times, the team remains sensitive to committing to only those deliverables it can and intends to deliver.

There is a definite marketing side to developing an effective strategy. Thus, as a guide, the team develops a listing of every conceivable reason why the customer might resist selecting its proposal, followed by a strategy to address each one. Consideration is given as to how each real or perceived weakness can be turned into an advantage, be repackaged, or be addressed in the proposal, as well as how to best showcase the team's strengths, competencies, and project-related experience.

WRITING THE PROPOSAL

With the strategy completed, the project manager and his team begin to write the proposal. The first step is to review the available data sources to isolate the "must" and "shall" statements in the RFP/RFQ or other contract documents. Data sources may include the:

- RFP;
- scope of work statement;
- specification or requirements document;
- performance or quality standards (ISO, QS, AS9000);
- implicit requirements from the interview with the customer;
- evaluation or ranking criteria;
- regulatory requirements or rulings;
- environmental impact studies;
- customer vision and mission statements;
- customer contract policy statements;
- former successful proposals with the customer; and
- former unsuccessful proposals with the customer.

All available sources of information are used to provide the team with important data with which to address the critical hot buttons and project requirements of the customer.

Once all "must" and "shall" requirements have been isolated, a comprehensive explanation of how each will be addressed or satisfied, technically and administratively, is then developed for inclusion in the proposal. It is vital to explain how the team will effectively plan and execute the customer's type and scale of project, monitor project performance, control potential failures, as well as apply proactive risk management techniques to control surprises that could compromise the project. The team focuses on conveying a comprehensive understanding of all the technical aspects of the project and provides logical, supportable evidence that the technical solution being proposed will address the root causes behind the customer's issues or opportunities.

It is important that the customer understand (and concur) as to why the project team has selected the proposed approach. The customer must be comfortable that the project team has given due consideration to the unique needs and requirements of the project by proposing a customized approach versus a canned one that may or may not work as proposed. The message to the customer is that the team has considered all feasible options and, from them, has selected the most cost-effective, risk-adverse approach possible for the project. Whenever possible, the team incorporates applicable past successes with similar customized approaches, as well as comparisons to other less successful approaches applied by competitors.

Once the approach or methodologies that will be applied have been defined, the team creates an outline (see Table 3-6) to guide the writing of the proposal. Just like a work breakdown structure (WBS), the outline ensures a logical flow for the proposal while at the same time assuring that nothing will be left out.

As the project team members begin the development process for each section, they consider four questions to aid in guiding their efforts:

1. What are the key things that must be addressed in this section?
2. How will each be accomplished?
3. Why was each particular approach selected?
4. What strategy (or sub-strategy) will be incorporated in support of those actions?

With answers to these questions available, the writing of each section begins.

Just as many project professionals are not adept at verbal communications, many are ill equipped to write a comprehensive and concise proposal that is pleasing to the reader. Most proposals are excessively long, requiring the reader to spend an inordinate amount of time wading through page after page of irrelevant information in an attempt to identify the salient points. It is best to be as concise as possible. If something can be said in 20 pages, avoid the temptation to expand the proposal to 100 pages just to make it appear more impressive. On the other hand, the experienced writer never leaves open questions or fails to address all issues of prime importance to the customer.

One overriding fact is always paramount: someone is required to read every proposal. The experienced project manager and his team are keenly aware of the fact that human nature will prevail. If the reviewer finds a proposal difficult to read or understand, it will be set aside while others are being considered, or simply discarded. Either way, the opportunity to get short-listed is lost. Consequently, successful project managers follow a few simple rules when writing a proposal:

- Eliminate redundancy and unnecessary boilerplate copy.
- Dump the apple pie and motherhood statements.
- All references are directed toward "this" project only.
- Bullet points, graphs, and tables are used to minimize the volume of text.
- Simple, commonly understood words and phrases are used (the average person reads at an 8th grade level).
- Slang terms and acronyms are avoided.
- Paragraphs are kept to four sentences, sentences to no more than 10 words, and words to no more than 12 letters.
- The tone of the content is professional, but relaxed, like a good novel.
- Active tense is always preferred.
- Sizzle and excitement are incorporated into the document (if it is boring to the writer, it will put the reviewer to sleep!).

Page design and format also have an impact on the reader's willingness to read the document. As much "white space" as possible is incorporated to reduce text density and make the document more visually interesting. Headers and graphics are used for the same reason. Margins, for example, are maintained at approximately 1.0 to 1.25 in. for visual relief. A good comparison to demonstrate this point is to compare the front pages of *USA Today* against the old format of *The Wall Street Journal*. Sans serif fonts are used for the body of the document because they make the eye move faster, while serif fonts are used for headings and titles to draw attention. Novelty fonts are never utilized in a professional document, nor are more than two fonts ever used in a document.

Because flow and organization are critical to a professional proposal, page numbers are a must, as are section numbers, graphics titles, and a table of contents. Graphics are kept simple and incorporate one message or theme each. Those that best depict the point being made are selected; non-relevant graphics are always avoided. Color, too, is important. For text, black is preferred, with red used only to highlight negative or nonperforming factors. Thermal or wire binding is always preferred and off-the-shelf report covers are always avoided.

Cover Sheet

As the cover sheet is the first thing the reviewer sees, it immediately sets the expectation for the contents of the proposal. If it is interesting, eye-catching, and attractive, the reviewer is more likely to read on than if it is dull and uninspiring. As a result, successful proposal writers select a 30+ pound, glossy coated stock for their cover sheets. A high-quality print job is also mandatory. Another good technique is to subtly incorporate the theme or strategy selected by the project team into the cover sheet.

Cover Letter

The cover letter may well make or break a proposal. Thus, experienced proposal writers avoid using boilerplate copy, clichés, or the same old dry phrases used by everyone else. Statements like "Our organization is uniquely qualified to provide you with . . ." or "Our staff of highly qualified professionals can deliver what you need when you need it" are simply boring and trite. Instead, the cover letter is used to introduce energy and sizzle into the proposal, to differentiate it from the competition and grab the reviewer's attention and interest, and to make a bold statement concerning one or more of the customer's hot buttons. This will encourage the reviewer to read the proposal to learn how the project team intends to support that statement.

A cover letter always contains more references to the customer or the customer's project than to the project manager, his team, or his organization. As a general rule, the references to the customer outweigh those to the project team by at least a factor of 3 to 1. The experienced project manager recognizes that the project is all about the customer, not his team or his organization.

The cover letter is a focused, action-oriented, one- to two-page (maximum) introduction of the primary project issues and opportunities. It includes a recap of the customer's key hot buttons or concerns and a summary of the results the project team will deliver to address each. For example:

> "You and your staff will enjoy a 35% return on investment from the $3.2 million savings that will be generated from your project over the next three years as a direct result of CAG's commitment to your process cycle time improvements. In fact, over 15 clients from diverse industries have actually realized well in excess of that amount due to rigorous attention to detail and design excellence on their projects.
>
> "You will be the beneficiary of this strong tradition of excellence in project and design management through:
>
> - industry-acclaimed scheduling and budgetary controls to ensure total compliance with your project requirements (see page 3).
> - dedicated project personnel with the expertise and the authority to make on-site decisions that will minimize the risk of unexpected design and process failures throughout your project's life cycle (see page 5).
> - custom-designed cost containment and monitoring techniques that will ensure your targeted reduction of 23% in operating expenses (see page 6).

- state-of-the-art engineering change order control processes that have been designed exclusively for your project to ensure no more than a 3% change order rate throughout the life of your project (see page 9)."

In this example, the project manager supports his statements through the use of references to specific pages, which invite the reader into the body of the proposal where detailed explanations are given. His use of active versus passive tense gives credence to his statements, as well as confidence to the reviewer that there is substance to this proposal that warrants further, more detailed review and consideration.

The closing of the cover letter is equally as positive, leaving no doubt in the reviewer's mind that the project team is ready, willing, and able to deliver on their commitments. Again, for example:

- "Our project team will contact you to address your questions and schedule a kickoff meeting with your project personnel," or
- "Our project team has begun the preliminary development of the project schedule in anticipation of your favorable response to the proposal."

As it is an integral part of the proposal, as well as a major piece of the marketing effort, the cover letter is always bound into the proposal to ensure it will not get separated from the body of the proposal and lost.

Title Page

As with the cover letter, the title page establishes the "look" of the proposal and thus reinforces the level of expectation established in the cover letter. It is an ideal place to incorporate one or more elements of the team's strategy or theme into the proposal title. As a consequence, the use of company letterhead is discouraged. The title page incorporates limited graphics, and only those that are appropriate. For maximum impact, the title page is kept clean, professional, and simple.

Table of Contents

The reason the project manager incorporates a table of contents into the proposal is to assist the customer in locating specific sections quickly. Proposals are typically reviewed by more than one individual, and every reviewer will have a different hot button or area of interest. The table of contents directs each reviewer to those sections of greatest individual interest, thereby facilitating the total review process and enhancing the probability that the proposal receives favorable consideration.

The table of contents is not overly detailed; it is usually a single page that contains the section titles and subtitles along with their corresponding page numbers. On large proposals (100+ pages), the project manager incorporates index tabs for each major section, as well as an index at the back of the proposal. The objective is to make it as easy as possible to find information.

Executive Summary

The executive summary is a condensed version, a one- to two-page synopsis, of the salient points of the proposal. It is intended for those executives who have neither the time nor the inclination to read the proposal in its entirety, but who want to know enough to make an informed decision. As a consequence, this is an extremely important section requiring much skill in its preparation.

By design, the executive summary is a 25,000-foot overview of the proposal stated in as few words as possible, much like a legal brief. This user-friendly section states known or expected problems or issues and how each will be addressed. Again, to facilitate the review process for these senior reviewers, it includes references to specific sections (and pages) within the proposal where more detailed descriptions of each issue resolution are discussed. It contains:

- a statement of purpose for the proposal;
- a statement of the scope of the proposal;
- restatement of the project requirements and specifications in brief;

- a statement of approach or methodology selected by the project team for the project and why that approach is best for this project;
- a statement of the results that the project team will generate for the customer (be careful, this is a commitment!); and
- a conclusion statement.

A checklist (see Table 3-8) is used to guide the project manager and his team in writing this critical section to ensure every key element is captured and nothing omitted. Even a small omission or mistake in the executive summary will be devastating as it will leave the executive reviewers (decision-makers) with questions or concerns about the project team's ability to effectively manage the project.

The following is an example of a well-written executive summary. Not only is it targeted on the key hot buttons of the executives who will review the proposal, but it also sets a level of expectation by stating specific deliverables along with the methods that will be utilized to achieve them. It further incorporates specific references to sections within the body of the proposal where the reviewers will find more detailed explanations, thus reinforcing that the proposal contains a high degree of substance versus just hollow words or generalities.

> "Achieving a targeted improvement of 15% to 20% in ABC's operating performance within the Plantation Division is the intent of this proposal. To realize this objective within 18 months from ABC's acceptance of this proposal, specific actions have been identified for inclusion in the project plan. Those actions are consistent with the requirements outlined in ABC's RFP of December 22, 2008, and include the following:
>
> - a comprehensive situational assessment and reengineering of ABC's manufacturing processes within the electronics operations of the Plantation facility,
> - an aggressive value engineering of all product families currently produced within those same manufacturing processes,

Table 3-8. Executive summary checklist.

Questions to Consider	Yes/No
Are the expected results or deliverables well defined?	
Are all problems and opportunities well defined?	
Is the approach to the problem or opportunity well defined?	
Are the reasons why the approach was selected well defined?	
Are all technical requirements defined and addressed?	
Are the customer's technical concerns effectively addressed?	
Are the customer's managerial concerns effectively addressed?	
Are all RFP requirements and specifications addressed?	
Is the selection of the project team well supported and justified?	
Does it adequately define the strategic plan?	
Does it adequately define the tactical project plan?	
Does it define how risk management will be employed?'	
Does it demonstrate our capability to manage the project?	
Does it demonstrate our commitment to manage the project?	
Does it communicate the selected proposal theme in a clear way?	
Does it answer the questions the decision-makers will likely have?	
Is it logical?	
Is it easy to read and comprehend?	

- a comprehensive skills assessment of the Plantation personnel associated with the direct and indirect support of the manufacturing processes, and
- establishment of new baseline performance measurements for operating personnel within the manufacturing and support processes.

"The action items selected for the project were the result of extensive research into ABC's current operating performance and three-year historical trends that have demonstrated a marginal decline in operating throughput and product quality, coupled with a significant increase in operating expenses and inventory investment. The trends in these key operating metrics indicate a movement away from the positive improvements made by ABC's competitors. They are indicative of severe process-related problems requiring immediate attention before sizable losses in market position are realized. Refer to Section 4, page 27 for further details.

"Based upon multiple successes in reengineering complex electronics manufacturing processes similar to ABC's (references have been provided in Section 6, page 55), it is anticipated that the targeted improvements required by ABC in its RFP can be achieved within the time and budgetary constraints designated. Specifically, the deliverables for the project will include:

- 12% to 15% reduction in inventory investment in AA and A-class items,
- 20% to 30% reduction in process cycle time for all direct manufacturing processes within the electronics unit,
- 45% to 50% reduction in budget variances within the manufacturing unit, and
- 5% to 7% improvement in first-pass yields from the current baselines.

"The techniques that will be employed to generate these results are detailed in Section 5, page 42 of the proposal. These techniques have been recognized by Fortune 100 companies as "world class" and have been deemed "innovative and proactive" by MIT's Sloan Business School.

"To summarize, the requirements of ABC's RFP of December 22, 2008 can and will be achieved through an aggressive, well-managed project led by CAG's senior project manager and supported by the senior executive staff. CAG

> will utilize proven reengineering techniques applied by experienced professionals with a track record of success on multiple projects in similar industries."

Scope Statement

The statement of scope delineates for the reviewer specifically what the project contains and what it does not. While clearly stating what is specifically excluded from the project may seem somewhat redundant, it is important as it defines the boundaries under which the proposal is based. Including this statement will help to avoid misunderstanding or misconceptions about what is and is not included in the project team's intended scope of work.

The scope statement contains a statement of understanding, as well as a detailed scope of services statement. The statement of understanding demonstrates to the customer the project team's understanding of the project. It is not used to sell the project team's approach or the capabilities of the proposing organization. As with all sections of the proposal, brevity is paramount. Here is an example.

> "It is understood that ABC, Inc. expects conformance with MIL standard 105.1 in system design configuration and specification, at a project cost not to exceed $14.6 million. The expected project completion date is on or before June 17, 2009, and the expected project deliverables are:
>
> - Phase one prototypes of all primary systems as described in Section D-27 of the RFP dated March 6, 2009;
> - validation process definitions conforming to MIL standard 105.34 for all primary and subsystem elements described in Section D-38 of the RFP dated March 6, 2009; and
> - system compatibility analyses for all primary and subsystem elements described in Section D-38 of the RFP dated March 6, 2009, along with recommendations for process improvements for each system and subsystem element consistent with USAF value engineering standards 321.6 and 321.8."

A second example from another industry sector provides additional insight. The level of detail contained is important as it provides clarity of both what is expected from the project, as well as why those deliverables are expected.

> "The City of Wellington owns a 90-acre plot of land lying west of 103rd St., from 103rd to 167th, between Southern Blvd. on the south and Belvedere Rd. on the north. The City of Wellington, in close cooperation with the Palm Beach County Business Development Department, is proposing to develop a phased, high-technology business park on that plot of land. The Palm Beach County Business Development Department will rezone the land for commercial use to accommodate the City of Wellington's business park development.
>
> "The City of Wellington intends to retain the services of a professional development team to prepare the land use and reclamation master plan, an environmental impact statement, and preliminary engineering study for submission to the County Planning and Zoning Commission.
>
> "The major objectives of this project are:
>
> - to develop a master plan, which emphasizes compatible land usage;
> - to redevelop vacant, condemned land into tax-generating facilities, thereby enhancing the tax base for both the City of Wellington and Palm Beach County;
> - to provide 2,800 jobs for the residents of Palm Beach County; and
> - to improve the revenues flowing into the City of Wellington by 26% within 18 months of completion of the project."

The scope of services statement clearly and comprehensively delineates all activities planned during the project and all deliverables that will be generated. This critical statement sets the level of expectations for the customer, as well as the terms and conditions under which the project team will operate. The deliverables list is made as extensive as possible to reinforce the team's understanding of the customer's needs, as well as to ensure that there will be no downstream surprises should the customer have expected something other than what the team intended to provide. As with other elements of the proposal, bullet points are used not only to ensure brevity, but also because they do not imply any prioritization. The scope of services statement does not include "experience" language. It only describes those activities that will be included in the project, an approximate schedule for each, the assignments for each, and the control and monitoring techniques that will be employed by the project manager.

In the scope of services statement, the project team is free to introduce any additional activities that the research indicated will be needed to ensure successful project completion. So doing further emphasizes the team's understanding of the project environment and constraints, and why acceptance of the proposal will provide additional value that the competition will not. Care is given, however, to emphasize to the reviewer that these additional actions are optional so as not to give the impression that the team is padding the project to generate additional revenues. This section is also an excellent place to incorporate any non-cost activities that the project team will provide at no additional cost to the customer. Even minor "free-bees" are appreciated and make for good marketing.

In the event that the criteria contained in the RFP/RFQ are unclear or incomplete, the project manager incorporates the team's assumptions in the scope statement along with the logic used to support them. He reinforces in the statement that the proposal is based upon those assumptions and that altering those assumptions will result in a change to the scope of the project along with the project team's project definition and deliverables. A good approach is to propose a preliminary investigation to aid the customer in solidifying his specifications, requirements, and expectations. From that investigation, the customer will be able to develop a more effective RFP/RFQ. This approach will set the project team apart from its competition by demonstrating its willingness to work with the customer in ways that will ensure the success of the customer's project. Still another approach is to provide the customer with a menu of suggested activities from which to select those of most interest. Known as "microscoping," this approach provides the customer with the ability to tailor the project and its cost to specific business constraints.

Statement of Approach

Conveying the project's methodology, the statement of approach describes how the project team intends to execute the project for the customer. It corresponds with the statement of understanding by addressing each specific requirement stated therein with a specific plan of action that will generate the expected results. The statement of approach is designed to leave no doubt that the project manager and his team have done their due diligence and know exactly what to do to meet all project requirements. There is no boilerplate or canned business model used in the preparation of the statement of approach. This statement is unique to each project and, as such, is always drafted anew for every project.

The statement of approach is written as though the project team has already been awarded the project. Action-oriented, fact-based verbiage demonstrates a proactive approach to the project, leaving the reviewer with the confidence that this project team is ready, willing, and able to handle the project. The statement of approach also describes how and why the approach being proposed is different/better than that being proposed by the competition. This will assist the customer in understanding how to differentiate between proposals. It starts with an overview or summary, and then becomes progressively more detailed as each action is described.

Project Controls

The statement of control or compliance describes the quantitative project control or quality management techniques that will be employed by the project team to ensure that the desired results are obtained. Specific tools and methodologies are cited that have been used previously on similar projects, along with the results they generated. Commonly used control techniques include:

- preliminary failure analyses,
- failure mode and effects analyses,
- fault failure analyses,
- system failure analyses,
- statistical process control techniques,
- advanced quality planning processes,
- process capability analyses,
- quality function deployment techniques,
- design of experiments techniques,
- stage-gate monitoring techniques, and
- performance metrics and reporting techniques.

The team explains how these proposed techniques will be dynamically applied throughout the project to ensure continuous control versus a static, one-time review. Particular emphasis is again placed upon the customer's hot buttons. Reference is made to monitoring and reporting frequencies to reinforce the strong level of proactive control that will be applied during all phases of the project. While emphasis is placed on proactive management and control, the project team and the customer are cognizant of the fact that surprises do happen, especially with complex projects. Thus, in this section the project team explains the contingency planning techniques that will be utilized to control the impact of a failure should it occur.

Project Team Qualifications

Stating the qualifications of the project team members provides the project manager with another opportunity to sell his proposal to the customer. He opens with a brief one-page explanation of how the team members were selected for the project, how they will be organized, and how they will be managed. He includes personal profiles of each team member so that the customer understands whom they will be working with, as well as their individual and collective project-specific qualifications for the project. It is important that this section focus on the capability as well as the experience of each team member.

Figure 3-5 illustrates an effective summary tool. It indicates not only each project team member's project-specific experience, but his or her technical expertise and project experience as well. There are levels of redundancy for critical assignments and all critical skill sets have been effectively covered for the project.

	Project Team Experience	Jefferson	Jones	Biltmore	Cheney	Thompson
Project-specific Experience	Large system-based projects	X		X	X	
	Large structure-based projects		X	X		X
	Large government-funded projects	X	X	X	X	X
	Large budget-constrained projects	X	X	X	X	
	Large subcontractor projects	X		X	X	X
Technical Experience	Structures engineering and design	X	X			X
	Systems engineering and design	X			X	
	Design reliability		X		X	X
	Design producibility		X	X	X	X
	Concurrent engineering	X	X	X	X	X
	Value engineering/value analysis		X	X	X	X
	Quality engineering/control			X	X	X
	Safety, environmental, health compliance		X			X
Project Management	Human-machine engineering			X		X
	Contract administration		X		X	X
	Direct project management responsibility	X			X	
	Project planning	X	X			
	Project execution/implementation	X	X		X	X
	Risk management	X	X	X	X	X
	Subcontractor management	X			X	X

Figure 3-5. Project team expertise.

The personal profiles are written with a focus on project-specific accomplishments, results the individual has achieved in previous project assignments, and how those skills will be applied to the customer's project to generate similar results. For example:

> "Phillip Reed is an internationally recognized expert in the fields of electronic design and process reliability, with over 25 years of hands-on product development experience. Phil's personal involvement on the Time Warner project last year resulted in a 23% reduction in design costs and a 36% reduction in engineering changes. These are consistent with the results being sought on ABC's project."

Personal profiles are yet another marketing tool for use by the project manager in differentiating his proposal from that of his competition. The profiles are kept short, targeted, and include testimonials to further enhance their value to the customer. They begin with a summary of the individual's experience, capabilities, and past accomplishments. Included are awards or recognitions the team member has received, along with publications and acknowledgements created or received. The focus is on satisfying the customer's hot buttons by demonstrating that one or more project team members have the skills and experience to satisfy those expectations. Next, the project manager briefly describes the individual's relevant project experience along with a brief history of the results generated on one or more of those projects. For example:

> "When the project fell two months behind schedule because of unexpected delays in receiving approval from UL and CSA, Phil rescheduled the balance of the project plan to fast-track the remaining product, process, and tooling design activities, thereby bringing the project in on schedule and on budget."

Testimonials are great marketing tools for the project manager too. There is nothing better for building customer confidence than to read the words of praise from peers or former customers of the proposing company. To capitalize on that fact, testimonials are used frequently, but professionally, to reinforce each team member's capabilities and skills.

The customer is also interested in how the project team will be managed and what assignments will be made. Recognizing this, the project manager incorporates a proposed organization chart that illustrates the various assignments and reporting structures. Early identification of a project team structure provides additional confidence for the customer that this team is ready on day one to start. Figure 3-6 illustrates a typical project organization chart. The project organization chart is created anew for each project to ensure that all team members and corresponding assignments meet the needs of the project under consideration.

Project Schedule and Budget

It is essential that the schedule and budget included within the proposal be realistic and attainable. Once delineated within the proposal, the two become locked in concrete from the customer's perspective. It is, therefore, incumbent upon the project manager and his team to ensure that all factors impacting the project from planning through execution be thoroughly evaluated before incorporation into the proposal. Risk planning is factored into each as well. The remaining chapters of this text focus on project schedule development, budget, and risk management plans. Thus only the general guidelines will be covered here.

Use of graphics in the project schedule and budget section is preferred, but only in an overview sense. For example, a top-level Gantt chart is acceptable, as is a chronological milestone chart to illustrate the proposed project schedule. For the budget, a table of expenditures by category and date gives the customer the data required for preliminary cash flow planning. A preliminary failure analysis provides sufficient detail to demonstrate the project team's competency in managing foreseeable project risks. The project manager provides enough data to validate his numbers and projections, but avoids providing the details behind those summaries until either the team is short-listed or the project is awarded.

In addition, the project manager incorporates into this section a description of the change control, configuration control, schedule control, budget control, and contingency planning techniques and

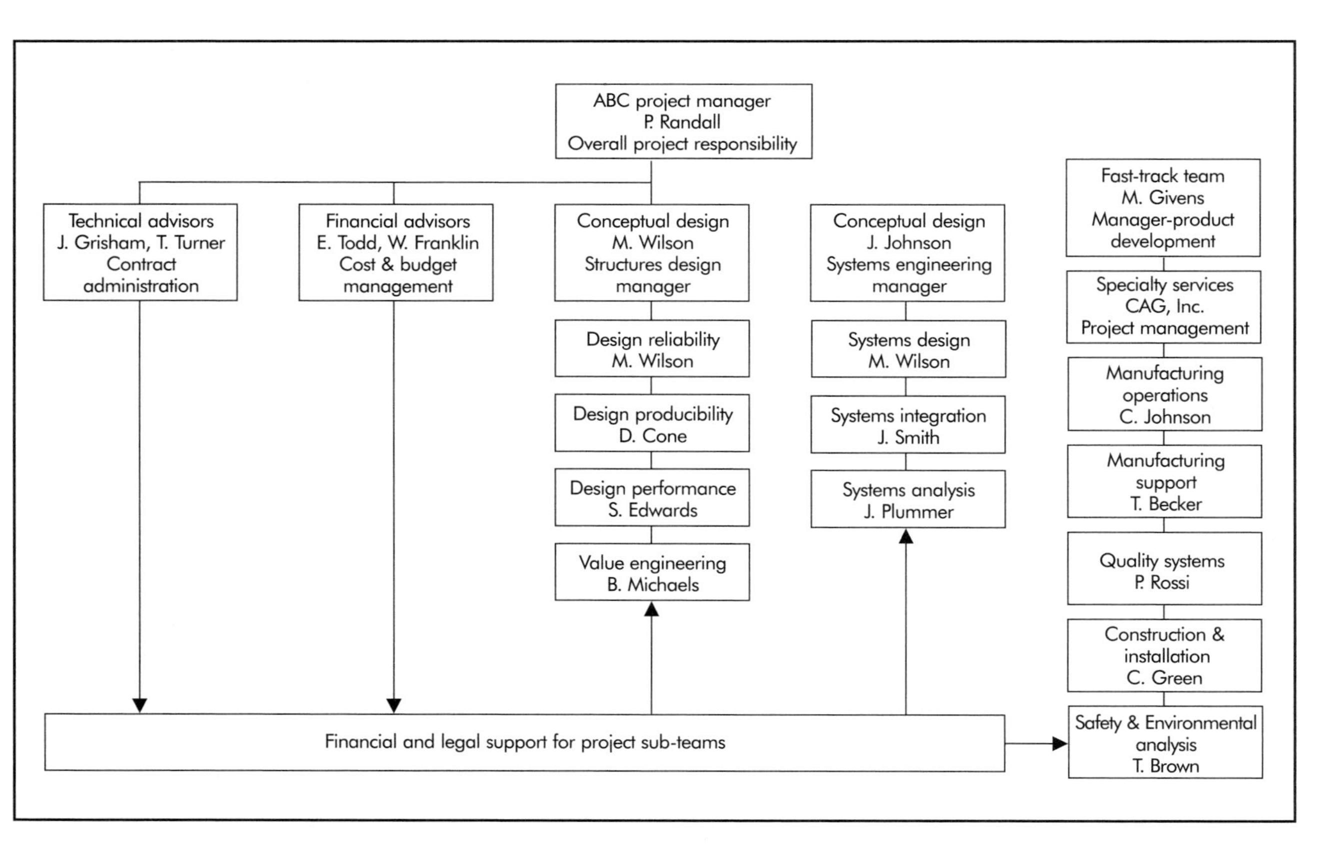

Figure 3-6. Typical project team organization chart.

systems that will be employed to ensure that all of the project requirements are met. Examples from prior projects of a similar scope and inclusion of testimonials are excellent sales tools in this section as they demonstrate the effectiveness of the controls in project environments like that of the customer.

Appendix

Appendices are used by the project team to house relevant supporting data, documentation, forms, licenses, certificates, legal requirements, company information, reference lists, sales literature, and other information that the customer will find of value in evaluating the team's proposal. This is not the place, however, for irrelevant filler materials or unrelated sales brochures. The general rule is: If the information is not of measurable value in supporting one or more sections of the proposal, omit it.

Reality Check

Once the first draft of the proposal is completed, the project manager and the team do a reality check to ensure that:

- All of the customer's hot buttons, requirements, and expectations have been addressed.
- The approach selected for each is realistic given all existing or forecasted constraints.
- The logic used by the project team is sound and easily understood by the customer.
- All options are adequately explained, as well as why the proposed approach was selected.
- All activities for completion of the project have been identified and any associated risks addressed.

Final Review

Prior to sending the proposal to the project "red" team, project management staff, or the executive steering committee for final review before submission to the customer, the project team completes one final internal review of the proposal. All elements must be complete and the look of the proposal must meet professional standards. It must flow logically and be easy to read, leaving nothing open to interpretation. A simple checklist, such as that shown in Table 3-9, can be used to assist the project team with this undertaking.

If in the course of the final reviews, one or more things are found deficient, the project manager ensures that they are addressed before the proposal is delivered. As stated previously, once the proposal is received and accepted by the customer, the project team is locked into the deliverables, terms, conditions, schedule, and budget. As a result, it must be right before it leaves the hands of the project team. More than just winning the project depends upon it.

SUMMARY

This chapter explains the process of writing a project proposal when in a competitive environment. While the focus throughout the chapter is on winning external customer projects, the approach is equally as valid when competing for internal funding against other projects under consideration for inclusion in the portfolio.

The process of preparing and creating a proposal is resource-intensive, requiring a high degree of attention to detail, along with professional planning and skilled execution. Much like building the project schedule and budget that will be discussed in later chapters, writing a successful project proposal requires the skill to communicate effectively, plan thoroughly, and control the external factors that will render the end result useless. As illustrated in Table 3-10, an effective proposal will address all of the customer's questions and concerns. On the other hand, a poorly written proposal generates more questions and concerns than it addresses.

The objective of a project proposal is to get short-listed by the customer, opening the door to allow the project team to formally present it to the customer. The only successful outcome is to win the business. Anything short of that is an exercise in futility. As a result, experienced project managers have learned to do it right the first time.

Table 3-9. Proposal evaluation checklist.

Proposal Evaluation	Yes	No	Revise
Is the main thrust of the proposal to sell our company's services and products?			
Does the proposal contain at least a 3:1 "you/us" ratio?			
Does the proposal hit the customer's hot buttons and their drivers?			
Does the proposal differentiate our company from the other firms who are bidding?			
Is the proposal boring or difficult to read?			
Is the approach clear, logical, and feasible given all constraints?			
Does the proposal demonstrate a comprehensive understanding of the customer's specifications and needs?			
Does the proposal provide convincing evidence that the required results will be achieved?			
Does the proposal demonstrate limited risk in working with our company?			
Does the proposal demonstrate our capability to manage the project effectively?			
Does the proposal clearly define the value we add to the project?			
Does the proposal provide attractive pricing?			
Does the proposal demonstrate an attractive cost/ value ratio?			
Will the proposal get our company short-listed?			

Table 3-10. Proposal evaluation tool.

Characteristics of Effective Proposals
1. An understanding of the customer's specific needs and the drivers behind them is demonstrated.
2. The project proposal is clear, logical, and easily understood.
3. There is demonstrable evidence that the project will work as planned with only limited risk to the customer.
4. The project management team has the requisite skills necessary to manage, control, and complete the project.
5. The cost/benefit comparison for the project is provided for the customer.
6. The cost/benefit comparison is attractive to the customer.
7. There exists a clear linkage between the proposal elements and the customer's evaluation criteria.
8. The proposal focuses on the project's value to the customer and the abilities of the project management team or its organization to deliver that value.
9. The project proposal contains elements of risk management and contingency planning.
10. The project proposal demonstrates agility and flexibility in the project team's approach to the project.

Characteristics of Poor Proposals
1. The proposal fails to demonstrate a comprehensive understanding of the customer's needs and why they exist.
2. The project proposal is difficult to read and comprehend.
3. The project proposal is filled with irrelevant facts, figures, statistics, and examples—simply as filler material.
4. The proposal provides only cursory information about the project management team, failing to show how its skills and experience match the project needs.
5. The proposal does not provide evidence that the project will address the customer's specific requirements.
6. The proposal fails to show the relationship between costs, returns, and risks to the customer.
7. The proposal does not correspond with what the customer requested or desires.
8. The proposal focuses on what the project team will provide versus the benefits the customer will derive.
9. The proposal format and content is obviously boilerplate, with little thought given to creativity or originality.
10. The concepts and ideas outlined in the proposal are not well conceived.

4
The Strategic Planning Model—Acceptance of Responsibilities

OVERVIEW

This chapter's objective is to provide an idea of the depth and breadth of the responsibilities that lie before the project manager. The strategic project planning model that will be employed (see Figure 4-1) begins with the expected project deliverables and expectations as defined through rigorous analysis and discussion with the customer or project sponsor. This initial stage in strategic project planning defines both what is and is not expected from the project and, therefore, begins to determine the project's scope. The intent of this stage is to define what the project is intended to produce; in essence, the results to be derived. Note that this does *not* define the project, only its intended output.

The model then moves into developing the rules and guidelines that define the operational policies and procedures the project team will follow throughout the project's duration. Next is refinement of the project's scope, along with a definition of the project's performance metrics.

The next stage in building the strategic project planning model is selecting the project team based upon the skill sets required for the project. While the project team is often preselected for the project manager by his or her executive management, responsibility for analysis and adjustment of the project team to meet unique project requirements remains with the project manager.

Once the project team is in place, the strategic project planning model requires an assessment of the project management environment to isolate the real and potential problems, issues, and opportunities the project team is likely to face during the

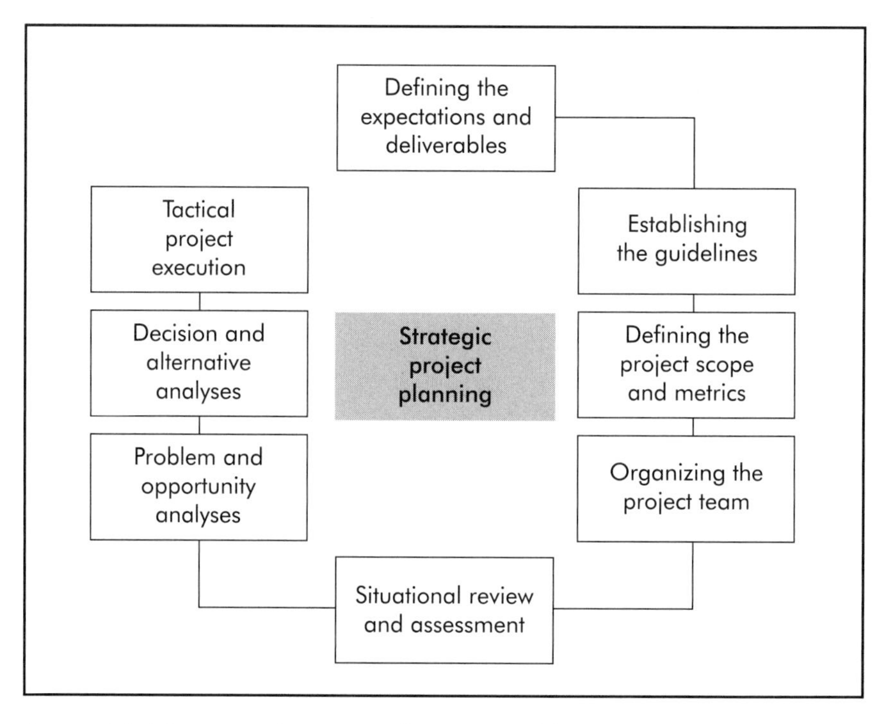

Figure 4-1. The strategic project planning model.

project's life cycle. A critical element in the project planning cycle, situational analysis seeks to identify what's happening now, what happened in the past that must now be dealt with, and what will likely happen in the future that could positively or negatively impact the project.

Problems and issues identified during the situational assessment are then addressed through structured problem analysis to determine the true root cause(s) behind them so that alternatives can be developed and assessed against the project objectives. This, like situational assessment, is part of risk management, focusing on identifying real and potential issues to be assessed and then addressed through contingency planning.

The next stage in strategic planning is to identify all alternatives available to the project team, determine their respective risks and costs, and then quantitatively analyze each alternative against the project objectives. *The alternative selected becomes the definition of the project. In essence, "how the project objectives will be met."*

The final stage in the strategic planning model involves tactical planning and execution as shown in Figure 4-2. Here the selected project alternative is detailed through development and execution tools like the work breakdown structure (WBS), cycle time modeling, PERT techniques, and Gantt charts. These become the tools used by the project management team to control and monitor the project, assess performance against established project objectives, and initiate corrective actions should a problem occur or a trade-off in one or more of the project variables become necessary.

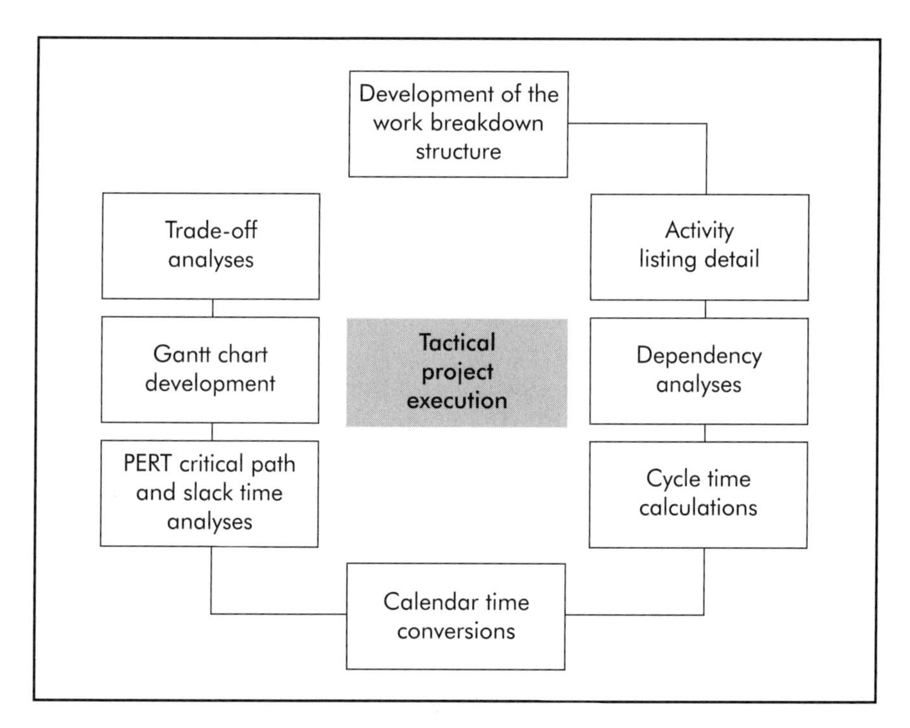

Figure 4-2. The tactical planning and execution model.

Strategic project management is a structured methodology for analyzing and managing complex projects that are, or will likely be, impacted by a multitude of variables, constraints, and internal or external influences. The secret to effective project planning is to utilize these tools to break down the project into several manageable, easy-to-understand-and-monitor subprojects or activities that can be effectively controlled by the project management team throughout the project's duration.

ACCEPTING RESPONSIBILITY

Project management does not mean simply giving orders and expecting employees or peers to blindly follow. The project manager typically has no direct-line management position over the project team members or the functional organizations impacted by the project; thus he has very little real power. The typical project manager has assumed or been given a great deal of responsibility and accountability by management, but is rarely granted the authority with which to force change throughout the organization. As a result, he is often called upon to employ a different approach . . . leadership.

A project manager looks at each situation realistically. To whom do the individuals on the project team report? To whom are they loyal? Who controls their paychecks? A project manager cannot *manage* people who do not report to him; this simply does not work in a project environment. Rather, the project manager must *lead* the team. This requires acceptance and trust from members of the team. And that dictates an entirely different set of skills than are typically utilized by traditional project managers.

> *Project managers must manage time effectively so that it works for, rather than against, the project team.*

Project management requires extensive technological and facilitation skills, the capability to comprehend and develop strategic organizational objectives, and the tactical skills to ensure their successful implementation. In addition, it requires the skills to accurately assess customer (internal and external) requirements and expectations, and then to effectively prioritize them to establish project baselines for future risk and trade-off management. Organizational skills are necessary to select, develop, and motivate personnel from diverse functional and organizational groups to ensure that they work together to attain established project objectives, while keeping the project on schedule and within budget through effective project control processes.

Project management also requires follow-through to ensure that corrective actions are taken quickly and decisively, guaranteeing that the project's objectives are never compromised. And finally, it calls for the skills to know when and how to make decisions that will impact the overall project performance, costs, and schedule.

Effective project managers are ready, willing, and able to make decisions even in the face of conflict or politics. It goes with the territory. To do so requires a thorough understanding of people. They know how to identify the multitude of motivational triggers inherent in every individual, and have the skills to use them effectively. They also understand the importance of establishing attainable milestones and the associated metrics to monitor progress relative to project requirements.

Employees are intelligent and up to a challenge. A project management team given a stretch goal will work diligently to attain it. They will put forth the effort and the hours to meet the challenge. However, they will soon recognize if a goal is unreachable. Then, they will stop trying because they know their limitations. Any individual or team will push for success unless they know that the task at hand is impossible to complete successfully.

SUCCESS OR FAILURE

One of two possible cultures will be established quickly within the project team—success or failure. It occurs with the first project milestone. If that milestone is met on schedule and on budget, then an expectation for future success is established within the team. Meeting the second milestone becomes easier. The third is even easier, and so forth. A culture of success has been established within the project team. The members know the objectives are attainable. However, if the first milestone is not met successfully, a culture of failure sets in. Doubt about the team's capabilities begins to infiltrate the individuals. When the second milestone is missed, the culture of failure becomes cast in stone; it is almost irreversible. That is why it is imperative that the project manager structure the project so that success is practically guaranteed on the first few milestones. This sets the tone for all future actions.

Rules and guidelines are then established for the project management team. Ultimately, every team member is held equally accountable for working within those parameters. It is through this framework that the project manager earns the trust of every team member by being objective, consistent, and fair. The team is able to count on its manager to follow the guidelines, stand up against confrontation, and shield them from political influences that could hinder the successful completion of the project. Team members are convinced that the manager will make the right decisions and stand firmly behind those decisions.

Equally as important, project mangers thoroughly and accurately understand themselves. They recognize and accept their own weaknesses, as well as strengths. They constantly endeavor to create synergy by building a project management team that complements those strengths and offsets weaknesses. That is an essential step in building depth and capability within the project team. It is what gives the project team the alignment and balance needed to ensure longevity and success.

Management style is important, but it is unique to individuals and the particular environment in which they operate. Successful project managers adopt a management style that fits them personally, as well as the scope and constraints of the project they have been assigned to manage. There is no "one size fits all" when it comes to project management. The key is to lead by example.

Project managers remain emotionally prepared for the stress that inevitably comes with a project management assignment, physically prepared for the long hours and grueling pace that will be required, and politically prepared for the turf battles that lie ahead. They are also socially prepared for the selling needed to push the project through the senior management approval processes.

EXECUTIVE HINTS

Before launching headlong into an assignment, project managers might do well to make time to discuss several issues with the customer or project sponsor. In essence, this is the first of many situational assessments needed by a project manager to understand fully what she is charged with. It is good to know up front what the ground rules are and what issues will likely be encountered along the way. The intent is to discover any hidden or implicit expectations that may signal downstream surprises.

1. Before beginning, project managers make it a point to clearly understand what is expected of them and the level of empowerment they and the project team have been granted. What authority do they have in making decisions, spending money, or changing existing processes, policies, or procedures? In many cases, the project will result in a change in the way business within the organization is currently conducted. If so, it is imperative to understand whether or not the project manager and the project team have the authority to implement, rather than simply recommend, those changes. There is a big difference in the two. This requirement is determined early in the project planning phases—what actions or decisions the project manager can make alone and what issues or decisions must be discussed with higher levels of management. The rules under which the project manager will operate are fully understood. And, once those rules are understood, the project manager communicates them clearly to the project team so that there are no misunderstandings.
2. Another question to be asked is, "How will success be measured?" This may seem like a dumb question, but it is not. For example, does success mean being on time to the day, week, or month? Does it mean being exactly on budget, or is plus or minus 5% acceptable? Can the expected deliverable

vary within certain acceptable tolerance limits? In many cases, there is an acceptable range in which project performance is judged acceptable. By knowing that range, the project manager is better able to manage project resources and make valid cost-benefit judgments should the requirement for trade-offs arise.

3. While exploring the nuances of the assignment with the customer or project sponsor, the astute project manager makes it a point to clearly understand which project requirements are *musts*, and which are simply *desired*. In every project there are certain deliverables and rules that must be complied with—no flexibility, no tolerances, no exceptions. These are the expectations and requirements that make or break the project. There is no compromise. They function as a baseline for the project. *If they are not met, the project will not be deemed a success*. Therefore, the project manager must know those expectations and requirements up front. There are other requirements in a project that are desired but not required. In essence, there is some level of flexibility. These are things that the project sponsor would like from the project, but can live without so long as the "musts" are achieved. Knowing them up front will assist the project manager in prioritizing work assignments, allocating resources, and conducting trade-off analyses.

Simply doing your best is not good enough when it comes to managing complex projects. Know what the customer's expectations are and know that they are achievable before committing to deliver them.

4. Project managers, along with project sponsors, work together to determine whether or not all project, organizational, and customer expectations have been clearly and completely defined. They focus on completely and accurately identifying the needs of the customer, as well as those of the organization before commitments are made. Conflicts are resolved with the organization, customer, and/or project sponsor before moving forward. If the expectations appear unrealistic

given known project or organizational constraints, the project manager negotiates with the project sponsor or customer to bring them into the reality zone. The project expectations are reassessed relative to schedule, resources, and budget. Negotiations continue until expectations and requirements are in alignment with the capabilities of the organization, project manager, and project team. Eagerness to please is never allowed to overshadow good commonsense.

5. What are the risks (to the organization, to the project, and to the project manager personally)? This is a critical issue that needs attention early in the project's concept development stage. The project manager along with the customer or project sponsor discuss the downside should the project not come off as planned. Will profitability, market share, or competitiveness be compromised? Could the organization be subjected to contingent liabilities, environmental impact, personal injury, or product liability litigation? These are not trivial matters, as history has demonstrated. By knowing the downside, and understanding its associated impacts on the project and organization, the project manager is better prepared to manage the project risks.
6. What are the possible rewards from the project? Can the organization achieve greater profitability, market share, or competitiveness? Will successful project completion reflect favorably on the project manager and the project management team when raises and promotions are under consideration? These are the motivators that can be used by the project manager with his project team. Team members will want to know, "What's in it for me?" This is a reasonable question that requires an honest answer.
7. From where is resistance likely to come, and to what degree? As discussed previously, many projects will require that organizational or business processes, policies, and/or procedures be changed as a result of the project. This means crossing organizational boundaries and impacting how other functional managers or disciplines do their work. Implementing change of this magnitude, especially

by someone from outside the affected function, is generally not well received, and is often met with some level of active or passive resistance. By anticipating where and from whom that resistance is likely to come, the project manager can avoid much of it through frequent discussions with affected functional managers and employees. Such contacts allow the project manager to sell the benefits of the project by incorporating various suggestions from these functional managers into the planning and execution of the project.

8. Who will mentor the project team to aid in overcoming possible political or functional resistance from sources above the project manager? Who can be counted on for help in times of crisis? There should be no shyness about asking these questions as they will likely be asked of the project manager later by project team members.

GAGING COMMITMENT TO THE PROJECT

In assessing the assignment, the project manager carefully gages the project sponsor's and senior management's commitment to the project. There are several ways to do so.

1. Sufficient resources must be allocated to successfully complete the project within the allotted time frame and budget. The use of a "lessons-learned" database provides insight at this stage to ascertain if the allocated resources appear reasonable given the scope of the project as it has been explained.
2. Resources must be deployed when and where they are needed. Allocation is one thing; deployment is another. Will the resources be provided when needed without delays, or will there be a constant battle with other functional managers for those limited resources? Delays in getting the promised resources will delay the completion of the project. However, the reason for the delayed completion often will be forgotten, leaving the project manager holding the bag.

3. The experienced project manager requires a commitment of capital along with the ability to employ those funds without redundant, unnecessary oversight and approvals. Therefore, the first question asked is, is there sufficient funding for the project given its scope and the actual constraints of the organization? At this stage, again, concern is with the reasonableness of the financial allocation to the project. Secondly, is the project manager able to move forward with normal project spending to launch the project in a timely manner?

It is great to be a hero—so long as you are around to receive the benefits that come from pulling a loser project out of the fire. In most cases, however, projects doomed from the start take the project manager down with them; so assignments are chosen carefully. In general, project management assignments should be taken only if there is both the ability and support required to be successful.

"Just say no!" This may seem a bold (foolish) statement. But the project manager is selected for an assignment because her superior or project sponsor has faith in her abilities. By expressing concerns professionally, along with the reasoning behind them, the project manager will gain, not lose, the project sponsor's confidence. Senior managers rely upon their project professionals to identify potentially hazardous business situations and projects so that alternative courses of action can be sought before commitments are made. Thus, it is a good idea to objectively assess a project before committing to it to ensure the project is on sound footing. Why spend time, money, and valuable resources on a project that cannot possibly be successful? It simply does not make good business sense.

People will complain and moan about how bad things are until a change is recommended. Then, almost miraculously, everything gets better.

To summarize, there are a number of questions that require answers before the project manager accepts an assignment. Knowing how management and the customer think, the upside and downside of the project, and being empowered to get things done are all essential to the project manager in his decision of whether or not to take the assignment. There are times when walking away from an assignment is the best course of action. Not all projects can be or will be completely successful. History is a good teacher. The pages of the *Wall Street Journal* are sprinkled each day with projects that have not come off as planned—and the personnel changes that have resulted from them.

5
Setting Project Expectations Early, Realistically, and Measurably

DETERMINING EXPECTATIONS

As part of project planning, it is imperative that the project manager ensure that the expectations set for the project are within her capabilities and those of the team considering all of the real organizational, operational, and financial constraints in existence.

In most cases, the initial project description is, at best, an incomplete description of the anticipated project deliverable(s), or the symptom(s) of a problem plaguing the customer or organization. If taken at face value, it will often lead the project manager in the wrong direction. For example, one company had lost over 12 percentage points in market share over the prior two-year period. Under the guidance and direction of a senior steering committee, the project manager was charged with the responsibility of developing and launching a project to return the company's lost market share. Based upon a cursory review of the situation by the steering committee, its members indicated that the market share loss had apparently resulted from either pricing or product quality. In reality, the market share loss was the direct result of the excessive cycle time customers were experiencing from the repair department when products were returned for repair or replacement. Had the project manager taken what the steering committee members said at face value, she would have launched a project that was doomed to fail because it did not address the real issue. This is not an isolated instance. In fact, it demonstrates the norm.

Why is it typical to do such a poor job in defining project expectations? The reasons are simple:

- Project managers too often fail to identify and then prioritize the project and customer requirements, as well as the drivers behind them before starting.
- They make unfounded assumptions instead of obtaining and validating facts.
- They fail to quantify and prioritize the customer or project sponsor's expectations.
- They put blind faith in the expertise and direction of those above them, and consequently find themselves faced with the requirement to change direction once into the project, introducing unacceptable risk along with added time and costs.

Successful project managers utilize quantitative versus qualitative methodologies to gage customers' expectations, or to assist customers in isolating their expectations before defining the project scope and methodology. Typical techniques, like voice-of-the-customer (VOC) analyses, quality function deployment (QFD), gap analyses, field surveys, and others are employed by many project managers in the early stages of project definition to quantify and prioritize customer requirements and expectations.

Quality and performance targets are then developed from data received through focus groups, customer clinics, market and customer surveys, interviews, and competitive benchmarking. What an experienced project manager looks for is solid data with which to establish the project baseline. The goal is to define exactly the expected deliverables, and then to prioritize them relative to the customer's specific requirements.

Before a project manager commits to anything, he meets with the project sponsor and/or project customers, following the guidelines in the model illustrated in Figure 5-1.

To begin with, the project manager *asks* for a definition of, along with the relevant details concerning, the project requirements, expectations, specifications, cost and schedule targets, metrics, constraints, contingencies, compliance issues, etc. He then *listens* closely, taking notes of exactly what is said and how it is said. It is often necessary to go beyond listening, to read between the lines to better understand why issues are perceived to be as

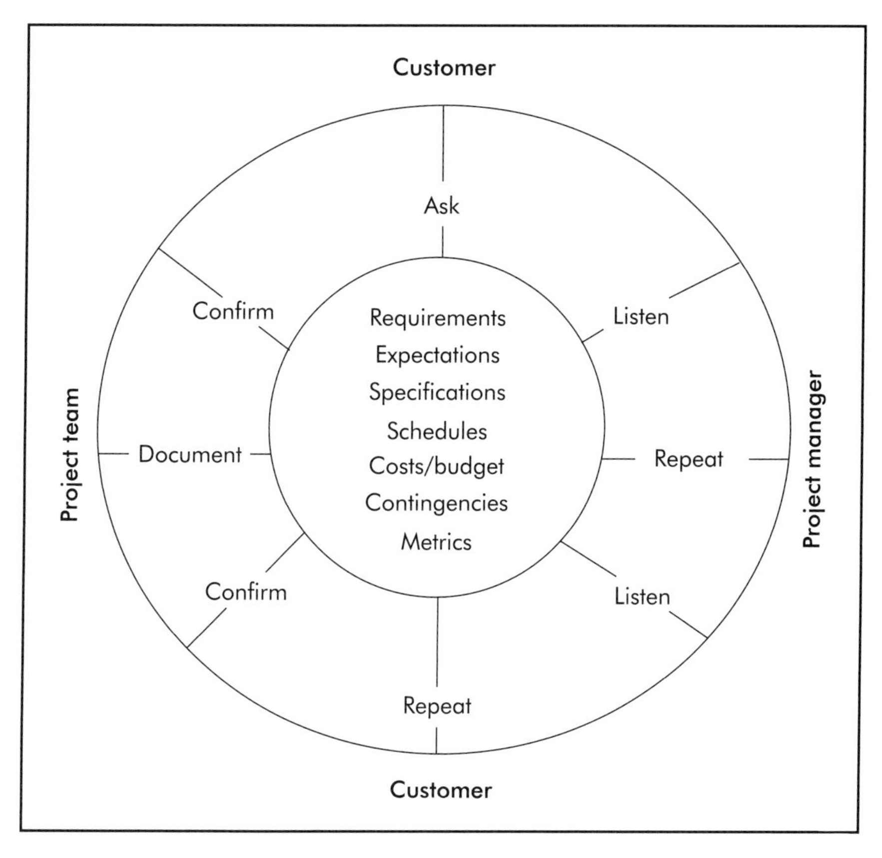

Figure 5-1. Illustration of method to define project expectations.

they are. Then, the drivers, definition, and details are repeated back to the customer, exactly as understood. Clarification is sought for any questions that arise. Again, the project manager listens, making any necessary adjustments and modifications to his notes. Then the drivers, definition, and details are repeated back exactly as understood again. At this point, a *confirmation* of the project manager's understanding is requested from the customer. Once agreement is reached, the project requirements and expectations are *documented* for future reference by all parties. Upon completion of the documentation, a final review and confirmation is requested

A cardinal rule of project management: Under-commit, over-deliver.

from the project sponsor or customer. This simple model, in combination with the other quantitative methodologies mentioned, allows project requirements and expectations to be accurately defined and prioritized in the beginning, thereby eliminating or minimizing the possibility of downstream changes and their associated impacts on the project's cycle time, budget, and performance.

Understanding what the customer (or senior management) actually expects from the project often involves more than merely listening to them describe the desired or expected project outcome. To ensure that the project is planned and launched successfully, the project manager conducts his own due diligence to better understand the reasons why the customer perceives the existing business environment to be unacceptable or an opportunity to exist. In essence, the project manager seeks to understand every aspect of the work that must be accomplished, as well as those circumstances that led up to the need for the desired change in the business environment.

It is equally important that the project manager understand the culture and value systems within the customer's environment. These implicit expectations or cultural issues are generally unspoken, but are critically important to the customer. They drive senior management's decision-making and set the direction of the organization. If a project manager inadvertently does something within the project to compromise a customer's culture or value system, the results are often catastrophic.

Setting the Project Scope and Deliverables

Setting the scope of the project is an interesting exercise. Experience (at times painful) shows that defining the scope of the project is as difficult to do as maintaining it. Both are critical to the project's success.

A project's scope is like our waistlines—as we grow older they mysteriously get bigger, often without our even noticing. Business projects are much the same. The project manager is often implored to: "Just add this one deliverable or requirement to the project. It is a small detail that should not have much impact on the project." Time and time again, those little details are added until, all of a sudden, the project manager recognizes that her project exceeds the budgeted resources and schedule. Then, no one seems to remember how all of those tangential details got included in the first place. Guess who is left holding the bag.

Here is a cardinal rule: Once the project scope is defined, it does not change without a complete analysis of the proposed change's impact on all elements of the project, and the subsequent approval of the project sponsor or customer. The results and approval of the impact analysis in many cases will dictate reworking the entire project plan, risk management plan, procurement plan, communications plan, and project budget. In other cases, a complete restart is required. Or alternatively, a second project is run in parallel with or subsequent to the original project. Just adding a few more personnel or increasing the budget is generally ineffective if the total impact is not well understood.

In defining the project and its deliverables for the project team, it is essential that the project manager clearly describes and communicates the project's scope, direction, and focus. The better the project team members understand the project's expectations, the better they will perform. In addition, the project manager clearly delineates the intent and purpose of the project to convey its importance and level of urgency to the organization.

Benefits to be derived from the project are described and quantified during the project manager's initial meeting with the project sponsor, along with any environmental issues that will likely impact the project. And, as with all elements of business, the metrics that will be used to gage progress and project performance are clearly defined as part of the overall project description. It is, therefore, wise for the project

Once the project scope is defined, it does not change without a complete analysis of the change's impact on the project. The results may mean reworking the entire project plan.

manager to carefully consider all project expectations, along with the actual constraints the project team will face before committing to a baseline. The experienced project manager always avoids being either overly optimistic or pessimistic. Rather, his focus is on achievement of a set of realistic deliverables, costs, and timelines for the project.

Also essential to the success of the project at this stage is a comprehensive description of the operating rules and guidelines governing the project—the rules of engagement for *this* project. Questions like the following are typical of the type of information that experienced project managers seek at this stage of their initial due diligence:

- Are any of the project objectives or expectations in conflict?
- What are the rules, policies, or procedures under which the project team must operate?
- What operational, financial, resource, technology, facility, equipment, or geographical constraints exist?
- What qualifiers (business, environmental, regulatory) must be considered?

ANALYZING THE PROJECT SCOPE FOR CONFLICTS

Every project must be analyzed to better understand the business constraints that may exist. Again, this is part of risk management—taking a proactive look at all facets of the business, and its environment, before taking action. Here is an example that illustrates the point.

A new project manager in a pharmaceutical company was assigned to reduce the base material cost component in one of the company's largest product lines. She was also asked to simultaneously improve corporate cash flow by minimizing the company's inventory investment. Given that her background included brief stints in purchasing and materials management, she appeared well suited for the assignment.

The project manager's first action was to review the cost files on those items that represented approximately 80% of the material cost content of the product, using a simple Pareto analysis. She then established a new cost target for the buyers—a 6% material cost reduction using world-class metrics derived from a competitive benchmarking study. The metric she employed to measure the performance of the buyers against the project deliverable was purchase price variance (PPV).

The company's inventory investment in designated product areas was then reviewed. The project manager found severe inventory surpluses in many raw material categories. In discussing her findings with the controller, she learned that overall inventory performance had been on the decline for the last several years, and inventory was now a serious drain on cash flow.

The project manager decided to introduce a second project deliverable into the scope of the project—reducing inventory investment by 17% in 18 months. After calculating the financial impact of such a reduction on cash flow and inventory carrying costs (a component of the base material costs), she concluded that her targeted performance would, indeed, fit well with the other project deliverables. Thus, she introduced a second project metric to monitor performance—inventory turns. Her target deliverable was an improvement from 2.4 to 14.0 inventory turns annually.

To summarize, the project manager selected two deliverables:

1. A 6% reduction in material costs in 12 months.
2. An improvement in annual inventory turns from 2.4 to 14.0 in 18 months.

On the surface, all seemed well thought out. As the project got underway, however, numerous disagreements among the project team broke out about the planning and approach that would be employed for the project. The project manager found herself between two camps, each with an apparent agenda of its own. Her efforts to reach a consensus between the two opposing factions fell flat. She, therefore, decided to move forward with the project and micromanage it until all parties cooled down and began working together.

At first, everyone appeared to have the expected deliverables well in mind. Things did calm down, for a while. Then the buyers began to receive a rash of price increases from key suppliers as a result of supply-demand pressures in the market. In an evasive action, the buyers began negotiating for larger quantity price breaks to keep overall material costs at the targeted 6% reduction levels. As the practice became more widespread, inventory began to build up, driving turns lower instead of higher. The project manager, keyed by her project metrics, began to put pressure on materials management personnel to reduce inventory levels through more effective planning. As she increased the pressure, the camps became more vocal. Finger-pointing started, then open warfare. Her frustration began to show as things got worse, ultimately causing her to lose total control of the project.

What happened? A look behind the scenes reveals the obvious answer. It was a simple case where the project manager failed to see the trap that she, herself, created. The project deliverables, reinforced by the performance metrics that she established, were in direct conflict. Can you not reduce inventory investment and material costs simultaneously? Certainly, it is possible if the proper metrics are used. In this project, however, the project manager selected conflicting metrics, creating a win-lose situation. When things started to come apart, the project team members began scrambling to be on the winning side. Working at odds with one another, the team members focused on achieving the project deliverable under their direct control at the expense of the others. The result was total chaos. The project manager failed to select the appropriate project metric: total cost. Total cost would have provided a means for both camps to be successful (and, thus, the project).

The moral of the story is this: Before initiating a project, the experienced project manager, through his analysis and due diligence, thoroughly understands all existing constraints and conflicts. Based upon his understanding of same, a common direction and approach is selected that establishes win-win targets. This is supported by using the appropriate project metrics designed to focus all team members on a common deliverable utilizing a common approach.

The Reverse Image

When defining the scope of the project, it is as important to define what is *not* to be included as a deliverable as it is to define what is. Assessing and defining those expectations not included within the scope of the project prevents the inclusion of unnecessary project requirements and activities that often introduce additional costs and resource consumption. By considering what is not to be included in the project, duplication of effort and redundant activities are avoided. Project limitations thus become clearer and assumptions regarding the project are highlighted so that they can be validated before a final course of action is decided upon.

Get the Customer Involved

Whenever possible, it is wise to involve the project sponsor or customer in defining the project deliverables and scope, as well as the schedule, budget, and compliance criteria (see Figure 5-2). This ensures customer ownership of the project prior to its launch. That ownership is critical. This point is expanded on in greater detail in a later chapter. For now, suffice it to say that getting the customer's buy-in to the project scope at this stage of the project is of great value in effectively managing downstream proposals for scope changes (scope creep).

Establishing Metrics

As discussed earlier in this chapter, project performance and tracking measurements (metrics) are critical to accomplishing project and business objectives alike. Simply stated, that which is not measured and monitored will not change or improve.

In setting metrics, the project manager recognizes that his project will be judged by:

- performance—the quantifiable, measurable results derived; and
- perception—a subjective view of the project manager's effectiveness in meeting the requirements and expectations of the customer or project sponsor.

Effective project management addresses performance and perception by exploring numerous project and customer-related issues. For example:

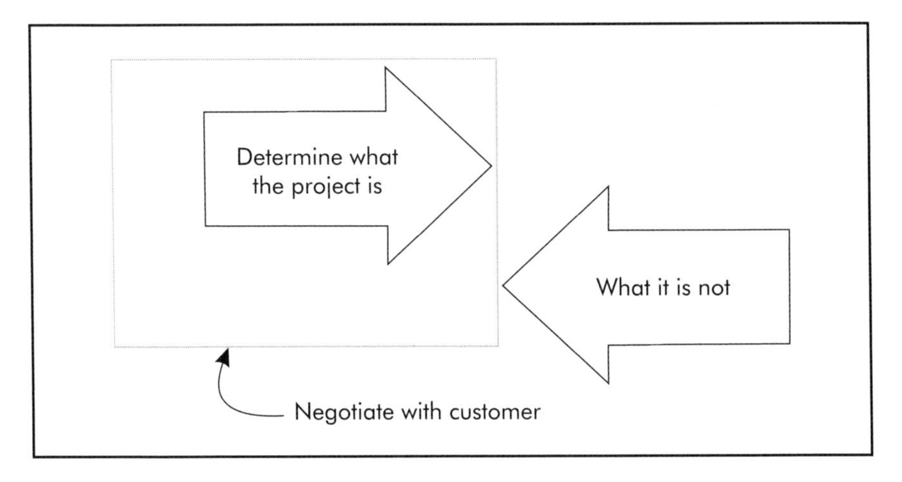

Figure 5-2. Project managers should work with customers to determine a comprehensive, exact understanding of their expectations.

1. What is to be measured?
2. How will it be measured (methods, tools, procedures, etc.)?
3. How often will it be measured?
4. By whom will it be measured?
5. What data will be required to meet project and customer requirements?
6. What data collection systems will be required?
7. What corresponding data conversion systems will be employed?
8. What data system compatibility issues must be addressed?
9. What reporting mechanisms will be required?
10. What will be the reporting frequency?

When establishing performance and compliance metrics for her project, an experienced project manager follows a few basic rules.

1. Everything can be measured, although some things are more subjective. When developing subjective measures such as index-type metrics, management approval is sought before applying them to the project. The goal of metrics is to guarantee consensus among the project team members,

supporting functional managers, and senior managers. Metrics themselves should not promote conflict. The best bet, whenever possible, is to develop and utilize objective, quantifiable metrics.

2. Effective metrics are user-friendly. The harder they are to apply and track, the more time consuming and problematic they will be to the project management team.
3. A frequent review period (weekly) is established for the key project metrics. If those reviews reveal the need for a change, corrective actions will be made without hesitation. Metrics are, by their very design, intended to be dynamic. Thus, changes are likely to occur during the life cycle of the project. However, before any change is made, buy-in from all parties is required.
4. Successful project managers recognize that it is generally a good idea to present project metrics in graphical format. Doing so makes them easier to read and comprehend by all project stakeholders. As discussed in Chapter 8, effective communications planning allows the project manager to better manage perception and avoid unnecessary redundant reporting that adds little value to the project or its stakeholders.
5. Whenever possible, existing corporate metrics are utilized for the project. This saves the time and effort of developing new measures, and avoids the required system changes often necessary to generate them. This will also facilitate acceptance from those who must approve and use the metrics.

The perception of professionalism often stems from how well the project manager anticipates a required corrective action, and then initiates it before the actual need occurs. And that, of course, is why metrics are so vital to the project manager. Their function is to identify potential failures or out-of-control situations so that the project manager can be proactive in eliminating or minimizing their impact. In essence, metrics are another form of project risk management, referred to in Chapter 11 as the *probability of detection*.

On the subject of eliminating common surprises, experience has shown that an assessment of the data collection systems is generally in order in the early stages of the project. It typically includes an evaluation of the timeliness, accuracy, and accessibility of current data collection systems, along with a comparison of what they measure against actual project requirements. Of prime concern is the timeliness of the data collection systems: are they real-time or batch processes? Without timely, accurate data, decisions cannot be made and progress cannot be measured.

Project Documentation and Charter

After the project's deliverables and scope have been clearly defined, including its metrics and data collection systems, the project manager commits the data to writing in the form of a project charter. This final step is critical, as it formalizes the project baseline for all concerned. The project charter includes:

- approved project scope and deliverables;
- approved performance specifications;
- targeted project schedules and budgets;
- preliminary project team or skill set requirements;
- expected resource requirements and the timing of their use or consumption;
- project metrics and their associated data support systems;
- reporting mechanisms and their frequencies;
- decision and corrective action procedures, including scope control systems;
- the assigned level of empowerment;
- all project approval requirements; and
- a preliminary work breakdown structure (WBS) to serve as a pictorial overview of the project scope.

After all factors are documented, it is time for everyone to sign on the bottom line—the project manager, project team, project sponsors or customers, any critical suppliers to the project, and the appropriate members of senior management. Project ownership is now mutual.

SUMMARY

Establishing customer expectations for a project is neither easy to do nor to maintain. It requires a high degree of due diligence on the project manager's part, along with a high degree of customer cooperation. As a project becomes increasingly complex, setting its expectations and scope will become even more difficult, making the need for quantitative methodologies even more important.

In all projects, it is critical that the project manager observe the following precepts:

1. Be careful never to over-commit on the project. Be realistic in setting the project's expectations and scope. Understand what the customer expects and why, then compare those expectations against the funding, resources, and schedule allotted to the project. The earlier a discrepancy is resolved, the higher the probability that its impact on the project will be minimized. It is always better to over-deliver than to fail to live up to even one of the customer's expectations.
2. Frequently revisit the customer's expectations and the project environment. Determine if anything has changed that may render the project undoable. The earlier these issues are uncovered, the more options are available without a total compromise of the project. Like many of the other techniques discussed in this and earlier chapters, this is a form of risk management that every project manager is expected to employ.
3. Remain sensitive to environmental conditions within the customer's and the project manager's organization that could introduce potential liability for either or both parties. The project manager's main responsibility is to manage his project ("the business") effectively and efficiently. That means being aware of all external and internal factors that could render the project, and the parties, subject to litigation of any kind. Maintain the scope of the project and its expectations within reasonable boundaries so that misconceptions are minimized or eliminated up front.

4. Constantly communicate the project's scope and expectations to all project team personnel, management, customer personnel, functional managers, etc. Also communicate what is not to be included or expected. The more familiar everyone is about the project scope, the fewer the surprises when only exactly what was committed is delivered and nothing more.
5. Always align the project budget and schedule to the project expectations and scope. If a misalignment exists, problems will result. Once set, the project's scope and expectations should be guarded like a checkbook. Avoid scope creep, if possible. If unavoidable, control it. So doing adds an improved probability of success in delivering a successful project. As stated previously, prevention of a problem is always more likely to generate acceptable results for the project and the project team than attempting to react once the problem occurs.

6
Organizing and Leading the Project Team

THE PROJECT TEAM

Today, customers, senior management, and support groups expect more from project managers and the projects they govern: product or service quality approaching zero defect levels; those same new products and services at an increasingly faster pace; a higher degree of customization to customers' unique expectations or applications; elimination of premium pricing for any reason; and products and services whose creation and use will not negatively impact the business environment.

New technologies expand the project manager's ability to do more for the customer. But no project manager can keep up with the increased complexities of global technologies, project and business requirements, industry and market dynamics, and technological innovations alone. It simply is not possible.

To be effective, project managers must utilize all available resources to their maximum potential. That means forging the human resources within the organization, as well as those available from external sources, into an effective project management team to achieve the benefits of cross-functionality, synergy, and an organizational perspective. The successful project manager uses team dynamics, team chemistry, and organizational development techniques to motivate a diverse group of professionals to adopt a common approach and common metrics to meet or exceed defined project requirements. It is equally as important to create the dynamics of an effective project team as it is to design a comprehensive strategic and tactical project plan. In many cases, it is even more important.

THE BENEFITS OF TEAMS

The use of project teams has multiple and multi-faceted benefits.

1. Project teams typically generate a greater number of ideas, and often better ones, because each team member brings a different background, different experiences, and different perspectives.
2. Cross-functional project teams are generally more creative in developing cost-effective, risk-adverse solutions to operational and performance problems.
3. Project team members are better at analyzing large amounts of data and complex situations in shorter time frames than individuals acting alone.
4. The perspective of cross-functional project teams tends to be more organizational than functional, focusing on what is best for the project and its stakeholders versus what may be best for individual departments or employees. As such, project team decisions focus on optimization of all applicable business functions toward the achievement of project goals versus the optimization of any one function at the expense of another.
5. Communication is enhanced because every function impacted or influenced by the project is represented in the up-front planning phases of the project, as well as in the final solution or recommendation. In the same respect, risks are minimized as the team perspective is broadened regarding the potential problems that these individuals, through their experience, bring to light early in the project's planning phase.

It Does Not Always Work Out as Planned

In many situations throughout both government and industry sectors, project teams have proven ineffective. Why? Many of the employees placed in a team or decision-making situation lack the desire, skills, or experience to function effectively within the structure of the team environment. Because most organizations fail to recognize this critical fact, many teams are organized and sent into action without the least understanding of how they will achieve their goals, much less how to work together as a unit. Still another contributing factor to this unacceptable phenomenon is that many teams are organized under the auspices of a project manager with little, if any, formal managerial training or experience. The project manager lacks the skills to:

- make effective project-level or business-level decisions;
- develop strategic plans that consider all situational constraints along with project objectives;
- lead a diverse team of knowledge workers who, in many cases, are more technically competent than the project manager (and they have no formal reporting linkages to the project manager).

As a result, creativity, synergy, and the ability to "think outside the box" are typically not part of the team's readily available skill sets.

MANAGING THE "WATER LINE"

From a managerial standpoint, a project can be compared to a ship on the high seas. As the ship churns through the water on a calm, sun-filled day, everything is okay. Similarly, so long as the project remains on schedule and on budget, everything is fine . . . the seas are calm.

Suddenly, the ship strikes something in the water, opening a large hole approximately 25–30 ft (7.6–9.1 m) above the water line. Are the ship and crew in trouble? In our analogy, will the project sink (fail)? Not if everything else is under control. As with the ship's captain, there is time in these circumstances for the project manager to address the problem without panic. But what if the hole is beneath the water line? That is a different story. Now the problem is of a critical nature—one that will likely sink the ship (project) if decisive corrective actions are not taken immediately.

Who on the project team is capable, comfortable, and willing to make those below-the-water-line decisions? More than likely, the answer is only the project manager. And that is perfectly acceptable because she is the one ultimately responsible for the project; the one who is trained and experienced enough to make those project-critical decisions. Then why have a project team? The answer is simple: to make the *above-the-water-line* decisions. These decisions are those that team members can, and should, effectively make with the proper training, coaching, and experience. They are important, but not critical to the success of the project. These are the decisions that the team members will be "ready, willing, and able" to make. With team members in place who are capable and willing to make those above-the-water-line decisions, the project manager is free to concentrate on the *below-the-water-line* decisions where her experience and expertise are best utilized.

Simply stated, project managers are not typically capable of making all of the decisions required in the execution of a project, nor should they be required to do so. There are decisions that are simply better made by team members who are closer to the issues. These are the people with the experience and skill sets most suitable for resolution of everyday issues or situations. Consequently, it is the project manager's responsibility to ensure that these people are resident on the project team, trained and ready to step forward to help when called upon.

THE SCIENCE OF SELECTION

Often a project manager is permitted to select team members for particular project assignments based on their skill sets, project-specific experience, or other talents. In other cases, senior management preselects the team members before assigning the project to a particular project manager. In either case, it is the project manager's responsibility to ensure that the unit can and will function effectively together. If there are problems with the chemistry or skill sets of the project team members, it is the project manager's responsibility to address them by making the appropriate personnel changes. This

Creating synergy in a project team comes from the right chemistry. Chemistry is a science, not an art. Luck plays no part in it. So, the project team must be designed before the project!

is a below-the-water-line issue, and must be dealt with even in the face of politics or resistance from upper management. Project success is dependent upon it.

No project or business manager is successful until he is surrounded by capable employees ready and willing to fulfill key roles. "You will never be promoted until there is someone ready and willing to take your place." (Termini 2007) The same holds true in a project management assignment. The success of the project is dependent upon the effective planning and execution of every assignment by every team member. While there is no secret formula for success in dealing with team members in a project environment, there are a few proven guidelines on how to identify and recruit people who will have a high degree of chemistry with one another. Chemistry is essential. Without the ability to work together effectively, the team members will never develop the synergy and trust necessary to manage complex business projects.

There are several techniques used by professional project managers to build an effective project management team. The following are some of the more important elements of their selection strategies:

1. Select individuals who have the ability and willingness to contribute to the project team as a team member, not as a superstar. True team members focus on the success of the project team versus individual glory. Without that focus, trust among team members never develops and team synergy is sacrificed.
2. Select individuals who bring complementary skills that will increase the overall strength, balance, and capabilities of the project team. Doing so ensures that all needed skill sets are covered and, most importantly, the weaknesses of one team member are compensated for by the strengths of another.
3. Select individuals who will perform well under pressure and who are results oriented. Within a project environment, pressure and stress are always prevalent. Some individuals do not work well in that "pressure-cooker" type of environment. The fast pace cannot be eliminated or avoided as

project assignments are required to be completed on time as scheduled. Thus it is essential that only individuals who are capable of thriving in a fast-paced environment be resident on the team.

4. Select individuals who are capable of leading as well as following. Select role players who are multifaceted in their capabilities and who demonstrate a willingness to accept new responsibilities and challenges. This type of team member gives a project manager a great deal of flexibility in assigning project-critical tasks.
5. Select individuals who are committed to testing the boundaries of the status quo, those who thrive on thinking in unconventional terms, but who are controllable. There is a difference between team members who constantly seek better solutions to project challenges and work in consensus with others, and those who are best described as loose cannons breaking rules and creating political problems for the team.
6. Select individuals who are willing to learn new skills from other team members and who at the same time are willing to share their expertise with those same individuals. Synergy and trust grows within a team when individuals share their knowledge in an attempt to help others improve their own skills and capabilities. A sense of honor and respect quickly develops as individuals feel a personal obligation to live up to the gift of knowledge that has been bestowed upon them from a peer.
7. Avoid selecting politicians; let them run for office elsewhere. There are, however, times when these skills are critical assets for the project team. In cases where access to key decision makers is severely restricted, these individuals have the ability to open doors so that the project team is granted an audience with those individuals who are key in resolving issues restricting the project's progress or success.
8. Select individuals with both technical and interpersonal skills. The balance of the two skills is critical to building communication and cooperation among team members.

9. Select individuals from across the organization, top to bottom. Try to get as much breadth as possible on the project team to ensure organizational, rather than functional, thinking.
10. Finally, ensure that all critical skill sets required for the entire project are identified and that personnel with those unique skill sets are resident on the team. Never leave holes in the staffing of a project where the required skill sets are overlooked or left unfilled.

BUILDING A COHESIVE TEAM

Once the team is selected, successful project managers:

1. Develop depth on the project team through cross-training, managerial and technical skills training, and intergroup mentoring.
2. Establish rules and guidelines with the team for decision-making, problem-solving, corrective actions, group interactions, dispute resolution, and assignment completion that apply equally to all team members. All team members are held accountable for policing themselves and each other relative to those policies and guidelines.
3. With the input of all team members, establish realistic objectives, metrics, schedules, budgets, resource needs, expectations, and deliverables for each phase of the project. All team members are involved in strategic and tactical planning activities to build ownership in the final approach.
4. Tightly control external and internal politics to shield the team from negative influences that will disrupt harmony and trust. Team members must be free to do their work without interference or micromanagement. The project manager clearly understands that "the buck stops here" applies to himself and him alone. Accolades go to the team while criticism goes to the project manager.
5. Communicate clearly and concisely. The project manager never assumes that his team knows exactly what he is thinking or what is expected. Communication always precedes action to achieve effective results.

6. Refrain from the temptation to micromanage team members. Many team members are more technically competent in specific areas than the project manager is himself. Therefore, whenever possible, the team is allowed to manage itself under steady-state conditions. Successful project managers facilitate versus manage these knowledge workers for maximum results. It is only in times of crisis that the project manager takes charge and then, only until the crisis is resolved.
7. Consistent in direction, approach, and scope, the project manager communicates effectively so that the team always knows his expectations and positions on key issues. It is not required that the team members always agree with him, but everyone must know his position. It is equally as important that the project manager's actions remain consistent with his words. Trust and team unity depend upon it. (Termini 2007)
8. Set project-critical priorities and maintain them unless conditions make a change necessary for the success of the team's objectives or mission. That change is communicated in advance along with the logic behind it to ensure understanding and buy-in of team members.

Creating Balance

A successful project manager is able to envision his project. Much like a jigsaw puzzle, his vision is only complete if all pieces are in place. Every piece of the puzzle is unique, just as the skill sets and personalities of every individual on the project team are unique. They must all fit together in a complementary fashion before the vision is realized. Similarly, it is only with individuals who possess the unique and complementary personality profiles and functional skill sets required for THIS project, that the project team is in balance.

Every team member has strengths and weaknesses. The successful project manager recognizes that fact and builds upon it to strengthen the project team. For example, if everyone on the project team is strong in the areas where the project manager is highly competent and, similarly weak in the areas where he lacks expertise, what kind of project team would it be? It would be a narrow, misaligned one with little, if any, balance. Every successful project team needs balance to see it through the difficult times. Complementary skill sets bring such balance to the project team.

Leading and Following

A particularly valuable team member is someone who has the ability and willingness to both lead and follow, a person who can be relied upon to carry the leadership load at different stages of the project. The team functions much like a flock of geese. When the leader tires, he falls back into the formation where the resistance from the air is less so that he can rest to ultimately resume his leadership position later. As the lead goose rotates back into formation, another moves forward to take the lead. Even though the project manager is the head goose, there are times when he will need assistance in performing tasks. In cases like this, team members must be willing and able to lead so that the project manager can attend to other pressing issues.

Effectiveness in project management relies as much on social science as it does on technical expertise . . . perhaps more.

In evaluating the complementary skill sets of candidates for the project team relative to their applicability for a particular project assignment, experienced project managers consider the individual's readiness profile. Every project is unique. As such, even individuals with prior project management experience may find themselves unready for a particular project or assignment. The more of the load the project manager carries, the more difficult it will be to effectively manage the project. The project manager was not selected to do everything, but rather to see that everything gets done. There is a difference.

Table 6-1 contains four readiness profiles that provide guidance on how and why to select certain individuals for a particular project assignment. It also provides guidance relative to the

Table 6-1. Four possible readiness profiles describing potential project team members.

R1	R2	R3	R4
Unable, unwilling, or insecure	Unable, willing, or confident	Able, unwilling, or insecure	Able, willing, or confident
Telling, guiding, directing, establishing	Selling, explaining, clarifying, persuading	Participating, encouraging, collaborating, committing	Delegating, observing, monitoring, fulfilling
Leader directed		Follower directed	

methodologies employed to lead and motivate those individuals. Every individual has a different motivational trigger that causes specific reactions under certain circumstances. To effectively lead these individuals, the project manager identifies and utilizes their unique motivational triggers to achieve the desired reaction. Using the wrong trigger will cause the individual to pull against the project manager instead of pulling with him. In complex projects and competitive business environments, it is particularly critical that all team members be on the same page throughout the life cycle of the project.

In many cases, project leadership involves mentoring team members to ensure that they are capable of handling specific project assignments. Mentoring can be done by the project manager himself or assigned to one or more team members with extensive experience or expertise in a particular discipline. In either case, it is a useful tool for motivating less-experienced team members to accept specific assignments, as well as in preparing them for more complex ones as the project progresses. Table 6-2 illustrates the degree of mentoring required for project team members with varying levels of experience or who demonstrate a given personality profile.

The amount of project management interface and mentoring varies with each readiness profile (see Table 6-2). As a result, the

Table 6-2. Amount of mentoring time needed for each profile.

Readiness Profile	Willingness	Ability	Amount of Mentoring Required
R1	Unwilling	Unable	Significant
R2	Willing	Unable	Moderate
R3	Unwilling	Able	Some
R4	Willing	Able	Little, if any

experienced project manager factors this into the selection process as he considers how much time will be required to train and mentor a particular individual for a specific role in the project. Recognizing his own limitations in this area, the project manager also considers assigning mentoring roles to the more senior members of the project team. In doing so, he recognizes that there are multiple benefits. Not only is the junior or less experienced team member brought through his learning curve more quickly, but relationships of trust are also formed among these individuals. It is a proven approach that builds unity among the team and allows the more seasoned team members to take on added responsibility in running and managing the team.

Superstar Mentality

Every project manager wants the best, most talented individuals for her project team. But sometimes those personality types do not fit well in a team environment. All the talent in the world is useless unless it can be applied effectively in support of a common approach to achieving a common goal. Thus every individual must work well with the others on the team. If an individual does not work with and support the project manager and other team members to create team chemistry, the end result will be the requirement for the project manager to perform more personnel management than project management (not the most effective use of her time and energy). The team will pull apart rather than together. Consequently, experienced project managers know to look for team skills first and technical skills second. This ensures that individuals on the project team focus on the team's success rather than personal glory.

Consistent Discipline

To be effective, there can be no question about what is expected from the project team and its individual members. Team members must be comfortable that the project manager will be consistent and fair, and that she will establish reasonable rules and expectations for the team, holding everyone to those same rules with no exceptions. So long as the project team is operating within those rules and guidelines, no micromanaging is needed. Team members are free to set their own direction and make their own decisions—in essence, to be truly self-directed. If, however, anyone strays from the team rules, the effective project manager becomes a predictable disciplinarian . . . taking quick and decisive action. By so doing, her entire team quickly becomes self-disciplined to the greatest extent possible, making her job easier and more enjoyable.

Tolerate Mistakes

In all business environments, especially challenging project roles, individuals must feel free to make a mistake without suffering major repercussions or unreasonable disciplinary actions. Deming put it best, "Drive out the fear of failure in your organization." If team members feel that their project manager views their mistakes as learning experiences, they will be more creative in their approaches to achieving project objectives. If, however, they feel that any mistake will be viewed negatively, they will never take a chance, never think outside the box, and never do anything not specifically asked of them.

By balancing the risk of mistakes and their potential impact on the project against the requirement to give individuals the freedom to take chances, the project manager effectively manages the downside of a mistake while maximizing team and individual creativity. Team members are encouraged to take chances, but are also required to consider the potential downside risk to the project if mistakes occur. This is done by reinforcing the team rules mentioned earlier, as well as requiring extensive due diligence to study the pros and cons of a proposed approach, especially in high-risk scenarios. Generally, if mistakes are made within the framework of the team's rules and guidelines, the downside effects are minimal and containable. However, if allowed to get outside those rules, mistakes are often devastating to the project as well as to individual careers.

Identifying the Essential Skill Sets

The experienced project manager recognizes the need to identify and recruit all of the individual skill sets required to ensure alignment with project requirements and expectations early in the project's planning phase. It is common practice to initially build a cross-functional core team that will lead the project, followed by a cast of supporting team members who will be needed on a more limited basis throughout the project (Figure 6-1). As most project team members are employees of fellow functional managers who have their own operations to run, experienced project managers clearly understand that selection of team members is a negotiated process rather than a dictated one. Minimizing the impact on the operations and personnel of these key operating managers through prudent use of those shared resources ensures their continued support of the project instead of their ongoing resistance. Project managers recognize that these functional managers are doing them a favor by supporting the staffing requirements of the project. Gratitude for this is demonstrated by being flexible in selecting team members who will meet the needs of the project while, at the same time, minimizing the impact on the supporting organization. Working together, the two managers find a solution that benefits both.

Without the ability to work together effectively, the project team will never develop the synergy necessary to manage complex business projects.

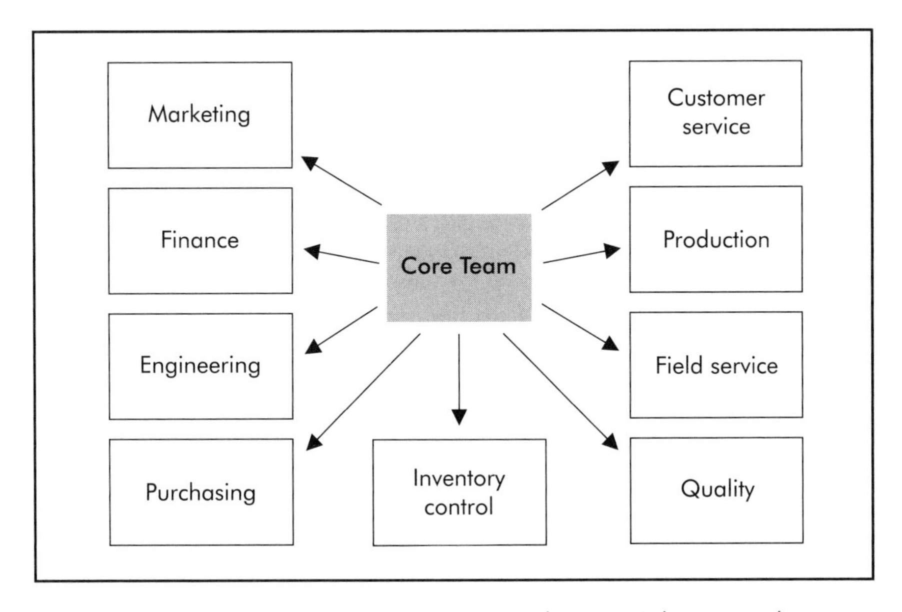

Figure 6-1. Core project management team and tangential support elements.

Table 6-3 illustrates a sample matrix used by professional project managers to structure their search for the right combination of skills and experience. The search is typically conducted within as well as outside the organization. Searching outside the organization is done for many reasons: the needed skills are simply not available within the organization, because of cost, or simply to avoid the negative impacts on organizational units that the use of internal personnel will create.

When looking at the required skill sets for the project, the experienced project manager also considers the personality-driven skills (Table 6-4) that are often essential in making the project team successful. These are not necessarily an individual's technical or operational skills, but rather those personal skills that allow the individual to consistently generate outstanding results, sometimes despite a lack of extraordinary technical capabilities.

Table 6-3. A checklist to help structure the search for the right combination of skills and experience for the project management team.

Functional Skill Sets	Required	Not Required	Candidates
Information technology			
Systems engineering			
Research and development			
Project management office staff			
Finance			
Accounting			
Administration			
Materials			
Purchasing			
Design engineering			
Process engineering			
Industrial engineering			
Manufacturing engineering			
Operations management			
Supplier quality engineering			
Quality assurance			
Process quality assurance			
Sales			
Marketing			
Field service			
Customer service			
Order entry			
Logistics			

Table 6-4. Descriptions of various personality-driven skill sets.

Skill Set	Competency
Customer advocate	This person takes the role of supporting the customer, the customer's needs and requirements, and the customer's priorities. He or she always wants to do what is best for the customer.
Business advocate	This person takes the role of monitoring the business and industry trends, along with their associated issues and opportunities. A big-picture thinker, this person keeps the team focused on near-term and longer-term issues.
Team advocate	This is a person who takes responsibility for actively supporting the course, direction, and vision of the project and team. He or she communicates openly and positively; listens intently; coaches, mentors, and teaches; and is self-disciplined and motivated.
Action advocate	This person is a "doer." Driven to handle even the most minute of detailed assignments, he or she consistently gets the tools and resources lined up to support the team in achieving its objectives.
The attack dog	This person is the driver who finds ways over, under, around, or through barriers and roadblocks. A creative, out-of-the-box thinker who is bottom-line focused, he or she owns the problems rather than placing blame on others and is not afraid of conflict or controversy. This person is not always politically sensitive.
Informal leader	This person is respected by all and is honest, straight talking, and sincere. He or she exhibits genuine concern for others and keeps everyone informed. Technically competent and consensus oriented, this person leads by example and presence and tries to influence others by actively involving them in the decision process.

Matching Skill with Activity

Once the essential skills have been identified, the next step for the project manager is to match them against the corresponding project activity in which they will be required. In addition, it is now appropriate to begin identifying potential team members from inside and outside the organization for those critical skilled positions.

The selection of candidates is often filled with bias and subjectivity if left to one individual. Therefore, experienced project managers seek several opinions from sources such as functional managers, the project sponsor or mentor, human relations professionals, peers, and executive staff members. The best-qualified candidates possessing both technical and interpersonal skills are sought. *The most important ingredient in building a successful team is chemistry.* All the skills in the world will be useless if the team members selected lack the ability to work together.

Next, the training needs for the individual team members are identified to ensure their skills are up-to-date and their thinking contemporary. In some cases, the project requires skills that are out of the norm, or are unique, and not commonly practiced within the organization. In those cases, as well, additional training of one or more team members is required to ensure all necessary skill set requirements for the project are satisfied. Table 6-5 is a simple matrix to aid in this task. In utilizing this tool, the project manager includes the time and costs for the training in the project schedule and budget planning.

All the talent in the world is useless unless it can be applied effectively in a business environment.

When planning for team training, the project manager contracts with training professionals who bring real-world experience into the sessions—experience that applies directly to the scope and requirements of the project being planned. Project management professionals clearly understand that theory is good only when coupled with hands-on, applications-based training that teaches team members how to apply specific project-related tools and techniques to their own roles on the project.

As with all up-front project planning, the project manager carefully considers the needs of the project as his first priority. The following questions are typical in ensuring that all aspects of this extremely important first step have been covered.

Table 6-5. Matrix to help determine the training needs of team members.

Project Activity Budgeted	Required Skills	Training Required	Dates Scheduled	Amount Budgeted	Team Member(s)

1. Have all the skill sets required for all phases of the project been identified?
2. Have the appropriate personnel, possessing the required skills, been identified and committed to the project?
3. Has the individual's personal commitment to the project, and that of his functional management, been received?
4. Does each team member possess the necessary interpersonal skills to achieve the required chemistry?
5. Have all training requirements been identified and sessions scheduled?
6. When will each project team member be needed? Will each be a permanent team member or simply an as-needed resource to the team?
7. For what duration is each member expected to support the project?
8. In what location will the members regularly meet?
9. Is collocation of the project team a requirement?
10. Has senior management's commitment to the project been received?

If the answers to these questions indicate that all bases are covered, then the project manager moves forward to the next step in the process. If not, additional groundwork is performed.

Benefits and Challenges of Proximity

One key element in ensuring the success of a project management team is collocation. While concurrent project management practices are now recognized as vital to the success of strategic business projects, adoption of those techniques is often unsuccessful. Why? Because as companies have grown larger and more complex, internal hierarchical organizations (silos) have evolved to manage the increased organizational size and infrastructure. Technological complexity has increased a hundred-fold, and process specialization that comes with growth has become a way of life. In addition, company growth has frequently resulted in geographic dispersion of people and functions, creating the need for enhanced expertise in managing project team members from a distance (a topic that will be covered in more detail later in this chapter). Any one or all of these factors are likely to inhibit the formation of many of the informal relationships essential to foster effective communication and cooperation on a project management team, thus exacerbating the challenges facing the project manager.

Cross-functional Teams

Departments often focus inwardly on specific functional objectives, metrics, and priorities, creating a silo effect. The resulting hierarchical organizational structures, with day-to-day activities directed by functional managers, are generally not effective in coordinating the many cross-functional projects and activities required to support simultaneous process improvement, and product and service development projects, along with normal day-to-day activities. To offset these infrastructure deficiencies, many world-class enterprises are forming and collocating cross-functional project management teams. Collocated project teams provide a broader, more complete understanding of the multitude of business issues and alternatives because team members bring enterprise-wide perspectives. This broad-based perspective guarantees that all critical elements of the business, from product, process, and service design through distribution, are given due consideration. Unlike the hierarchical structure of most traditional project management efforts, strategic project management's goal is to satisfy the external customers' product, service, and support requirements, along with the internal customers' operational requirements.

Learning to Interact

An important factor in guaranteeing the success of the project management team is to provide the opportunity for members to meet regularly to learn how to interact as a real team rather than just another committee. The majority of communication during the project is informal, and informal communication happens best when project team members are in close proximity.

When employees are physically placed together with barriers to communication eliminated, a relaxed atmosphere eventually develops in which differing opinions are freely exchanged without the negative influences of functional priorities or hidden agendas. However, when the project management team is first brought together, there is often a period of uneasiness because of differing experiences and perspectives. Fortunately, this passes quickly as group bonding begins to take place.

Collocation can take many forms. Project team collocation, typically the best approach, occurs when project team members are collocated in a single project area, with no physical barriers, no outside influences, and no conflicting priorities or agendas. Reporting lines are direct to the project manager versus functional managers for the duration of the project. Because of that, the project team members are free to make decisions that are best for the entire project management effort, without fear of political reprisals.

In smaller companies where full-time resource allocation simply is not possible, project team collocation remains feasible for part-time or short-duration project team members, so long as they have a singular location in which they always meet at a dedicated time. The hours are committed to the project team by senior management, with no functional manager given the authority to override the dedicated project team meeting times or agendas. For example, John is allocated to the project team between the hours of 8:00 a.m. to 10:30 a.m. daily. As far as John's superior is concerned, John does not exist between those hours and his work must be scheduled accordingly or redistributed to others within the department.

Physical collocation promotes close working relationships and friendships between the project team members, which are essential to building a winning chemistry. The chemistry among the members of a project team enhances the frequency and quality of communication and feedback. In addition, because of the close physical proximity of the individual team members, coordination of team activities is made easier. Infrastructure requirements, such as information and data networks, document distribution, administrative support, etc., are less demanding, thereby streamlining the project management process by accelerating information flow.

In many large, multinational organizations, there are valid reasons why project team collocation is not possible. Whenever that is the case, the use of virtual collocation is employed. With virtual collocation, managerial resistance and politics, as well as company size and physical dispersion of departments and facilities, can be detrimental to the project team if not given due consideration and constant observance. Thus the project management team must plan accordingly to use the political advantage of a senior mentor who is in a position to break through political barriers and effectively minimize outside influences on the project team and its individual members.

To push the project team to its limits entails some degree of risk. A project manager should not push beyond the team's limits, but push up to them.

With virtual collocation, some of the benefits of true project team collocation are achieved through the use of technologies such as:

- voice mail;
- internet or intranet connections;
- satellite uplinks;
- shared data networks;

- e-mail;
- video conferencing;
- interlinking through groupware and shareware of personal computers and workstations via increased bandwidths and data compression techniques;
- integrated services digital networks (ISDN); and
- product data management systems that support access control, coordination, and release of data, and make data available to project team members at appropriate times over a network controlled by electronic passwords or signatures.

Limits of Team Autonomy

Over time, many project teams become essentially self-managed. Team members make all or most of the above-the-water-line decisions governing their actions, based upon rules and guidelines mutually established between the project team and project manager. As a result, much of the responsibility and accountability in such instances rests with the project team, making it essentially autonomous. That autonomy, however, is never allowed to be construed by the project team as the freedom to act independently.

Typically, the team's actions are restricted to the formulation of project goals, performance metrics, timing, and approach. Senior management, in most cases, defines the structure and expectations for the project team, including the overall rules and guidelines under which it will operate. A seasoned project manager never allows the project team to overstep its level of empowerment. Such mistakes tend to become career limiting.

Team Growth

In the beginning, the new project team will not be a team at all. Rather, it will be a grouping of employees with individual objectives, agendas, and approaches. They will, in reality, be only a committee, no matter how well they are selected. With some projects, a committee is perfectly adequate. If the project is narrowly focused, short-term in nature, and clearly defined, then in many cases the project committee is preferable.

The project committee is simply there to provide the data and information required for the project manager to make all decisions and direct the project through to completion. If, on the other hand, the project is complex, longer-term in nature, and crosses many organizational boundaries, then a more preferable organizational structure is a formal project team.

Project management teams are distinctly different from committees. Forging a project team takes effort and time, typically several weeks to a few months. The following are a few of the signs that the committee has matured into a team:

1. A committee has a strong, clearly recognizable leader—the project manager. Teams, conversely, have shared leadership roles that change from time-to-time as the project progresses.
2. Committees have individual responsibilities and accountabilities—those assigned by the project manager. Those on teams, on the other hand, have both individual accountability and shared accountability as part of the project team structure.
3. Committees have individually focused project goals established by the project manager. Teams have collective project objectives, goals, and expectations.

The transition from committee to project team requires commitment from the project manager, as well as the individual team members. Hidden agendas must be flushed out and resolved; the project team must adopt a common purpose, common approach, and common objectives. The project team must adopt and accept shared risks and shared rewards as the basis of its charter. And, it must develop a unified identity.

As the project team begins to encounter adversity and difficulty, it will unite and galvanize much more quickly. Generally, the tougher the assignment, the stronger and quicker the team members will bond together into a real team. But miracles do not happen overnight. The transition takes time and patience, with several predictably rough phases of development.

Should the project manager be in a position in which a project team structure is essential, but time does not permit the normal

1–3 months required for a typical project team to evolve, consideration is then given to utilizing an experiential training center. These centers focus on creating personal relationships of trust between individual team members. They strive to break down the facade that most people use at work and allow the true person to become visible to the individuals on the team. These centers can be effective to speed the formation of a project team. But there are a few considerations that should be kept in mind.

1. There is a cost for these services, typically around $5,000–$10,000 per person, depending on the center. This cost becomes part of the project budgeting process.
2. These centers create an artificial environment for the project team. While offsite at the center, there are no business influences to disrupt the formation of the team relationships. Upon returning to the office, however, environmental factors will quickly erode the personal relationships formed at the experiential center unless the personal relationships are continuously reinforced. Collocation is of value here, as are pizza lunches once or twice weekly, or breakfast meetings on the way to the office. It is critical that the personal as well as the professional relationships be maintained.
3. Either everyone on the project management team goes to the experiential center, or no one goes. If only part of the team attends, those individuals will ultimately distance themselves from those who did not attend because personal relationships were never formed with the absent members. In essence, the team becomes permanently polarized and synergy is lost forever.

MANAGEMENT VERSUS FACILITATION

So what role does the project manager take during the transition period? Success comes from being accepted as one of the team, as well as its official leader. That often requires a completely different set of skills than the traditional project management approach. It requires facilitation skills, taking the role of aiding rather than directing, in an effort to help the project team achieve the desired results. Facilitation requires that the project manager recognize how her personal behavior impacts the project team's performance and outlook. In all aspects, the project team will be a direct reflection of the project manager, her attitude, and approach—for better or worse. If the project manager is negative, for example, the project team will likely see this as an indication of doubt or frustration. If the project manager is optimistic, the team will in turn be aggressive and bold in its approach to achieving the desired project objectives. The project team looks to its leader for managerial and emotional guidance, making it essential that she lead by example.

Monitoring Progress

As a facilitator, the project manager maintains open communications with the project team members, and an open mind to their input and suggestions. Rather than giving specific assignments like a sergeant, the facilitator makes suggestions regarding the actions required and encourages individuals to take on each assignment. As a facilitator, the project manager constantly monitors the project team's progress and makes necessary adjustments and corrections to guide it back on course when required. The project manager constantly fosters confidence by supporting the project team's needs. She makes sure the necessary tools and resources are available to the team to complete each project assignment on schedule. As goals and objectives are met, the team (not individuals) is recognized, rewarded, and encouraged to continue. Throughout the project, the project manager recognizes and acknowledges the effort put forth by the team and its members, but constantly reinforces the fact that *success is measured by the results the team generates, not the effort they put into the project.* There is a critical difference between the two.

Successfully facilitating a project team requires that decisions be made promptly to support the team's requests and recommendations. Indecision is deadly. To facilitate the decision-making process, the project manager clearly defines the criteria required for a decision and holds the team members to those guidelines. In addition, the project manager ensures that the direction, scope, and expectations for the project are clearly understood by each project team member. Once everyone is pulling in the same direction, routine decisions become less controversial.

Facilitation also means monitoring interactions among team members that impact team cohesion and performance. For example, team members with strong personalities or a high degree of technical expertise can, at times, become overbearing, dictatorial, and loud. Such actions are quickly addressed through one-on-one sidebar discussions between the offending team member and the facilitator/project manager. The offender is reminded that everyone on the team has an equal say and that all ideas are of value to the team in achieving its objectives. If the disruptive conduct does not subside quickly, then the project manager takes more aggressive disciplinary action—up to and including exclusion of the offender from future team activities and termination of his participation on the team.

As team members become more comfortable with each other, there is often a tendency to accept opinions as fact rather than challenging their authenticity and insisting upon validation. In such cases, the project manager reminds the team of the requirement to confirm all data sources to ensure complete objectivity in its conclusions and ultimate recommendations.

At times, the project team may begin to flounder, lose direction, or its sense of urgency. In cases like this, the project manager quickly reestablishes the project milestones and metrics, and refocuses the team's attentions on the ultimate objectives and expected phase-gate deliverables. There may be the inevitable confrontation that results from a lack of personal chemistry between team members, or from internal politics and the associated hidden agendas. In those cases, the project manager takes an even stronger role than in the previously mentioned situations by quickly bringing forth the issue to the team and asking for its support to resolve the problem. If the problem continues, a change of players is often the only solution. While dramatic, such actions are normally effective in resolving this and all future problems of a similar nature.

Leadership Imperatives

The fundamentals of leadership apply to a project management assignment just as they do with any other managerial role. To begin with, credit and recognition always go to the project team, not the project manager. Simply put, no project manager is ever successful alone or in spite of his team. It is only through true teamwork that is created from a focus on the team and its entire membership versus any one individual that project success is possible. Put simply, project managers who are internally focused are often seen by team members as arrogant. That arrogance promotes a sense of antagonism between the team members and their leader. In addition, by placing his accomplishments above those of his team, the project manager is self-promoting, which in turn means he is demoting his team. When this occurs, it quickly becomes transparent to the project manager's superiors, as well as his teammates, making neither the project nor career success likely. The first imperative is *team first*.

The second imperative is that the project manager constantly makes an effort to *showcase the team's accomplishments*. Note the emphasis on "accomplishments" versus effort. As stated previously, effort alone does not ensure project success. It is the results that the team generates that guarantees success of a project. Given the proliferation of communication technologies, the project manager has a multitude of tools available to maximize the exposure of the team's accomplishments. These range from project web sites, e-mails, newsletters and progress reports, e-room access, and formal project presentations, to informal communication between the project manager and project stakeholders. Typically, the experienced project manager will utilize one or all of these avenues to ensure that his team receives recognition for its accomplishments.

The third imperative is that *discipline is a requirement*. Without discipline, project activities will quickly degenerate into second place in the team's priorities; risks will be exacerbated as shortcuts are taken or due diligence requirements are compromised for the sake of expediency; and focus will be lost as personal agendas infiltrate team interactions and decisions. Discipline gives the project team a common focus. It enables the team to execute its responsibilities effectively, reliably, and consistently. With discipline comes trust among team members, pride in the team's accomplishments, and personal integrity in meeting individual obligations and commitments for the benefit of teammates and the project. But for discipline to be effective, it must be enforced by the project manager—fairly, consistently, and when needed, immediately.

Few project teams are self-disciplined at first. It is the project manager's responsibility to set the stage through development of team rules and guidelines that will apply to all members equally. It is then the enforcement of those rules that solidifies the team's operating structure, setting the stage for a common focus on a common approach that all will follow. Experienced project managers are well aware that without discipline, employees will fall back on the existing organizational culture. When they do, project momentum is lost. In the end, project team discipline boils down to three simple expectations that apply to each team member.

1. Complete assignments on schedule and on budget, which is, in essence, doing what needs to be done consistently and accurately.
2. Work within the rules of the team to ensure that common goals are achieved.
3. Make personal sacrifices for the benefit of the team. Exercise self-control to ensure that team needs overshadow individual wants.

Keeping the Team Sharp through Leadership

Any time individuals work together in close proximity or on difficult assignments, problems are likely to occur. It is human nature. Experienced project managers recognize this fact and pay close attention to intergroup dynamics and group processes, with particular attention paid to personality conflicts that have the potential to disrupt team chemistry. They watch for the signs that will indicate a potential problem: ineffective resource and time utilization; noncompliance with milestone or activity requirements;

lack of team cohesiveness in addressing routine project issues; lack of attention to detail in completing assignments or in carrying out day-to-day responsibilities; poor judgment in routine decision-making; or an unwillingness to challenge another teammate when that teammate is obviously incorrect. Other indicators of disfunctionality within the team include: discouragement; burnout; frustration; individuals withdrawing from team activities or discussions; politicking; or the formation of camps. Once identified, the project manager quickly and decisively addresses each issue on a team or individual basis—or both. Focus and momentum cannot be allowed to be lost.

The ability to maintain focus and momentum is key to a successful project team. Thus, to keep his team sharp, the experienced project manager makes a concentrated effort to:

1. Provide team members with a clear understanding of what must be accomplished at each phase gate throughout the project while giving them the opportunity to take part in deciding how to accomplish the project goals and objectives. He lets the team members take an active role in developing the project strategies and techniques employed throughout the project. This approach greatly enhances their confidence in themselves, the project, and the project manager.
2. Provide a sense of direction and purpose. The members of the project team must have a sincere belief that the project is beneficial for the customers, the organization, and themselves. They must believe that the project is under control and correctly focused. And they must be convinced that the correct skill sets are represented on the team to ensure success. Often, direction and control are enhanced through the metrics set by the project management team. Those performance metrics quantitatively measure not only how the project team is progressing against the project milestones, but also how efficient the team is in accomplishing those project objectives. Earned value techniques (see Chapter 10) are typical of the approach used for this purpose, as are variance or trend analyses, gap analyses, and process analyses.

3. Constantly rotate assignments and the leadership of the project team. In doing so, all team members will remain focused on the status of the project, the assignments due, critical path compliance, and performance. Recognizing that they will ultimately be responsible for running certain aspects of the project, they will take more ownership in the project at all levels.
4. Ensure that the rules and guidelines that the project team are expected to operate under, from tracking performance to transferring the project leadership role, are well defined, and understood by all project team members.
5. Maintain high visibility for the project and constantly promoting it to peers and superiors. The project manager communicates with all of the functional managers and supervisors who will be impacted by the project to seek their input relative to their departmental needs and requirements. He constantly communicates to them the actions that the project team is taking to ensure that their needs and requirements are being addressed. This is also an opportunity to sell the benefits of the project at all levels within the organization.
6. Address conflict and resistance quickly and thoroughly. Every project team eventually encounters some degree of internal resistance. After all, project teams are often chartered to alter current business processes, policies, and/or procedures. In other words, the team will likely break some, if not several, organizational rules. That means, by definition, there will be those who are not enamored with the team's efforts. If the best efforts fail to win the support of those individuals, or heavy resistance is anticipated due to the nature of the project, then experienced project managers solicit one or more mentors who will provide the political muscle required to push critical issues through. There are times when this outside support is vital to keeping the project moving.
7. Shield the project team from negative outside influences that will disrupt the team's unity or focus. Project management

is like a one-way valve. When there are compliments and accolades to be handed down, they pass directly through the project manager to the team members. If, however, there is criticism or controversy directed at the project team, it stops with the project manager. Not fair? No one promised that project management, nor any management position for that matter, would be fair. It comes with the territory.

8. Address problems early. Rules will likely be broken by the project team. To the extent possible, experienced project managers get prior approval to head off problems. The project manager also points out to the project team members that processes, systems, and policies cannot be changed overnight, and he encourages them to be patient.
9. Encourage "followership" among all team members. This requires each team member to: demonstrate initiative; align his or her efforts with those of the project team; personally commit to team goals and project objectives; support the project manager and other teammates; make positive contributions to the project and team on a consistent basis; and take a stand when circumstances so dictate for the benefit of the team.
10. Recognize that projects require a significant amount of individual commitment and contribution from team members, which often takes away from their personal time away from the office. In a project environment, 60-hour weeks are common. As such, it is incumbent upon the project manager to ease the burden and stress that continuous long hours place on team members. One approach, where possible, is for the project manager to authorize flex time around predefined core hours. So doing will ease the burden and stress on team members by providing a degree of flexibility in the scheduling of project-related as well as personal demands.

OVERCOMING LIMITATIONS

As discussed previously, problems will occur in almost every project, even with the most comprehensive planning. This is especially true when dealing with projects that are very complex, multidimensional in scope, or that involve leading-edge technologies, processes, or systems. In cases like these, the demands placed on the project team by business constraints, the customer, or the project stakeholders appear unrealistic to the project team. The more apparently outlandish these demands seem to the project team, the higher the likelihood that team members will withdraw from active participation or will simply go through the motions without making the required personal commitment to the project. Either way, the project manager is faced with a perplexing dilemma. Experienced project managers have learned to deal effectively with situations like these by recognizing and altering the triggers behind human nature that create the team's initial paradigms. They have learned:

1. Focus and doggedness will lead to breakthrough ideas and approaches that are often buried within the frustrations caused by these unique challenges. They do not allow the team to waste time trying to change the project requirements and expectations, but rather focus the team on the demands of the project to seek innovative, unique solutions. They reinforce Plato's belief that "necessity is the mother of all invention" by pointing out to the team that nothing of true value or significance has ever been created by content people. It is only when pushed up against a wall that individuals truly become creative in seeking solutions to the most difficult problems. When the project requires radically new or high-risk approaches, the project manager encourages the team to consider multiple creative solutions, thereby reducing the risk should a single approach fail.
2. Innovation is a conscious choice. Team members are encouraged to take an active role in seeking new, innovative solutions rather than sitting back waiting for an epiphany to occur. These project managers use time to force creative thinking and out-of-the-box solutions often by establishing artificial deadlines for action. Still another approach used by experienced project managers is to ask the team to make

a list of the 10 most logical reasons why the project cannot be completed as defined. Once the team has completed the task, the project manager requests that they now complete a listing of the 10 most logical reasons why the project can be completed as defined. This simple exercise forces team members out of their comfort zones by requiring them to consider their paradigms from another perspective.

3. Innovation evaporates as quickly as it appears if not acted upon. Experienced project managers understand the necessity of actively exploring the pros and cons of all creative concepts and ideas versus allowing them to be tabled for discussion at a later date. A simple example illustrates this point. How often has the solution to a particularly difficult problem at the office come to you during your sleep? Why did it not occur during normal working hours? What happens if you make a mental note of it and go back to sleep without writing it down? More often than not, that creative solution is forever lost. Active and timely involvement prevents these great ideas from instantly evaporating.
4. Sustaining innovation will often require a change to the baselines that measure and reward individual or organizational performance. It is, therefore, frequently necessary that the project manager adjust the reward and recognition systems, process definitions, company policies, or procedures to ensure that old behaviors do not reappear.
5. To meet the challenges of unique projects, it is often not enough for the project team to simply enhance existing systems, processes, procedures, or products. The project manager encourages his team to actively seek completely new methods or approaches, experiment, benchmark against best practices from a multitude of industry segments, and take a clean-sheet approach to the resolution of the problems. To do so, team members are encouraged to challenge one another professionally. This will force individuals out of their comfort zones and into creative thinking. Team members are encouraged to push the envelope with their thinking, but at the same time, to identify and address the

risks that those creative concepts may introduce utilizing quantitative techniques.

BUILDING CONSENSUS

The success of a project team hinges on its ability to achieve consensus on project-critical decisions. Consensus-based decisions carry the collective weight and support of the entire project team and have a higher probability of success when it comes to implementation than is possible through more dictatorial approaches.

Project managers are results-oriented people who, by their very nature, believe that if you want a job done right, you do it yourself. But they are not free to take that approach. The complexity of projects coupled with ever-changing business dynamics make it impossible to handle the load alone. The project manager must work through the team to achieve results. That means keeping *all* team members functioning as a team; supporting the direction the team is taking; and the solutions the team is proposing. And that, quite frankly, requires consensus.

But before consensus as a team can be reached, the members must all agree on what consensus means. So here is a simple definition. *Consensus* means agreement on an approach or course of action that, while possibly not perfect in the minds of every team member, is an acceptable compromise that all members will accept and agree to support. In essence, it is the best available alternative, given all things considered.

How long does it take to reach consensus? That depends on many things:

- the nature and complexity of the issue before the team;
- clarity of the goal or objective;
- urgency in reaching a conclusion or solving a problem; and
- the mood or cooperation of individual team members.

Normally, reaching a consensus takes more time than a simple majority vote. But by striving for consensus, the project manager is assured that all team members have accepted the approach and that they will continue to work together for the common good.

Building consensus requires a methodical approach that begins with agreement on what consensus means, followed by establishing a time limit for making the decision. As the discussions (debates?) progress, the project manager gages the overall level of agreement between the team members and focuses the discussions on only those issues where agreement has not been reached. The team is not permitted to constantly rehash issues that have been resolved, or consensus may be lost. The project manager establishes the ground rules early: if a team member disagrees with a decision or approach, she is required to explain why and to offer an alternative.

Should a stalemate develop, the project manager makes the final decision. One of his key responsibilities is to maintain the project's momentum. Before moving forward with the decision in a case like this, he gathers as much data as possible given the time and/or economic constraints. All sources of data and information are validated. The project manager listens openly and objectively to all of the alternatives being proposed by the team members, as well as the reasoning behind each. He employs fundamental problem-solving and decision-making techniques to highlight the best possible alternative, then makes the decision and advises the team of the solution and how it was derived. The project manager requests the team's support and moves aggressively forward to implement the decision. This action promotes confidence in the project manager as a decisive decision-maker. The project team will appreciate the opportunity to participate in the decision-making process and will feel a degree of comfort in knowing that their project manager will make the hard calls if the team falters. The next time consensus is needed, the team will work harder to achieve it.

MANAGING FROM A DISTANCE

The challenges of managing a project team continue to grow in complexity. This is driven by growing trends in:

- outsourcing;
- telecommuting;

- virtual companies, divisions, franchises, departments, or functions;
- multinational acquisitions;
- partnering and strategic alliance agreements; and
- international sourcing.

While technology has provided the project manager with an expanded array of tools with which to communicate with team members not physically located together, technology alone has not proven to be the complete answer in effectively managing and motivating team members located in distant places. Certainly, there are advantages to an organization derived from maintaining multiple locations for its employees, often on a global scale, which are far-reaching. Those advantages include: greater market branding and positioning options that allow the organization to draw from a much larger pool of potential employees and contractors; lower costs and overhead when employees work from home; and enhanced lifestyle options for valued employees who prefer to live in a location other than that where the office resides. Will these trends change over time to a more traditional organizational structure? This is not likely.

Regardless of the advantages to the organization, the pitfalls for a project manager faced with the requirement to manage from a distance are many—and serious. Communication difficulties are at the top of the list. Most of the communication that occurs within an organization occurs informally (up to 95%) between employees who work in close proximity of one other. When team members are geographically disbursed, that informal communication link is lost. Even with the vastly enhanced communication technologies available to the project manager and his team, the personal aspect of sharing ideas and approaches with the team member next to you is lost.

Next on the list of challenges is the feeling of isolation experienced by disbursed team members. They are not part of the normal office or team meeting rituals, routine, or culture. They are isolated, alone. They do not feel included or accepted as part of the project team and, as such, do not make a concentrated effort to take an active role in the project. Third, there is a predictable loss of team camaraderie in addressing the challenges of the project, decreasing the project manager's ability to foster the critical chemistry required of a synergistic project team.

So how does a project manager overcome challenges to effectively and seamlessly manage his disbursed project team? The answer lies in relationship building with those disbursed team members. Successful project managers follow a few simple rules:

1. Set clear, measurable goals and objectives for all team members. At the project kick-off meeting, as well as at each phase review or more often, they discuss all project expectations, results, issues, and challenges. By utilizing quantitative metrics that are clear and well understood by all team members as the basis of team performance measurement, the project manager draws contrasts between actual and expected project performance, depersonalizing those issues creating the variances, and seeking input on approaches to close the gaps. By focusing on the resolution of the issue or variance versus who created it, all team members feel free to become part of the solution. The focus is on fixing the problem versus assigning blame.
2. Establish and maintain a regular reporting routine and structure that considers the work hours, culture, and language limitations of all team members.
3. Utilize video conferencing whenever possible to maintain "face" contact; e-mail communications to share project-critical information quickly; instant messaging to maintain an informal communication link with team members in remote locations; frequent telephone calls to reinforce personal bonds and minimize miscommunication problems that often arise from written communication; and personal meetings to reinforce and build personal relationships and trust. Team members working in a distant location greatly appreciate involvement in project communications and decisions, especially when their input is used.

4. Clearly define all roles and assignments for each team member, and the team as a whole, including schedule and budgetary constraints, compliance measures, performance targets, and expected deliverables.
5. Provide objective feedback to all team members on a frequent basis. Feedback is based in fact derived from quantitative metrics applied and available to all team members.
6. Define the limits of empowerment and discretion for each team member, and the team as a whole, along with all operating rules under which the team must operate. Policies, procedures, authority limits, roles, and responsibilities are documented to avoid any confusion or misinterpretation.
7. Employees in distant locations are never micromanaged. They are trusted to get the job done within the constraints of their locale, and are given a wider range of discretion in how they generate results because of those constraints.
8. Controls are put in place to monitor results, not because employees in distant locations are not trustworthy. If the project manager is unable to trust an employee, then other actions are required to address that personnel problem.
9. Not everyone is suited for a distance role in support of the project. Distance employees are, by nature, self-motivated with a high degree of drive and results orientation. As such, it is incumbent upon the project manager to staff carefully to ensure that the employees selected for a distance role possess the correct personality, experience, track record, and skills required to ensure project success. In the same respect, not all assignments are appropriate for or adapt well to the constraints of a remote site. Roles and assignments must be clearly thought out before they are made, again to ensure the highest probability of success for the project and the team member. Activities that are dependent upon local support are good examples of assignments that should not be given to a remote team member unless allowances are made to ensure the required levels of communication and cooperation between the local and distant parties exist.

10. Maintain a personal side of the working relationship with distant team members by remembering birthdays, holidays, and family activities. Birthday cards, flowers, or simple notes from the project manager mean a great deal, especially to those team members from different cultures. In the same respect, experienced project managers are always sensitive to local customs and cultures, and make an effort to recognize them in communications and working relationships.

WHY PROJECTS FAIL

Projects fail for a number of reasons, some under the control of the project manager, some outside of his control. There is, however, a recognized pattern of failures that will give the project manager insight into those things that require a watchful eye. Typical failure modes for a project include:

1. The project manager does not make project requirements and objectives clear enough for the project team, thus limiting its understanding of the project's direction, scope, and purpose.
2. The project manager does not effectively promote the project to other functional managers, thus failing to ensure that the project's benefits are well understood by all affected parties.
3. Buy-in and support from other functional managers do not exist because functional needs and concerns were not effectively addressed by the project team during the project plan's development.
4. The project manager fails to build a project team that works well together. Individual team members fail to take ownership and lack commitment to completing the project on budget, on time, and with the expected results. In short, the project manager does not achieve the necessary buy-in from the project team members.
5. The strategic direction of the project is not aligned with that of the organization or the customer.

6. The project manager and his project team fail to effectively develop and execute the strategic and tactical plans for the project.
7. The statement of work under which the project scope was developed is not comprehensive or achievable.
8. The capabilities of the project team are not aligned with the requirements of the project.

SUMMARY

An effective project team requires talented, capable individuals who will work together, as well as with outside resources and functional managers, to get the project tasks and objectives completed in the most cost- and time-sensitive manner possible. It requires effective leadership from its project manager along with committed "followership" from every team member. As such, every individual associated with the project must:

1. Demonstrate a sense of ownership by accepting responsibility and accountability for the project, actively participating in its every facet, and meeting commitments to the project stakeholders and fellow team members.
2. Exhibit a sense of purpose and direction through a clear understanding of the project team's rules, guidelines, and responsibilities. And, along with this, develop a sense of independence associated with her role and responsibilities within the team setting.
3. Trust each other: know she can rely upon other team members to get things done, and call things as she sees them without becoming overly sensitive to personality issues. She must respect the confidences of her fellow project team members and be supportive rather than judgmental of their opinions and actions.
4. Provide honest and candid feedback to others on the team, structured in a constructive versus destructive format, so that all team members can learn from their mistakes without the fear of retribution or embarrassment.

5. Display a sense of urgency in getting the project planned and executed, as well as in implementing corrective actions when required.

Effective project leadership requires that all team-related issues and requirements be satisfied before the subsequent phases of the project are launched. As such, it is common for seasoned project managers to utilize simple checklists or similar tools to guarantee closure of this phase of project planning. Revisiting the basics is always wise before moving forward.

- Have all of the skills required for all phases of the project been identified?
- Have the appropriate personnel, possessing the requisite skill sets, been identified and committed to the project?
- Are the necessary interpersonal skills present to ensure the proper team chemistry?
- Have all training requirements been identified and sessions scheduled?
- Have the schedules and durations of the project team members been established?
- Has the location in which the project team members will work been identified, and will it be available as needed?
- Is collocation a requirement? If so, has it been approved?
- Has management's commitment, and that of the project team members, been obtained?

Once it is apparent that the team infrastructure is firmly in place, it is time to build a project communications plan and begin assessing the project environment to ascertain what minefields lie ahead.

REFERENCE

Termini, Michael J. 2007. *Walking the Talk: Moving into Leadership*. Dearborn, MI: Society of Manufacturing Engineers.

7
Managing Contractor, Consultant, and Supplier Relationships

OVERVIEW

Whenever an "outsider" is introduced into the project team, an entirely new set of dynamics occurs. Whether a contractor, consultant, or supplier, the project team often rejects them outright or discounts the value these professionals bring to the project. From a management perspective, this situation creates a significant degree of complexity for the project manager in building the required chemistry and synergy within the project team. It introduces a degree of risk into the project that cannot be either dismissed or discounted.

This chapter explores many of the issues facing the project manager when dealing with the requirement to introduce outside support members into his project team. To begin, an understanding of the drivers behind individual and team behavior in situations like this is in order. In essence, the initial question is, "Why do team members reject these assets out-of-hand without first considering the value they bring to the project?" The answers vary by organization and by project, but can be summarized as follows.

- Project team members prefer to work either alone as individual contributors or with known peers. The comfort of working with individuals they are familiar with from other projects or daily functional interactions provides them with a safety net that, they believe, protects them from unknown problems or risks. Trust for them is based upon experience and knowledge of how an individual will react in a given situation. Without this foreknowledge, trust is withheld and solid working relationships are never formed or, at the very least, they require more extensive management to create.

- Many project team members lack the interest or experience in managing a project. Thus they are not familiar with how to develop the relationships required to build a synergistic team or with identifying and filling in existing skill set gaps that cannot be addressed by strictly internal personnel. Without this experience, they fail to recognize the need for these valuable resources, and thus reject the project manager's efforts to bring the needed skill sets into the project.
- Then there is the belief that these outsiders make significantly more money than the internal team members do. Questions like this quickly arise, "If they are so good, then why do I have to train them or oversee their work?" Professional jealousy enters the picture—and commonsense leaves.
- Still another question arises. "Why outsource these activities or hire contractors to do them versus hiring more full-time personnel?" The belief (often unjustified) is that internal team members are capable of performing the required tasks more quickly and at less cost, at higher quality levels, and with little training. Issues like budgetary constraints, upturns and downturns in business, capacity, competency, and capability factors are not clearly understood or accepted by the internal team members. They are not familiar with the concept of maintaining technologically critical or project critical skill sets internally, while outsourcing mundane or routine activities to keep fixed costs or overhead low. They simply view these activities as a waste of time and money.
- When outsiders do arrive on the scene, there is often a misconception about the terms and conditions under which they will be retained and operate. Internal team members expect these outsiders to be held to the same standards, rules, and expectations as they are. This, however, may not be possible for either legal or contractual reasons. Again, because they are frequently not experienced in the complexities of contract management, contract law, or federal labor laws, the internal team members quickly conclude that the outsiders

> are being treated differently, often better, than the internal team members are. Load factors may be lighter, work hours shorter, and assignments easier. Resentment quickly sets in as the seeds of revolution are sown.

Issues like these, whether real or perceived, will negatively impact the project team along with its expected outcomes. If not addressed early and decisively, such issues will doom the project or, at the very least, create a true leadership challenge for the project manager.

ENSURING PROJECT AND TEAM ALIGNMENT

When staffing the project team, the first consideration is whether or not the needed resources are available internally. For many reasons, ranging from existing load factors to competency considerations, the project manager may conclude that the needed skills or resources are not available internally. Thus he elects to retain the services of professionals or outsource part or the entire project. In so doing, the project manager is ensuring that alignment between the requirements of the project and the capabilities of the project team in delivering those requirements exists. When the decision is made to seek outside support, various commodity or service strategies are enacted. As illustrated in Figure 7-1, these commodity strategies are based upon two factors: risk and value. Ranging from easily procured products and services to those that are unique and difficult to source, decisions are made as to which will be acquired externally and which will be assigned to internal resources.

As is expected, strategies vary by segment based upon project-specific factors unique to each business situation. Unique commodities or services are those that represent a high risk to the project schedule but low budgetary impact. These are products or services that are provided or produced to unique specifications to ensure the provider maintains a significant competitive differentiation among his peers. As such, these commodities and services are difficult to source, requiring longer than usual lead times or notice that will, if not properly managed, impact the project schedule. Critical commodities or services, on the other hand, represent

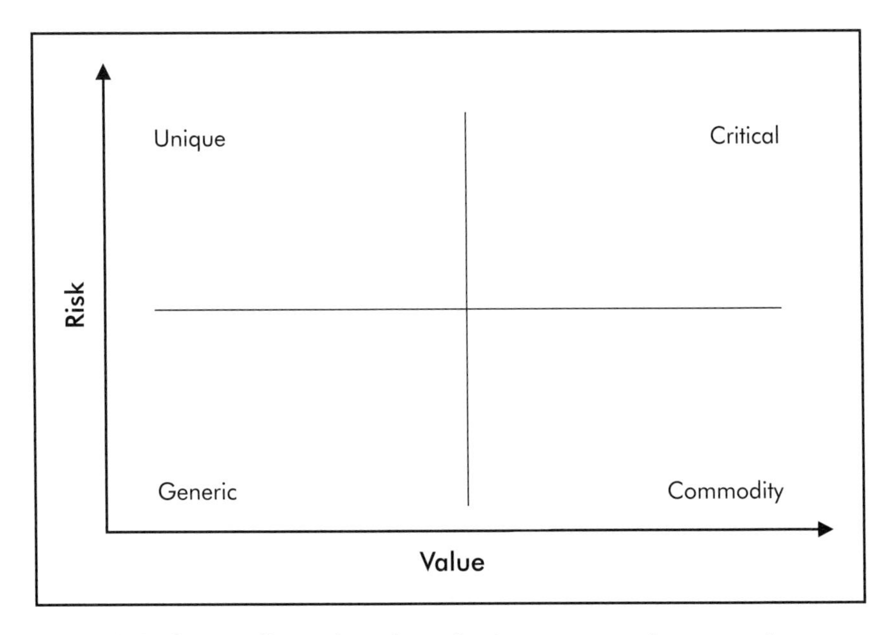

Figure 7-1. Commodity and service selection segmentation strategies.

high risk to both the project schedule and budget. They too are designed or provided to critical specifications, making them difficult to acquire within a short lead time or at a favorable cost. In many cases, these products or services are only available from a single provider or, at best, a limited number, thus driving up the cost of acquisition. Generic products and services are those that represent little schedule or budgetary risk to the project. They can be sourced from numerous providers with little effort or lost time. Their commonality makes pricing competitive. Commodities represent equally low risk to the schedule but often carry a higher risk to the project budget. Sourcing effort is not problematic but the unit pricing or hourly rate is often high.

Selection Strategies

As Figure 7-2 illustrates, selection strategies are based upon a multi-phased process that considers the gap between resources

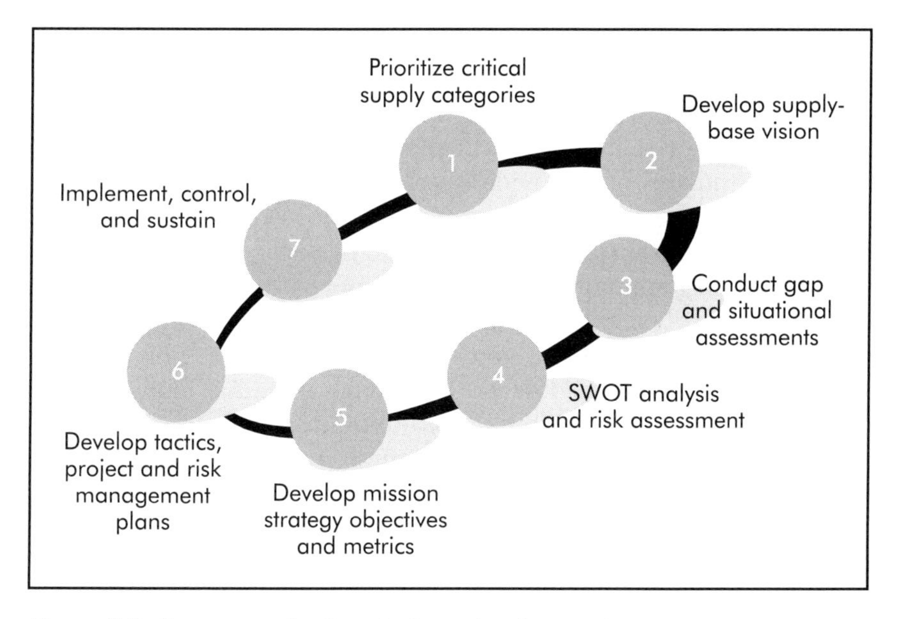

Figure 7-2. Resource selection strategy development.

or skill sets available internally and those that must be sourced externally.

Once a decision is made to acquire external resources, the project manager prioritizes the project-critical product or service categories based upon schedule and budgetary risk. In concert with the acquisition and/or supply management professionals, the project manager discusses the expectations and constraints surrounding the project with which the external resources are expected to comply. Together, they then conduct quantitative assessments of the situation, examine the gap between prior deliverables from key suppliers and what was actually expected/provided, develop specific project deliverables and performance metrics to measure compliance, integrate appropriate risk management techniques, and then select the best providers based upon the 3C approach:

- process *control*,
- process *capability*, and
- continuous *compliance* with project expectations.

This process is designed to identify specific project deliverables that these external resources are contracted to fulfill, define specific actions that are to be taken by the supplier to bridge the gap between project-specific requirements and those available from internal resources, and provide a real-time monitoring mechanism to ensure consistent compliance with no eleventh-hour surprises that have the potential of derailing the project.

The project manager, with the support of his team and the acquisition professionals, considers the risks introduced when external resources are introduced into the project. Then specific strategies are developed to address each one. As Table 7-1 illustrates, expected problems, challenges, and their associated risks are identified. Contingency plans and risk management techniques are then developed along with their expected cost and schedule impacts, and a quantitative risk measure is calculated (detailed in a later chapter).

For high-risk situations, alternative actions, products, or resources are sought to minimize the threats to the project or to capitalize on the opportunities available to enhance the project outcomes (see Table 7-2).

Table 7-1. Assessment of expected risks, issues, and challenges.

Expected Issues/ Challenges	Contingency Plans	Expected Costs and Timing	Risk Assessment Results

Table 7-2. Alternatives and options to minimize risks or threats and capitalize on opportunities.

Alternative Actions, Products, or Commodities	Threats and Opportunities

A Step-by-step Approach

The process begins with a comprehensive review of the project scope statement, defined expectations, deliverables required by phase, and specific project constraints. From that assessment, the project manager determines which skill sets and/or resources are required for each phase of the project, both direct and indirect. The tool utilized in this step of the process is outlined in Table 7-3. Each critical activity (derived from the work breakdown structure [WBS]) is listed along with the required skill sets necessary to ensure that it is completed as planned. Dates when these skill sets will be required are noted, as are any logistical requirements. Team members are then selected and assigned for each of these critical activities—first from internal resources, then for those unable to be filled internally, from external resources.

Once the resource or skill-set gaps are identified, the project manager determines the most cost-efficient, lowest-risk approach to fill them. If the gap is a personnel gap, questions like the following are considered.

1. Is there time to train internal resources?
2. If not, is there time to recruit resources for the project with the needed skills?

Table 7-3. Resource selection process.

Activity	Required Skills	Dates Required	Location Required	Employee or Contractor
Brand plan	Market strategist	4/1–6/30	Miami	Jordan
Market plan	Financial strategist	6/1–9/15	Miami	Thomas
Public relations plan	Consumer strategist	6/1–9/15	New York	Contractor
Sales plan	Sales strategist	6/1–10/1	Miami	Kirk
Field campaign	Field sales	10/15–11/5	West Coast	Miles
Data analysis	Analyst	10/15–11/5	Miami	Miller
Ad campaign	Graphic artist	1/10–3/31	New York	Consultant
Launch coordination	Project management	4/1–6/6	Los Angeles	Edwards

3. If not, are there other internal resources available through other corporate divisions or operations with the required skill sets?
4. If not, which external sources are available from which the needed skill sets can be acquired?

Supplier and contractor failures remain two of the most significant risk factors for most projects. Thus it is incumbent upon the project manager to select resources, whether human, product, or technological, from providers with a known track record in the type, scale, and scope of project under consideration. Simply because the provider demonstrated exceptional performance on other projects of a different type, scale, or scope does not mean the company can or will perform similarly on "this" project. Apples-to-apples comparisons are critical to ensuring that risks are minimized. The best approach is to select sources from the organization's certified or qualified provider listing. These sources have been through an extensive quantitative evaluation that statistically measures their capability and performance on a broad-ranging scale of assessment criteria. Other considerations include issues relating to:

- source type: dual, single, or sole;
- total cost versus unit price or hourly rate;
- availability and lead time;
- compliance-dictated or industry-dictated registrations;
- reputation or performance history;
- size and capability; and
- years of experience with this type of project.

In summary, the selected supplier is required to provide a bridge between the project team's capabilities and the requirements of the project. As illustrated in Figure 7-3, strategic alignment is achieved only if the project team's capabilities and

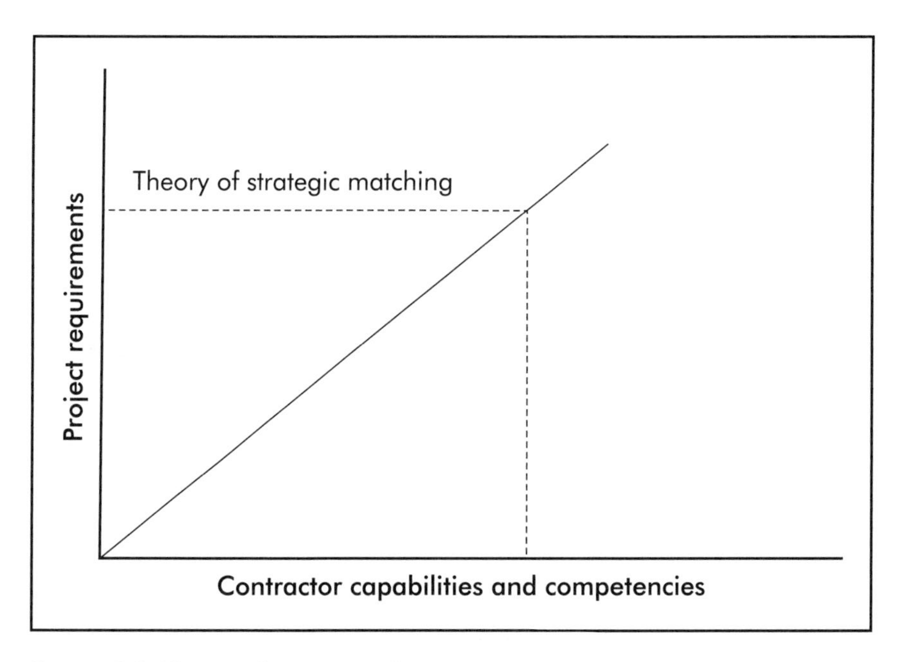

Figure 7-3. Theory of strategic alignment.

competencies match, one-for-one, with each and every requirement of the project.

Strategic Alignment

With strategic alignment, the needs of the project are balanced (in perfect alignment) against the capabilities of the internal and external members on the project team. There is a seamless base of skills and experience to ensure that all project requirements are fulfilled as planned. The same concept applies for acquired products, services, technologies, etc. By ensuring strategic alignment, the project manager effectively offsets internal weaknesses and limitations with the strengths available from the external resources. This is particularly important when there is not time or capital to develop internal resources for the project or when the need is only temporary.

As illustrated in Figure 7-4, the opposite situation occurs when misalignment exists between the project requirements and the team's capabilities and competencies. When this situation is allowed to develop, the project team members lack the ability to successfully deliver the project, irrespective of how dedicated they are or how hard they work. Simply put, the team lacks the skills necessary to deliver the expected project deliverables in the time frame or at the cost expected. Mistakes are inevitable. Delays are predictable. Budget overruns will occur. In short, the project will fail to meet expectations in one or more areas. In a case like this, the typical response is to blame the external resources. Rest assured; that story will fall on deaf ears. It is the responsibility of the project manager to fulfill all required skill sets through internal or external sources to ensure that a seamless, synergistic, competent project team is available and deployed to the project. Failure is not an option. With project team's competency comes lower risk, lower cost, and maximum performance.

Baseline Performance

The next step in the process is to quantitatively baseline the requirements of each assignment, then match them against the pool

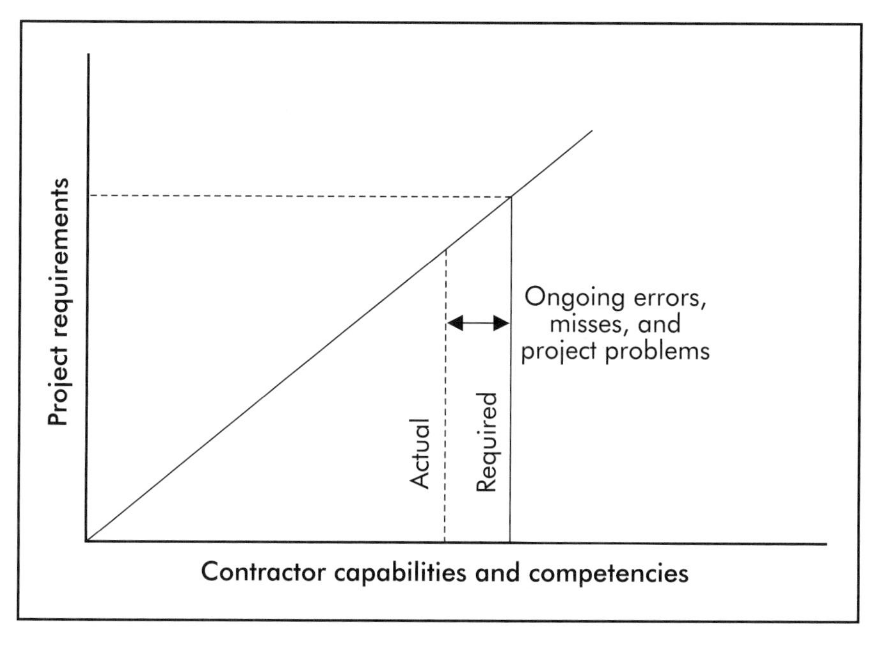

Figure 7-4. Strategic misalignment and its effects.

of known resources, comparing each possible source against that baseline, as well as against the baseline of performance of their peers. There are numerous certification and qualification tools available to the project manager for use in this process. Many of those selection and ranking tools exist within the purchasing or contract management disciplines within most organizations and can be applied effectively in a project environment for the selection of contractors, consultants, or suppliers.

A typical ranking tool is outlined in Table 7-4. As the example illustrates, the contractor scored 94 against the baseline of 90 points required for the project. Compared to all other contractors under consideration for this project, the contractor scored 8 points higher. However, the contractor scored 5 points lower than required against the baseline of 90 for change performance. If the project manager determines that this is a critical aspect of the project, consideration will be given to other contractors who

Table 7-4. Source ranking and competency modeling.

Competencies	Score for Contractor	Average of All Contractors	Gap (+/–)	Project Requirements	Gap (+/–)
Schedule performance	90	85	5	90	0
Quality performance	95	85	10	90	5
Budget performance	90	90	0	90	0
Specification performance	95	90	5	90	5
Change performance	85	80	5	90	–5
Service reliability	95	85	10	90	5
Flexibility	100	90	10	90	10
Technical support	100	90	10	90	10
Customer service	100	85	15	90	10
Regulatory performance	90	80	10	90	0
Total	94	86	8	90	4

may be somewhat lower in total score, but who meet the minimum score for all of the baseline competency requirements.

Many organizations apply weighting factors to the various competency categories to better reflect the level of importance or prioritization to their specific organization. As business conditions change, the weights are adjusted to better reflect current requirements. This "living" ranking methodology allows the project manager to remain in sync with the prevailing business climate during all phases of the project's life cycle.

The scoring mechanism used is consistent with most certification processes.

- 90–100%: Contractor consistently meets all project requirements and expectations. The contractual relationship is maintained.
- 80–89%: Contractor meets most project requirements and expectations. The project manager and contractor revisit the contract requirements, scope, terms, and conditions and refocus on all areas requiring improvement.
- 70–79%: The contractor is failing to consistently deliver expected results for the project. The project manager discusses with the contractor the deficiencies in meeting the project requirements and contract terms. Project performance metrics and measurement criteria are reviewed, and then the project manager initiates a 60-day probationary period (or one that is contractually defined). If performance fails to meet the 90% level within 60 days, the contract is terminated.
- Under 70%: The contractual relationship is discontinued pursuant to the cancellation clauses of the contract.

There is another tool used by the project manager to select among contractors or providers who have been previously certified or qualified by the organization's procurement processes. In this case, a more general comparison is utilized as illustrated in Table 7-5. In this example, four contractors or providers are compared against the baseline of the current project requirements. Specific strengths and weaknesses are highlighted as they apply to the project under consideration. Unique concerns are also factored into the comparison. Based upon this rough-cut approach, the two providers who do not possess the capabilities needed for the project are immediately removed from further consideration, leaving only the two (in this example) remaining providers for further analysis and final selection. This is an acceptable methodology only when all providers under consideration have been previously certified on projects of a similar scale, scope, and type.

Once the field of potential providers has been narrowed, the project manager then compares the actual performance history of

Table 7-5. Contractor comparison worksheet.

Contractor	A	B	C	D
Certified	Yes	Yes	Yes	Yes
Rating	90%	92%	85%	84%
Competencies	Product design	Time to market	Testing and reliability	Product manufacturing
Weaknesses	Capacity booked	Slightly more $	Limited capability	Limited capacity
Concerns	Ability to handle project at this time	None	Not capable	May stretch them too far

the remaining providers. Again, he is cognizant of the scope, scale, and type of projects under review to ensure a supportable basis of comparison. As Table 7-6 illustrates, particular consideration is given to performance issues that introduced project performance, budget, or schedule difficulties, as well as to how the providers reacted and ultimately controlled the overall impact of any unexpected work delays or unplanned costs. In this example, the project manager establishes a baseline of 23 project performance criteria that are unique to his business. For each, he compares the remaining potential providers against one another on the basis of three factors:

1. the number of hours required to resolve a problem that occurred in one or more of the baseline criteria,
2. the fully burdened cost to resolve each of those issues, and
3. the total cost of the nonconformance (individually and collectively) when factoring in all actual schedule, direct, and indirect costs.

By so doing, the total schedule, resource, and financial costs to the prior projects are considered, thus providing the project manager with a clear understanding of the risk factors that are unique to each potential provider.

Table 7-6. Contractor performance scorecarding example.

Nonconformance	Hours to Resolve	Fully Burdened Cost to Resolve	Cost of Nonconformance
Receiving inspection			
In-process inspection			
Final inspection			
Design errors			
Specification errors			
Bill-of-material errors			
Purchase order errors			
Requisition errors			
Rejections			
Rework/sorting			
Returns processing			
Premium freight			
Surplus inventories			
Obsolete inventories			
Scheduling errors			
Inventory count errors			
Warranty claims			
Field campaigns			
Packaging errors/failures			
Invoicing errors			
Expediting time			
Logistical errors			
Excess lead times			
Total			

DEFINING EXPECTATIONS AND RESPONSIBILITIES

Once the external support providers are selected and contracted, the stage is set for mutual cooperation, understanding, and performance in a project kickoff meeting. Establishing a baseline of understanding early, along with addressing any contractual, operational, or legal constraints, allows every team member to clearly understand what is expected of themselves and every other team member, as well as the collective responsibilities of the team itself as they relate to schedule, budget, and deliverable performance. This initial communication sets the performance expectations for the team and reinforces that the success of the project is dependent upon every team member delivering on their assignments consistently and completely.

To ensure that all team members understand what the outside resources (contractors, consultants, suppliers, etc.) have been retained and contracted to provide, the project manager summarizes each assignment (see Table 7-7). Specific deliverables for each external provider, whether it is a service, a product, or function, are identified, along with the performance specifications and metrics that will be used to monitor and confirm compliance. Included are the schedule, budgetary, or performance requirements associated with each assigned task or activity. The project manager is as specific and detailed as possible to ensure that there are no misunderstandings or misconceptions to cause downstream problems between the internal and external team members. Questions are encouraged and honestly answered to force discussion and surface hidden agendas or ill will. In short, the intent is to get all team members (internal and external) on the same page before the project is launched.

Statements of Work as the Basis of Communication

One of the most effective ways of eliminating misunderstandings with contractors and suppliers is to document in a comprehensive statement of work (SOW) exactly what is expected of them, as well as the terms and conditions under which those expectations will be measured. As with any team member, individuals respond positively

Table 7-7. Contracted assignments, roles, and responsibilities.

Product or Service to be Provided	Definition or Specification	Schedule, Performance, and Cost Requirements

when they clearly understand what is expected. The opposite holds true as well. As Figure 7-5 illustrates, the SOW provides the basis of the purchase order terms and conditions used to retain contractors and suppliers. Expectedly, the SOW is different for each specific contractor or supplier.

The focus of each SOW is thus to accurately and comprehensively define what products or services each contractor or supplier will provide for *this* project: In other words, the exact scope of their deliverables that are being purchased. The SOW further states as accurately as possible what tactics or methodologies will be utilized to measure achievement of each assignment. If the scope statement is incorrect or incomplete, team communication and project performance problems will assuredly arise downstream in the project. In essence, the SOW emphasizes performance that can be contractually defined. Thus, the results of the contractor or supplier's efforts can be measured in terms of technical and quality performance, schedule progress, and budget or cost compliance.

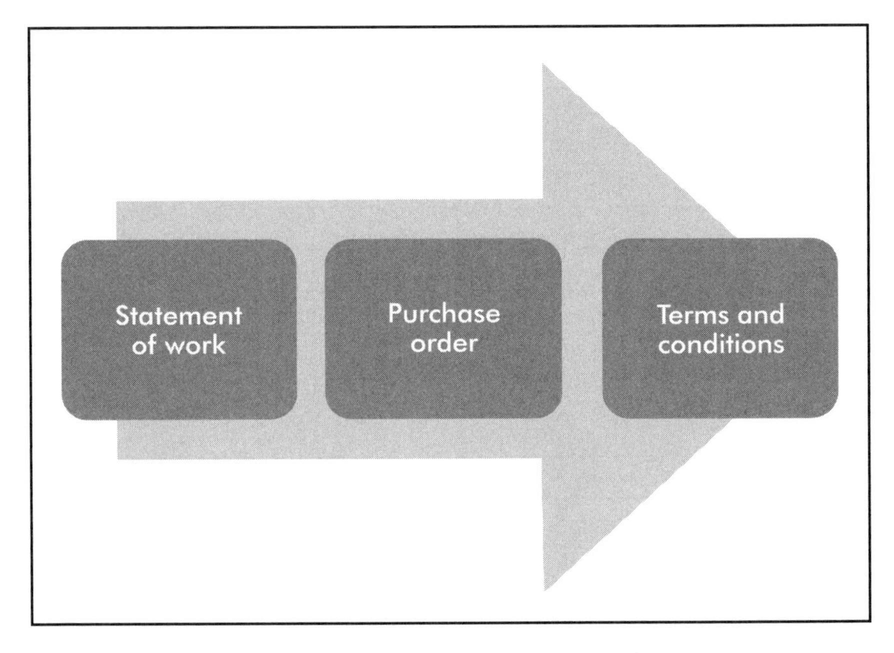

Figure 7-5. Statement of work as the purchase order driver.

Roles and Responsibilities Defined

During the kickoff meeting, the scope of the contractor or supplier's work is discussed with all team members. Once the scope and extent of the contracted services are understood, the next step is for the project manager to clearly define the specific roles and responsibilities of each team member for each phase of the project. By so doing, team members, internal and external, understand how they will impact the project, as well as the activities of their peers. Failure to take this step is one of the most common causes of conflict between internal and external resources—the lack of understanding of how each is to interface and interact with their peers, who is responsible for what, and the specific direct and support responsibilities each has during every phase of the project's life cycle. By knowing what each team member is to deliver and what role they will play, other team members are better able to assist and backup one another when needed to prevent problems that have the potential to spread through to the subsequent activities or phases of the project. As Table 7-8 highlights, both direct and support responsibilities for each team member are defined for every phase of the project; this ranges from accountability for the overall results of each particular phase of the project to the support and review roles each team member is expected to perform.

For example, Edwards will be accountable for delivering results in three separate phases of the project (data development, red team review, and district review), making her the project lead for those three phases. In addition, she is expected to act in a support role during the data compatibility and program and testing phases of the project supporting Jones and Contractor Two, respectively. Finally, she is slated to perform review functions during the data conversion and compliance review phases of the project in support of Contractor One and Smith, respectively. Each team member's roles and responsibilities are subsequently delineated. This level of detail promotes understanding, cooperation, and coordination among all of the team members because nothing is left open for interpretation. The assignment questions are answered up front.

In addition to the assignments, other critical project criteria are discussed during the kickoff meeting, including:

- project scope;
- project personnel reporting structures;
- communication channels and methodologies;
- levels of empowerment;
- organizational, financial, and political limitations and constraints;
- status reporting frequencies, formats, and content requirements;
- explicit and implicit expectations of the project stakeholders;
- specific operating rules and guidelines under which the team will operate;
- schedule and budget tolerances along with acceptable ranges;
- specific project challenges, forecasted failure modes, and expected risk factors;
- corrective action procedures;

Table 7-8. Roles and responsibilities defined.

Project Phase	Edwards	Jones	Smith	Contractor One	Contractor Two
Data development	Accountable	Support	Review	Support	
Data conversion	Review	Support	Review	Accountable	
Data compatibility	Support	Accountable	Review	Support	
Program and testing	Support	Review	Support		Accountable
Compliance review	Review	Support	Accountable		Support
Red team review	Accountable	Support	Support		
District review	Accountable	Support	Support		

- decision criteria and methodology;
- project performance metrics;
- conflict resolution policies and procedures;
- phase-gate deliverables along with compliance requirements of each;
- schedule and budget requirements;
- confidentiality issues or security requirements;
- logistical issues facing or influencing the team; and
- business or operating constraints including attire, policies, procedures, work hours, safety-related requirements, access restrictions, security passes, parking, work areas, work tools and equipment, etc.

Why cover so much detail at the kickoff meeting? The detail is to guarantee that there is no misunderstanding, no miscommunication, and no bias that will lead to downstream team chemistry or cooperation problems.

As illustrated in Figures 7-6 and 7-7, communication strategies are also discussed with the team during this kickoff meeting to ensure that the needed data gathering requirements and assignments are clearly defined, as well as to clarify specific stakeholder communication requirements in the way of format, content, or frequency. The intent is to seamlessly bridge the communication gap between the team and project stakeholders in a way that meets stakeholder requirements in the least cumbersome manner possible for the team. Exception reporting techniques often satisfy this requirement, especially for more senior stakeholders who are interested only in the issues facing the project team, what they are doing to address and resolve those issues, and the results the team has achieved to date against each issue.

The flag report in Figure 7-6 illustrates the cumulative number of deliverables actually completed for each phase of the project contrasted against the number planned, as well as their associated trends over time. It also illustrates how far behind schedule each of these deliverables is against the phase-gate requirements, and the number of deliverables that will be required in the upcoming period. This gives the project stakeholders a backward and a

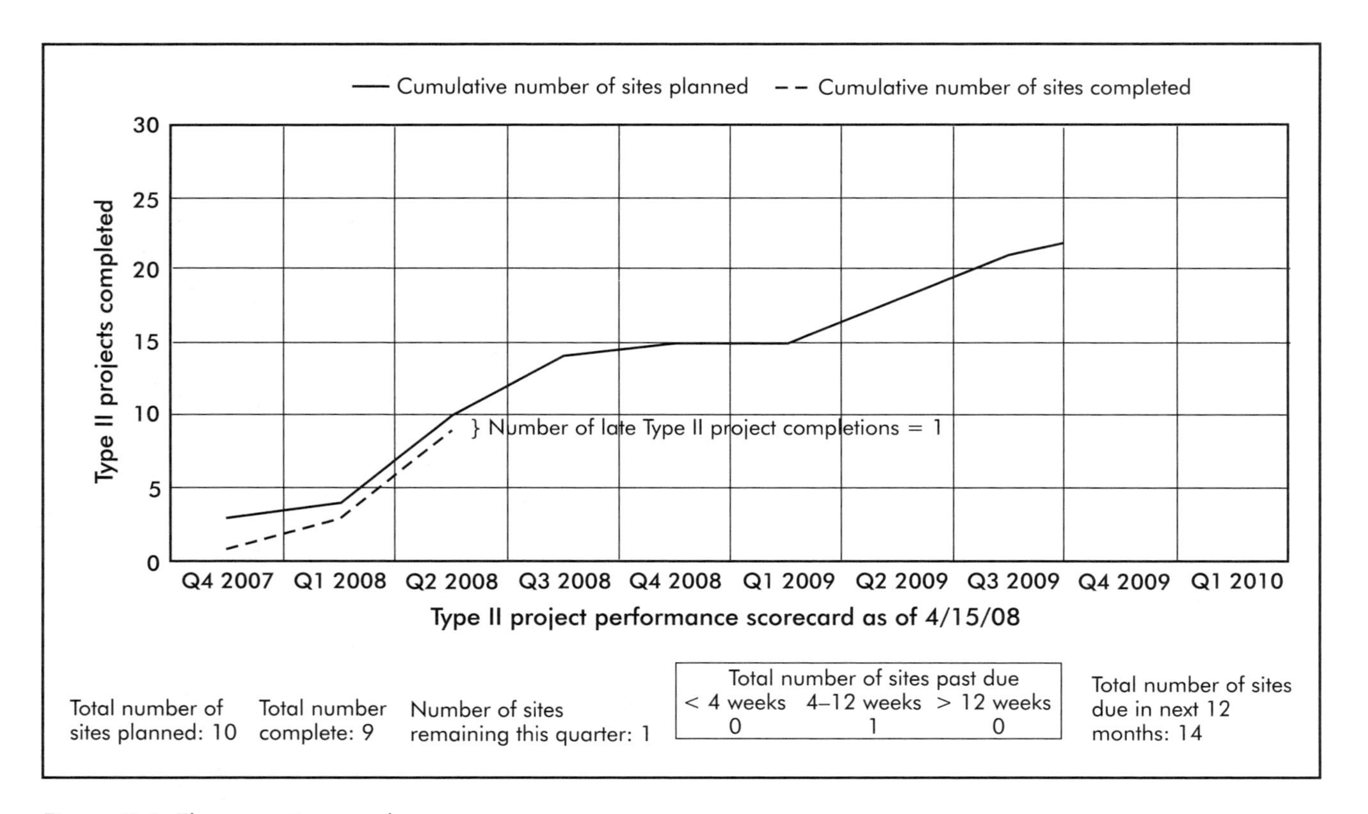

Figure 7-6. Flag report example.

forward look to ensure an accurate perspective of how the project team is actually performing.

Figure 7-7, on the other hand, provides more specific detail regarding each deliverable including the planned completion date, the revised completion date, corrective actions taken, results realized to date, and any remaining risks to the project that have resulted due to the delinquency of the deliverable.

Whatever format is ultimately selected, it is imperative that it be simple, easily understood by all parties at all levels, and accurate. Three-dimensional charts and graphs, while they look professional, are often difficult to read. Graphics that relay more than one message are equally difficult to understand because they are too busy and often confusing. The best practice for all involved is to keep it simple and leave the sophisticated artwork for another purpose.

Performance Measures Defined

Next, specific performance requirements are detailed for each deliverable at each phase of the project and quantitative performance metrics are applied. The project team members are given these requirements in terms of the required results, and are provided criteria for verifying compliance. As shown in Table 7-9, project deliverables are defined along with their expected due dates, budgeted costs, quality or compliance specifications, the quantitative metrics that are to be applied, and the data sources from which the compliance measures are to be taken. For the external resources, these criteria are also delineated in their contracted scope of work, or the terms and conditions section of the contract. Why so much detail? Again, this approach ensures a comprehensive understanding of exactly what is to be expected from each internal and external team member to eliminate any confusion or misconceptions downstream.

COMMUNICATION

Most project and many business professionals are not adept at written communication. And, in all forms of communication,

Project: Prinston Type II Pipe Plant

Project manager: Curt Tylor

Date submitted: 04-15-09

Scheduled completion date: 1-30-09

Status:
- < 4 weeks behind schedule: _____
- < 4–12 weeks behind schedule: __X__
- > 12 weeks behind schedule: _____

Expected completion date: 05-25-09

Actions & corrections: Construction lagging due to Metro services crew being pulled from site for 4 months. Produced punch list of outstanding items. Construction crew is back at site.

Results to date: Construction is underway on all phases of site and building projects.

Risks: Unless additional Metro crews or other subcontractors are assigned to the site, the delay may impact other site start dates due to the limitation of available manpower.

Figure 7-7. Exception report example.

Table 7-9. Performance metrics example.

Project Deliverable	Due Date	Cost	Compliance Requirements	Metrics Applied	Data Sources
Architectural design	5/15/08	Not to exceed $155,000	IAI121.57	Geometric dimensioning and tolerancing	SME 123.9 IEE 345.3-10 IAI 664-9
Construction drawings	7/10/08	$28,750	VDOT135.98 & VAHOA21.754	Geometric dimensioning and tolerancing	ANSI 123.51 1
Project budget	8/5/08	$7,500	+/– 2.0%	USD	Account code: P06-220
EPA site permit	10/25/08	$5,500	EPA336.2 & HASMAT21.77	Federal and Virginia state regulations	EPA inspection
Building permit	12/21/08	$5,500	Full state and local code compliance	Virginia state and city of Richmond	Virginia building code enforcement
Certificate of occupancy	1/1/09	$1,950,990	Full state and local code compliance	Virginia state and city of Richmond	Signed/sealed certificate

perception, as well as content, must be effectively managed. So, dump the e-mails. The problem with e-mails is that they are impersonal and are often interpreted differently than the writer intended. Tone and content are often inconsistent with the intended message. As such, they leave many unanswered questions to be filled in by the receiver—either correctly or incorrectly. So, whenever possible, project managers communicate in person.

It is important that communications between and among all team members and the project manager be candid so that conflicting ideas or objectives are addressed through isolation of a common approach that allows all parties to agree. Too often, the "outsiders" feel their opinions and suggestions are ignored or not valued. When disagreements arise, these external resources believe they will take the brunt of the blame for project difficulties, whether or not they are at fault. They often believe that the corrective action process put in place by the project manager will not provide them with equal consideration when disagreements arise. In short, they believe the communication channels are unidirectional, favoring the internal team members at the expense of them.

It is thus critical that the project manager reinforce at every possible opportunity that *all* team members will receive the same consideration and respect; no person will be given advantage over another. Corrective action processes favor no one, but rather are focused singularly at resolving project problems. When individual team members believe their opinions and suggestions are given equal weight, communication problems between internal and external members are minimized.

Understanding Limitations

One of the most significant sources of communication problems between team members is a lack of understanding regarding why contractors and suppliers are frequently treated differently than company employees. The legal and contractual constraints that limit the project manager's ability to level the playing field are rarely understood and rarely discussed. As before, a little time in the kickoff meeting taken to discuss these limiting factors will go a long way in defusing many common problems and misconceptions.

The courts have clearly defined the differences between a company employee and an outside contractor. In their rulings, several factors are used to differentiate the two and no single factor is deemed exclusive. All factors are considered equally when deciding whether or not the line between outside contractor and employee has been breached. In general, three categories are considered:

1. behavioral control;
2. financial control; and
3. relationship of the parties.

Beginning with behavioral control, a contracted team member is considered an employee when:

- The project manager has the right to direct and control the contractor.
- The project manager provides extensive instruction regarding *how* the assignment is to be accomplished or performed (that is, how, when, or where to do the work, what tools or equipment to use, or where to purchase supplies or services). This suggests to the courts that an employer-employee relationship exists.
- The project manager provides training on required procedures and methodologies that indicates the project manager wants the work to be done in a specific manner.

However, if the contractor receives extensive instruction regarding *what* is to be done but *not how* it is to be done, the courts deem this to imply an independent contractor status.

Financial control is the second category the courts consider. Here:

- If the contractor has a significant investment in his or her business that is at risk, contractor versus employee status is indicated.
- If the contractor is reimbursed for some or all business expenses, a contractor relationship is indicated.
- If the contractor realizes a profit or a loss from the relationship, a contractor relationship is indicated.

Relative to the relationship of the parties, the courts have ruled that:

- If the project manager provides the contractor with insurance, pension, or paid leave, an employee status is indicated.
- If the project manager provides the contractor with a written agreement indicating the contractor is not an employee, a contractor relationship *may be indicated*, based upon the other criteria herein.

Why do we care? If adjudicated an employee, the contractor is entitled to all of the benefits and considerations, as well as company-paid obligations afforded an employee. So then, what restrictions can be reasonably placed on a contractor? Obviously, compliance with all federal labor laws, company safety and general working rules, state and local public records laws, company confidentiality restrictions, contract terms and conditions, and regulatory compliance restrictions are all reasonable and expected. However, the number of work hours per day or period, the actual hours worked daily, holidays and vacation schedules, etc., are likely to differ from those of internal team members. They are governed solely by the contract terms, which renders them outside the control of the project manager.

Conflict Between Employees and Contractors

Effective communication is the key to harmony between internal and external team members. Recognizing this fact, the project manager prepares in advance by developing and later communicating the project plan and budget, expected project deliverables, change control processes, performance tracking processes and, of course, conflict resolution procedures that will apply to all team members.

While conflict resolution is never the most pleasant aspect of project management, it is certainly one of the most important. By addressing issues that create conflict quickly and completely, the project manager ensures that problems are resolved on a professional versus a personal level. Once an issue is allowed to become personal, it is far more difficult to resolve.

While harmony is the obvious goal in team interactions, conflict is not unexpected. It is, in fact, a normal and inevitable aspect of team dynamics. Unlike what is commonly believed, conflict is rarely a result of personality differences as personalities do not conflict. Rather, it is the team members' behaviors, biases, and opinions that conflict. Conflicts and disagreements, while they may seem to be the same, are not. Disagreements are simply differences of opinion, while conflicts are often more serious because they are driven by emotions. And as we all know, emotion is a blinding force to commonsense. In many cases, conflicts between project managers or internal team members and contractors are the result of:

- a lack of or incomplete communication,
- value or professional interpretations,
- poor decision-making or leadership on the part of the project manager,
- discrepancies in the perceived performance or productivity of the contractor,
- unresolved prior conflicts, and
- constant changes in direction or scope of the project or contractor's assignments.

Most conflicts are minor and easily resolved while others require more involvement and interaction on the part of the project manager. The rule of thumb for project managers is to resolve the issues quickly before they become a conflict of wills. When personalities are allowed to enter the situation, commonsense becomes almost impossible to inject back into the discussions.

When faced with conflict, a little analysis serves the project manager well. First, it is important to isolate the nature and type of conflict that exists between the contractor and team member. Answers come from asking direct questions, listening intently and openly to the answers provided by both parties, and collecting facts to differentiate between opinion and reality. A thorough analysis of the issues and the drivers behind them is made, and the conflict is resolved in the most equitable way for all parties involved. The analysis includes candid assessment of the following questions:

- What problems are the contractors causing the team?
- What problems are the internal team members causing the contractor?
- What is the single most important goal to be achieved for all parties in resolving this conflict?
- What common ground exists that will allow both parties to reach a consensus on the resolution of the issues in conflict?
- What other actions can be taken to encourage positive relationships between all parties?

In all cases, open and candid communication is the catalyst for a timely resolution. A meeting of the minds is often possible if the issues are addressed quickly and honestly, and if there is a sincere desire for resolution existing with all parties.

Several techniques are available to the project manager to resolve the conflict: collaboration, compromise, negotiation, mediation, and arbitration.

Collaboration

The goal of collaboration is for all parties to win by working through differences to achieve creative solutions that satisfy both parties. This consensus approach is useful when there is a high degree of trust between the parties and when all parties are willing to change their positions with the introduction of new information and/or options. The main drawback is that it often takes a significant amount of time and energy on the part of everyone.

Compromise

With compromise, the parties agree to give ground on some of their positions, while maintaining their position on those issues of most importance to them personally. In other words, winning something and losing a little is an acceptable outcome. This is a good approach when parties of equal status are committed to reaching intermediate settlements to save time, especially on individual aspects of more complex issues. Drawbacks to this approach are that important values and longer-term objectives may be derailed and it may prove ineffective if the initial demands or differences are too great.

Negotiation

Negotiation endeavors to separate the personalities, opinions, and bias from the problem, thus depersonalizing the issues in conflict. The parties are encouraged to be respectful, professional, and nonjudgmental when considering opposing views. With this approach, the parties focus on aggressively attacking the problem while remaining courteous to the other party. The focus is on "why" the problem occurred rather than on "who" caused it. Thus, fear is eased and commonsense is allowed to play a significant role in the resolution process.

The project manager encourages the parties to avoid taking a hard position, but rather to focus on the requirements of the project as well as the contractor's contract terms and conditions of engagement. Common interests and areas of common agreement are constantly stressed throughout the discussions with a focus on mutual problem solving versus creation of an adversarial atmosphere. The main drawback is that previously agreed upon areas of conflict often creep back into the discussions if care is not taken.

Mediation

In the mediation approach to conflict resolution, the project manager submits the dispute to a neutral third party for review and advice. After listening to all parties, the mediator offers unbiased suggestions rather than binding solutions for the parties to consider and discuss further.

Arbitration

When conflicts rise to the level of arbitration, the project manager submits the dispute to an impartial third party for a final and binding decision. The intent is to avoid costly and time-consuming litigation, while at the same time giving all parties a fair and equitable hearing of their positions.

SUMMARY

It is not the avoidance of a conflict that is critical to team synergy and success. Rather, it is dealing with the conflict when it does occur. Team members will disagree: that is expected and acceptable. It is only when the disagreement is allowed to become personal and antagonistic that the conflict becomes difficult or even impossible to resolve.

In summary, managing contractor and supplier relationships requires:

- the ability to make fair and equitable decisions on the project,
- the ability to differentiate between problems resulting from internal personnel and processes versus contractor personnel,
- the ability to view issues from both company and contractor perspectives,
- the ability to communicate effectively with all parties,
- the ability to resolve conflicts quickly, without bias or prejudice, and
- the ability to establish reasonable expectations for contractors and internal personnel alike.

Contractors and suppliers are given specific expectations and deliverables that can be confirmed through quantitative metrics. Their contributions to the project, along with their ability to inject suggestions and recommendations, will enhance the project outcome. Contractors and suppliers are involved in and rewarded for their contributions to all phases of the project in which they participate. They are accepted and treated as equal team members, with the same respect and consideration given their internal counterparts.

8
Project Communications Management

OVERVIEW

One of the often forgotten elements of project planning is the requirement to effectively plan for the required communications between various project stakeholders from the launch of the project through each phase until completion. Every project stakeholder has a different set of expectations and requirements relative to the project. If those expectations are not effectively met, the natural tendency of each stakeholder is to micro-manage the project manager and his team until those expectations are satisfied. That micro-management will take several forms ranging from the requirement to submit more frequent comprehensive reports to daily briefings from the entire project team. Ultimately, the project manager in this situation will find herself and her team spending more time making presentations and attending nonproductive meetings than in working on the project itself. The project will suffer, not because of poor planning or execution, but because the project team is unable to focus on the critical elements of the project in a timely and efficient manner. The solution is to incorporate stakeholder communications requirements into the project planning from day one, just as is done for every other deliverable of the project.

The same need for planning holds true for internal communications between the project manager and her team. Experienced project managers recognize the need to effectively and thoroughly plan the format, frequency, and content of the communications that will take place—from the kickoff meeting to completion of the project. To aid the project manager in addressing these critical communication requirements, this chapter will focus first on communication planning for external stakeholders, followed by communications planning requirements when dealing with the project team.

COMMUNICATIONS PLANNING FOR EXTERNAL STAKEHOLDERS

The intent of communications planning is to assure the timely generation, collection, dissemination, storage, and disposition of critical project information throughout the life cycle of the project. In other words, the project manager is to provide a critical communication linkage between the project team and the project stakeholders, without burdening the project team with redundant, nonproductive reporting requirements. To do so requires a comprehensive analysis of the information needs of each stakeholder. This is followed by the integration of each requirement into a reporting mechanism that provides timely and accurate dissemination of information to address stakeholder questions before they are asked. This proactive approach provides a high degree of comfort and confidence among stakeholders by reinforcing the perception that the project team is professionally managing all aspects of the project. This perception is then reinforced by the reality of the results generated throughout each phase of the project. When there is an air of confidence, the project team is unencumbered with the requirement to constantly report results, answer irrelevant questions, or make time-consuming presentations.

If senior management or the project sponsor are unaware of what the project team is doing, why, or the results that are being achieved, they will surely micro-manage the team to death.

Many of the basic project-planning tools provide the team with critical information, status reporting, and action requirements:

- Gantt charts,
- budget worksheets,
- earned value analyses,
- gap analyses,

- trend analyses,
- process analyses,
- milestone listings,
- situational assessments, and
- risk assessments in the form of preliminary failure analyses or risk criticality analyses.

The problem with these frequently used communication tools is that, while they are easily understood by the project manager and his team members, they are often too detailed to be easily and quickly absorbed by most project stakeholders. It is not that these stakeholders are not intelligent enough to comprehend these documents, but rather that they will not take the time to do so. As a result, they push back with questions, additional reporting requirements or, worse yet, additional meetings. The secret to effective communications planning is to keep the reporting simple in content and format. To do so requires effective:

- communications planning to isolate the needs of all stakeholders including the amount, format, content, and frequency of the information expected from the project team;
- distribution planning to ensure the information reaches each respective stakeholder when and where expected; and
- performance tracking and status reporting systems that make critical project information available to all stakeholders on a real-time basis.

The ultimate objective of communications planning is to create a single mechanism that will satisfy the needs of all stakeholders utilizing readily available systems and communication technologies within the organization.

Inputs

In general, the total information requirements for communications planning are not readily available from the project sponsor or project stakeholders. The project manager is forced to conduct a degree of up-front due diligence to ascertain the specific requirements for each stakeholder, as well as the communications technologies available within the organization. This is because most stakeholders have differing requirements. For example, most senior executives expect quick, concise reports that answer questions such as, "What is the problem?"; "What actions have been taken to address the problem?"; and "What results have been realized to date?" They expect the project manager to "manage" each situation to ensure that the project remains on plan. Senior executives do not have time for, nor interest in, the details behind the actions taken, alternatives selected, or problems encountered. They simply want to know what the project manager and his team have accomplished. Middle managers, conversely, will often require more detail in specific operational areas or information regarding organizational impacts. Further, technical experts will require extensive data on specific problems, assessments, and actions.

The secret to success for the project manager is to take the time to interface with each stakeholder early in the planning stages of the project so that all communication requirements are boiled down to their common denominator prior to the kick-off meeting. By so doing, the project requirements are clearly delineated for all internal and external project stakeholders, conflicts resolved, and formats set before the project is launched. Completing this process often requires a comprehensive understanding of both the explicit and implicit desires (hot buttons) of each stakeholder, as well as why he or she might have reservations about the project or reject it outright. Much like a good sales professional prepares for a sales presentation to a prospective customer, the project manager completes his due diligence before approaching each stakeholder. To prepare, he reflects upon the following questions:

- Is there a real need that this project satisfies from the stakeholder's perspective?
- How much will the project cost to implement and maintain?
- Is the project team's proposed approach better than current practices?
- Are there non-financial impacts that have not been considered?

- Are the expected benefits from the project truly significant? What is the cost/benefit ratio and what is the risk or likelihood of achieving those benefits?
- How will the project impact current operations? What are those potential impacts?
- How will the project impact future operations? Can it be supported post-implementation?
- Is the project team truly capable of delivering on their promises? If not, what long-term risks or impacts will project failure have on the organization or its customers?
- Does the project budget and cash-flow projection meet all financial baseline criteria of the organization or customer? Does it complement the organization's financial vision?
- What non-financial benefits will be derived from the successful implementation of the project? Are they significant in the eyes of the customer?
- Is this the best use of organizational resources at this time?
- How will the project impact the organization's customers in both the short and longer terms? Will the project negatively impact customer commitments, expectations, or service?
- Are there any existing or potential conflicts between this and other planned or active projects? Are there any between this project and ongoing business operations?
- Are the proposed project schedule, budget, and deliverables acceptable and achievable given the real organizational constraints?

Figure 8-1 illustrates a typical worksheet used by the project manager to organize communication needs for the project.

Much like any sales process, the project manager seeks to understand what requirements or reservations a key stakeholder may have so that those concerns are addressed during the project planning process, and by the corresponding communication requirements integrated into the team's communications plan. Typical areas of concern include: budget or capital requirements; project timing; benefits versus risks the project introduces; the impact on organizational resources; the size of the project and the team's ability to manage it effectively; customer or market impacts; politics;

	Benefits of Project	Costs to Them	Conflicts They See	Risks to Them
Senior management				
Operational management				
Support groups				
Customers/ stakeholders				

Figure 8-1. Stakeholder preparation worksheet.

concerns about the level of up-front due diligence; impact of or reception to change; history of the project manager or his team on similar projects; existing or projected organizational constraints; or current operating or financial problems within the organization. In addition, there may be parochial interests underlying a stakeholder's reluctance to support the project. Whatever the existing or potential concerns, the experienced project manager realizes that they must be addressed quickly and completely to avoid the potential for downstream resistance from any functional or support organization. Just like any form of quality management, prevention of a misunderstanding or problem is always less costly than failure.

As before, preparation is key in acquiring the needed information, so a plan of action is devised to assist the project manager in his efforts. Figure 8-2 illustrates a typical sales preparation tool designed specifically for this purpose.

Stakeholder or Manager:	Comments/Due Diligence
Impact on the project	
Areas of concern	
Other reasons for resistance	
Tactics to overcome resistance	
Outside influences on stakeholder	
Internal influences on stakeholder	
Approach	
Follow-up timing and issues	
Conclusions	

Figure 8-2. Project sales tool.

TYPICAL REPORTING MECHANISMS

In addition to top-level Gantt charts, the most common forms of communication for project stakeholders typically include:

- gap analyses or situational assessments, which are typically utilized early in the planning stages of the project to illustrate the differences between expected levels of performance and those currently being experienced;
- process analyses to demonstrate how business processes are actually performed (as-is) compared against either current procedures or protocols (should-be), or other possible alternative approaches (could-be or to-be);
- variance reports comparing actual to planned performance in schedule, budget, and compliance;
- trend analyses illustrating project performance over time against the datum of planned performance;

- earned value analyses to provide current and forecasted status of the key project variables based upon a datum of actual performance to date in the project; and
- impact analyses to isolate the potential or real impact on the project variables of a proposed or actual change in scope, schedule, design, or compliance requirements.

Visual Communication Tools

In general, visual forms of communication provide the best level of understanding for project stakeholders with the least amount of effort for the project team. Visual communication tools include charts, graphs, pictures, tables, bullet listings, story boards, Oobeya charts, etc. When using these or any other form of communication mechanism, however, it is imperative to use only terms that are commonly used within the business environment. To do otherwise introduces a high degree of risk for the project manager as it leaves issues open for interpretation (or misinterpretation as is often the case). For example, to incorporate "earned value" terminology into reports when this phrase is not commonly utilized or understood within the organization will cause confusion among stakeholders as they struggle to understand how it applies to the project or business. It is common for a project manager, in an effort to look more professional, to utilize unfamiliar terms in a presentation to impress his stakeholders or superiors. When that happens, the project manager finds himself questioned and challenged on even the most mundane issues as stakeholders interpret the message differently.

Prior planning prevents wasted effort.

There are a few simple, yet unbreakable rules when it comes to communicating to stakeholders:

- be accurate and concise;
- never leave anything open to interpretation;
- anticipate questions that could be asked and be prepared with a response;

- be particularly sensitive to politically charged issues and be prepared with the facts that support the project team's approach; and
- never introduce an issue that has not already been thoroughly researched and evaluated.

Watch Out for Hard Numbers

Project managers can unknowingly introduce problems into a report by only using hard numbers. The secret to avoiding hard-number misunderstandings is to always provide relevance through comparisons to expected levels of performance. For example, to report a project to be $10,000 over budget and three weeks behind schedule is a recipe for disaster unless the stakeholders receiving this information understand that these numbers represent reasonable variances from the expected project's plan. For example, if the project is $10,000 over budget on a $150,000,000 project, the variance represents only a small percentage of overage and is, thus, insignificant. On the other hand, if that $10,000 represents a 25% variance to expected budget levels at a particular stage of the project, then a significant amount of explanation is to be expected, along with a comprehensive corrective action plan.

Formatting

With today's graphic presentation tools, there is a tendency for project managers to succumb to the temptation to make reports and presentations overly fancy by incorporating three-dimensional charts and graphs, or utilizing nontraditional colors or overly ornate fonts. The best practice is to keep reports, graphs, and charts simple:

- Use one concept or data set per graph.
- Use two-dimensional bars or lines on a graph.
- Assign colors that follow commonly accepted norms: black sans serif fonts, white or light blue backgrounds, etc.

If stakeholders must stop to study a graphic to understand it, they will simply dismiss the project manager's message and interpret their own. When they do, trouble begins. Keep the graphics simple and the message will be easily and quickly understood (Figure 7-6 is a good example).

Exception reports are yet another tool used by project managers to provide a summary of project status in a format that is easily understood by all stakeholders (see Figure 7-7 for an example). These reports focus the stakeholder's attention on those issues or problem areas within the project that require immediate attention. Following the concept of quick, concise information dissemination, the exception report format identifies the particular problem, what impact it is or is likely to have on the project, the actions that have been initiated by the project team to address the problem, and the results realized to date. This format is excellent for interim phase-gate performance reporting, especially for senior managers, because it highlights the areas of risk to the project proactively, thus eliminating eleventh-hour surprises that often blindside stakeholders.

INTERNAL PROJECT TEAM COMMUNICATION PLANNING

While much of this chapter has focused on communication planning for external project stakeholders, it is equally as important to plan internal communications to ensure that the team is always apprised of the project status and those issues that could derail project performance. Effectively managing a project team requires constant communication between the project manager and his team members, both individually and collectively. Projects will fail, often times, simply because assignments are not well understood or are misinterpreted by a project team member. Unfortunately, many project management professionals are not blessed with good communication skills. But because effective communication is an essential element in building a synergistic project team, today's project managers are forced to learn this critical skill set.

The up-front assignment of individual roles and responsibilities is a good start to outlining the specific responsibilities and expectations for each team member. The kickoff meeting provides a forum for team discussions to ensure a common understanding of the project requirements early in the planning stages, thereby ensuring that everyone is on the same page before the project is launched. But communication is not restricted to just the planning stages of the project. Communication between the project manager and his team continues throughout each phase, because every plan must be thoroughly communicated before action is initiated.

Early pioneers in the areas of human psychology often focused on ways to improve employee performance by altering managerial methods. One of the most noted discoveries in this area was the Hawthorne Effect, which proved that if an employee knows her performance is being measured against a known baseline, she will improve it to meet that expectation often with little input or oversight from her superior. The Hawthorne Effect applies equally as well to project team environments. If the project manager constantly communicates individual and team expectations in measurable terms, the team members will respond. It is only when those expectations are unclear or poorly communicated that failure occurs. This is where visual controls become important. Visual controls and communication tools provide guidance and focus for the team members on project-critical issues, rather than allowing their attention to be diffused across a myriad of issues that while important, are not critical to the overall project success. This prioritization of action forces the project members to address those issues that require immediate or near-term resolution before moving on to other activities—those critical path activities that will make or break the project, as well as those issues that have introduced or have the likelihood of interjecting an unacceptable level of risk.

Understanding Barriers to Communication

Within a project team, communication takes many forms: written, verbal, and non-verbal. All are equally important and each has unique risks and benefits. While most project managers focus their attention on written and verbal communications, it is often the project manager's non-verbal communications that create the majority of the problems between him and his team.

The project manager's body language, facial expressions, physical gestures, even his eyes often send a different message than the words he speaks. Project team members quickly recognize these subtle differences and this creates a sense of uncertainty and discomfort. Again, the experienced project manager has learned to actively control his body language so that it sends the same message as his words. It takes practice because we think ten times faster than we can speak. As a consequence, words spoken from the project manager's mouth are light years behind his thoughts. Complicating matters even more, the project manager's body language reflects the current thought cycle, so it is likely to be completely out of sync with what he is saying at any given time, sending the wrong message. It is no wonder that misunderstandings occur. So how does a project manager overcome this physical phenomenon? By consciously slowing down the thought cycle to concentrate on the topic at hand, he is better able to synchronize his words with his body language. This means that the project manager will be required to give the team member, or team as a whole, his undivided attention during project discussions—no thinking about another issue or problem, a presentation that is due to senior management tomorrow, or what he is supposed to buy at the grocery on his way home—just the issues before him.

Other real or perceived barriers to effective team communication exist to an extent in every organization. They include:

- politics,
- organizational structure (localized versus decentralized),
- team demographics and geographic location (time zone differences),
- cultural or value system differences among team members,
- emotion,
- gender,
- age (mix of baby boomers, generation X, generation Y, etc.);
- bias;
- functional or disciplinary terminology; and even
- differing communication styles.

It is essential for the project manager to factor these challenges into his communications planning activities so that they are addressed before problems arise. Team synergy will depend upon how effective he is with this task.

Figure 8-3 illustrates a typical tool used by project managers to identify and address real and potential communications problems within the team. It is intended to be a proactive tool, but it is also effective in a reactionary mode should communications problems develop during the course of the project.

In all cases, communication between the project manager and his team is honest and candid, but never brutal. Successful project managers have learned to be sensitive to the recipient to ensure that their message gets through as intended. They know that to be effective, their message must be both "heard" and understood by the recipient. Otherwise, misinterpretation is likely to lead to additional personnel problems downstream.

Issues/Observations	Actions/Comments
Identify actual or potential communication stoppers	Who: What:
What is the intent or hidden agenda behind the comment?	Political: Personal:
How can the issue be diffused or addressed effectively?	Action:
Is there a common ground that will allow consensus?	Metrics: Approach:
Can this or similar issues be prevented in the future?	Approach:
Are "camps" forming?	Why:
Is there a chemistry problem?	Who:
Is there a trust problem?	Why:
Are personnel changes needed?	Who: When:

Figure 8-3. Communications planning tool.

PROJECT KICKOFF MEETING

For most project teams, the bulk of the communication begins in the kickoff meeting. Team members are introduced; lines of communication defined; project goals, expectations, and constraints delineated; preliminary schedules, budgets, and compliance requirements outlined; and project review techniques and reporting requirements defined. In addition, project performance metrics, the results of the preliminary risk analysis, individual roles and responsibilities, and stakeholder or contractual "shall" requirements are discussed in detail along with preliminary phase-gate milestones and deliverables. The intent of the kickoff meeting is to ensure that all team members understand the project expectations as well as their specific assignments.

During the kickoff meeting, the project manager defines the structure and location of the team's communication nerve center, along with the supporting technologies. The intent of the communication nerve center is to provide a clearinghouse for information collection and dissemination so that all team members and stakeholders receive timely and accurate updating on all critical elements of the project on a real-time basis. It acts as a quality control point to ensure the accuracy and relevancy of all information coming into and out of the project team. Figure 8-4 is illustrative of the type of information handled.

Oobeya (Visual Control) Techniques

Developed by Toyota, oobeya techniques are used by project managers during team meetings to provide a "story-board" visualization of the current status of a project. The oobeya technique provides an important mechanism to direct the discussions among team members during meetings to only those issues requiring immediate action, thus reducing meeting times and increasing involvement. Much like the concurrent product development approach, the oobeya approach uses a cross-functional perspective and focuses discussion among team members on resolving project-critical issues. The net result is that project-critical issues receive the highest priority, and thus support, from all team members.

Project compliance teams
Phase I deliverables: 3/19/09

Product Validation	Deliverables	Due Date	% Complete
	Process analysis	2/16/09	100
	Voice of the customer analysis	2/25/09	100
	Collect and review baseline data (audits, historical data, etc.)	2/28/09	100
	Audit manufacturing operations	3/3/09	100
	Benchmark of validation processes	3/10/09	100
	Gap analysis (U.S., Japan)	3/10/09	100
	Develop control plan for operations (U.S. and global)	3/19/09	100
	Develop and implement site training	4/1/09	50
Overall		11/18/09	62

Figure 8-4. Communication center communiqué example.

Resolution is quick and accurate because the "team" now takes responsibility for resolving the problem versus just a single team member. An example of a typical oobeya chart is illustrated in Figure 8-5.

Each team meeting includes project team members and critical support group members, as well as senior management in cases where project-critical issues require approval and support for actions typically outside the scope of the project manager. Prior to the meeting, the project manager updates the oobeya chart and supporting data. He then develops a focused meeting agenda to ensure solutions-oriented discussions. During the meeting,

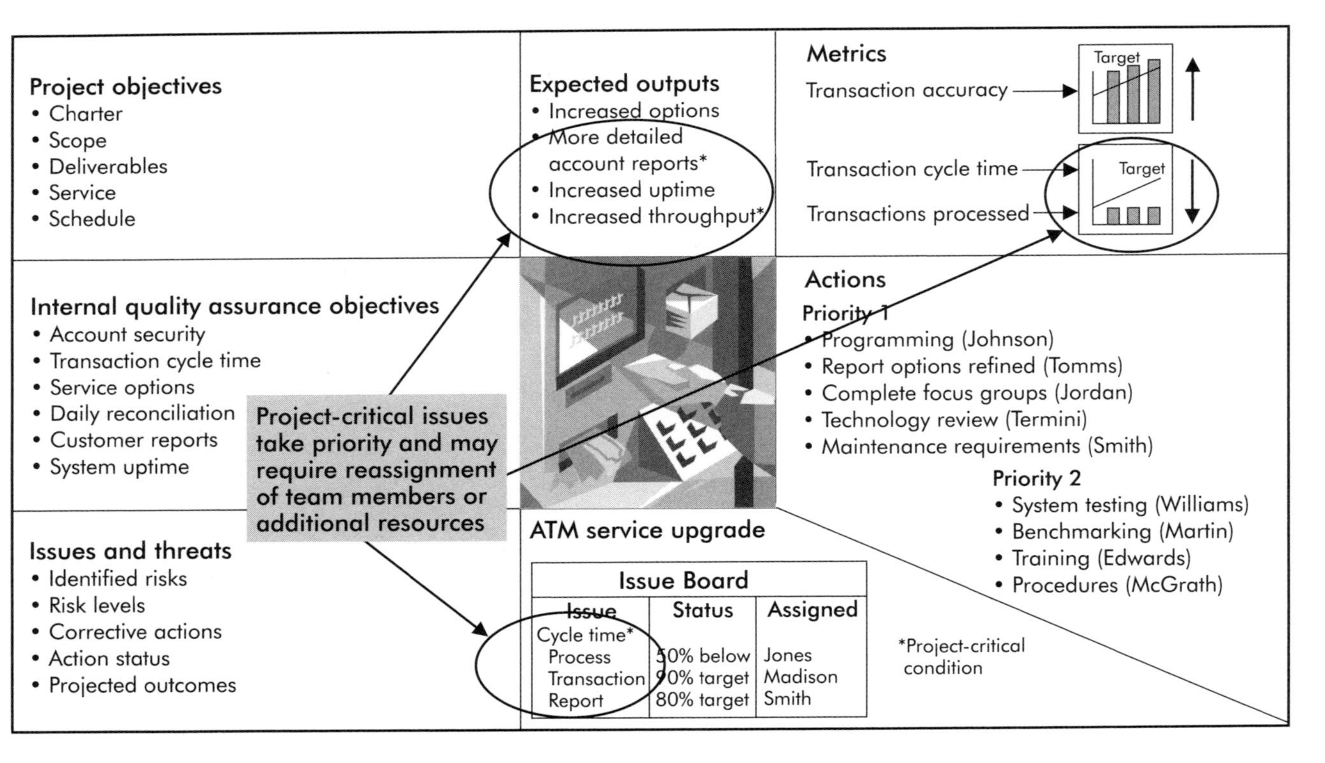

Figure 8-5. Oobeya chart.

discussions are reserved for only those project-critical issues identified on the oobeya chart. Should a team member identify a non-critical issue during the discussions, she adds that issue to the oobeya chart after the meeting rather than disrupting the meeting while in progress. Utilizing the strengths, weaknesses, opportunities, and threats (SWOT) approach, which considers all facts and risks to the project from these project-critical issues, the project manager seeks a consensus solution from the team that will ensure a successful resolution for each item. Input from all team members is required to ensure a truly cross-functional, multidisciplinary perspective.

SUMMARY

The often-overlooked secret to effective project team performance is communication, both within the team and with external project stakeholders. Like every other aspect of a project, communication must be planned and executed with a high degree of skill and foresight. The message, format, and timing of communications are all equally important in ensuring that the information being disseminated is received by all stakeholders as it is intended. It takes only one stakeholder misinterpretation to bring the project to a stop until that misunderstanding is clarified. Project team productivity is maximized only when team members spend their time working on the project activities versus attending non-value-added meetings or writing redundant reports that often are never read.

9
Assessing the Project Environment—Past, Present, and Future

OVERVIEW

It is a fact. Less than one third of all projects launched by companies and government agencies are concluded successfully. One of the primary reasons for this phenomenon is the lack of understanding of the project environment and the drivers behind it. Inexperienced project managers make initial assumptions without confirmation of their validity based upon past experiences, hearsay, or bias, setting the stage for unsupported conclusions and actions. Risk becomes exacerbated because the basis of the decisions made for the project and the ultimate actions taken are incorrectly focused. The end result: the project is compromised from the start.

Unfortunately, when projects fall behind schedule or exceed their budgets, project managers often site unexpected problems or unforeseen factors. The truth is, the vast majority of these project derailments are foreseeable up front in the planning stages IF the project manager does an effective situational assessment to uncover the true issues facing the project. By knowing what problems are likely to occur throughout the life cycle of the project, the project manager is positioned to effectively deal with them through project scope realignment, contingency planning, or risk management techniques. In short, those "unexpected surprises" can be avoided and the project completed successfully through a thorough situational assessment in the early planning stages.

SITUATIONAL ANALYSIS AND ASSESSMENT

To begin with, experienced project managers assess a given situation to determine what problems, issues, and opportunities exist, or if any have the potential of developing during the life cycle of the project. Situational assessments focus on determining why current conditions exist and the drivers behind them. By understanding exactly what is happening and why, the project manager is better prepared for the risks that may lie ahead. Thus, he can effectively develop contingencies to either offset the likelihood of their occurrence or minimize their impact. This is yet another aspect of project risk management. In essence, situational assessments seek to answer three questions:

1. What do I know? (In other words, what facts do I actually have?)
2. What do I not know? (What validated information or data do I not have?)
3. What do I need to know? (What data or information is needed to draw supportable conclusions that will enable the project team to move forward to a successful conclusion?)

In many cases, current conditions result from an unrecognized or unmanaged problem, issue, opportunity, or change in:

- organizational, functional, process, or individual performance;
- market, industry, or business dynamics;
- personnel attitudes, behavior, culture, or morale;
- customer service;
- the quality or reliability of the organization's products or services;
- profits, cash flow, or other financial metrics; or
- operational or process cycle times.

In essence, there may be issues, problems, or opportunities in any or all critical elements of the project, business, or industry. These issues may have occurred in the past. Or, there may be indications of an impending problem or opportunity in the foreseeable future. Either way, the experienced project manager recognizes the need to identify these critical issues and address the impact that they now have or will have on the project in the future.

Probing Questions

The project manager begins his situational assessment, process analysis, and/or gap analysis with a series of probing questions. They are designed to highlight the potential change or deficiency that created the problems or opportunities his project team will face in planning and implementing the project. Specifically,

- What has changed?
- When did it change?
- How much has it changed?
- Where did the change occur?

Armed with the answers, the project manager begins to probe into why the change(s) occurred and what can be done to identify its root cause so that an effective plan of action can be developed and implemented. He understands that every project is unique. Thus, his assessment focuses on those conditions surrounding each particular issue affecting *this* project. The project manager realizes that relying on past successes from other similar projects may not result in the same outcome. As a result, he assesses every project from available facts.

Past and Present

The project manager delves into the past to determine what unresolved problems or opportunities may, or will likely have a significant impact on the conditions identified in the present day. In addition, he explores the actions that may have been taken in the past to address those problems or opportunities, along with the reason(s) why those attempts failed. Obviously, the last thing anyone wants to do is to repeat failure. This is simply not a smart career move. The project manager then turns to the present to identify the current actions employed to address these same problems or opportunities so as not to duplicate efforts or inadvertently hamper the progress of other functional or project managers.

Manageable Components

Once the current conditions have been thoroughly defined and assessed, all related issues or opportunities are broken down into manageable components. Remember the old adage, "You eat an elephant one bite at a time!" The same is true for organizational or process problems. Using process problem-solving techniques, each is decomposed into its smallest elements so that a more thorough understanding of each element can be developed and the common links between elements identified. One of the first questions explored by the project manager is, "Is there more than one problem or opportunity impacting the project environment, or is there a single issue manifesting itself in different areas at different times, in different ways?"

Decision-making is the responsibility of the project manager—even in the face of conflict and politics.

Because resources are typically tight, it is necessary for the project manager to prioritize which issues, problems, or opportunities to pursue first, based upon:

- the potential impact each problem, issue, or opportunity has on completing the project on schedule and within budget;
- the potential for performance improvements or financial returns to the customer;
- the level of risk in the near and longer term for the project;
- the impact on resource consumption or utilization during the project; and/or
- the impact on customer satisfaction or customer expectations from the project.

The next step is to apply the fundamental problem-solving techniques (discussed later in this chapter) to identify the drivers behind the problem or opportunity impacting the current situation and determine the best solution.

When assessing the situation, the project manager will be working with a significant amount of data. Before an action plan is devised, he and his team will assess and validate all of the relevant data and convert it into usable information. By so doing, the project manager maintains objectivity and minimizes the likelihood that bias will lead him to draw incorrect conclusions.

Assumptions

The initial assessment of the situation will be based upon certain assumptions. Before moving forward, it is always wise for project managers to validate those assumptions to ensure that they are sound and have not been affected by personal or organizational biases. The validity of the initial assumptions will impact the ultimate success, costs, and timing of the project, as well as individual careers.

One way to confirm assumptions is through a simple analysis, as illustrated in Figure 9-1.

All assumptions that the project manager and his project team make in assessing the situation are listed. Those assumptions are then ranked by degree of risk to the project. The levels of risk are defined as:

1. *High*: If incorrect, these assumptions will result in probable failure of the project. There is little chance that a successful recovery will be possible at any cost. These are the most critical assumptions, and thus carry the highest priority for analysis.
2. *Medium*: If incorrect, these assumptions will adversely impact the project budget, timing, and/or deliverable. A degree of recovery is possible, but only with significant impact on the project variables and resources. In most cases, the customer will experience some degree of dissatisfaction. These are the number two priorities for the project team to assess.
3. *Low*: If incorrect, these assumptions can be contained with normal project management control methodologies and techniques. Their impact is typically modest, thus relegating them to the lowest priority for assessment.

Once the assumptions have been ranked, the next step is to assign the responsibility of validating each assumption to a member of

Assumptions	Risk Level	Sources of Data	Confirmation Assigned to	Valid?	Action Plan
	High				
	Medium				
	Low				

Figure 9-1. A chart to help validate assumptions.

the project team. Validation is a fact-finding activity. It is not intended to support the assumptions made by the project team, but rather to confirm their accuracy or inaccuracy. These analyses must be done carefully. The data sources used to substantiate or show the error of an assumption are included on the assumption and risk analysis worksheets for two reasons:

The decision on which course of action to take in effect defines how the project objectives or deliverables will be met.

1. To ensure the accuracy of the validation process was done accurately, and
2. To support the project team's actions relating to that assumption. There is no guessing in this analysis.

An actual completed risk-assumption analysis worksheet is shown in Figure 9-2. It contains all the relevant information used by the project team to support its assessment of the situation impacting the implementation of an integrated business system.

CASE STUDY—AGI/ACEG

To illustrate the application of many of the project management tools discussed from this point on, an actual case study is introduced. The company's name, locations, as well as several facts have been altered. However, the basic situation has been retained.

Alliance Consumer Electronics Group, Inc. (ACEG), a division of AGI International, is headquartered in a major city in the United States, with five regional distribution and repair centers located strategically throughout North America. The production of AGI's products takes place overseas and the products are shipped directly to point-of-sale mass merchandisers for sale to consumers. ACEG is chartered as the repair and aftermarket parts operation for AGI throughout North America. Structured as a profit center subsidiary of AGI, ACEG maintains other similarly chartered subsidiaries in other parts of the world.

Producing several lines of printers, computers, and computer peripherals for the international marketplace, AGI has had an excellent following for numerous years as a result of its innovative,

Assumptions	Risk Level	Sources of Data	Assigned to	Valid?	Action Plan
1. Systems hardware is adequate to support implementation.	High	IT manager and system specifications	S. Edwards	Yes	
2. Systems support from MIS and vendor will be adequate to ensure user readiness.	High	MIS skills set analysis	S. Shanks	Yes	
3. New applications software can be implemented and tested within 6 months.	High	Vendor user group analysis	B. Johanson	No	Reschedule for 10 months
4. Users will accept new software.	High	MIS survey	C. Schmidt	Yes	
5. Database conversion can be completed within 3 to 4 months with 99%+ accuracy.	Medium	CAS data user group analysis	M. Termini	Yes	
6. Y2K issues have been resolved by vendor and in-house MIS personnel.	Medium	IT manager and software specifications	J. Armstrong	Yes	
7. User training can be completed by in-house MIS personnel.	Medium	MIS skills set analysis	J. Kimbrough	Yes	
8. Vendor will deliver software on or before contracted date.	Low	Contract terms and penalties	C. Calcara	Yes	

Figure 9-2. A completed risk-assumption analysis worksheet.

high-quality, competitively priced products. AGI's products are used in business, educational, and home applications. Like its three major competitors, AGI has enjoyed a growing market over the last 10 years as the demand for computer-based products skyrocketed. But over the most recent 3-year period, AGI has seen its market position erode by almost 13%. Recognizing that even though the company remains profitable and competitive, a continuation of such a loss in market position could be devastating, AGI's senior management commissioned a voice-of-the-customer (VOC) analysis to ascertain why customers seemed to be moving to the competition. The results of the VOC analysis indicated a growing discontent among customers owning older equipment because of the repair time quoted by ACEG.

In response, AGI's senior management created a project team comprised of AGI and ACEG personnel to determine the facts and take corrective action to regain the lost market share. The project team immediately launched a situational assessment to ascertain what was happening so that some conclusions could be drawn. The first step taken by the project team was to conduct a focus group study to understand customer expectations regarding the repair process.

The study revealed that customers expected their products to be repaired and returned within 5 business days, but would prefer having them back within 3 days. The project team then conducted an analysis of the repair process to determine how long it actually took for comparison to those expectations. The results were shocking. On average, it took ACEG some 45–50 days to complete repairs and return the products to customers.

The project team then conducted a third study to benchmark competitive repair times as a basis for comparison. The results of this competitive benchmarking study revealed that the competition averaged somewhere between 8–10 days to complete similar repairs and return the products to customers. The project team concluded that a major problem existed, although it did not know what it was or its source. Senior management was convinced that the problem was a loss in market share. The project team was not so sure. Perhaps the market share loss was more of a result of something else, like the repair cycle time.

There appeared to be a relationship between customer displeasure regarding the repair cycle time and loss in market share, but this, the team concluded, was certainly a high-risk assumption. In addition, the initial data seemed to indicate that even the competition, although much better at repair timing than ACEG, appeared to be far in excess of customers' expectations. Did that give them a competitive advantage over AGI? And where did this expectation of 3–5 days come from? Were customers asking for too much? There were simply too many unanswered questions for the project team to draw any meaningful conclusions. More information was needed.

Several key assignments were made relative to the project team's initial assumptions. The first assumption, considered high risk, was that there was a relationship between the cycle time of ACEG's repair process and the loss in market share. A member of the project team was assigned to commission a second VOC analysis to more accurately determine the answer to that question. The results of the analysis revealed that the customers were genuinely frustrated with the repair process and, because of that, were discarding their old products and buying new equipment from another manufacturer in hopes of getting better service. And, the frustration was growing as the population of older products grew. Obviously, the relationship was real.

The second assumption requiring validation was that the customers' expectation of a 3–5-day turnaround was necessary, even realistic given that the competition was at 8–10 days. The project team assigned a member to initiate another focus group study to probe customers about what would be an acceptable repair time, in their minds, regardless of the manufacturer. The team knew that its ultimate actions would be far different if it targeted meeting the competition's 8–10 day performance instead of the customer's expectation of 3–5 days. Even the transit times would become an issue at the reduced target levels. The team also knew that just meeting the competition's benchmark, if it was found to be unacceptable to the customers, would do nothing to return the company's lost market share. There were some major risks here that needed to be managed.

The results of the project team's study were revealing. The customers did, indeed, expect a 3–5-day turnaround. Anything beyond that created the necessity for the customer to buy a replacement product because of use demands. Even though the team had succeeded in uncovering the 3–5-day expectation and knew of the competition's 8–10-day performance, it was not happy about the task of trying to reach either level of performance. The competition was used as a benchmark only because it was markedly better than ACEG. In fact, the customers confirmed that the only major market differentiation between brands, in their minds, was service—not price—not functionality—not design. The fact that the provider offering the best service was going to get the business became crystal clear in the discussions.

The next assumption was that ACEG could improve its performance sufficiently to meet customer expectations. In an attempt to validate this high-risk assumption, the project team conducted a complete situational assessment of ACEG's repair processes. Here is what they found.

When a product breaks down in the customer's location, the customer is required to call ACEG's 800 hotline for a return goods authorization (RGA). A customer service representative handles the call and determines if the return is to be authorized and if it should be a warranty or non-warranty item. An RGA number is assigned to the customer from a log maintained by the customer service representative and the customer is given the address of the service and repair center where the products are to be returned. This is normally a 10–15-minute process. After the customer has hung up, the customer service representative manually prepares an RGA with the appropriate customer, product, and requested service information. This is a 5-minute process. Once the RGA form is prepared, the customer service representative sends the RGA form to his or her supervisor for approval. There is generally a 4–8-hour turnaround.

Once signed by the supervisor, the RGA form is returned to the customer service representative who enters the data into the computer system and generates six copies for distribution (a 10-minute process). Copies are distributed to Customer Service, the Repair Department, Accounting, Receiving (where they are filed for later referral), and the customer (another 10–15-minute process). Once products are received from the customer, they are delivered directly to the Repair Department by the receiving clerk after the RGA number is confirmed and matched against the copy of the RGA form in the receiving file (15 minutes).

If an RGA has not been issued, the receiving clerk places the customer's products in a waiting area and prepares an unauthorized customer return form in duplicate, which identifies the customer, customer address, product identification code, and requested repairs. One copy is mailed to the customer service representative for the customer's region, and one copy is maintained in the receiving files (25–30 minutes for the receiving process, and 36–48 hours before the customer service representative handles the document and takes the next action). Upon reviewing the unauthorized customer return form, the customer service representative contacts the customer to discover the nature of the problem and determine what repairs are being requested. An RGA form is then prepared and processed as before. (There is a total cycle time of approximately 45 minutes if the customer can be reached on the first try. The average, however, is 8 hours.) In addition, the customer service representative prints and mails a written warning to the customer regarding the RGA policy in effect at ACEG (15 minutes).

After receiving the RGA in the inter-company mail from the customer service representative (8–12 hours), the receiving clerk relocates the customer's products in the waiting area, matches the RGA copy against the customer's packing slip, updates the RGA log, prepares a receiving report, and forwards the customer's product on to the Repair Department. Copies of the receiving report are distributed to the Customer Service Department, Accounting, and the Repair Department (with the customer's product), and a copy is retained for the receiving files. Because of the cramped workspace in the Receiving Department and the heavy workload, often customer products are lost or misplaced for up to 7 days, making the total cycle time of this step of the process 7–10 days.

Upon receipt of the receiving report from the Receiving Department, the Customer Service Department clerk prepares a sales order for internal processing of chargeable and non-chargeable costs (15–20 minutes). Eight copies of the sales order are prepared and then distributed to the Manufacturing, Quality, and Engineering Departments at AGI, the Shipping Department at ACEG, the Accounting Department at ACEG, and the Repair Department at ACEG, with two copies retained in the Customer Service Department for filing in the customer file and product file (30 minutes).

When the customer's product gets to the Repair Department, a visual inspection and component-level analysis is conducted. The nature of the problem is identified along with whether warranty or non-warranty repairs are required. Any visual damage that will void the warranty is photographed for retention in the job folder (8–16 hours). A job folder is then prepared with a returned goods report (RGR) detailing the required repairs, the RGA, the sales order form, and any photographs taken. If non-warranty repairs are required, but not approved on the RGA, the job folder is returned to the customer service representative for resolution with the customer. When the customer service representative receives approval from the customer for the cost of the repairs and an account to charge the repairs to, the RGA is updated and returned to the Repair Department (4–6-day process).

The Repair Department then repairs the customer's product and notes the associated costs on the sales order form. When the product repairs are completed and tested, the job folder is updated, the sales order form is updated with the material and labor costs, and the returned goods report is completed with the test results and actions taken to repair the customer's products (15–20 day process for repairs, 2–3 days to prepare all documentation). The customer's product is then taken to Shipping with a copy of the RGR and the RGA. One copy of the sales order form with the repair costs is sent to Accounting for invoicing, and a second copy is sent to the Customer Service Department for filing. The job folder is then filed in the Repair Department for future reference (30 minutes).

When Accounting gets the sales order form, it prepares a customer invoice for non-warranty repairs. The charge is discussed with the customer service representative for final determination of whether or not to charge the customer for the full cost of the repairs (30 minutes). If it is determined to charge the customer for all or part of the repair costs, an invoice is prepared and sent to Shipping for inclusion with the customer's product upon return (15 minutes). If it is determined not to charge the customer, a "no charge" invoice is prepared and sent to Shipping for inclusion with the customer's products. In either case, two copies of the invoice are sent to the Customer Service Department for filing in the customer's file and the product file (15 minutes).

When he receives the customer's repaired product, the returned goods report, the RGA, and the invoice from Accounting, the shipping clerk prepares the packing slip, bill-of-lading, and freight invoice; packs the customer's product in a suitable container for shipment; and notifies the carrier for pickup (30–45 minutes). The RGA and RGR, along with the shipping documentation, are filed in the Shipping Department and copies are sent to the Customer Service Department (10 minutes). When the documentation arrives in the Customer Service Department from Shipping, the customer service representative updates the customer and product files and then closes the sales order file (30 minutes). At this point, the process is complete.

The project team, armed with the foregoing process description, discussed the possibility of modifying ACEG's existing process to reduce the process to the 3–5-day targeted performance. It concluded that no further consideration could be given to that proposed action until it could accurately identify the root cause behind the cycle time drivers and the volume of repair requests being received. A further complication arose from the process analysis. The project team found that the cost of repairs under the current process actually exceeded the cost of producing a new product by two to three times. This analysis revealed that, coupled with the overhead from ACEG's organizational structure and the cost of those repair activities, not only were ACEG's money-losing operations causing a substantial loss in market share for AGI, but they were also burdening AGI's bottom line. The project team decided that a root cause analysis was necessary to help develop the remainder of the strategic and tactical project plans.

PROBLEM-SOLVING

The basis for an accurate evaluation of a given issue, opportunity, or problem is cause-and-effect reasoning—determining what has gone wrong or what has caused the identified situation. A problem, or an opportunity, is the visible effect of a cause (an event or action) that has occurred at some time in the past. The key for the project manager is to relate that exact cause to the effect being observed, because only then can the problem be effectively resolved and kept from recurring in the future. Again, for example, the market share loss experienced by AGI was not the problem, but rather a symptom of an internal product, process, or system defect. The project team's focus, therefore, was not on regaining lost market share, but rather on identifying and resolving those internal problems.

Define the Problem

Problem-solving begins with a concise, accurate definition of the problem, which seeks to answer the following four questions:

1. Exactly what problem or issue is being observed?
2. Where was the problem first observed?
3. When did the problem first appear?
4. What is the significance or magnitude of the problem?

The answers to these questions will yield important information for the project manager to use in determining the extent of the problem or issue, and thus the size of the project. For instance, if the gap between what should be happening and what is happening is small, then the project likely will be more of a process improvement effort. If, on the other hand, the gap is large, then the project will probably take more extensive reengineering or redesign efforts, with more resources, time, and money required.

True Root Cause

In defining the problem, it is essential that the project team determine what *is* and what *is not* happening, the gap between the two, and the factors that have impacted the deviations.

The project team looks for changes that have occurred in each of the "should-be" conditions or performance. Once the changes are identified, the team explores the what, where, when, and magnitude of each. The true root cause of the problem will answer each of the four questions identified above. The project manager realizes that only the singular root cause of the problem will create the effect being observed. Therefore, once the root cause is identified, it is confirmed through simulation techniques. Only then are the project manager and his team assured they have found the true basis of the problem.

Simulation

With technical problems, quantitative simulation techniques are employed to determine if the true root cause has been identified. With business projects, process modeling or business modeling techniques are utilized, especially when they are reasonably scalable compared to similar techniques on similar projects evaluated in the past. However, in some cases, simulation techniques are just not available or are overly complex. In such cases, commonsense is used to ascertain if the cause identified by the project team will realistically create the same effects as have been observed. In all cases, the deviations are carried back in time as far as necessary to isolate when the problem was first observed. This will lead to the changes that occurred, and ultimately to the root cause.

The Root Cause Model

The objective of the project manager and the project team is to isolate the singular root cause from the field of multiple, probable, possible root causes. As illustrated in Figure 9-3, the objective is to arrive at the singular root cause, ultimately eliminating all of the other possible root causes associated with the issue or problem under analysis.

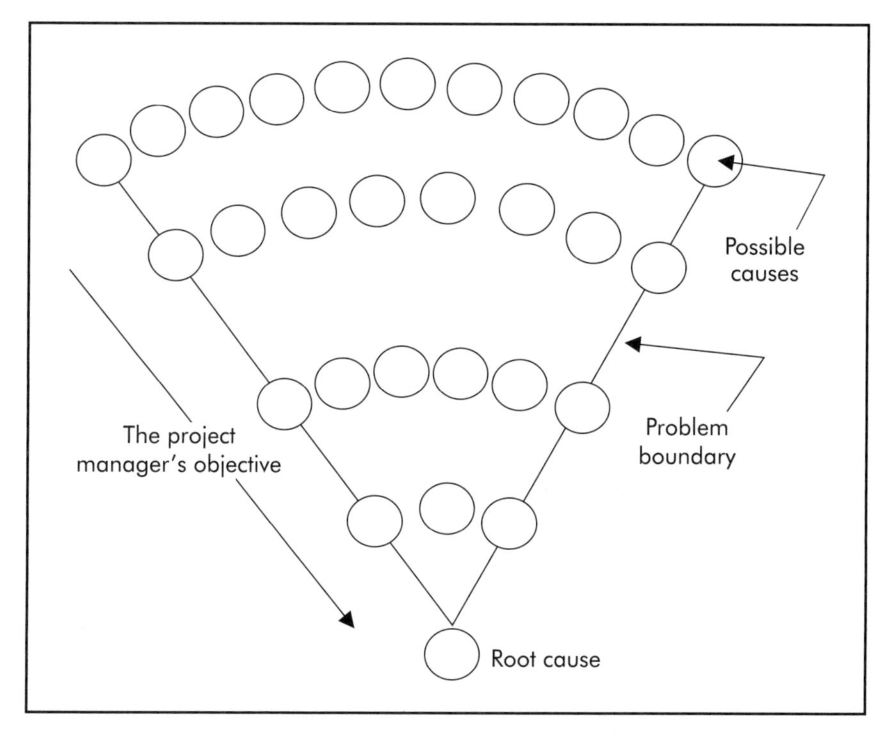

Figure 9-3. The root cause model.

In arriving at the root cause, the project manager is faced with three possible constraints that could possibly prohibit the project team from reaching the singular root cause.

Constraints

The first constraint is *time*. In some cases, the project team is forced to stop at a level above the singular root cause because time constraints are forcing more immediate action. For example, the project manager may find that it will take one month to come down the model to a level where there are three possible root causes, and an additional 10 months to come down to the singular root cause. In such a case in which time is constrained, the project manager is forced to stop at a higher level within the model and, as a result, incorporate solutions to all three possible root causes into the project's planning. Attempting to select just one of the possible root causes is risky and ill advised.

The second constraint is *financial*. With many projects, the financial costs associated with arriving at the singular root cause may outweigh the benefits of the effort. Again, it may be the wisest choice for the project manager to stop at a level above the singular root cause and include all remaining possible root causes in the planning. The implementation may be more costly and complex, but the total return on investment will generally be much greater.

The third constraint is *technology*. For example, when TWA 800 was lost, the American Transit Authority (ATA), Federal Aviation Administration (FAA), Federal Bureau of Investigation (FBI), Central Intelligence Agency (CIA), and several other government agencies began analyzing the flight data to determine what had occurred. From the multitude of possible root causes, they quickly reduced the possibilities to three: missile, bomb, or mechanical failure.

Due to the nature of the catastrophe and its potential impact given the number of 747s in service at that time, the agencies quickly concluded that stopping at this level of the root cause model was unacceptable. They began an extensive search of the sea floor to find and retrieve all possible pieces of the plane. Once found, each piece was carefully examined and the plane reconstructed. Evidence revealed that a missile was not the cause of the crash. They moved down the model one more level: bomb or mechanical failure. Wave front and flame propagation studies were conducted along with a series of other chemical analyses. The results confirmed that the crash was not the result of a bomb, but rather a mechanical malfunction in the center fuel tank. Immediate actions were then taken to implement the required retrofits on all remaining 747s and other Boeing planes with similar fuel tank configurations. If the investigators had merely guessed at the root cause of the disaster, many more such incidents may have occurred.

A much different scenario, however, faced NASA's engineers after Challenger was lost. The engineers were constrained by the fact that much of the physical evidence burned up in re-entry. As a result, they were forced to stop at a higher level in the model and, through a more complex and extensive project, address all possible causes of the disaster.

Time, financial, and technological constraints are real and must be addressed by the project team in the project analysis phase so that a supportable decision is made regarding the course of action to take during the tactical planning and implementation of the project.

Techniques and Tools

Most project managers from technical disciplines have a background in using basic problem-solving techniques to resolve technical problems. However, they often forget that those same techniques can be used to resolve project and business management issues. Those same basic problem-solving techniques are essential to finding the problems and/or issues (and their associated drivers) that must be addressed during the tactical planning and execution phases of the project. Commonly used problem-solving tools include:

- evaluation and planning tools (gap analysis, process analysis, cause-and-effect diagrams, failure mode and effects analysis [FMEA], design of experiments [DOE], preliminary failure analysis, etc.);
- data collection tools (quality function deployment techniques, voice-of-the-customer analyses, surveys, focus groups, questionnaires, interviews, measurements, and observations); and
- data display tools (run charts, histograms, check sheets, and Pareto charts).

The use of these tools is widely understood and practiced by most project managers in their work, but they are generally applied too narrowly to be useful for project-level decisions. In general, a combination of these techniques is better suited to aid the project manager in working his way down the root cause model. Figure 9-4 illustrates how different combinations can be employed to yield tangible results.

The analysis begins with a brainstorming session to identify all potential root causes of the problem or issue. The project team

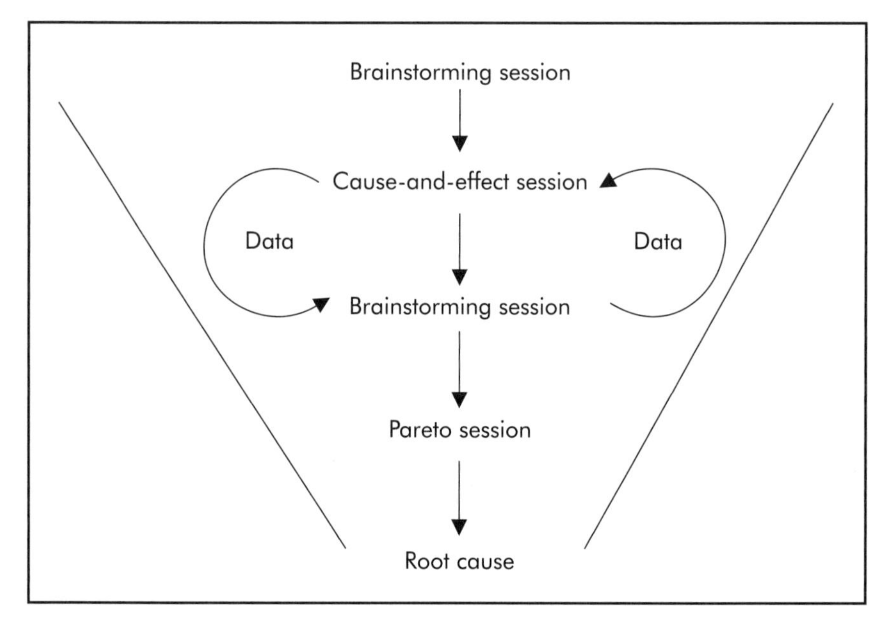

Figure 9-4. Different combinations of problem-solving techniques often deliver the best results.

then begins to combine and categorize the possible root causes through a cause-and-effect (fishbone diagram) analysis. With each iteration, data is collected to support the project team's analyses and assumptions. After several iterations, the results will take the form of a standard Pareto distribution yielding the one or two most probable root causes. The project manager then determines if time, technology, and money allow the team to conduct further analyses to derive the singular root cause.

Collecting Data

Often the data used during problem-solving sessions is found to contain a significant amount of error. There are several rules the team should follow in collecting data to ensure additional variables are not introduced into the evaluation process.

1. Identify exactly what is to be known or learned, and then determine the type and amount of data necessary to support the problem-solving efforts. The collection of data costs money and consumes project time. While data is an essential element in the problem analysis phase, the collection of redundant or irrelevant data is a waste of resources and time. Therefore, restricting the project team to collecting only the essential data necessary to make a sound decision is wise (What do I need to know?).
2. After the data is collected, it is sanitized by correcting obvious errors and filling in gaps. Caution should be exercised. It is never assumed the data is accurate as collected, even if it is computer generated. Inaccurate data can be misleading, allowing the project team to reach the wrong conclusions and initiate invalid corrective actions.
3. The data is then organized by type, category, time, frequency, etc., and ultimately condensed by computing statistics such as averages, mean, or range. Finally, the data is converted into usable information using the aforementioned data display tools.
4. While the team is collecting and analyzing the data, the project manager continues to monitor the situation to ensure that nothing has changed that could render the initial analysis invalid. This is an essential part of ongoing risk management.

All work is again documented to ensure that the project is correctly base-lined for future review and analysis, including:

- the assumptions the team made and how they were validated;
- the data collection methods;
- the data conversion methods and their results; and
- the steps taken by the team to arrive at and validate conclusions regarding the root cause of the problem or issue.

CASE STUDY—AGI/ACEG REVISITED

Here we pick up again on the project team's assignment. Through the team's analysis, a number of possible root cause drivers surfaced for the situation at ACEG. So, the team members decided to conduct a root cause analysis in an attempt to identify the true root cause of ACEG's cycle time problem. This analysis is illustrated in Figure 9-5.

From its initial brainstorming session, the project team concluded that there were three categories of root causes for the problems being experienced at ACEG: cycle time, quality, and product design. The team members reasoned that any of the three general categories could generate the effects being experienced. They also concluded, however, that those categories were too broad to be meaningful, so they conducted a more detailed analysis (What

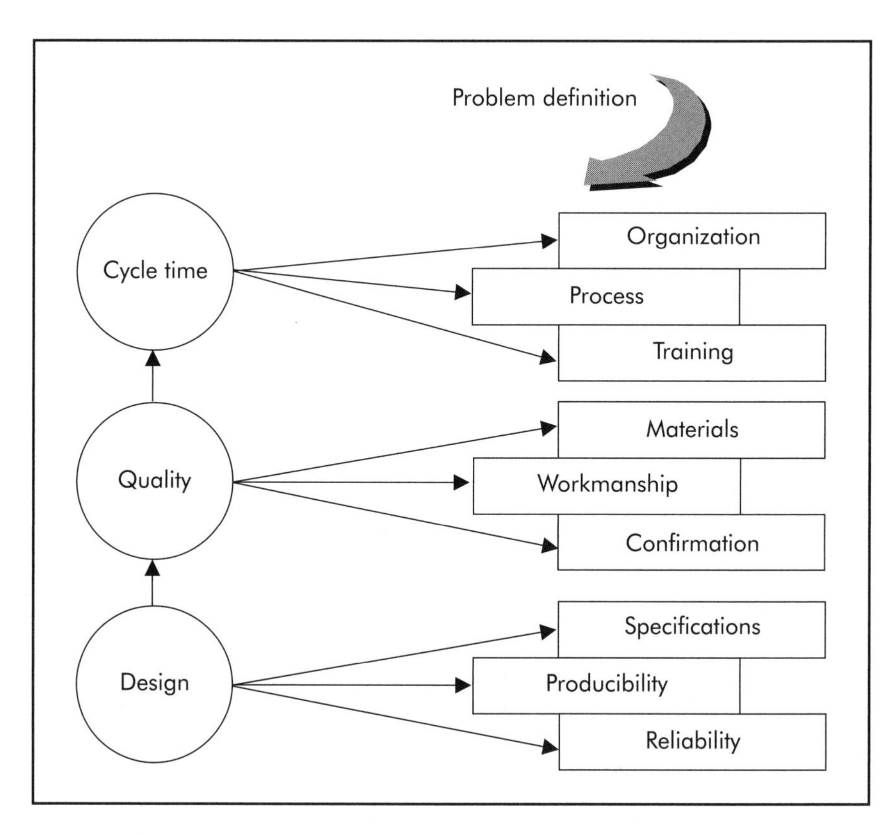

Figure 9-5. Visual presentation of the project team's root cause analysis.

do I not know? What do I need to know?). They began with cycle time, which, they concluded, was a key issue in the eyes of the customers. But, was cycle time a cause or an effect? For example, cycle time could be impacted by the design of the process itself, by the training that the repair process personnel had received (which could affect their productivity), or by the multi-location organizational structure of ACEG and all of the associated communication issues that this often creates.

The team then analyzed quality with the same cause-and-effect perspective and concluded that quality could be a factor in the cycle time of the process and in the customer's perception of the company's products. Team members reasoned that if the quality were poor, then more products would fail during use, creating a higher volume of returns that eventually would backlog ACEG. They also reasoned that customers might be frustrated with the general quality of AGI's products, causing them to purchase competitive products perceived to be of higher quality. But poor quality, itself, might be an effect of other root causes rather than the root cause itself. For example, the team speculated that poor quality could be the result of nonconforming components and assemblies that AGI received from its suppliers. Or, poor quality could result from unacceptable workmanship by AGI's assembly personnel. Or, equally possible, it could stem from ineffective confirmation systems at AGI that should identify and correct nonconforming products before they are shipped to point-of-sale locations.

Finally, team members concluded that the product design also could be a factor—either a root cause or an effect. They surmised that the products could be failing prematurely, creating the huge volume of repair requests. Further, the design deficiencies could be the result of poor or inaccurate product specifications, which caused the products to fail before their expected lifetime. They speculated, as well, that the design could be good on paper, but not producible in a manufacturing setting given AGI's process capabilities and controls. Or, the design could simply lack the reliability factors to ensure that it would live long enough in use to satisfy customers' expectations. In fact, any of these theories could have been the true root cause. But which one was it? That is what the project team had to find out.

To begin, the team members created a root cause model. Then, using the tools and techniques discussed in this section, they began to work their way down the model addressing the design categories first. They analyzed product reliability data along with competitive benchmarking data and concluded that AGI's products did live as long as they were intended. In fact, they actually had a longer mean time between failures than the competitors' products. So, reliability was ruled out.

Team members then looked at the design's producibility and compared it against the manufacturing process capability studies that they requested. Those analyses revealed that the designs were consistent with both in-house and externally purchased process capabilities, and that their design tolerances did not exceed what was reasonable for the industry. So, the producibility question was put to rest.

The project team then moved on to the question of product specifications, commissioning an independent study of the accuracy and applicability of all product documentation, specifications, and tolerances. The results revealed a high level of accuracy in all documentation and specifications. The design, the project team concluded, was sound.

The project team then moved down the root cause model to quality. It analyzed the incoming quality levels of the components and assemblies that AGI purchased from outside suppliers from historical inspection reports and random sampling of products being received. It found the quality level of all incoming materials to be excellent. Coming further down the root cause model, team members analyzed the quality of the workmanship in AGI's assembly processes and found it, too, to be exceptional (six sigma levels). They then looked at AGI's quality confirmation systems for any noncompliance or weakness. The statistically based quality confirmation systems were analyzed through statistical process control measures, reliability and repeatability studies, and failure mode and effects analysis (FMEA) studies. The project team concluded that the quality conformation systems were well within the compliance levels set for AGI, and for the industry as a whole. Quality, it concluded, was not the root cause.

The project team next looked into the training received by ACEG's repair and customer service personnel to determine if productivity and capacity were the drivers behind the cycle times. It found that ACEG conducted frequent training and testing of its personnel in all areas. That data, coupled with actual observations conducted by the project team and conformation testing conducted by the operating management staff, confirmed that the personnel at ACEG were capable of handling their assignments and tasks effectively.

The next step was to look into the organizational structure and the process design. But this is where the project team had to make a critical business decision. Time was becoming an issue for the company. Projections of nonlinear market share loss were being received by the project team from marketing and senior management. It was clearly time to move forward.

Based upon prior analyses, and the level in the root-cause model, the project team concluded it was safe to move forward by including both remaining possible root causes into the ultimate solution for the project—the process design and organizational structure. These are the types of business decisions that the project manager and his project team must often make. There is always, however, an extensive enough analysis done before the project team moves into the tactical stages of the project to clearly know the situation and its likely drivers. This, too, is part of effective risk management.

DECISION-MAKING

Once the root cause of the problem has been identified, a decision is made regarding the best alternative for resolving the problem or addressing an opportunity facing the organization. The alternative selected by the project team provides the project manager with the final definition of the project and must represent the lowest risk, lowest cost, least impact approach for the company. Simply throwing people and money at a problem is unacceptable.

In many cases, this ultimate definition of the project will differ from the one the project manager was originally assigned. This is because, in most cases, senior management or outside customers only work with symptoms or loosely defined desires. How those issues are ultimately addressed is rarely of concern to the project initiators. They are looking more for results. The professional project manager realizes the difference and works to accurately define the project before initiating its tactical planning phase.

Avoiding Decision-making

Many project managers avoid making decisions because of the controversy and direct confrontations commonly associated with the decision-making process. Often, the project manager's decision results in a contest between differing points of view. Politics are often a factor. The person with the most political clout often prevails and the loser suffers the embarrassment of defeat in front of her project team, peers, and superiors. So decisions are avoided. But one of the roles and responsibilities of the project manager is to make decisions, often times critical, sometimes unpopular ones. As was said earlier, indecision is deadly to the project team's efforts and the project manager's credibility.

Any good decision is based upon a comprehensive understanding of the project requirements, coupled with the results of thorough situational assessments and problem-solving efforts that have identified the root cause of the problems or issues impacting project performance, expected deliverables, project schedule, resource consumption, costs, budget, etc.

The next step is a comprehensive assessment of the possible alternative courses of action available to address the problem or opportunity, followed by an analysis of the results possible from each of the alternative solutions—both good and bad.

No Perfect Decision

There is simply no perfect decision. The best decision is one that selects the solution closest to fulfilling all project requirements and expectations in the most cost and time-effective manner possible, with the least risk. Current conditions must be given due consideration. There are times when doing nothing is the best course of action.

For example, in late 1997, one company's MIS project team recommended to the CEO that the company scrap its existing business systems and purchase a fully integrated package from one of the leading business software providers. It believed that the old systems were simply incapable of supporting the company into the 21st century. An outside consultant advised the CEO not to proceed at that time, since the fix for the year 2000 (Y2K) problem had not yet been implemented in the selected software.

Despite the consultant's advice, the company decided to move ahead with the purchase, based upon the project manager's assurances that the Y2K issue was under control. The company was warned by the consultant not to modify the software in any way so that the fixes ultimately developed by the software company could be implemented without delay or problem.

In early 1999, the CEO was informed by the IT manager that the new business systems would not operate in 2000 as a result of delays experienced by the software developer in resolving many of the Y2K problems. There were only two feasible solutions available at that time:

- buy another fully integrated business system with the Y2K fixes in place and scrap the one purchased two years earlier; or
- hire as many mainframe programmers as possible and begin reprogramming the existing software to fix the coding problems—despite the warning, the company had modified the programs once installed so the software provider now had no way of knowing what had been done.

Initially, the correct decision would have been to wait until the Y2K fixes were in place. Now, the alternatives available to the company were costly and embarrassing. Ultimately, senior management bit the bullet and started fresh with new software. What about the original project manager? Let us just say he became free to pursue other career endeavors.

Decision-making is a responsibility that cannot be avoided by a project manager, and she must accept the downside accountability of that decision should it be flawed.

The Decision Process

The decision process begins with an accurate description of what the decision is intended to resolve (project objectives, issues, opportunities, and problems), along with the known alternatives available to the project team.

The tool used by most project managers is a typical decision matrix (see Figure 9-6). Its application is straightforward. The objectives and deliverables established for each phase of the project are listed by the project team and divided into two categories:

1. The project objectives, which *must* be achieved to guarantee success of the project.
2. Those *desired* objectives the project team would like to achieve, though they are not necessarily mandatory for successful completion of the project. The desired objectives are those used to compare one alternative against another. They become the differentiators in the decision process.

All objectives are quantifiable and measurable. The must objectives function as a go/no-go filter for all alternatives. Unless an alternative (course of action, methodology, approach, etc.) fulfills all "must" objectives, it does not meet the baseline criterion essential for successful project implementation; thus it is immediately removed from consideration.

Alternatives

While there are only two alternatives shown in Figure 9-6, there will be many more for the project. Alternatives are typically brainstormed from a clean sheet of paper, *without* the objectives in view. If the project objectives are in sight, the project team will unconsciously try to force-fit alternatives, possibly overlooking some creative solutions to the problems and issues facing the project.

Objectives matrix for: (project or decision description)					
Objectives		**Alternative A**		**Alternative B**	
Musts		**Data**	**Y/N**	**Data**	**Y/N**
A					
B					
C					
Desired	**Weight**	**Data**	**Score**	**Data**	**Score**
D					
E					
F					
Total					

Figure 9-6. This kind of matrix helps project managers glean information about project objectives so they can be better prepared for future decision-making.

As a point of clarification, the objectives represent *what* is to be accomplished with the project (deliverables). The alternatives represent *how* they are to be accomplished (approach). The alternatives are the courses of action to be considered in accomplishing the objectives set forth for the project.

Figure 9-7 illustrates a decision matrix used in an actual project. While it contains only two of the original 10 alternatives that the project team considered, it does illustrate the mechanics for developing the tool.

Every decision has consequences, both positive and negative. Those consequences are thoroughly considered and assessed for their potential impact on the successful completion of all project objectives. In all cases, they are considered *before* a final decision is reached. This is the project team's final opportunity to address negative consequences at little or no cost to the project.

Prevention is always less costly than failure. Negative consequences will always introduce additional problems into the project. As has been said, "The evil that men do lives after them; the good is oft interred with their bones." The same can be said for a poor decision at the project level. It will outlive all of the good work done by the team and the project manager. The business journals are filled with examples every day. Overlooking negative consequences that make a decision unworkable or the project objectives unreachable is a fundamental and potentially career-limiting mistake that no project manager wants to make. Do you remember New Coke™ or Crystal Pepsi™?

Pros and Cons

A simple, but effective practice will aid the project team in evaluating alternatives. All pros and cons associated with each alternative are listed by the project team. This exercise forces the team to think clearly about all of the upsides and downsides of the alternatives under consideration.

Once all alternatives and objectives have been identified and listed, they are then compared against the "must" objectives. These are black-and-white issues; either an issue meets each of the

Objectives matrix for: *Alliance Consumer Electronics*

Objectives		Alternative 1: Reengineer process		Alternative 2: Outsource function	
Musts		**Data**	**Y/N**	**Data**	**Y/N**
Reduce cycle time to 5 days		CT data	Yes	CT data	No
Ensure a 15% margin		VE study	Yes		
Reduce overhead by 50%		VA study	Yes		
Desired	**Weight**	**Data**	**Score**	**Data**	**Score**
Reduce cycle time to 3 days	10	CT data	10.0		
Implement in 180 days	8	PM study	7.2		
Ensure 55% ROI	8	VA study	7.2		
Return MS in 180 days	7	Market study	3.5		
Address "mine"	5	IE study	5.0		
Total			32.9		

Figure 9-7. Decision matrix used in an actual project.

must objectives or it does not. A "no" means that the alternative is no longer under consideration.

The data field is a reference field for the project manager. It contains the sources of information regarding each alternative's conformance or nonconformance to the respective "must" objective. It is a reminder of how the decision regarding that alternative was made. For example, if a large number of objectives carry a "must" designation, the expectations may well have been set too high given the actual project constraints, and vice versa. If none of the alternatives selected meet all of the "must" objectives, and those "must" objectives are deemed necessary for the successful completion of the project, then consideration is given to combining one or more alternatives to generate an acceptable hybrid solution. Often, this approach provides the project team with the best solution by offsetting the weaknesses of one alternative with the strengths of others.

Desired Objectives

In addition to the "must" objectives, the decision matrix contains a listing of the "desired" objectives, along with a prioritization scale or weighting factor that differentiates each "desired" objective from the others, based upon their relative importance in meeting the overall project requirements. Unlike "must" objectives, which carry no prioritization, "desired" objectives are weighted on a ten-point scale, with a weighting of ten indicating the highest level of importance and a one indicating the least significance to the overall project or decision requirements. After the alternatives are compared against the "must" objectives, each remaining alternative that satisfied each of the must objectives is then scored against the desired objective, using the following scale:

- 100% conformance to meeting the desired objective = 1.0,
- 90% conformance = 0.9,
- 80% conformance = 0.8,
- 70% conformance = 0.7,
- 60% conformance = 0.6,
- etc.

Scores for each alternative are calculated by multiplying the point totals times the weighting factor for each "desired" objective, then totaling all scores for that alternative. The alternative that best conforms to the decision or project objectives, based upon the highest score, is the recommended course of action.

The Reality Check

A reality check is always applied by the project manager and his team members once the final alternative is selected. While the selected alternative may look good on paper, the project team seeks to determine if it is really workable within the existing project and business environment. Can it be implemented within the organization in a reasonable time frame? Is it economically feasible? Have all functional, organizational, and political barriers been breached? Have all necessary management approvals been received? If so, the team moves forward to implement the decision. If not, further review and additional actions are taken.

To aid the project team in the reality check, often more in-depth questions are in order. The following questions are only used to illustrate the approach. The actual questions the project team uses will depend upon the conditions, environment, and constraints surrounding the project. As stated previously, every project is unique and must be analyzed on its own merits.

1. Will the alternative selected provide the expected level of performance or financial return required for this project?
2. Will the alternative selected meet project cost targets?
3. Can the alternative selected be implemented within the desired project schedule without introducing unreasonable risks?
4. Will the alternative be accepted by the customer and/or this company's senior management?
5. Can the alternative selected be maintained by the customer or the company's own operating personnel without undue burden, overhead, or life-cycle costs?
6. Is the alternative selected robust enough to withstand current and future business or market environments and constraints?

7. Will the alternative selected project the desired image for the customers, organization, and project team?
8. Will the alternative selected generate an acceptable return on investment for the organization and the customers?
9. Will the alternative selected require an investment in personnel, facilities, technology, or equipment and is the investment realistic and acceptable to the organization?
10. Does the customer or organization have the essential skill sets to implement and maintain the selected alternative?
11. Will the alternative selected expose customers or the organization to any undue business, financial, or competitive risks?
12. Is the alternative selected compatible with current core competencies, operations, and distribution methodologies?
13. Will the alternative selected allow the company to expand business within current markets?
14. Will the alternative selected allow the company to expand business or operations into additional markets?
15. Will the alternative selected provide demonstrable market differentiation for this company or for customers?

CASE STUDY—AGI/ACEG CONCLUSION

It was now time for the project manager and team to analyze all available courses of action to resolve the cycle time and organizational structure issues surrounding AGI's loss of market share. The project manager and his project team met again with the senior management at AGI and ACEG to report status and obtain a clear direction relative to management's "must" and "desired" objectives. While they knew that regaining market share was paramount to senior management, they also knew that there would be other objectives to achieve.

With senior management's assistance, the following objectives, both "must" and "desired," were developed.

"Must" objectives:

1. Regain the lost market share (12.7%) within 24 months.
2. Make ACEG, as an operating division, profitable. A minimum profit margin of 15% was set as a floor.

3. Reduce the overhead of ACEG by 50% within 24 months to further improve corporate cash flow and earnings before taxes.
4. Meet the customer's request for a 5-day turnaround on repairs.
5. Ensure a minimum return on investment of 32% on expenditures undertaken in association with the project by the project team.
6. Total expenditures associated with the project cannot exceed $10 million.

"Desired" objectives:

1. Meet the customers' request for a 3-day turnaround for repairs (weight factor of ten).
2. Gain additional market share of 5–8% from competitors within 36 months from implementation of the project (weight factor of seven).
3. Complete implementation at AGI and ACEG within 180 days (weight factor of eight).
4. Reduce ACEG's overhead by 78% within 36 months (weight factor of four).
5. Improve ACEG's margins to 25% within 36 months (weight factor of four).
6. Utilize the existing automated business system to eliminate/minimize manual documentation processing and ensure internal control (weight factor of eight).
7. Maintain published warranty policies (weight factor of ten).

With the objectives clearly defined and quantified, the project team next set out to develop a series of alternative courses of action to address the customers' and senior managers' "must" and "desired" objectives. In creating its decision matrix, the project team considered that, because of the significant gap between the actual and the desired levels of performance, out-of-the-box solutions likely would be required. Its conclusion was based on the fact that the current process, as designed, could simply not be refined enough to close the gap sufficiently.

The project team's initial brainstorming session yielded the following alternatives that the team would ultimately include in the decision matrix. No ideas were critiqued before inclusion. The team knew that all alternatives should be analyzed "by the numbers" so that each ultimate solution could be justified quantitatively.

1. Consolidate all centers into one.
2. Create specialty centers, using each of the five service and repair centers for one specific type of repair.
3. Reengineer the existing component-level analysis and replacement methodology to incorporate a more modular repair methodology.
4. Provide customers with a replacement unit taken from a stock of repaired units.
5. Send the customer a new unit, irrespective of warranty period.
6. Set a flat rate for all repairs.
7. Outsource the entire repair process to point-of-sale centers.
8. Outsource the entire repair process to "mom-and-pop" shops in all major cities and metropolitan areas.
9. Implement traveling repair services whereby a technician could be dispatched from the service and repair centers to the customer's site for repair.
10. Send repair parts to the customer for do-it-yourself repair.
11. Reengineer the entire repair process to eliminate all redundant approvals and documentation.
12. Offer the customer an incentive to buy a new unit rather than repairing the old unit (a discount coupon for 10% off the retail price of a new unit).
13. Extend the warranty period to three years for parts and labor.
14. Redesign the products to further enhance quality and reliability.
15. Do nothing.
16. Combine alternatives 1, 3, 6, and 11.
17. Combine alternatives 2, 3, and 6.
18. Combine alternatives 2, 3, 6, and 11.

19. Combine alternatives 1, 3, 4, 6, and 11.
20. Combine alternatives 1, 3, and 6.

With all of the various alternatives defined, the project team then set out to create the decision matrix illustrated in Table 9-1. The data fields have been left off intentionally, but were included in the team's analysis.

Alternative 19 was the clear victor in the project team's analysis. The implementation plan was developed around the criteria in alternative 19 and was successfully implemented within 6 months. In summary, from a customer's perspective, here's how the process now works.

The customer places a call to an 800 number. A recorded message opens with a brief apology for any inconvenience that the customer may have suffered as a result of their equipment being out of service. It then asks for two pieces of information: date of purchase and serial number.

The recorded message advises the customer that a customer service representative will speak with them within 30 seconds. If customers have the requested information readily available, they remain on the line. If not, they hang up, retrieve the needed data, and then replace the call. Within 30 seconds, a customer service representative comes on the line and again apologizes briefly for any inconvenience that the customer may have encountered. The customer service representative then offers the customer one of two choices:

1. For a flat fee (based upon ACEG's reengineered repair costs, transportation costs, and a 15% margin) ACEG will have a replacement unit delivered to the customer within 24 hours. The customer is instructed to take the replacement unit out of the shipping carton and place the defective unit back into the same carton. ACEG provides tape and return shipping labels. The customer is further instructed to place the boxed (defective) unit in a convenient location so that ACEG can make arrangements to have it picked up within 1–2 days. So, for a modest flat rate (usually 20% to 25% of the cost of a new unit), the customer is back in operation within 24

Table 9-1. Decision matrix

Objectives	Alternatives																			
Musts	1	2	3	4	5	6	7	8	9	10	11	12	13	14	15	16	17	18	19	20
1	N	Y	Y	Y	Y	N	Y	Y	Y	N	N	N	Y	Y	N	Y	Y	Y	Y	Y
2		N	Y	N	N		N	N	N				N	N		Y	Y	Y	Y	Y
3			N													Y	N	N	Y	Y
4																Y			Y	Y
5																Y			Y	Y
6																Y			Y	Y
Desired																				
1																10			50	0
2																28			35	14
3																32			24	32
4																20			20	8
5																16			16	8
6																40			40	8
7																50			50	50
Total																196			235	120

hours. The customer suffers no additional inconvenience associated with transporting the defective unit to a drop-off or repair location or the hassle of finding suitable shipping containers. ACEG takes care of it all.

2. Return the defective unit to ACEG for repair and get it back within 5 working days—at no cost. Under this scenario, ACEG ships packaging materials to the customer within 24 hours and makes arrangements for the defective unit to be picked up that same afternoon. The unit undergoes a modular repair and test, and is then returned to the customer.

Obviously, if the customer can wait the 5 days, it is an attractive offer. What ACEG has found, however, is that over 98% of its customers select option 1, as time is always a critical consideration and the cost of that option is extremely reasonable. Within 24 months, AGI regained its lost market share plus an additional four percentage points from its competition. Overhead was reduced by over 80% and margin targets were realized. What about the project management team? They received sizable bonuses.

10
Project Budgeting and Cost Management

OVERVIEW

Budget development occurs in two stages during the project. First in preliminary form, the target budget is developed for the overall project during the portfolio-planning phase. At this stage, the budget represents a target for financial planning purposes only. It is usually based upon a review of the company's lessons-learned database or may be a rough figure developed by a senior staff member or project management office member. Once the project team completes its situational assessment and decision analysis to determine specifically what approach will be utilized to deliver the expected outcomes, a detailed plan is developed for each phase of the project. It is at this stage that the final project budget is prepared and cost controls instituted. These processes are done in parallel following the concept of concurrent or left-side planning.

The portfolio management process was covered in Chapter 2, so a quick overview will suffice to remind the reader of how the process is used to select and prioritize projects. As illustrated in Figure 10-1, the initial budget is derived through the first three phases of idea generation/strategic alignment, opportunity assessment, and product/service evaluation. It is in these stages that each concept is evaluated based upon one to several criteria ranging from:

- expected returns;
- cash flow impact;
- resource impact;

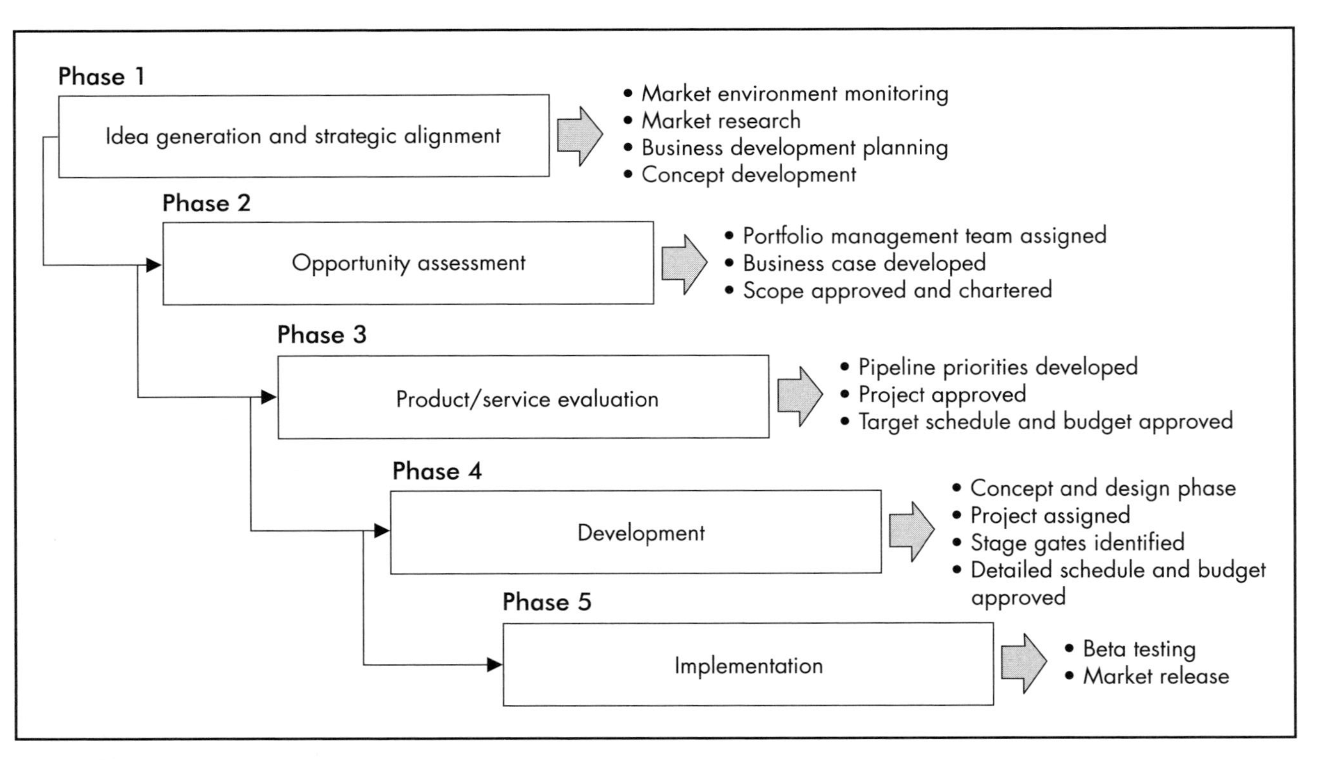

Figure 10-1. Budget development takes place over the first three phases of the project.

- risk;
- customer, stockholder, or market impact;
- market segmentation;
- brand and positioning strategies, etc.

Once the formal project management planning begins, these rough estimates and target budget figures are fine-tuned into actual operating budgets that will drive additional cash-flow impact analyses and the overall budgetary control processes for the project.

In this chapter, the process of developing a detailed project budget will be defined from the initial estimates to the final cash-flow impacts. Control mechanisms ranging from earned value techniques to impact assessments will be illustrated along with the basic financial management and investment decision tools. In essence, the project manager is concerned with the "total costs" of all resources, materials, capital equipment, utilities, etc., utilized to meet expected project outcomes. This life-cycle or activity-based costing approach includes resource planning, cost estimating, cash-flow estimating, control measures, and specific management requirements such as return on investment, internal rate of return, cost-benefit, and risk management.

It is senior management's responsibility to protect corporate assets. As a consequence, every project investment is required to generate a reasonable and predictable return. It is, thus, incumbent upon the project manager to ensure that the capital and human assets allocated to the project are managed and controlled properly to ensure maximum return on their utilization.

PROJECT BUDGETING

In the real world, it is common for any organization to have several projects in the active portfolio competing for limited capital and human resources. As such, it is management's responsibility to select only those projects that will produce the greatest return for the organization after considering all risks. Thus, every project manager is required to develop detailed budgets and associated control mechanisms to guarantee that those returns are realized. This fiscal responsibility cannot be delegated or ignored by project managers. To waste or misuse limited corporate assets is predictably career limiting.

Budget Inputs

Inputs for the budgeting process are derived from the project planning and portfolio management processes, including:

- project proposal terms and conditions, purchase order, contract terms and conditions, or project charter;
- fixed-price contracts, cost-plus-fixed-fee contracts, cost-plus-expenses contracts, time-and-materials contracts, time-and-materials not to exceed contracts, contract incentives and penalties, insurance premiums, etc.;
- project work breakdown structure (WBS) and the activities included in the final project schedule;
- resource pool descriptions along with salaries, benefit costs, burden, etc.;
- acquisition cost planning for external resources, services, materials, logistics, etc.;
- lessons-learned database cost and operating budget cost variance information on similar projects as well as daily operations;
- organizational policies and procedures;
- project investment or capital requirements and constraints;
- organizational cost of capital;
- travel expenses;
- testing, certification, or validation costs;
- regulatory or environmental compliance costs;
- tariffs, duties, royalties, dockage, and pipeline costs;
- facilities and utilities costs; and
- risk management costs, etc.

In short, every element of cost that will be experienced during the life cycle of the project is considered at this stage of the budget development process. Because the budget includes an estimate of all anticipated costs, it forms a working document that provides financial guidance for future project decisions and actions taken by the project team. So, in essence, the budget serves two primary functions for the project manager: it is a tool to accurately monitor and record expenditures relating to the project, as well as a tool to maximize control over those expenditures to ensure they are appropriate, justified, and approved.

The project budget contains both direct and indirect costs. Direct cost categories include things like personnel costs, contracted or purchased services and materials, equipment, travel, communications tools and systems, etc. Indirect cost categories, on the other hand, include cost elements like overhead and burden. These are real and tangible costs that will be applied against the project. There are also fixed and variable costs to be considered—those costs that either change or remain constant with activity levels.

As most project managers have only limited experience in the financial arena, it is often wise to solicit the assistance of a cost accountant or financial analyst to assist in the preparation of the budget. These professionals are knowledgeable about how these costs are applied, the typical variances encountered through the course of normal operations, as well as how they are reported. For example, return-on-investment calculations come in a number of variations, each resulting in a distinctly different outcome. The financial professionals are familiar with how each organization calculates these financial metrics, as well as the accepted cut-off levels for project funding at each phase gate. Their guidance, as a result, is often invaluable.

For many projects, cost categorizations provide an easy way to identify, consolidate, and monitor costs. For example, costs can be broken into major categories:

- product, process, or service costs (for example, materials, labor, overhead, etc.);
- capital costs (for example, equipment, tooling, spare parts, finance charges, support systems, design, installation, transportation, texting, validation, user or employee training, taxes, royalties, duties, etc.);
- operating costs (for example, energy, utilities, perishable materials and tooling, maintenance supplies, maintenance training, technical and operational support, occupancy, lease or mortgage, overhead, burden, etc.); and

- project management costs (for example, project personnel, miscellaneous travel, project management tools and systems, communications, analysis and data acquisition, security processing, safety apparel, and administrative costs).

Other categories may include:

- sales, general, and administrative costs;
- proposal costs;
- research and development costs;
- change and configuration management costs;
- service costs; and
- guarantees, warranties, or contingent liabilities.

Budgeting Impact Example

On a recent pharmaceutical industry project, the steering committee made the decision to outsource much of the compliance and project management responsibilities to two teams of consultants. Because the company was required to comply with Food and Drug Administration (FDA) mandated procedures and protocols, each consultant was required to comply with those same standards. To make this possible, the company was forced to provide each of the 100+ consultants with laptop computers and cases marked with company logos, secured network access codes and electronic keys, telephone extensions, workspaces, security badges, and parking facilities. The immediate (and unplanned) budget impact was well over $1 million. Should these costs have been planned during the budgeting process? The obvious answer is "yes." Once again, any cost that will be applied directly or indirectly against the project is to be included in the budget's development to ensure that there are no surprises later.

Building the Budget

The budgeting process begins with resource planning (identification of required resources and the quantities of each needed for each activity); an estimate of those resource costs considering escalation, demand, and availability factors over the life of the project; allocation of costs to each activity; and distribution of those costs over time in compliance with project needs and organizational constraints. As illustrated in Figure 10-2, this structured approach guarantees that all costs are captured and applied correctly.

Resource Planning

In the resource planning phase, the physical resources needed for each activity and the quantities of each are identified. Completed in conjunction with the development of the final project schedule pursuant to concurrent or "left-side planning" techniques, this phase considers:

- the resources that will be needed;
- when they will be needed;
- in what quantities they will be needed; and
- any lead time or sourcing considerations.

Data for resource planning is available through the project schedule, WBS, the lessons-learned database, project scope statement, project charter, proposal terms and conditions, contractual terms and conditions, resource pool descriptions, personnel load and productivity factors, organizational policies and procedures, activity duration estimates, purchasing and logistics databases, product bills of materials, process descriptions and routings, job descriptions, topic matter experts, internal and external publications, sales forecasts, market research, etc.

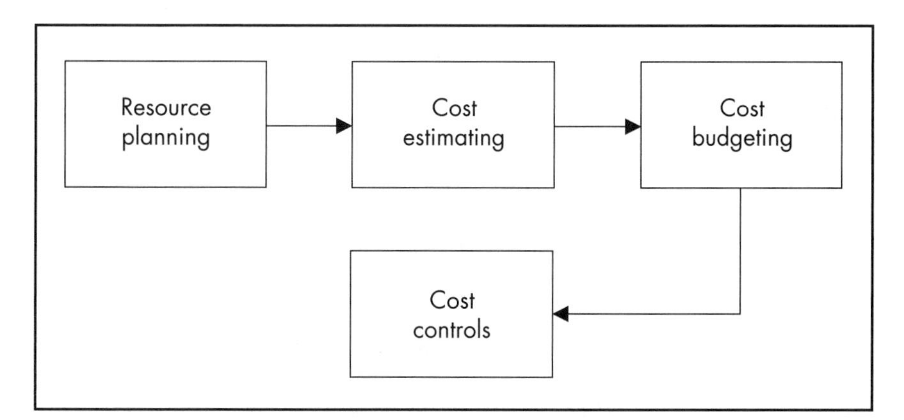

Figure 10-2. Budget development process.

Once all resource needs have been identified, costs are applied to each.

Cost Estimating

The cost estimating process involves the development and application of all cost factors to each of the resources identified in the resource-planning phase. In so doing, consideration is given to the "total cost" of each resource, as well as possible causes of variance to the expected costs. For example, the price paid for a given commodity often represents only a fraction of its total cost. Other factors to be considered and included are insurance, transportation (normal and premium), taxes, handling, duties, royalties, packaging, up-charges for less-than-lead-time orders, quality sorting, quality control, rejection and rework costs, inventory carrying costs, overhead, and burden, to name just a few. In addition, price and cost changes over time are also considered, especially for products and services whose pricing is tied to more volatile commodities, labor contracts, or global supply/demand dynamics. Certainly, any commodity or service provided by a singular or limited number of suppliers is always subject to volatility in pricing and availability. When in doubt, the experienced project manager solicits the aid of purchasing and logistics professionals.

During this phase of budget development, consideration is also given to alternative, lower-cost materials, methods, sources, technologies, and labor sources through the application of value engineering or value analysis techniques. In all cases, the project manager is charged with introducing the lowest-cost, lowest-risk solutions. Working closely with the activity detail development underway in schedule development, value analysis techniques often drive changes in schedule and cost to minimize total activity and project costs. This trade-off process is necessary to identify the best total solution considering both time and money.

Tools and techniques available to the project manager for the cost estimating phase of budget development are described as follows.

- *Analysis of financial and operational variance accounts.* Variances to expected material, labor, or expense budgets and their causes are available through general accounting reports. They are typically captured monthly for companies with standard cost accounting systems and in real time for companies with activity-based cost accounting systems. The information is available through either accounting personnel or operations-level managers and supervisors.

- *Analogous estimating.* Based upon similar projects or activities, historical data provides moderately accurate data relative to the expected cost of resources. Because this is back-looking versus forward-looking data, it is generally acceptable for general planning purposes but not for the final budget.
- *Bottom-up estimating.* Similar to a bill of material cost roll-up, this technique begins with an estimate of the costs of each lower level resource accumulated to successively higher levels until all elements of the activity are included.
- *Scaling or parametric modeling.* When the primary project cost elements are easily scalable (upwardly and downwardly), parametric modeling is used to predict the scaled activity costs. This technique is most valuable when historical data is accurate, applicable, and external or internal cost escalation factors are minimal. When significant volatility is common in material, service, or labor costs, this technique rarely provides the degree of accuracy required for the budgeting process.
- *Industry periodicals.* In some industries, such as construction, published periodicals and cost estimating tools are available, which accurately predict cost factors for many project elements. These sources are updated on a frequent basis to reflect the most current costs, so retaining the most current revision is a requirement. Additionally, the project manager utilizing these tools is well advised to confirm compatibility before relying on the data they provide. For example, the use of a construction estimating tool developed for the Northeast U.S. may not accurately reflect the costs that can be realistically expected for a similar project in the Southwest U.S.
- *Zero-based budgeting techniques.* An excellent tool for the budgeting process, this technique takes a clean-sheet approach to

cost estimating. All cost factors are developed from current versus historical data, making it one of the most accurate tools available for budgeting.

- *Vendor bid analysis.* This technique utilizes current vendor and contractor bids to forecast costs for volatile or project-critical resources, materials, and services over time. Much like the zero-based budgeting technique, vendor bid analysis incorporates costs that can be contractually confirmed throughout the life cycle of the project, thereby minimizing or eliminating the potential for unplanned or unforeseen cost escalations.

The outcome of the cost estimating phase of the budgeting process is a realistic, supportable estimate of the cost of each resource needed for the project. Costs are based upon quantitative analytical tools that predict the most likely cost of each of the required resources, including risk and contingency planning costs. Where fixed costs are not possible, estimates of the most likely range of costs are used. In such a case, the project manager is well advised to be conservative.

In summary, it is imperative that the project manager and his team capture all costs as accurately as possible considering the possible and likely changes in those costs throughout the life cycle of the project. When comparisons are utilized, they must be logical and scalable. Indirect costs, burden, overhead, and similar charges to the project cost structure, as well as any external costs, also must be captured. In all cases, the use of actual versus average costs is required, especially in the project-critical areas of labor, materials, logistics, outside services, etc.

Cost Budgeting

The cost budgeting phase involves the allocation of the overall cost estimates to the individual activities to build a time-phased cost baseline with which to measure ongoing project financial performance, as well as to highlight the cash-flow impacts on the organization derived from the project. In some cases, multiple baselines are required to satisfy the diverse requirements of the project stakeholders and sponsors. Table 10-1 presents typical project budget expense categories.

Table 10-1. Typical expense categories.

Overhead	Burden	Interest	Reporting	Utilities
Energy	Perishables	Maintenance	Support	Occupancy
Lease	Mortgage	Insurance	Allocations	Equipment
Purchased services	Purchased materials	Acquisition planning	Sourcing costs	Certification costs
Quality testing	Quality compliance	Quality control	Quality planning	Corrective actions
Labor (salary)	Labor (benefits)	Labor (burden)	Labor training	Labor acquisition
Travel	Software	Supplies	Spares	Testing
Systems	Systems support	Logistics	Installation	Taxes
Royalties	Duties	Handling	Shipping	Regulatory compliance
Risk assessment	Contingency planning	Risk abatement	Corrective actions	Risk reporting
Communications costs	Technology costs	Miscellaneous costs	Legal costs	Entertainment costs
Direct materials	Indirect materials	Indirect labor	Disposable materials	Expensed materials
Hazardous waste remediation	Hazardous waste disposal	Environmental impact studies	Politics	Customer approval

The use of a budget worksheet, as illustrated in Figure 10-3, facilitates the capture, analysis, and monitoring of the various budget elements. A simple spreadsheet provides an adequate basis for the development of this planning tool. The intent is to capture the various expense categories for each activity including their associated cost per period, periods in which the expense is incurred, and the total cost. Multi-faceted reporting capabilities are available as derivatives of the budget spreadsheet when the data is sorted. Table 10-2 is an example of a completed budget worksheet.

By totaling the costs for each activity for each period, the project manager is able to identify the periodic cash-flow impact of the project on the organization. This data allows Accounting to set aside funds for the project on a period-by-period basis as part of their cash-flow planning (see Table 10-3). As Table 10-4 illustrates, from the same data, the total budgeted cost per activity is calculated to highlight the activity cost distribution: in other words, where the major cost factors for the project lie. Or, the

Activity	Expense Category	Cost per Period	Period (Day, Week, Month)	Total Cost

Figure 10-3. Budget preparation worksheet.

Table 10-2. Budget worksheet example.

Activity	Expense Category	Cost per Period	Period (Month)	Total Cost
Product development	Direct labor	$12,000	1–10	$120,000
	Contracted labor	$5,000	5–8	$20,000
	Overhead	$1,000	1–10	$10,000
	Materials	$25,000	6–9	$100,000
Project funding	Capital costs	$2,000	1–10	$20,000
Product validation	Travel	$2,500	9	$2,500
	Outside testing	$15,000	9	$15,000
	Food and Drug Administration approval	$10,000	9–10	$20,000
Marketing	Public relations firm	$25,000	11–12	$50,000
	Marketing plan	$30,000	12	$30,000

same data can be used to generate a visual control and reporting tool such as the Pareto chart in Figure 10-4.

As another example, for further refinement and control, the project manager can sort the data by expense category to identify what portion each category contributes to the total project cost, as shown in Table 10-5. For visual control and reporting, charts such as those in Figures 10-5 and 10-6 are generated.

BUDGET AND COST CONTROLS

Once completed and approved, the budget and its associated cost elements require constant monitoring and control to ensure the project remains within financial constraints on a phase-by-phase basis versus simply in overall terms. This is because the project expenses directly impact the organization's cash flow. By remaining vigilantly focused on expenditure control, the project

Table 10-3. Budgeted costs per period.

Budget Period	Budgeted Costs
1	$15,000
2	$15,000
3	$15,000
4	$15,000
5	$20,000
6	$45,000
7	$45,000
8	$45,000
9	$67,500
10	$25,000
11	$25,000
12	$55,000

Table 10-4. Total cost per activity.

Activity	Total Budget
Project funding	$20,000
Product development	$250,000
Product validation	$37,500
Product marketing	$80,000

manager ensures that the funds needed to support his, as well as other organizational projects and activities, are available when and as needed. Consequently, control measures are introduced to:

- identify influencing factors that may create changes to the cost baselines,
- determine if and when a change to the cost baseline occurs or is eminent, and
- effectively manage those changes if and when they occur.

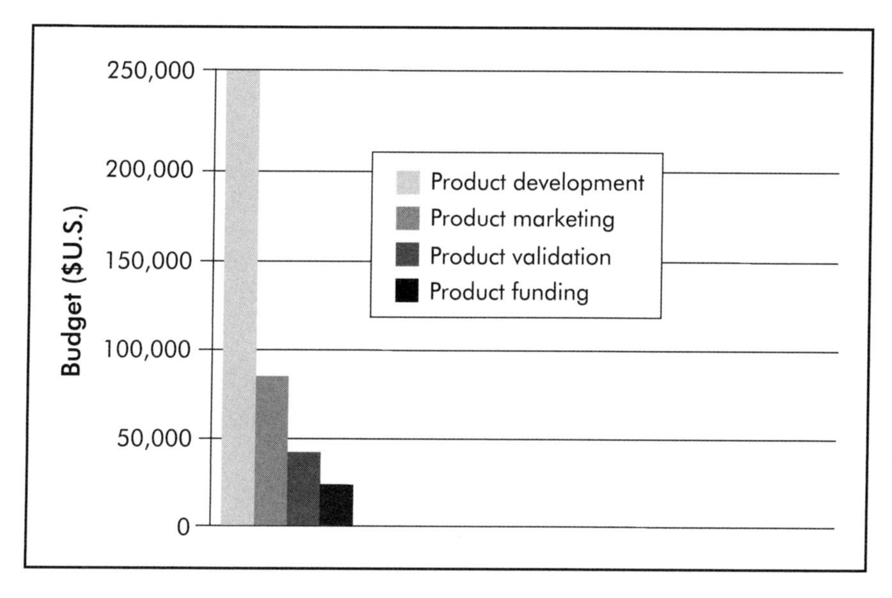

Figure 10-4. Pareto chart of total project budget by activity.

Table 10-5. Project budget by expense category.

Expense Category	Budget
Direct labor	$120,000
Contracted labor	$20,000
Overhead	$10,000
Materials	$100,000
Capital costs	$20,000
Travel	$2,500
Outside testing	$15,000
Food and Drug Administration approval	$20,000
Public relations firm	$50,000
Marketing plan	$30,000

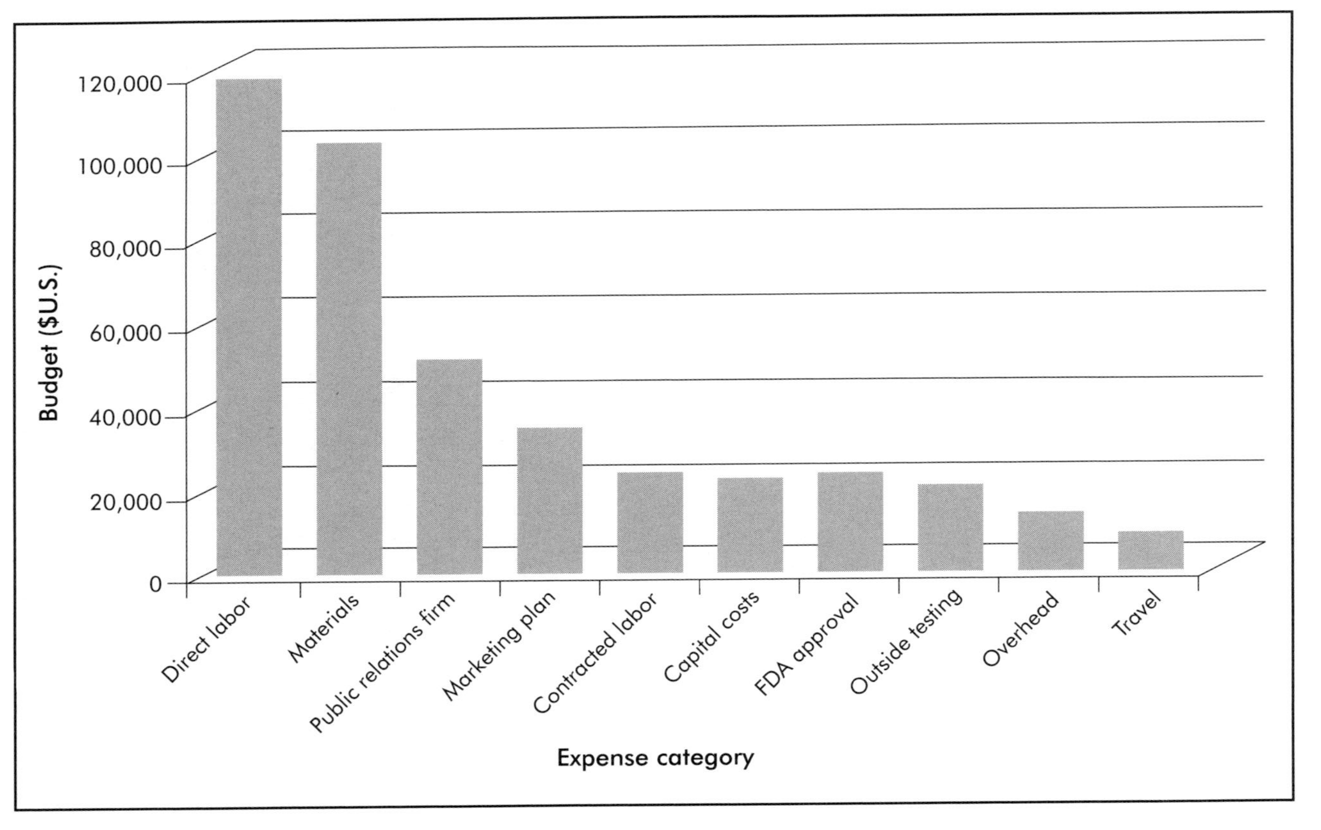

Figure 10-5. Project budget by expense category.

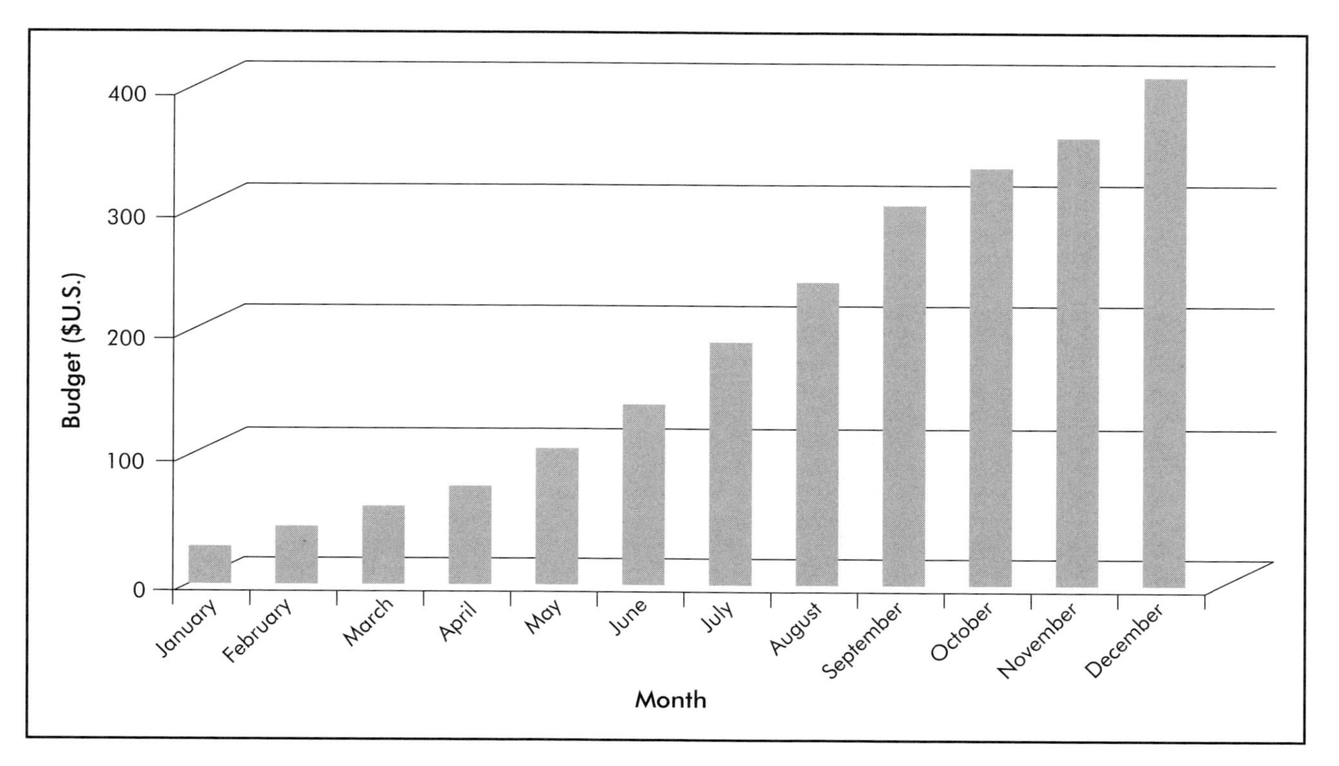

Figure 10-6. Planned budget throughout the project life cycle.

Just as with a scope, methodology, or schedule change, the responsibility for acceptance or denial of a change to the project budget rests with the project sponsors or senior management, not with the project manager or his team. It is the project manager's responsibility to identify potential changes to the project that will impact the budget, quantitatively assess the potential impact of those changes (including direct and indirect risks), and formulate the team's recommended course of action. If the project sponsors approve the change, it is implemented and documented, with corresponding changes to the budget and schedule baselines made. If the proposed changes are denied, however, the project manager documents the rejection in the lessons-learned database and moves forward with the project as previously scheduled and budgeted. Figure 10-7 illustrates the process.

The control processes implemented are designed to address both positive and negative variances to the project cost baselines. While not always apparent or fully understood by many project managers, excessively positive variances to the project cost baselines are equally as detrimental to the organization as negative

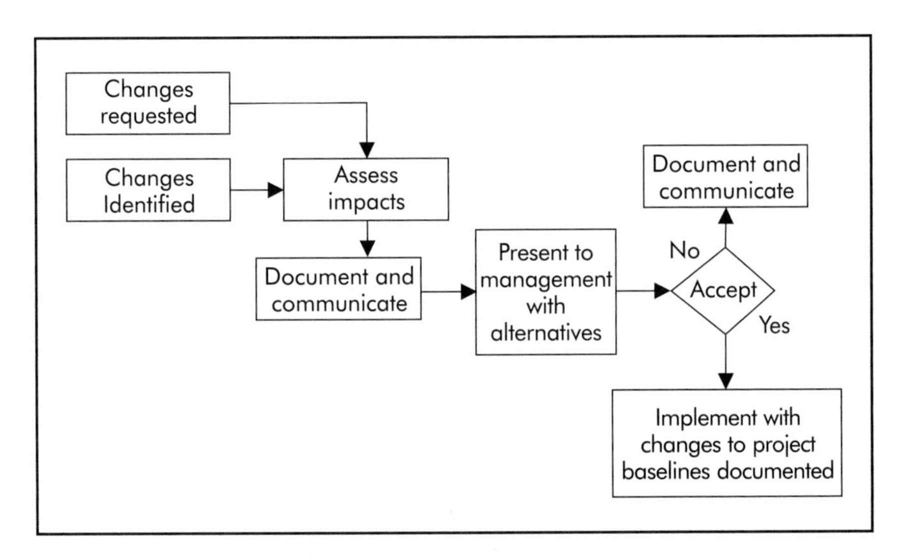

Figure 10-7. Budget and cost control process.

ones. The reason why goes back to the fact that the organization has set aside funds for this project versus other purposes. Failure to utilize these funds as planned effectively limits the organization from pursuing other endeavors that may be as, or nearly as, important to the long-term needs of the organization. This is yet another reason why it is critical that the budget planning process be as accurate as possible.

There are reasons why positive variances can occur unexpectedly. For example, the project team, anticipating significant risks in one or more areas, often builds in (and rightly so) contingency plans to address the expected failures when and if they occur. If those failures are not realized, the time and money set aside for their eventuality are no longer required. Once recognized (often at a phase-gate review), the project manager notifies the project sponsor of the excess funds so they can be reapplied to other organizational activities. Squirreling those funds away for a rainy day is inappropriate and harmful to the best interests of the organization.

For many organizations, formal cost control systems already exist that can be applied effectively by the project manager in his efforts to control the project budget. Cost accounting, auditing, configuration management, value engineering, value analysis, process management, quality management, materials management, and existing operational budget management systems are common examples. In essence, the project team's focus is on those factors that introduce "change" or the potential for it to the project. With change comes the opportunity for cost increases, as well as decreases. Thus, at times, change actually will be beneficial for the project. In other cases, it will be detrimental. It is the responsibility of the project manager and his team to ascertain the impact each potential or real change will have and then to react accordingly.

A typical control tool is illustrated in Figure 10-8. Much like the spreadsheet-based tools discussed previously, it provides running totals of costs, along with the budget variances. The reason percentages are included is to provide a frame of reference for the project manager and project sponsors. For example, a $100,000

Activity	Budgeted Costs	Actual Costs	Variance ($)	Variance (%)	Percent Complete	Comment/ Corrective Actions

Figure 10-8. Cost control system tool.

variance stated singularly will certainly raise immediate concerns with accompanying calls for detailed analyses and corrective actions. However, if that same $100,000 variance represents only a 2% variance from the project budget, the level of concern will be greatly diminished.

Costs for Expediting Projects

A common question posed to the project manager is "What will it cost to reduce the schedule?" To answer that question at any stage of the project, the project manager relies upon his control systems to provide a supportable and realistic answer. As indicated in Table 10-6, expediting costs (similarly called "crash costs") are calculated utilizing a general accounting technique that identifies the penalty per period for bringing the project to completion earlier than scheduled. Considerations in this calculation include cost penalties associated with:

- overtime for internal and external personnel;
- premium freight for expedited deliveries or "less-than-load" shipments;
- expedited handling;
- expedited setup or scheduling from suppliers;
- more expensive materials, technologies, or methods; and

Table 10-6. Project expediting tool.

Activity	Budgeted Costs	Budgeted Duration	Crash Costs	Crash Duration	Excess Cost/ Day
Testing	$5,000	5	$10,000	2	$4,000
Review	$1,000	2	$2,000	1	$1,500
Revise	$2,000	5	$4,000	3	$933
Retest	$5,000	5	$10,000	2	$4,000
Review	$1,000	2	$2,000	1	$1,500
Total	$14,000	19	$28,000	9	

- risks associated with the expedited scheduling, both internal and external.

While these considerations are by no means all inclusive, they do illustrate the requirement to consider all factors as well as their feasibility before moving forward with the expedited actions. However, tools such as that shown in Table 10-6 entertain the fallacy that "anything is possible." Experienced project managers always include a heavy dose of reality when making these calculations to ensure that what looks good financially on paper, in actuality, can be delivered.

Earned Value Metrics

Earned value measurement techniques provide the project manager with ongoing insight into how project performance, at any stage of the project, impacts current and future costs. Earned value measurement tools are based upon three independent variables:

- *planned value*—an estimate of the value of the physical work scheduled to be performed and defined as the budgeted cost of work scheduled (B_{CWS}) at any stage of the project;
- *actual value*—the actual cost of work that has been completed at any stage of the project, which is defined as the actual cost of work performed (A_{CWP}); and
- *earned value*—the budgeted value of the work actually completed at any stage of the project, which is defined as the budgeted cost of work performed (B_{CWP}).

From these factors, values are calculated to assist the project manager in addressing real or potential variances to the project budget, and to monitor future performance and report project status to the stakeholders. Again, as these tools are intended to provide real-time feedback, they can be effectively applied at any stage of the project.

Schedule variance (S_V):

$$S_V = B_{CWP} - B_{CWS} \qquad \text{(eq. 10-1)}$$

Schedule performance index (S_{PI}):

$$S_{PI} = (B_{CWP}/B_{CWS}) \quad \text{(eq. 10-2)}$$

Cost variance (C_V):

$$C_V = (B_{CWP} - A_{CWP}) \quad \text{(eq. 10-3)}$$

Cost performance index (C_{PI}):

$$C_{PI} = (B_{CWP}/A_{CWP}) \quad \text{(eq. 10-4)}$$

As evident from the application of these metrics:

- If $C_{PI} = 1.0$ and $S_{PI} = 1.0$, the project is on schedule and on budget.
- If C_{PI} and S_{PI} are both less than 1.0, the project is over-budget and behind schedule.
- If C_{PI} and S_{PI} are both greater than 1.0, the project is under-budget and ahead of schedule.

The following example clarifies how earned value metrics are applied and the information they provide.

The project manager and her team had planned to be completed with the marketing activities for their project effective today. The scheduled cost of those activities was budgeted at \$10,000. The project team has spent only \$9,000 to date, but has only 90% of the required tasks completed. What is the team's schedule and cost variance and what does that mean to the team?

$$B_{CWS} = \$10,000$$

$$A_{CWP} = \$9,000$$

$$B_{CWP} = (B_{CWS} \times 90\%) = \$9,000$$

$$C_V = B_{CWP} - A_{CWP} = \$9,000 - \$9,000 = 0$$

$$S_V = B_{CWP} - B_{CWS} = \$9,000 - \$10,000 = -\$1,000$$

Conclusion: The project is on budget but behind schedule.

Another set of earned value control metrics provides the project manager with projections of anticipated changes to the original project budget based upon the actual performance to date at any stage of the project. These control metrics include:

- budget at completion (B_{AC})—the original estimate of the planned total cost of the completed project;
- estimate at completion (E_{AC})—the revised estimate of the total project cost based upon current progress and performance at any stage of the project, calculated as B_{AC}/C_{PI}; and
- estimate to completion (E_{TC})—the amount of capital required to fund the project to completion from a particular point in time during the project life cycle, it is often an answer to the question, "How much more money is required to complete the project?" E_{TC} is calculated as $E_{AC} - A_{CWP}$. This is a particularly important metric for cash flow planning.

As an example, assume the original budget estimate for a particular project was $200,000. If the budgeted cost of work performed to date for the project is $100,000, and the actual cost of work performed to date is $25,000, what is the revised projection for the total cost of the project? To answer this question, the project manager simply calculates the new E_{AC} as follows:

$$C_{PI} = B_{CWP}/A_{CWP} = \$100{,}000/\$25{,}000 = 4.0$$

$$E_{AC} = B_{AC}/C_{PI} = \$200{,}000/4.0 = \$50{,}000$$

To answer the question, "How much more?" the project manager simply calculates the new estimate of costs required to complete the project as follows:

$$E_{TC} = E_{AC} - A_{CWP} = \$50{,}000 - \$25{,}000 = \$25{,}000$$

The previous examples are predicated upon a steady-state environment. However, if the project manager is faced with actual or potential changes to the project, those associated risks are considered when revisions to the forecasted project costs are calculated. For example:

- If the original assumptions made during the development of the project plan or during its implementation have proven to be erroneous, then the E_{AC} reflects a revision in the execution of the remainder of the project. It is calculated as $E_{AC} = A_{CWP} + E_{TC}$ or the actual costs experienced to date plus a new estimate for all remaining work to be performed.

- If the variances that were experienced early in the project are considered to be atypical, then $E_{AC} = A_{CWP} + (B_{AC} - B_{CWP})$, or the actual costs experienced to date plus the remaining planned budgeted costs.
- If the variances experienced during the project to date are considered to be typical of those that will be experienced during the balance of the project, then E_{AC} is calculated to reflect the actual cost of the project to date plus the remaining project budget modified by a performance factor that reflects those variances. In other words, $E_{AC} = (A_{CWP} + (B_{AC} - B_{CWP})/C_{PI})$.

Figure 10-9 and Table 10-7 are used to illustrate an actual product development project in which the project manager and his team found themselves facing a series of questions. The project was scheduled to be completed on or before May 31, but as of that date, it was only partially completed. Senior management called

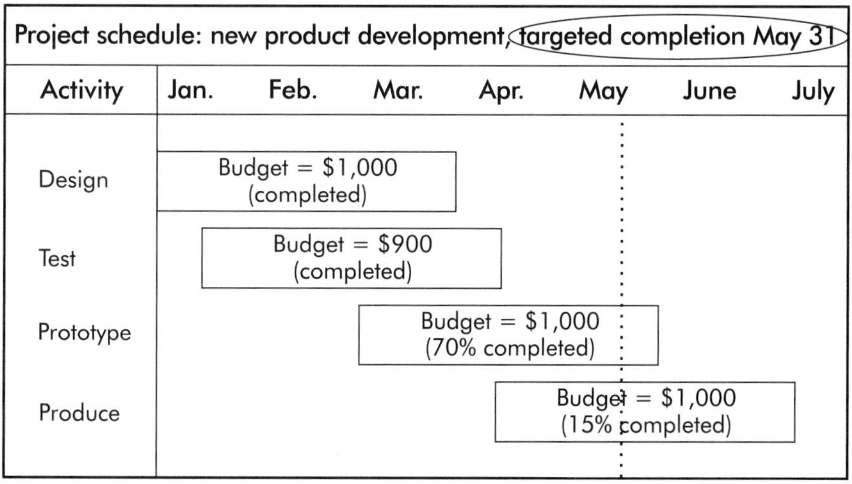

Figure 10-9. Project status as of May 31.

Table 10-7. Project expenditures and completion status as of May 31.

Activity	Actual Cost to Date	% Complete
Design	$950	100%
Test	$725	100%
Prototype	$830	70%
Produce	$0	15%

an immediate phase-gate review meeting to get to the bottom of the situation. Predictably, the questions asked revolved around the team's budgetary and schedule completion concerns.

- "How much more capital will be required to complete the project?" and
- "How much will the project cost in total when complete?"

To answer these questions, the project team completed the following calculations:

B_{CWS} = \$1,000 (design) + \$900 (test) + \$1,000 (prototype) + \$1,000 (production) = \$3,900

A_{CWP} = \$950 (design) + \$725 (test) + \$830 (prototype) + \$0 (production) = \$2,505

B_{CWP} = \$1,000 (\$1,000 × 100% for design) + \$900 (\$900 × 100% for test) + \$700 (\$1,000 × 70% for prototype) + \$150 (\$1,000 × 15% for production) = \$2,750

$$B_{AC} = \$3,900$$

$$C_V = B_{CWP} - A_{CWP} = \$2,750 - \$2,505 = \$245$$

$$S_V = B_{CWP} - B_{CWS} = \$2,750 - \$3,900 = -\$1,150$$

$$C_{PI} = B_{CWP}/A_{CWP} = \$2,750/\$2,505 = 1.10$$

$$S_{PI} = B_{CWP}/B_{CWS} = \$2,750/\$3,900 = 0.71$$

$$E_{AC} = B_{AC}/C_{PI} = \$3,900/1.10 = \$3,545.45$$

$$E_{TC} = E_{AC} - A_{CWP} = \$3,545.45 - \$2,505 = \$1,040.45$$

Conclusions:

- Project is behind schedule and under-budget.
- Total project cost is estimated to be $3,545.45 versus the original estimate of $3,900.
- The team will require an additional $1,040.45 to complete the project.

FINANCIAL INVESTMENT CONSIDERATIONS

In the budget planning cycle, several financial and capital investment considerations often come into play for the project team in relation to the project. These include, but are certainly not limited to:

- make or buy decisions;
- purchasing or leasing new equipment, facilities, or technologies;
- replacement or upgrade of existing equipment, facilities, or technologies;
- closure of facilities, either permanently or temporarily; and
- addition, enhancement, or elimination of personnel, services, products, processes, or business units.

The typical decision process considers the return on investment from each option compared against the organization's cost of capital. Thus each option is ranked accordingly. The focus is obviously on selecting the investment alternatives that generate the highest expected net return for the organization. The net return is the revenues or savings generated by the project after the gross revenues or savings have been reduced by the cost of capital. The rule of thumb is that an investment should not be made unless its returns exceed the marginal cost of investment capital as illustrated in Figure 10-10.

Other considerations to be included in the investment analysis are taxes, depreciation, fixed costs, variable costs, sunk costs, opportunity costs, avoidable costs, and risk costs.

Sound investment and acquisition decisions are based upon quantitative due diligence and proven financial principles. If in

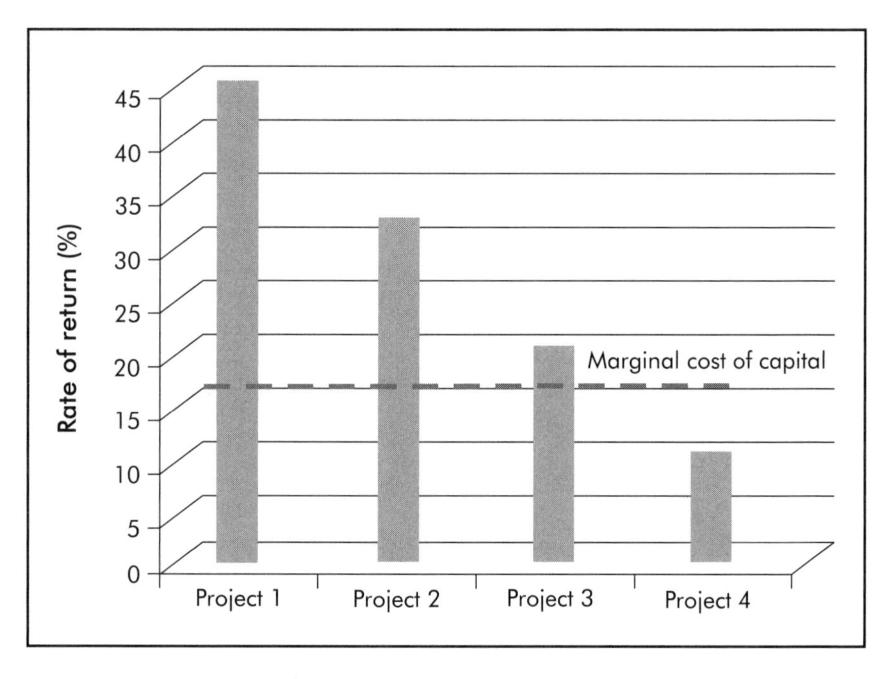

Figure 10-10. Project selection criteria.

doubt, or if not fully versed in the application of financial decision criteria, a project manager is wise to solicit the aid of a financial expert to guide the decision process. Doing so will save not only capital but also possible embarrassment downstream.

Present and Future Value

The problem often faced by the project manager and her team is that the alternatives under consideration often have differing economic lives. If the economic lives were the same, comparisons could be based on the same criteria. However, because they are not, the project manager is required to consider the time value of capital when selecting among various investment alternatives. To facilitate the decision process, project managers utilize the concepts of present and future value to bring all investment alternatives back to the same baseline for comparison purposes. Because these standard investment techniques are well published and understood by most project managers, only a brief summary will be included herein.

Both present and future value calculations are based upon the principle of compounding, or compounded value, which is the value of a sum of capital after it has earned an annual rate of interest over a specified time frame. In essence, the capital invested earns interest each period on the principal plus the interest earned during each preceding period. The *present value* of an investment option represents the current value of the invested capital that is expected to be received at some point in the future after consideration of its compounding at a specific interest rate into the future. In short, the present value of a sum of capital invested over a period of time includes compounding at a given interest rate. The same is true for *future value* calculations, only in reverse. As a result, this is often referred to as *discounting*.

*Under-commit—
Over-deliver*

Payback

A second commonly used investment criteria is payback. The *payback* method ranks investments according to the amount of time required to return earnings or savings equal to the total cost of the project or investment. In other words, investments are ranked by how long they take to break even. When considering the payback method, however, the project manager is wise to remember that this technique has two serious drawbacks:

1. It does not consider the time value of capital.
2. It does not consider possible revenue streams beyond the payback period.

Thus, for most project investment decisions, the net present or future value techniques are used to ensure a more accurate comparison of investment options.

SUMMARY

Building and managing the project budget requires a significant amount of attention to detail, research, and follow-through. Like building the project schedule, the approach is structured with no shortcuts or shooting from the hip. Every aspect of cost is considered and included—both direct and indirect. Price and total cost variations are anticipated and built into the time-phased budgeting process. Cash flow impacts are factored in to ensure the project can be funded as planned through each phase. Cost controls are implemented dynamically and empirically to ensure that only those expenses appropriate to and approved for the project are applied against the budget.

Fiscal management is as much a critical aspect of project management as schedule development and project performance. All fall within the responsibilities of the project manager and his team; and all influence the outcome of the project. Failing to deliver in any of these three areas will lead to project failure, often resulting in serious career repercussions.

11
Managing Risk

OVERVIEW

If there is a single given in the business world today, it is simply this: business executives are, by nature, risk adverse. The more risk a particular project introduces into the business, the higher the probability that senior management will expect more professionalism in the way the project is managed and in the results that the project manager achieves. That is why risk management is of such critical importance. Judgment calls, made daily to ensure that the project is not compromised, must be based upon solid risk management techniques that focus on quantitative rather than qualitative data whenever possible. When risks can be reasonably foreseen, there must be a plan to address them in a cost-effective, time-sensitive manner.

Every project contains some degree of risk. And yet, most project managers are ill prepared when it comes to identifying or adequately addressing those potential risks. For project managers, risk is dual-faceted: it introduces the opportunity to improve a project's performance and deliverables, but also has the potential to negatively impact them.

TYPES OF RISKS

Management Risks

The following discussion highlights just a few of the typical management risk factors introduced into the project as a result of the project manager or the project team. Often, these risks are a direct result of the effectiveness with which the project manager performs his duties. For example, too often the project manager fails to follow the structured methodology required of the strategic planning model in the development of his project schedule and budget. Thus he makes invalid assumptions or takes shortcuts in the mistaken belief that, based upon experience, he can safely navigate into the tactical planning stages of the project. In other cases, he fails to build into the project plan the internal controls necessary to proactively warn of out-of-control situations.

Still another common project management failure stems from the project manager's failure to monitor the critical path of the project frequently enough, or to take timely corrective actions when a problem arises. All the planning in the world cannot compensate for a lack of timely follow-up and follow-through.

In still other cases, project managers do an inadequate job of identifying, quantifying, and prioritizing the customer's requirements, or in aligning expectations with team or organizational capabilities, capacities, or competencies, or by assuming that they know more than the customer does about what the project should and should not address or deliver. A failure to correctly identify and prioritize the customer's expectations and requirements will often lead to poor decisions and trade-offs that will ultimately result in project failure from the customer's perspective.

Further, if the project manager fails to correctly analyze the skill set requirements of the project, or if he does not ensure that the appropriate chemistry exists among the project team members, then a higher than normal risk of project failure will result due to the imbalance that exists on the project team.

Finally, there are legal risks associated with breach of contract terms, copyright or patent infringement, product liability, and personal injury, to name only a few.

Product or Service Design Risks

Product or service design risks are numerous, but are often either overlooked or not given due consideration during the planning stages by the project manager or his team. Among the most common is the failure to meet customer specifications or expectations relative to reliability, quality, functionality, or cost. Other factors include producibility, availability, product liability, safety, and technological obsolescence. Customer, brand, and market acceptance issues are also a consideration, as are competitive factors and market positioning. Issues surrounding hazardous waste disposal and environmental impact are considerations as well with more of the global community now focused on "green" technologies, products, and services. Process errors also introduce additional risk factors into a project. They include a lack of control over design or configuration changes, tooling and equipment design failures or cost overruns, and poor operations planning. Last, but not least, potential supply base failures are never overlooked as they typically introduce the most frequent and severe source of failures in a project across every industry segment.

Unexpected Events

Unexpected surprises will often exacerbate the risks associated with a project. For example, the risks associated with each of the following factors are always considered by experienced project managers, as well as the magnitude of their impact should they occur:

- suspension of project funding;
- withdrawal of project team resources or support resources;
- internal or external support system failures;
- changes in project team make-up or leadership;
- changes in technologies or compliance standards;
- changes in market or competitive conditions;
- changes in the customers' economic conditions; and as has been evident during the last decade,
- war or natural disasters.

Of these, suspension of project funding is one of the most common either at a predefined stage gate or at the end of a fiscal term due to business reasons outside of the control of or knowledge of the project team. Fortunately, most of these failures are foreseeable if adequate due diligence is done by the project manager and his team in the early planning stages. Coordination and consultation with functional managers and experts, other project managers, and the organization's lessons-learned database will provide insight into typical project failure modes. In fact, over 95% of the "surprises" that occur during the life of a project are actually foreseeable if this type of preventive action takes place in the evaluation and planning stages of the project.

Table 11-1 lists some of the typical project risk factors in the order of their probability. Each is considered as part of contingency planning, based upon past history with other projects and the amount of data available regarding each factor in the business environment.

There is no such thing as a perfectly safe, failure-proof project. Even the best project management practices do not guarantee that an unforeseen problem will not arise that will impact one or more project variables. It is, therefore, imperative that the project manager and the project team identify as many potential risks as possible, quantify their probability of occurrence and their potential impact on the project, and then build contingency plans into the project based upon those considerations. If the identified risk factors do not occur, the project will simply finish sooner and

Table 11-1. Typical project risk factors.

1. Supplier or contractor performance failures or cost overruns
2. Engineering or design changes/product or service design errors
3. Project management errors
4. Production process errors
5. Tooling or equipment design errors
6. Product reliability errors
7. Product or service costing errors
8. Start-up problems/excessive learning curve
9. Personnel skill set deficiencies
10. Administrative and operational cycle times
11. Distribution channel failures
12. Consumer and environmental safety issues

under budget. Failing to build these factors into the contingency plan, as can be expected, is a recipe for disaster—for the project and potentially for the project manager's career.

Even after the risk factors associated with each potential failure mode are assessed and contingency plans developed, the project team keeps a watchful eye on the project scope, variables, and objectives. The operating conditions and project environment are assessed constantly to ensure they remain consistent with the initial planning and situational assessment. If the baseline assumptions under which the project was launched change over time, the direction or scope of the project will no longer remain constant. These external influences will often compromise the integrity of the project plan, project budget, and project deliverables, requiring a complete reassessment of the project.

DECISIONS THAT INFLUENCE RISK

Every project manager is called upon to make a number of trade-off decisions regarding the project on a regular basis. The results of those decisions inevitably influence the project risk factors, either positively or negatively. The following examples are illustrative of the complexities associated with what may at first appear to be a simple decision.

Act or Postpone

Routinely, project managers decide whether to initiate an action or to postpone it until other facts become available. By doing nothing, the project manager can become trapped, unable to take action at a later date. On the other hand, by acting too quickly, the project manager might be missing an opportunity to meet or exceed the expected project performance. For example, a project manager must decide whether to purchase a new piece of capital equipment in anticipation of greater than expected demand, or wait until the demand becomes quantified through actual customer orders. In decisions like this, there is often no definitive data to guide the project manager, nor is there any guarantee that either decision will be successful. If the project manager waits on the purchase and the demand materializes, there is a high likelihood that the organization will not be able to fulfill its commitments to its customers, thus losing potential business to competitors.

When Chrysler's PT Cruiser® was introduced to the public, demand immediately exceeded expectations because the platform introduced new levels of functionality and economy. But rather than capitalize on a market niche that it had created, Chrysler had to ultimately settle for a smaller slice of the market because its production capacity was too low. The decision its management had made to forego spending for new facilities and equipment had inadvertently created the project failure. Conversely, had Chrysler invested heavily in equipment and facilities only to find that demand fell short of expectations, it would have been faced with excessive overhead, negatively affecting the company's profit line. Neither scenario is pleasant. A degree of risk exists with either decision. In many cases, the astute project manager will avoid this type of trap through a comprehensive situational analysis, or seek other, more appealing alternatives available through more creative, "out of the box" thinking. To do so, however, requires the project manager to discard old paradigms and biases in favor of the quantitative conclusions derived from a situational analysis, which separates fact from assumption and root causes from symptoms.

The experienced project manager evaluates the impact on the project brought on by an incorrect decision and then weighs each alternative accordingly. There are times when the alternative with the least downside risk is the better action. This means that the project manager must be realistic and unbiased in her analysis. What is the urgency of a decision? Is there time for more analysis or is action needed immediately? If a more immediate decision is called for, then it is important that the project manager seek the assistance of as many experts as possible, weigh their suggestions and the reasons behind them, then make a decision. As stated earlier, there is no such thing as a perfectly safe decision. Even doing nothing has its risks. The goal is to minimize the risks and maximize the potential benefits to the project with each decision made. In most cases, minimizing risks carries the highest priority. There are times, however, when taking a controlled, calculated risk early in the project, even though it introduces the potential for a minimal failure, may be better than waiting until later when the failure will most certainly be catastrophic.

One final thought: if the decision to continue with the current course of action is paramount to the project's success, then experienced project managers recognize the requirement to "burn the bridges" to ensure that the project team and the organization always look forward rather than second-guessing prior decisions. They do so by changing corporate policies and procedures, process and product definitions, even job descriptions and performance evaluation criteria.

Present or Future Opportunities

Another important decision concerns whether to capitalize on current opportunities or to wait for those that may become available in the future. For example, should the risk management team at AIG have waited for other suitors to pursue them in hopes of a better financial arrangement and greater global market share, or have gone with the offer made by the U.S. Treasury Department? This is an interesting question to ponder.

As Figure 11-1 illustrates, most project managers have a tendency to place a higher value on current benefits than on future benefits. The old adage, "A bird in the hand is worth two in the bush," is the logic used to justify such a decision. But is it always the correct decision? When deciding on a course of action, the successful project manager always considers both the near-term and longer-term objectives of the project. Future benefits are not arbitrarily dismissed because they may far exceed the near-term returns. Similarly, most project managers downplay future losses when compared to the potential of a near-term failure, opting to believe that by waiting, the downside will somehow be minimized. To be consistent, the project manager discounts current gains and losses to realistically compare them against conditions in the future.

Still another influencing factor in the decision process is that the acceptability of near-term risk is never directly proportional to the amount of stress or pressure being placed upon the project manager and the project team. As Figure 11-2 depicts, as

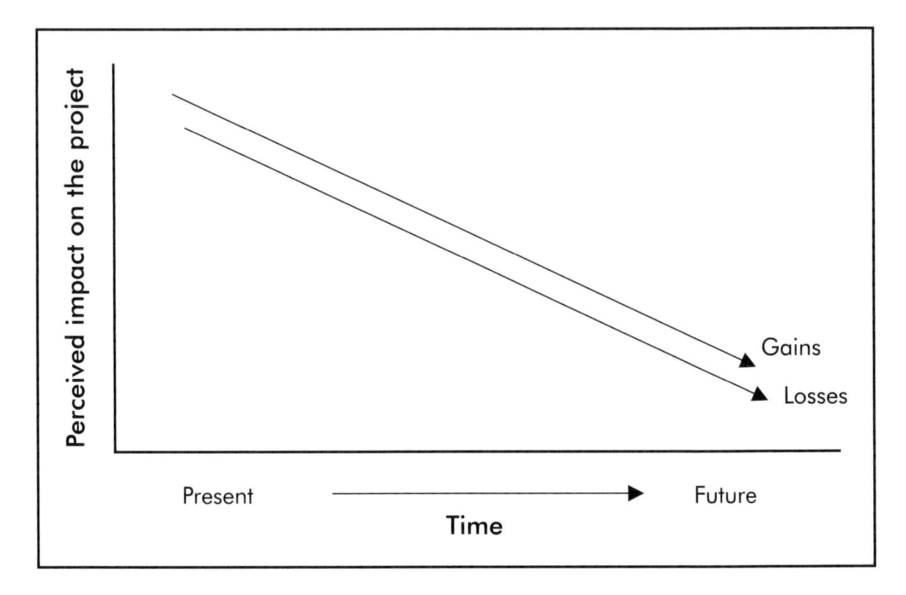

Figure 11-1. Most project managers tend to place more importance on current, rather than future, benefits.

the amount of pressure and subsequent stress on the project team increases, their willingness to accept risk increases at a proportionally faster rate, often eliminating commonsense altogether.

Situational Dynamics

When things are going as planned, most project managers are risk adverse. It is only when things start to go wrong that risk becomes acceptable. So, before initiating an action, the successful project manager comprehensively assesses the pros and cons of all near-term and longer-term actions, as well as the reasons behind the perceived benefits and losses associated with each action. There is no guarantee of absolute safety in any decision made by the project manager. Every situation is unique and is therefore evaluated on its own merits, constraints, and environment. The degree of safety can be enhanced, however, through:

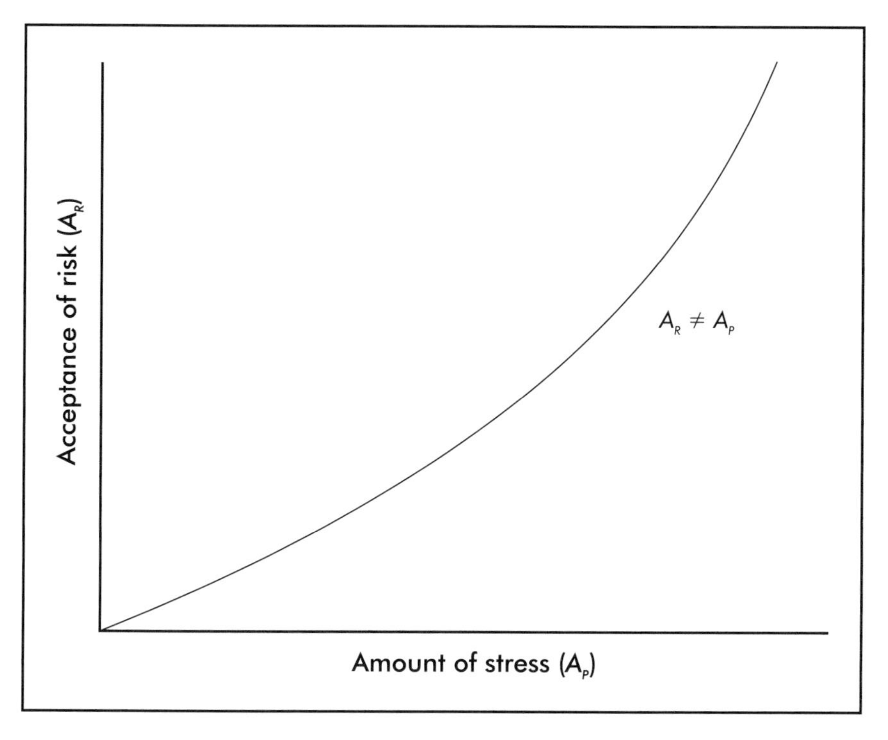

Figure 11-2. As the amount of pressure and pain increases, the willingness to accept risk increases at a proportionally faster rate.

- effective contingency planning;
- effective situational and alternative analyses;
- comprehensive analysis of the drivers behind the selected course of action;
- thorough pro and con analysis of the alternative selected;
- quantifying the decision process; and
- utilizing parallel solutions to minimize associated risk factors in cases of high risk.

How Much Risk Planning is Required?

A third decision faced by project managers concerns the amount of contingency planning and risk management warranted for a given situation. Contingency planning and risk management are designed to address areas of "predictable" failure. When such failure modes can be reasonably predicted by the project manager and/or the project team, it is logical to prepare a contingency plan in case they actually materialize during the life cycle of the project.

But what about purely random events with potentially devastating impacts on the project? Can effective contingency planning actually account for *all* possible chance factors, thus ensuring complete safety? While the desire for total control can be a valuable asset to the project manager, at what point does the desire for total safety become overshadowed by its cost? The simple answer is: no amount of internal control can offset purely random events. To develop contingency plans for every conceivable event or failure is simply unrealistic and costly. In most cases, unforeseen failures result more from faulty situational assessments that fail to recognize problems and their associated drivers than from pure chance.

Emotional Dynamics

Still another decision that most project managers are forced to address concerns whether or not to take an action when emotions are running high versus postponing that action until the dust settles a bit. Emotion is a powerful force that frequently clouds the judgment of project managers. It takes a strong project manager to resist the urge to jump into an action driven by emotion and table the decision until additional clarification or facts are received. Rational decisions are based on the identification and analysis of all possible alternatives, their probability of success, and the potential pros and cons to their timely implementation. As a general rule, an experienced project manager lets commonsense set the direction, then utilizes emotion to drive the implementation of the selected course of action (similar to the approach used by coaches in professional sports).

When weighing a course of action while in an emotional situation, an individual's own bias will greatly influence the way he perceives and assesses each alternative. Fear, for example, often amplifies the project manager's perception that a faulty decision will be catastrophic to the project, while anger acts in just the opposite way. If an immediate decision is essential, it is best to rely upon an unbiased third party for help before a course of action is selected and implemented.

THE DYNAMICS OF RISK

Risk is dynamic. Even though things were under control yesterday, there is no guarantee that anticipated or unanticipated risks might not materialize tomorrow. Thus, it is wise to conduct risk management as a routine part of the project's strategic and tactical planning stages. During the strategic planning stages, contingency planning takes the forefront in identifying the actions (along with their associated costs and resource impacts) that the project team will employ should a failure occur. Downstream, during the tactical planning and execution stages of the project, risk management is used to constantly monitor the project plan, project metrics, and the assumptions upon which the project plan is based. Then, should a failure occur, risk management is used to determine the potential impact of the failure on the project along with ways to minimize those impacts.

In essence, risk management involves inductive and deductive methodologies to predict and manage factors that could result in a project failure. Figure 11-3 illustrates the timing and application of each of these methodologies.

Inductive methods are used in the early stages of the project to ascertain what could fail. In essence, these are the preventive or proactive measures available to the project team. The objective is to identify potential failure modes; and then, through contingency planning, minimize their likelihood or impact on the project. Deductive methods are used to determine what could cause an implementation-side failure to occur so that actions can be put into place at any point in the project to minimize those potential causes.

Figure 11-4a demonstrates the numerous techniques that are available in a typical product or service development project; Figure 11-4b depicts a typical process improvement project.

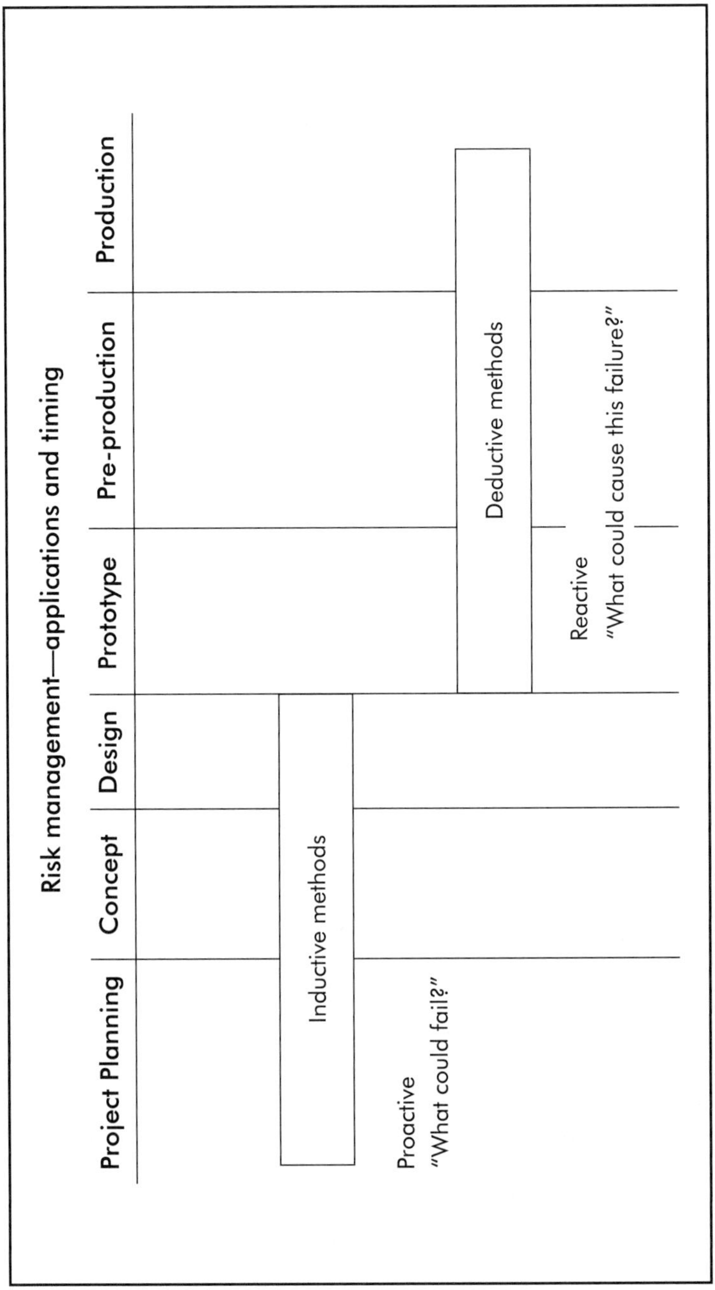

Risk management—applications and timing

Project Planning | Concept | Design | Prototype | Pre-production | Production

Inductive methods

Proactive
"What could fail?"

Deductive methods

Reactive
"What could cause this failure?"

Figure 11-3. Risk management involves inductive and deductive methodologies for predicting and managing factors that could bring about a project failure.

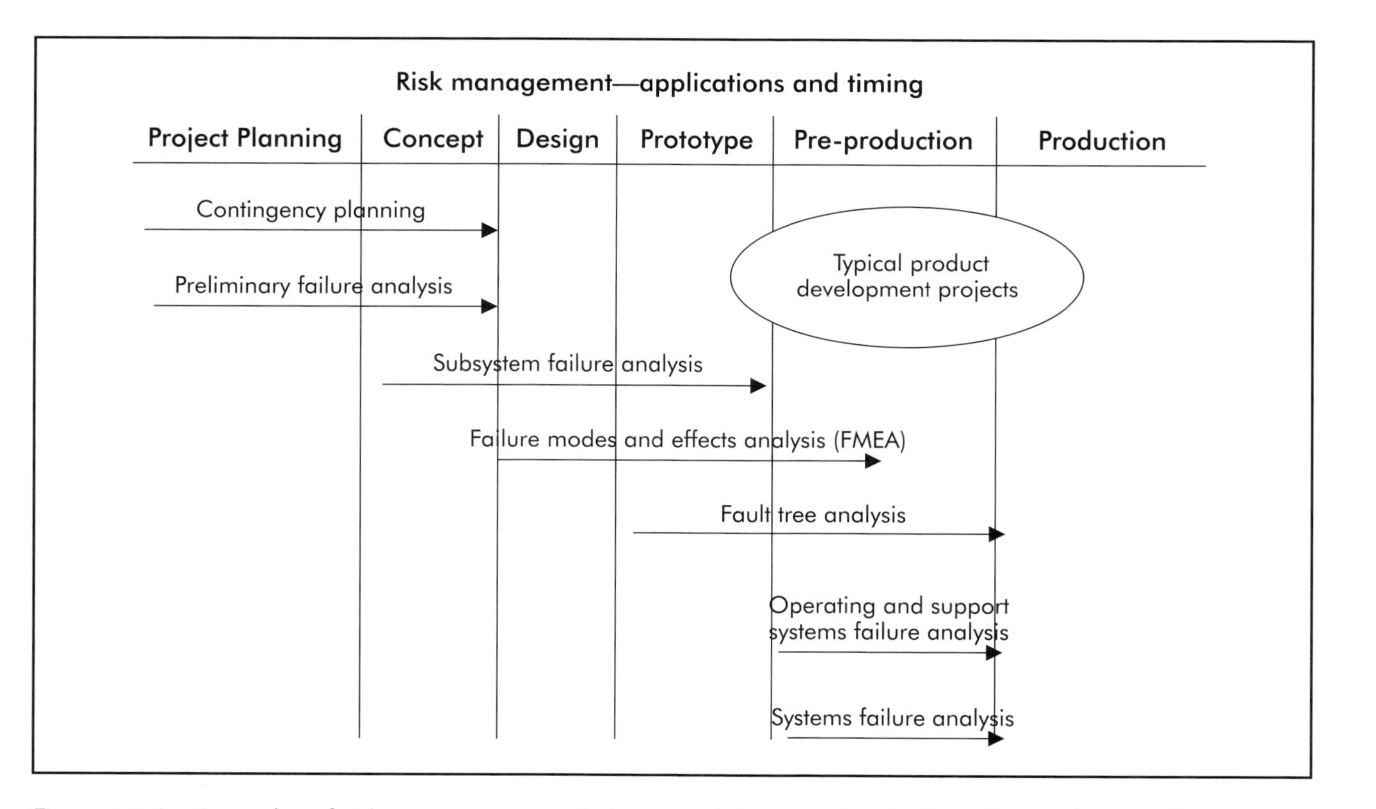

Figure 11-4a. Examples of risk management techniques and the stage in which each is implemented.

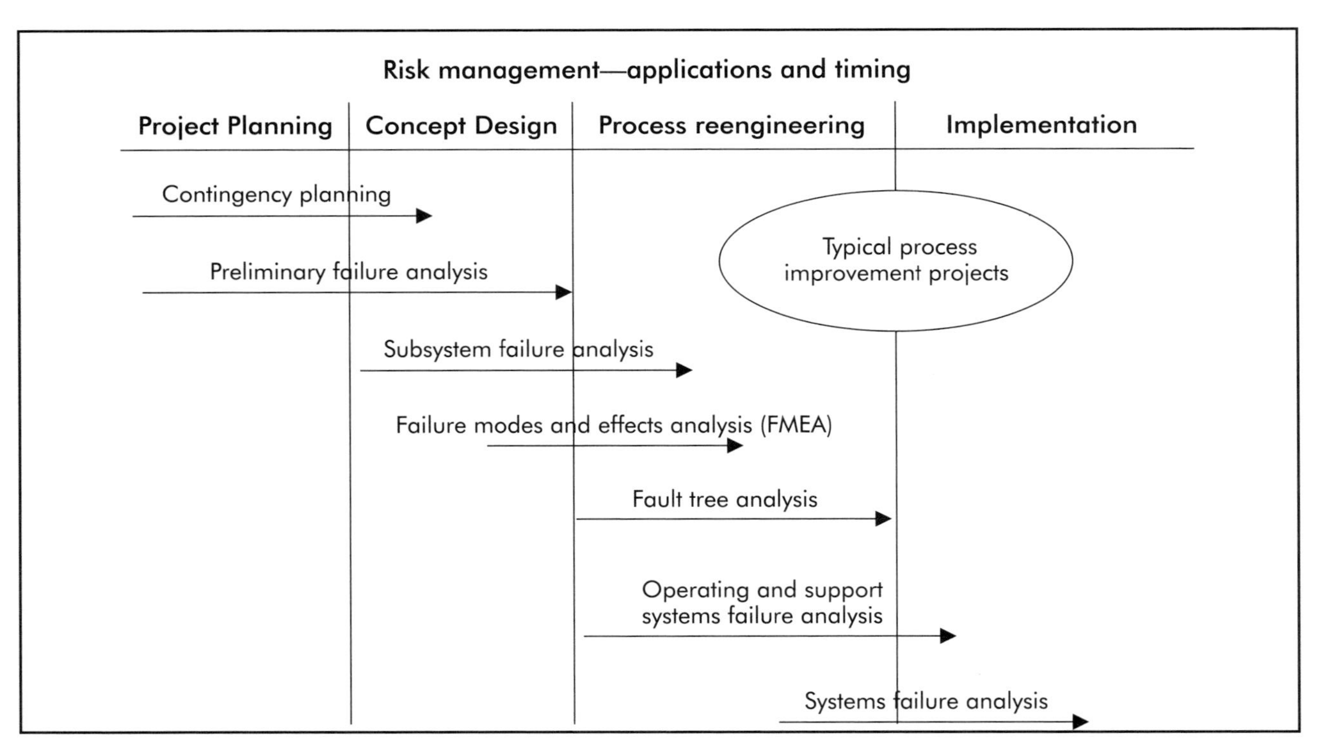

Figure 11-4b. Examples of risk management techniques and the stage in which each is implemented.

Failure Analyses . . . the Basis of Risk Management

Failure analysis is a systematic assessment of the various internal and external elements of a project, process, product, or service to identify existing or potential failure conditions. The intent is to identify and quantify risk elements to employ corrective actions in the most proactive manner possible given current project conditions and business constraints. The objective is to identify as many potential failure modes as are economically and technologically feasible given the time and budgetary constraints facing the project team. The project manager seeks to maintain control of the project by eliminating or minimizing the impact of the identified failure modes as early in the project planning cycle as possible. As with all project management actions, time is of the essence.

Risk Modeling

All failure analyses are based upon three fundamental risk factors:

1. the probability that a failure will occur;
2. the probability that the failure can be detected in sufficient time to minimize its impact on the project; and
3. the magnitude of the failure should it occur.

Risk, therefore, can be calculated for any potential failure mode through quantitative measures as follows:

$$R_P = P_O \times (1 - P_D) \times M_F \times 100 \quad \text{(eq. 11-1)}$$

where:

R_P = risk priority number (quantitative level of risk)
P_O = probability of occurrence
P_D = probability of detection
M_F = magnitude of failure

In many cases, project managers apply subjective measures to the risk factors. But using subjective factors on complex, bottom-line projects is simply not sufficient to ensure that the risk of a particular failure is accurately predicted and adequately addressed. Effective risk assessments are quantitative rather than qualitative. Thus, professional project managers apply quantitative measures like those in Table 11-2 to their risk management decisions.

Using the quantitative measures identified in Table 11-2, the project manager calculates the risk priority (R_P) number for each potential failure mode and then ranks them in descending value. More detailed failure analyses (preliminary failure analysis, failure modes and effects analysis, or fault failure analysis) are performed for failure modes with R_P values over 10. In these cases, re-scoping of the project and/or extensive contingency planning are also conducted as these levels of risk represent certain failure of the project without immediate corrective actions by the project manager to reduce the risk levels to values of one or less. Trade-off analyses (altering one or more of the project variables—schedule, budget, or performance) are performed for failure modes with R_P values between 1 and 10 as these levels are reflective of moderate to unacceptable levels of risk for the project. Again, in these cases, the project manager is required to immediately implement corrective actions to lower the risk levels to one or less. For failure modes with R_P values of less than 1, the levels of risk are acceptable. However, frequent monitoring by the project team is required.

Case Study Example

In this example, the project team was assigned to design a high-speed digital accelerometer for release to the customer on or before July 30. Based upon experience with other product design projects and knowledge of the current supplier base, the project team determined that several possible failure modes existed, which were necessary to include as part of the project's risk analysis. Those failure modes included:

1. The supplier will fail to deliver the needed components and assemblies on time to meet in-house production dates. Based on experience with this supplier, the probability is quite high that delivery will be late and the probability is low that the

Table 11-2. Quantitative measures for risk management decisions.

Probability of Occurrence (P_O)	Quantitative Value
Remote (occurrence unlikely)	1 in 1,000,000
Low	1 in 20,000
Low to medium	1 in 4,000
Medium (occasional failures)	1 in 1,000
Medium to high	1 in 400
High (repeated failures)	1 in 40
Very high (occurrence predictable)	1 in 2
Probability of Detection (P_D)	**Quantitative Value**
Remote (detection impossible)	Less than 1%
Very low (detection unlikely)	1% to 10%
Low	10% to 30%
Medium (detection possible)	30% to 50%
Medium to high	50% to 70%
High (good chance of detection)	70% to 90%
Very high (detection predictable)	90% to 100%
Magnitude of Failure Effect (M_F)	**Quantitative Value**
Minor (no measurable effect)	1
Low (slight effect only)	2 to 3
Moderate (customer will experience a moderate level of dissatisfaction)	4 to 6
High (high degree of customer dissatisfaction probable)	7 to 8
Very high (failure of the project in the customer's eyes is a given)	9 to 10

team will find out about it in advance. Further, if it does happen, the impact on the project is likely to be very high.

2. The supplier will fail to meet product specifications. Experience shows that the risk is medium to high that this will

occur. If the supplier fails to meet specifications, however, there is a high likelihood that it will be caught early. If the discrepancy is not caught, the impact on the project will be very high.

3. The supplier will miss cost targets. This is a medium to high probability with a medium to high likelihood that the overrun will be detected in advance. The impact on margin will be high if it does occur, however.
4. The product fails reliability testing. This is a low to medium probability given the supplier's quality systems and statistical process control (SPC) techniques. Nevertheless, if it does occur, the impact will be moderate due to the robustness that was built in. The bad news is that the probability of detection is low.
5. The product fails accelerated life testing. This, too, is a low probability with a moderate impact should it occur. Again, the level of robustness that was built in should handle moderate swings in product characteristics. As before, there is a low probability of detecting it in advance. Maybe not knowing is good?
6. The product could prove to be unproducible during prototyping. The likelihood of detection of this failure is medium to high based upon design of experiments (DOE) and repeatability and reliability (R&R) analyses, but it is still of concern. The probability of occurrence is low and the impact minor because there would be time to react prior to production, and there is a parallel design in the works just in case.
7. Internal product cost targets could be missed. Experience shows the probability of this occurrence is high. There is a poor record of accuracy in predicting internal costs. Detection is medium to high, but probably on the lower range of the scale. The impact could be moderate, as there is a significant margin built in just in case.
8. Production capacity may not be sufficient to meet actual demand for the product. Based on the ability to go to a third shift, the impact of this would likely be low, and there would

be a high likelihood of detecting it with sufficient warning to make the necessary arrangements. And, since there is enough experience in this area, the probability is only low to medium that it would occur.

9. The product might not be completed in time for the scheduled prototype run. Here, the probability is very high given past problems with production and its associated tooling. The problem is that the probability of detecting the failure is low. The impact on the project will be moderate because additional resources will be thrown at the problem to get back to the scheduled production dates.
10. The product will not be ready for production as scheduled. Now this is a big one, with a very high likelihood that it could occur. If it does, the impact on the project will be severe. There is a high likelihood that it will be detected in advance, but it would still make things unpleasant.
11. The sales and marketing literature will not be ready on time to support shipments. This happens occasionally and the impact is typically low because there is the ability to respond quickly with in-house publications staff. There is a high likelihood that a miss in this area will be detected.
12. The price books will not be ready for distribution to the retail outlets prior to initiation of shipments as requested. This, too, happens occasionally and even though the impact on the project is only moderate, the retailers will not be happy about it. However, there is a good chance that the failure would be detected with sufficient warning.

Table 11-3 outlines the preceding data for comparison.

To better understand the risk management actions that will be taken, the project team lists the possible failure modes by descending value so that the actions required by the project team can be categorized. The results are outlined in Table 11-4.

The action plans defined in Table 11-4 illustrate the project team's approach to eliminate or, at the very minimum, reduce the likelihood of the identified failures through effective, proactive contingency planning. If an analysis of the corrective action reveals that the R_P value is not sufficiently reduced, then the project team

Table 11-3. Failure mode analysis.

Failure Mode	P_O	P_D	M_F	R_P
Supplier fails to deliver on time	0.5000	0.25	9	337.50
Supplier fails to meet specifications	0.0030	0.90	9	0.30
Supplier fails to hit cost targets	0.0030	0.50	7	1.10
Product fails reliability testing	0.0003	0.10	6	0.16
Product fails accelerated life testing	0.0001	0.25	6	0.05
Product design proves unproducible during prototype run	0.0001	0.70	10	0.03
Product cost targets not met	0.0300	0.50	6	9.00
Production capacity insufficient to meet expected demand	0.0003	0.80	3	0.02
Product not ready for prototype run	0.5000	0.25	6	225.00
Product not ready for scheduled production	0.5000	0.20	9	360.00
Product sales literature not ready	0.0010	0.80	3	0.06
Product price books not ready	0.0010	0.80	4	0.08

P_O = probability of occurrence P_D = probability of detection
M_F = magnitude of failure R_P = risk priority number

Table 11-4. Failure modes by descending value.

Failure Mode	R_P	Action Plan	Assigned
Product not ready for scheduled production	360.00	Monitor daily	Design engineering
Supplier fails to deliver on time	337.50	New source	Buyer
Product not ready for prototype run	225.00	Monitor daily	Design
Product cost targets not met	9.00	Monitor weekly	Cost
Supplier fails to hit target costs	1.10	Monitor weekly	Buyer
Supplier fails to meet specifications	0.30	Monitor weekly	Buyer
Product fails reliability testing	0.16	Failure mode and effects analysis (FMEA)/redesign	Design
Product price books not ready	0.08	Monitor monthly	Marketing
Product sales literature not ready	0.06	Outsource	Marketing
Product fails accelerated life test	0.05	FMEA/redesign	Design
Product design proves unproducible during prototype run	0.03	Value analysis/ redesign	Manufacturing engineering
Production capacity insufficient to meet expected demand	0.02	Outsource	Manufacturing engineering

R_P = risk priority number

will seek other, less risky, alternatives. This "before-and-after" method of risk assessment ensures that the project team is on the right track.

Criticality and Risk

In addition to the risk priority (R_p) number that was reviewed earlier in this chapter, there is another primary index used to measure and quantify risk. It is known as the *risk criticality index* (RCI). The RCI was initially developed for use in the aerospace, defense, and nuclear industries to measure risk. In this application, risk is considered a function of the severity of a potential failure mode and its probability of occurrence. The severity categories defined in Table 11-5 are used with this risk management methodology.

The failure probability index categories are defined in Table 11-6.

From the two indices, regions of acceptable and unacceptable risk are defined. Any failure mode that falls within the unacceptable region of risk requires further analysis and corrective action by the project team. Risks that fall into the acceptable region require careful and consistent monitoring to ensure that they remain acceptable as conditions surrounding the project change. Project and business environments are dynamic. No amount of good planning can offset poor follow-through on the part of the project manager and his team.

Figure 11-5 illustrates the risk criticality index methodology.

Figure 11-6 shows a typical RCI example taken from the trucking industry. The example represents an actual analysis of a

Table 11-5. Risk criticality index severity categories.

Category	Definition
I. Catastrophic	A failure of severe magnitude all but guaranteeing that the project will fail
II. Critical	A serious failure that will cause a major impact on one or more of the project variables
III. Marginal	A moderate failure that can lead to difficulties if not addressed in a timely manner
IV. Minor	A minor failure that can be addressed with normal project management maintenance procedures

Table 11-6. Failure probability index categories.

Category	Definition
Frequent probability (level A)	High probability (>20%) during the life of the project
Moderate probability (level B)	Moderate probability (10–20%) during the life of the project
Infrequent (level C)	Occasional probability of occurrence (1–10%) during the project cycle
Remote (level D)	Unlikely probability of occurrence (0.1–1.0%) during the project cycle
Extremely remote (level E)	Extremely rare occurrence during the project cycle (<0.1%)

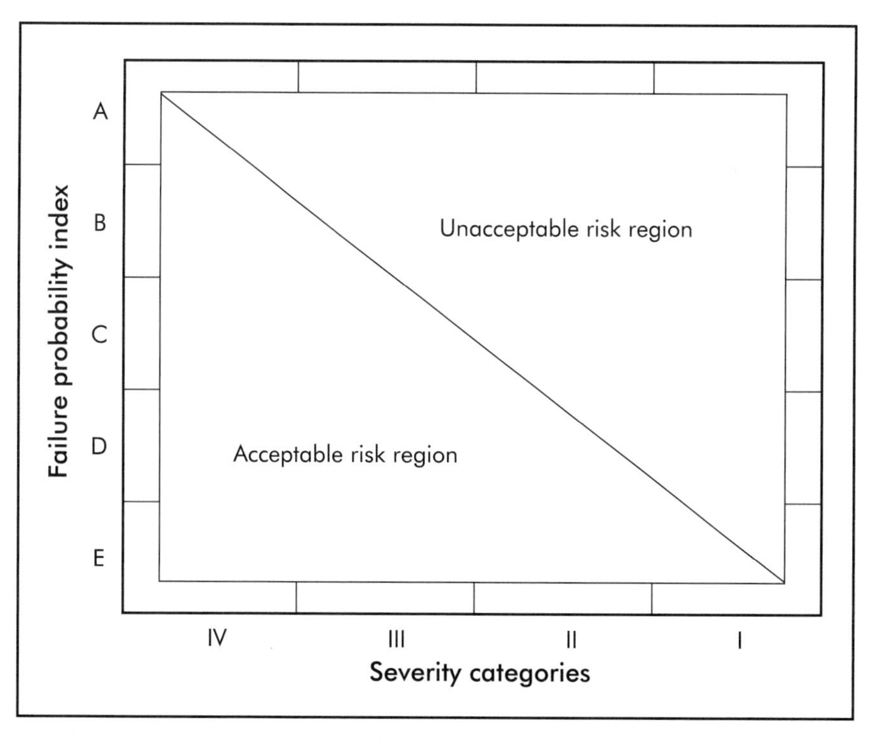

Figure 11-5. Risk criticality index methodology.

Risk Criticality Index	Effect of Brake System Failure	Repair Costs	Repair Time	Failure Probability Index A	B	C	D	E
Catastrophic I	Death likely—driver and others	$250,000 total loss	>6 months					
Critical II	Severe injury or death—driver and others	$150,000–250,000 major repairs	4–6 months					
Marginal III	Minor injury—driver primarily, others possible	$50,000–150,000 drive train repairs	1–4 months					
Minor IV	No injury to driver or others	$5,000—50,000 body work	<1 month					

Imperative that the risk be lowered through brake system DOE and FMEA activities

Back-up system controls to be added to reduce risk to acceptable levels

Current design acceptable—place maintenance instructions and warning label in owner's manual

Figure 11-6. This example of RCI shows an actual analysis of a potential braking system failure for a large truck.

potential braking system failure on a Class-8 diesel truck produced by a well-known truck manufacturer.

As shown in Figure 11-6, any potential failure mode that falls within the region of unacceptable risk is tagged for immediate corrective action by the project team to bring it to an acceptable level. Marginal region failure modes are also tagged for corrective action, although they receive a secondary priority and are typically less complex than those in the unacceptable region. Normal project management follow-up is then exercised for potential failure modes that fall into the region of acceptable risk.

RCI and R_p methodologies are the basis of most, if not all, of the more popular risk management techniques used in industry.

Preliminary Failure Analyses

Preliminary failure analysis (PFA) takes a 20,000-ft (6,096-m) view of the project to determine whether or not a more comprehensive analysis is warranted. In essence, this is a risk assessment that occurs early in the project planning cycle to evaluate the controls that have been put into place by the project manager to monitor:

- project variables (schedule, deliverable/performance, and budget);
- performance of the project team in meeting obligations and expectations;
- assumptions made by the project team and their continued validity; and
- any internal or external constraints or influences that could negatively impact the project variables.

Preliminary failure analyses (see Figure 11-7) are used for the initial go/no-go decision process early in the project life cycle as more definition of the project scope and approach are determined. PFA's typically include a definition of the potential project failure modes; areas of impact on the project the failure modes introduce; their probabilities, magnitudes, and risks; the corrective actions planned by the project team along with the associated risks introduced by the corrective actions; an implementation plan; and

Project title: ______________ Project number: ______________

Project manager: ______________ Date: ______________

Potential Failure(s)	Consequences					Risk (Before)				Corrective Actions	Risk (After)			
	Budget	Schedule	Deliverable	Safety	Other	P_O	P_D	M_F	R_P		P_O	P_D	M_F	R_P

Prepared by: ______________ Date completed: ______________

Figure 11-7. Preliminary failure analysis includes a definition of the potential failure modes, their probabilities and risks, possible corrective actions, the implementation plan, and an ongoing assessment of the results of corrective actions.

an ongoing assessment of the corrective action results to ensure compliance with project expectations.

The obvious intent of the preliminary failure analysis is to identify and quantify the overall level of risk (R_P) of an identified potential failure mode. This will allow the project team to isolate corrective actions or contingency plans that will reduce the risk to an acceptable level, as measured by the R_P value, *both before and after* the corrective action has been implemented. The greatest value the PFA provides is that it forces the team to evaluate the effects of corrective actions prior to implementation. If, for example, the corrective actions proposed by the project team generate only minor or no improvement in R_P value when it is recalculated after application of the corrective action, then the project team is well advised to seek other alternatives. If the level of R_P is significantly reduced, but still not to acceptable levels, then the project team adds secondary corrective actions to reduce the risk levels further. In some cases (unfortunately, this is common), the corrective actions proposed by the project team actually make the risk levels higher. Again, the PFA provides proactive guidance for the project team so that other actions can be taken to avoid the introduction of additional risk to the project. This "pre-post" perspective makes the PFA one of the most useful of the risk management tools available.

If there is a single given in the business world today, it is simply this: business executives are, by nature, risk adverse.

One final point is worthy of mention regarding the PFA. The calculation of the R_P incorporates three factors: the probability of occurrence, the probability of detection, and the magnitude of failure. The initial corrective actions typically considered by project teams address only one of these factors, the probability of occurrence. In most cases, to bring the level of risk down to acceptable levels, the team will be required to initiate corrective actions to address each of the other two factors as well. Simply attacking one of the factors versus all three will rarely bring the risk down to acceptable levels.

Subsystem Failure Analyses

Subsystem failure analysis is a technique utilized by project managers for expanding the preliminary failure analysis to address specific failures within subsystem elements or associated operations. In essence, it focuses the project manager and his team on those elements within the support and subsystems that could potentially be problematic so that specific, rather than general, corrective actions can be employed.

The format for subsystem failure analysis is similar to the preliminary failure analysis for most business and service projects. For product development projects, however, more specific formats are typically employed, such as fault failure analyses, failure modes and effects analyses (FMEA), or fault tree analyses. Each technique is useful in examining the effects of environmental and operational constraints on the project, procedures and policies, personnel performance and productivity, as well as equipment, facilities, and maintenance.

Fault Failure Analysis

Fault failure analysis is one form of subsystem failure analysis. It seeks to identify specific component failure modes, their causes, and their impacts on the subsystems of the project. An inductive approach, fault failure analysis seeks the answer to the question: "If this failure occurs, what will be the impact on the project?" Of particular note, as a personnel-focused methodology, fault failure analysis is often utilized to identify those failure modes that could result in an accident or potential personal injury.

The fault failure analysis format (see Figure 11-8) differs to some degree from that of the preliminary failure analysis in that it focuses the project manager on the component level where specific failures are most likely to occur. Further, it pinpoints specific operational modes that often contribute to the failure; external factors that could exaggerate, mitigate, or influence the failure mode; as well as any potential subsystem impacts that must be considered as part of any corrective action.

Fault failure analysis							
Component	Failure Mode	Operational Mode	Effect on Subsystem	External Factors	Influences	Risk (R_P)	Corrective Action

Figure 11-8. Fault failure analysis identifies specific component failure modes, their causes, and their impacts on the project's subsystems.

Figure 11-9 is an example of fault failure analysis taken from the airline industry after a recent crash involving a commercial airliner and a flock of birds. The component under analysis is an engine fan blade. In this example, each failure mode is described, dissected, and then assessed from various perspectives. The R_P value is the driver that signals the project team of the importance of initiating preventive measures to address this potential failure mode. As with all other risk management techniques, potential failure modes with high R_P values (greater than 1.0) must be addressed as early as possible to prevent the failure from occurring. Waiting until the failure occurs before initiating action is simply poor project management, and in cases like this, potentially deadly.

Failure Mode and Effects Analysis

Like fault failure analysis, failure modes and effects analysis (FMEA) is an inductive methodology that focuses on component failures, their causes, and their impacts on the project. FMEA not only seeks to identify the results should a component failure occur, but it also assesses the risks associated with that failure. FMEA techniques concentrate on those failure modes that will likely result in a complete failure of the project. Unlike fault failure analyses, however, FMEA is typically more equipment and product focused than personnel focused.

Even though the format (see Figure 11-10) appears tailored for technical projects, it can just as easily be applied to general business projects.

With FMEA, too, the R_P value sets the priority for action by the project team. It is always a good idea to test the R_P value before and after the corrective action is taken to ensure that the selected actions effectively reduce it to an acceptable level.

Figure 11-11 shows the application of FMEA in a business setting. The project in this example was to develop a new accounts receivable module as part of a major systems integration project. The project team assessed several potential failure modes based upon the prior experience of internal and external systems analysts. The corrective actions initiated by the project team were prioritized according to the R_P value, with the tax tables set as

Fault Failure Analysis							
Component	Failure Mode	Optional Mode	Effect on Subsystem	External Factors	Influences	Risk (R_P)	Corrective Action
Fan blade	Break	Take-off	Severe damage to engine Loss of all power likely Renders the engine unusable Loss of lift during critical operation	Weather Birds Temperature Debris Revolutions per minute	Materials Quality Maintenance Stress Load Temperature Design	57.5	Change to composite materials with increased tensile and shock load strength Alter design to accept material changes Apply localized electronic measures as bird deterrent

Figure 11-9. An example of fault failure analysis taken from the airline industry.

FMEA

Project: ____________________

FMEA number: ____________________ Date: ____________________

Item or Activity	Function	Failure Modes	Failure Causes	Failure Effects	Failure Detection	Risk (R_P)	Corrective Actions

Prepared by: ____________________ Date corrective actions implemented: ____________________

Figure 11-10. The failure modes and effects analysis format.

Project: New accounts receivable (A/R) module

FMEA number: 2345 Date: 3-1-XX

FMEA

Item or Activity	Function	Failure Modes	Failure Causes	Failure Effects	Failure Detection	Risk (R_p)	Corrective Actions
A/R module design	A/R tie-in to general ledger accounts	Loses date codes	Job control language (JCL) errors	Loss of tracking on A/R	A/R aging report—manual audit	55.7	Recode JCL with self-audit capability
		Loses invoice number	General ledger interface code(s) wrong	Loss of system recognition and update	Invoice log—manual audit	67.8	Recode JCL with fail-safe numerical issue
		Fails to account for local sales taxes	Tax tables missing or wrong	Internal Revenue Service and state underpayments	Manual calculation at month-end close	88.9	Add tax tables and set for quarterly updates to tax codes

Prepared by: G. Smith Date corrective actions implemented: __________

Figure 11-11. An example of FMEA in a business setting.

the number one priority, followed by numerical sequence codes, and then self-audit capabilities for the module.

In addition to the FMEA in Figure 11-11 utilized by the project team, a software failure analysis was also employed to review the software, hardware, system operator, and user interfaces to identify potential failure modes associated with each of the system elements. The software failure analysis was also used to analyze possible implementation failure modes, the logic flow diagrams of the system, and the potential impacts of anticipated system design changes. This specialty version of the FMEA technique is illustrative of how many project teams and many organizations have customized the various risk modeling techniques to suit their own specific internal needs and operating environments.

No amount of internal control can offset purely random events.

The typical FMEA format is applicable for software failure analyses, operating and support system failure analyses, process failure analyses, and system failure analyses in addition to the typical product failure analyses.

CASE STUDY EXERCISE

You have just been assigned the role of project manager for Alliance Telecommunication's new "Second Line Promo" project. The intent of the project is to capture a 20% growth in customer telephone line usage by offering an incentive to the customers to order a second telephone line for their homes to accommodate increased DSL-based Internet usage. Market studies have indicated that the infrastructure costs for installing cable in the targeted rural areas is not feasible, making DSL the only option for these customers. Marketing anticipates that 10% revenue growth is a probable outcome from the project, and senior management is eager to get the project implemented by early next year for maximum financial impact in the upcoming fiscal year. This gives the project team just 10 months to complete the project.

The risks to the corporation from this project are high given the local competition and overhead costs: project failure is likely to cause a market share loss of up to 35%, with corresponding revenue losses of 28% impacting earnings before taxes (EBT) by up to 54%.

A number of possible failure modes have been identified through an initial brainstorming session taking into consideration historical data on previous projects that the company has undertaken. Based upon that data, you have assigned numbers relative to the likelihood of those failures occurring, as well as their potential impacts on the project.

You have decided to conduct a preliminary failure analysis to determine actions that should be taken in the short and long term to minimize the risk of failure. The data is summarized in Figure 11-12.

You and your project team are requested to:

- prepare a preliminary failure analysis for senior management to review the risks and actions that the team anticipates before a final go-ahead is given for the project; and
- prepare a risk criticality index analysis illustrating all potential failure modes for the board of directors of the local public utility district who oversees the organization's operations in this region.

Based upon the data available, the results you have compiled are outlined in Figures 11-13 through 11-15.

The risks associated with the failure modes identified in the initial analysis were reduced successfully—with the exception of the calculation of demand by Marketing. The risk criticality and the preliminary failure analysis both indicate that more work is needed to ensure that this failure mode is reduced still further. You and the project team should review the recommended corrective action a second time to determine if other actions will reduce the risk to acceptable levels. If the determination is made that no further corrective action is capable of greater risk reduction, then you, as project manager, should initiate parallel actions. Put in place contingency plans that can be immediately

Potential Failure Modes	P_O	P_D	M_F	Risk Criticality Category
Inaccurate calculation of current capacity from Engineering	35%	10%	High	Critical
Inaccurate calculation of forecasted demand from Marketing	50%	2%	Very High	Catastrophic
Inability of Engineering to respond with new software specifications	5%	95%	Moderate	Marginal
Inability of Engineering to respond with new hardware specifications	20%	90%	High	Critical
Inability of suppliers to provide additional switch hardware on time	86%	20%	Very High	Catastrophic
Inability of suppliers to provide additional trunk hardware on time	10%	75%	Moderate	Minor
Inability to get funding approval for new capital equipment	25%	98%	Very High	Catastrophic
Potential Failure Modes	**Budget Impact**	**Scheduled Impact**	**Delivered Impact**	**Legal Impact**
Inaccurate calculation of current capacity from Engineering	Yes	Yes	No	Yes
Inaccurate calculation of forecasted demand from Marketing	Yes	Yes	Yes	Yes
Inability of Engineering to respond with new software specifications	No	Yes	No	No
Inability of Engineering to respond with new hardware specifications	Yes	Yes	Yes	Yes
Inability of suppliers to provide additional switch hardware on time	No	Yes	Yes	Yes
Inability of suppliers to provide additional trunk hardware on time	No	Yes	No	No
Inability to get funding approval for new capital equipment	Yes	Yes	Yes	No

Figure 11-12. Preliminary risk analysis for "Second Line Promo" project.

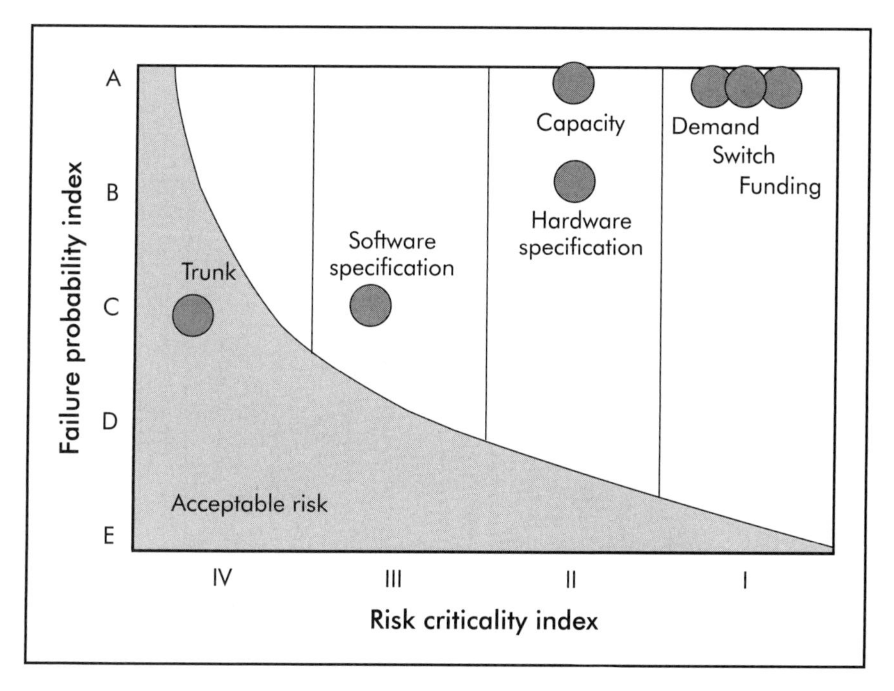

Figure 11-13. Criticality index for "Second Line Promo" project.

launched in the event that Marketing fails to accurately predict the market demand.

RISK VERSUS SAFETY

Whatever the risk management methodology, the cost impact of an accident or personal injury resulting from a project failure is always considered. While most of these costs are tangible, some are intangible until an accident occurs. Several of the most common safety-related costs associated with project management are outlined in the following list. It represents many, but by no means all, of the tangible and intangible costs relating to personal injury.

Typical tangible costs include:

- death, injury, or shock to a customer or employee;
- costs of rescue and medical personnel;

Project title: Alliance Second Line Promo — Project number: 98-456

Project manager: S. L. Edwards — Date: 9-18-XX

Potential Failure(s)	Consequences					Risk (Before)				Corrective Actions	Risk (After)			
	Budget	Schedule	Deliverable	Safety	Other	P_O	P_D	M_F	R_P		P_O	P_D	M_F	R_P
Inaccurate capacity calculation	Y	Y	N		Y	35%	10%	8	252	Conduct IE capacity study	10%	95%	3	1.50
Inaccurate demand calculation	Y	Y	Y		Y	50%	2%	10	490	Conduct focus group and VOC; match expansion to actual demand patterns; review weekly and adjust	10%	90%	5	5.00
New software specifications	N	Y	N		N	5%	95%	6	1.5	Outsource to second source	5%	95%	2	0.50
New hardware specifications	Y	Y	Y		Y	20%	90%	8	16	Add five systems engineers	5%	95%	3	0.75
Availability of switch hardware	N	Y	Y		Y	86%	20%	10	688	Order from second source and increase safety stocks	10%	95%	3	1.50
Availability of trunk hardware	N	Y	N		N	10%	75%	6	15	Order from second source and increase safety stocks	10%	95%	3	1.50
Funding approval	Y	Y	Y		N	25%	98%	10	5	Obtain preliminary approval and fund by phase based upon actual demand	5%	95%	2	0.50

Prepared by: S. L. Edwards — Date completed: 10-22-XX

Figure 11-14. Preliminary failure analysis identifying possible corrective actions.

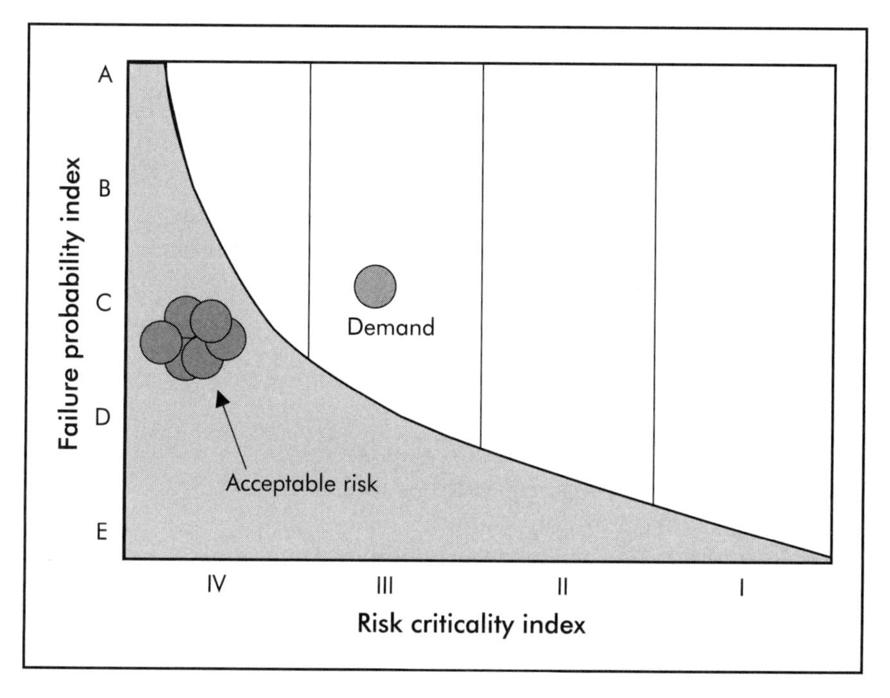

Figure 11-15. Criticality index.

- hospital and ambulatory costs;
- disability costs;
- rehabilitation costs;
- lost time of an employee or customer;
- pension for an employee or customer;
- retraining an employee or customer;
- productivity costs (loss of) for an employee or customer;
- death benefits and funeral expenses for an employee or customer;
- repair of property, equipment, facilities, or materials;
- replacement of property, equipment, facilities, or materials;
- recovery or salvage costs;
- obsolescence costs;
- accident reporting and investigation costs;

- corrective action costs to address the root cause of the failure;
- warranty costs, field campaigns, or product recalls;
- litigation and the cost of preparation;
- data collection costs;
- settlement costs with victims and their families;
- loss of income for the victims and their families;
- increased insurance rates; and
- contingent liability costs and penalties.

Typical intangible costs:

- market share loss;
- loss of business reputation and goodwill;
- lower employee morale and productivity;
- lower consumer confidence;
- loss of market or competitive advantage; and
- creation of a culture where failure is expected and accepted.

Case Study Example

Another example illustrates how the level of risk impacts the insurance premiums that an insurance company charges its policyholders on a home. Have you ever wondered how the premiums are determined? In most cases, the insurance companies calculate the probability of a loss and its associated costs (impacts) in much the same way as discussed earlier in this chapter. For a relatively new home in the hurricane belt of southern Florida, for example, the insurance company assesses the insurance premiums based on the risk of property loss. Factors like the type of construction, location, hurricane damage protection, and even the number of trees in the yard come into play. The insurance company objectively assesses the probability of a hurricane hitting the home based on historical data and meteorological trends for the area. The amount of damage that the home would likely sustain should a hurricane hit is estimated, ranging from only minor repairs to a total loss.

Prevention is always less costly than failure.

Table 11-7 considers the probability of everything from a minor crack in a window to a complete loss of the home. The amount of projected damage is categorized in probability ranges, then averages.

The statistical exposure or liability of the insurance company is calculated as the summation of the average costs times their probability of occurrence,

$$Exposure = \Sigma A_C (P_O) \quad \text{(eq. 11-2)}$$

where:

A_C = average costs
P_O = probability of occurrence

From Table 11-7, the exposure cost to the insurance company is calculated to be $8,375 considering all possibilities. The exposure cost is then multiplied by the probability of a hurricane

Table 11-7. Average exposure of hurricane damage for home in southern Florida.

Amount of Damage	A_C	P_O	$(A_C \times P_O)$
$1–1,000	$500	10.0%	$50
$1,000–10,000	$5,500	75.0%	$4,125
$10,000–20,000	$15,000	7.0%	$1,050
$20,000–30,000	$25,000	3.0%	$750
$30,000–40,000	$35,000	2.0%	$700
$40,000–50,000	$45,000	1.5%	$675
$50,000–60,000	$55,000	0.5%	$275
$60,000–70,000	$65,000	0.4%	$260
$70,000–80,000	$75,000	0.3%	$225
$80,000–90,000	$85,000	0.2%	$170
$90,000–100,000	$95,000	0.1%	$95
Total			$8,375

A_C = average cost P_O = probability of occurrence

hitting the area in the upcoming period. If the probability of a hurricane striking the area is 10% for the upcoming period, then the premium the insurance company will charge is $837.50 ($8,375× 10%) for that period.

After several years of premiums paid without claim incidence and no changes in historical storm patterns or severity, the insurance company is covered, statistically speaking. But then, there are occasionally those storms like Katrina, and all bets are off!

Legal Considerations

Ignoring the legal risks associated with project management is foolish. To begin this section, following are definitions of some terms from *Black's Law Dictionary* (Black 1991), which are applicable to many projects.

- a *liability* is an obligation to rectify any injury or damage for which the organization or project manager is deemed responsible, or for the failure of a project, product, or service to meet a specified warranty or guarantee;
- an *express warranty* is a statement by a project manager or provider, either written or verbal, in which a product or service is claimed to be suitable for a specific purpose, will perform in a certain way, or contains specific characteristics or capabilities; and
- an *implied warranty* is the implication by a project manager, manufacturer, dealer, or distributor that a given product or service is suitable for a specific purpose by advertising it for that purpose, selling it for that purpose, or indicating in operating instructions that it will accomplish that purpose.

Thus, when making either written or verbal commitments to customers or project sponsors, the astute project manager is keenly aware that those statements will be taken literally in a court of law.

Employee and Customer Safety

Every project manager must exercise due care concerning the safety of employees and customers. This implies that the project manager takes the same care that a reasonably prudent person or organization would exercise under the same or similar circumstances. It is somewhat of a judgment call, but commonsense will suffice under most circumstances. When in doubt, the wise project manager seeks advice from corporate counsel before deciding on a final course of action.

The experienced project manager also considers the impact of a failure, or an accident resulting from that failure, on rescue personnel. The law states that any foreseeable action that places a rescue worker in peril can be considered negligence on the part of the project manager or her organization.

In most cases, a project manager or an organization will not be held liable for actions resulting in personal injury or property damage if the dangers or risks associated with those actions could not have been reasonably anticipated. However, logic does not always prevail over a good lawyer, as was proven in the case against McDonalds involving the hot coffee. In all cases, a project manager and her organization must demonstrate due care in the design and manufacture of a product to avoid exposing an employee or customer to potential injury, death, or property damage.

If products or services contain or impose an inherent danger to employees or customers, then the project manager must employ reasonable diligence in warning them of those dangers. That is why warning stickers are pasted all over the inside of sport utility vehicles, as well as the outside of cigarette packages. Project managers in the pharmaceutical industry are forced to address this issue with each new product. But regardless of the industry, it is a legal requirement that cannot be overlooked.

The law states that any organization that maintains, stores, or transports hazardous or dangerous items or substances can be held liable for any injury or damage that results from those items, even if due care was exercised by the organization and it was not at fault. However, if the dangers associated with the use or consumption of a product or service are well known to the general public, then the provider is not required to warn employees and consumers.

Still another spin on this legal issue is that any retailer, wholesaler, or distributor must exercise reasonable care in the preservation and handling of the products that they offer to ensure that those products will not cause injury to their customers at a later date. This is why grocery stores rotate their perishable products on a regular basis, as do pharmacies.

If a product is produced with zero defects and performs within expected limitations, is it considered safe? Actually, there are a number of factors that can change the answer to this to "no." Typical factors that can render a safe product dangerous include human error, using a product in the wrong application, environmental factors, or simply the hazardous nature of the product itself. For example, if the project team develops a new ice pick that contains a thermal core to heat the blade for easier penetration, is that a guarantee that a customer might not stab his own hand with it? There is no such thing as "perfect safety." It is an excellent goal and definitely one that every project manager seeks to achieve. But reality prevails, forcing the project manager to take the necessary precautions.

DEDUCTIVE METHODOLOGIES

Deductive methodologies are those that focus on identifying the root causes of failures during the implementation phases of the project. These are downstream techniques that, by their nature, are reactive as well as proactive. While their main focus is on eliminating implementation-side failures, they are also used to minimize the impact of failures should they occur. Much like a root cause analysis, deductive methodologies seek to identify the root cause of a failure, the chain of events that led up to the failure, and the relationships between those events. Deductive methods concentrate on identifying the probability of failure occurrence and its impact on the project, as well as the corrective actions that can be taken by the project manager to minimize the impact on the project and the likelihood of reoccurrence.

Case Study 1

The following is an example that illustrates the application of deductive risk management techniques. You are leaving work one evening, and find that your car will not start. Before you can fix the car, you must first decide why it will not start. Using the Boolean logic relationships of deductive failure analysis, you quickly prepare a fault tree like the one shown in Figure 11-16. This, by the way, is exactly what the electronic system analyzers at the dealerships do to isolate a system fault in a vehicle.

To use the fault tree, you begin at the bottom of the shortest chain, eliminating each lower cause of the failure until the true root cause is identified and confirmed. Then the appropriate corrective action is initiated to get the car started. Had the Boolean relationships not been developed, any action taken would have simply been a shot in the dark. Maybe the car would have started, but maybe you would have missed dinner.

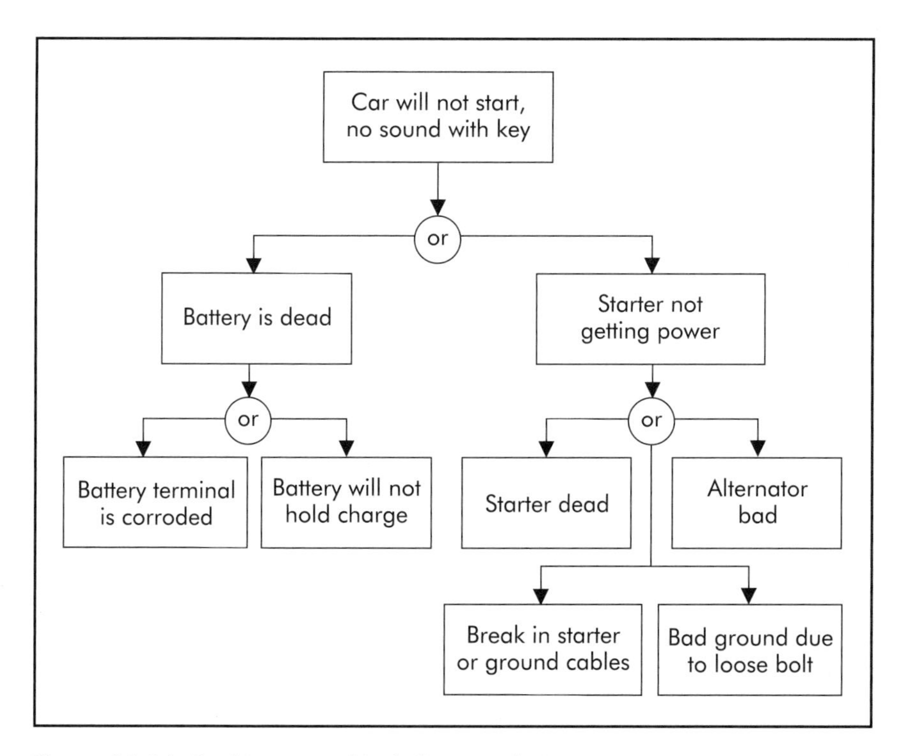

Figure 11-16. Fault tree used in failure analysis.

Case Study 2

A car rental company assigns a project manager the task of ascertaining the expected costs from various potential accidents so that the company can build those costs into their rental fees to avoid unexpected out-of-pocket costs later in the year.

The project manager begins by identifying the failure modes that have been experienced in the past, and then listing them along with the costs to the company (see Table 11-8).

Next, the project team creates a fault tree analysis to determine the relationships between various failure modes (see Figure 11-17). Also determined are the costs (magnitude of failure) and probabilities associated with each failure mode in the fault tree (see Figure 11-18). Next, each probability and impact are summed to arrive at a total exposure of $59,450. Given that an accident occurs only once in every 10,000 rentals, the company will charge $5.95 per rental day as part of the fee to cover their exposure.

Table 11-8. Rental car failure modes.

Action	Result
Rental car hits or is hit by another vehicle	No personal injury
Rental car hits or is hit by another vehicle	Personal injury
Rental car hits personal property	Causes damage
Rental car is damaged	No other vehicle or personal property involved
Rental car hits a pedestrian	Injury or death
Action	**Cost of a Failure**
Hitting another vehicle/cost to repair other vehicle	$15,000
Passenger injury, damage to rental car or second vehicle	$100,000
Repair of rented vehicle	$10,000
Damage to personal property (excluding repairs on rental car)	$25,000
Hitting a pedestrian causing injury or death	$50,000

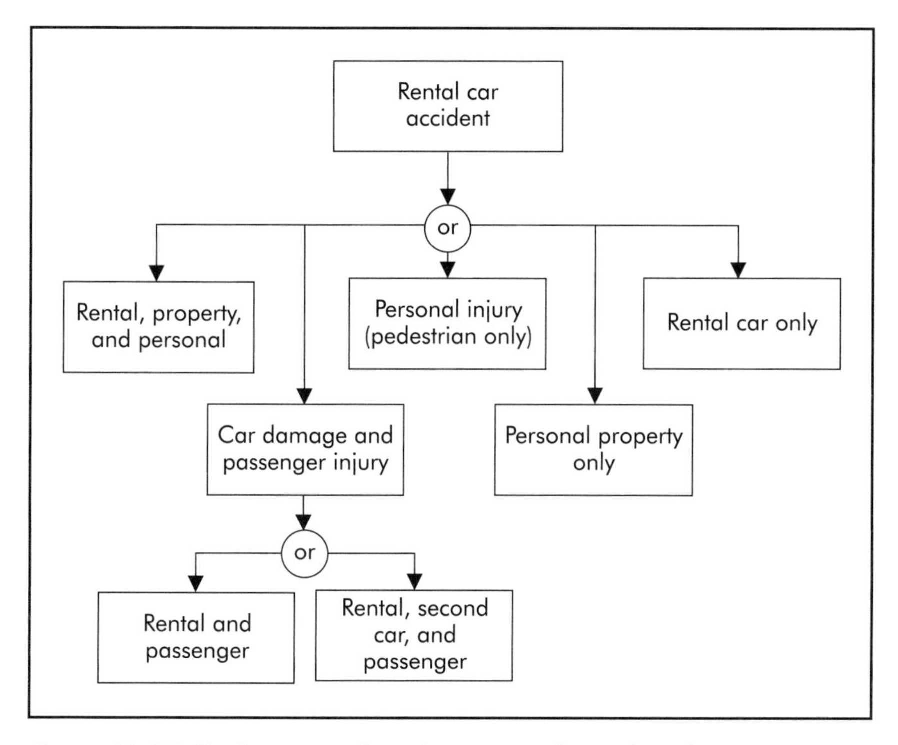

Figure 11-17. Fault tree used to determine relationships between various failure modes.

SO WHEN IS ENOUGH, ENOUGH?

Project managers constantly ask, "How much risk management is enough?" The answer is simple—it depends. The amount of assessment and risk management that each project manager undertakes is contingent upon a number of factors.

- Cost-benefit analysis: This is the point where the potential failure costs to the project are equaled by the cost of the risk management efforts undertaken. In other words, it is simply not good judgment to spend more on preventing a failure than what the failure would cost. In general, the numbers should guide the ultimate decision of when to quit.

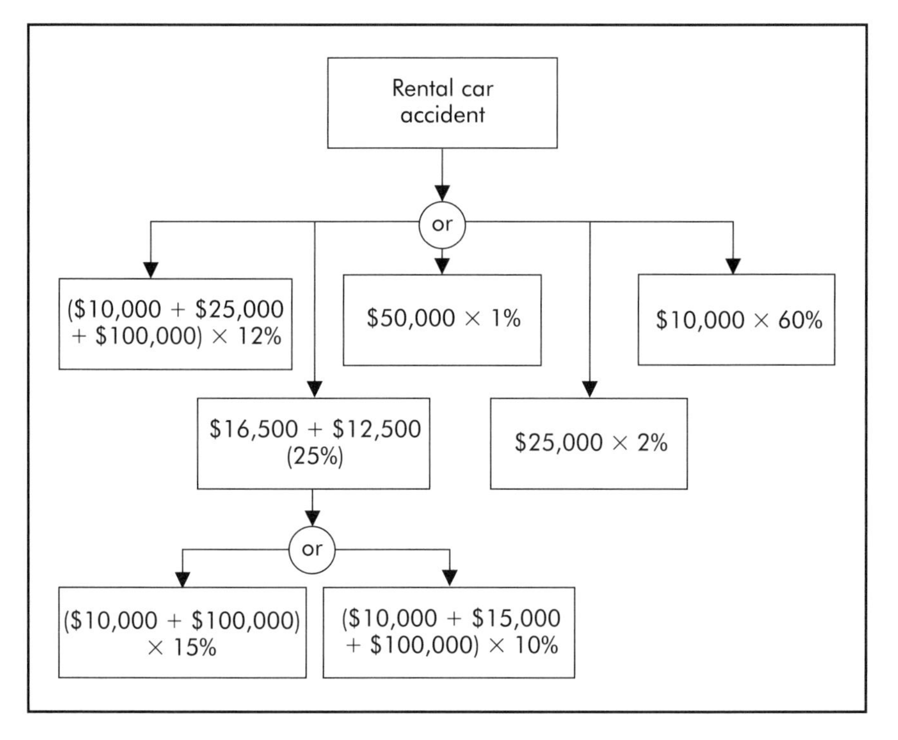

Figure 11-18. Fault tree showing the costs and probabilities of various failure modes.

- Goodwill: The potential costs associated with a loss of customer confidence in the organization as a result of a project failure should not be overlooked. These costs can be significant.
- Size of risk: Obviously, when the magnitude of a failure would be significant and its risk probability is great, then a little more time and money spent on risk management is typically a prudent investment. As with all business endeavors, commonsense and objective reasoning should be the guides.
- Tolerance: Many companies are simply adverse to any risk. Others are more open to a calculated risk. The level of risk tolerance acceptable to senior management will

always play a role in determining how much to invest in risk management.

- Pressure: Upper management, competitors, outside regulatory bodies, and even the economy often influence the amount of risk an organization is willing to accept. Pressures should not be allowed to force an improper decision that increases rather than decreases the risk. Risk management is intended to drive out subjectivity in the decision-making processes.

To minimize the risks to his project, the astute project manager is always informed about the customers' needs, expectations, requirements, and priorities, as well as the organization's competencies, capacities and constraints. Balance is always sought in satisfying customer priorities. Failure is never an option.

REFERENCE

Black, Henry Campbell. 1991. *Black's Law Dictionary: Definitions of the Terms and Phrases of American and English Jurisprudence, Ancient and Modern*, Abridged 6th Ed. St. Paul, MN: West Publishing Company.

12
Project Procurement Planning

OVERVIEW

The acquisition of outside resources, materials, and services is an integral part of the strategic planning process. Unfortunately, in many cases, the decision to outsource part or all of the project activities, or to source materials or services from outside contractors or suppliers, is a knee-jerk reaction to internal problems within the project or project team. The fundamental planning and control elements required to safely source these products and services are never thoroughly assessed, resulting in the introduction of extreme risk to the project.

Procurement planning requires a comprehensive assessment of the pros and cons to acquiring products and services from outside sources. Most organizations invest a significant amount of capital and resources into their supply base management and supplier development processes. These statistically based processes are founded on quantifiable measurement of key supply management ranking criteria that focus on a provider's process capability, process control, and continuous compliance to clearly defined performance criteria (the three C's). Providers are graded, ranked, and assigned levels of business based upon those supportable criteria. A dynamic process, the procurement professionals constantly monitor a provider's performance, taking decisive action whenever a provider fails to comply with the expected performance norms. In short, procurement planning and procurement management are key control elements in any organization. They are performed and managed by professionals who clearly understand their critical importance to organizational success.

Within the project environment, the decisions of what, when, and why to solicit outside products or service support are made early in the planning process. Decisions are based upon various factors, including:

- total cost;
- risk;
- resource availability;
- internal skill sets;
- organizational competencies, capacities, and capabilities;
- technology base;
- organizational impact;
- capital investment requirements, etc.

The decision of who to source these critical external resources from is equally as critical. Logic would suggest that if the organization's procurement professionals have completed a comprehensive and quantitative assessment of the organization's supply base and certified certain providers, then the project manager would be well advised to source from within that same group of certified providers. By so doing, the project team's risks are minimized to the greatest extent possible.

PROCUREMENT PLANNING PROCESS

The process of procurement planning involves the planning of what to procure, when to procure it, and what price to pay for those resources. It further includes solicitation planning to document critical specifications or performance criteria, as well as the preparation of a request for proposal (RFP) or request for quote (RFQ). Along with the RFP/RFQ is the need for a quantitative ranking system with which to measure all potential providers against a common baseline (Termini 1997), thus ensuring equity in the selection process.

Procurement planning also incorporates contract management processes (often defined procedurally within an organization to comply with both internal and external industry or business compliance or regulatory requirements), provider management processes to ensure ongoing compliance to contract requirements, and internal control systems to measure the quality levels of the products and services received. Other considerations in the procurement planning process include logistics, lead time, organizational sourcing policies, quality specifications and compliance methodologies, total cost factors, payment terms and conditions, delivery terms (freight on board [FOB]), confidentiality, risk, as well as contractual terms and conditions, to name just a few. In short, procurement management is a professional's arena from both an operational and a legal perspective. Thus, the project manager and his team are wise to solicit the assistance of a procurement professional to aid them in the procurement planning and possibly the procurement management aspects of the project.

Tools

Tools of the trade are numerous and varied. Each industry segment utilizes procurement tools, controls, and processes that have been honed over time to ensure maximum performance and safety for the organization. As a result, there are many similarities, as well as several significant differences, in the tools used by different industry sectors. For consistency, the project manager and the project team should utilize those tools and methods that have been adopted by their own organization. In the event that the organization has not developed a supply-base management process, the project manager can seek input and guidance from the Institute for Supply Management (ISM).

In general, procurement planning tools include:

- Make or buy analyses—a quantitative assessment of the total internal costs of providing a product or service against the total cost of acquiring those same products or services from an outside provider. The total cost basis is used to ensure that the comparison is an apples-to-apples one that considers all direct and indirect costs on each side of the equation.
- Request for quotation—a solicitation tool that defines in a concise and accurate manner the scope of work being procured or provided (detailed versus performance-based specifications); the cost basis for the acquisition (fixed cost,

time and materials, cost plus, cost plus not to exceed, unit price, etc.); the evaluation or ranking criteria that will be used in source selection; performance measurement criteria and systems utilized for same; schedule of delivery; terms and conditions of contract award; lead-time considerations, etc.

- Certified or qualified provider listing—a listing of providers that have been approved by the procurement department for use by internal operations based upon a statistically supportable ranking system.
- Industry quality, compliance, or validation regulations (Food and Drug Administration [FDA], Underwriters' Laboratories [UL], American National Standards Institute [ANSI], Canadian Standards Association [CSA], musical instrument digital interface [MIDI], etc.).
- Value analysis (VA) and value engineering (VE)—a detailed analysis of the cost versus value that each commodity, activity, product, or service provides. The intent of VA or VE is to eliminate all unnecessary, redundant, or non-value-added costs with an ultimate goal of acquiring the same product or service at a lower cost, or acquiring a higher quality product or service at the same cost. With both techniques, all elements of cost are fair game, and ultimate elimination of all cost factors the theoretical objective.

CONCLUSION

Project procurement planning is an arena that is particularly sensitive to risk, requiring professional planning and management from start to completion. If the project manager or his team is not skilled or experienced in this arena, it is wise to solicit the assistance of a procurement professional. So doing reduces the risks introduced into the project from supplier failures, cost overruns, delivery delays, quality problems, and more.

If the decision is made to acquire outside resources, it is imperative that the statement of work or scope of work (SOW) wording be accurate and comprehensive. This is one of the greatest failures in procurement management. The provider has a legal obligation to deliver specific services or products that have been agreed upon based upon the SOW's terms and conditions provided by the project team. If the SOW is inaccurate or incomplete, the burden of coping with non-complying deliverables rests solely upon the project team, as does the impact those failures will have on the project. Again, this is a serious process requiring professionalism and experience.

Finally, incorporation of the "total cost" of the products and services acquired for the project must be included in the team's cost estimating and budget planning, including any anticipated cost escalators that will likely occur over the duration of the project. Close only counts in horseshoes!

REFERENCE

Termini, Michael J. 1997. *The New Manufacturing Engineer . . . Coming of Age in an Agile Environment*. Dearborn, MI: Society of Manufacturing Engineers.

13
Project Quality and Compliance

OVERVIEW

Every project is intended to generate one or more deliverables, whether they are process enhancements, services, new products or processes, or simply the resolution of a business problem. Regardless of the deliverable, or combination thereof, the project manager and his team are responsible for ensuring that those deliverables comply with the expectations of the project sponsor in measurable terms. Thus, it is incumbent upon the project team to develop and implement a comprehensive quality plan to establish a baseline of quality standards against which compliance will be measured, as well as establish quality control systems to measure specific results. Throughout the project, the team utilizes quality assurance processes to evaluate performance dynamically to ensure that non-conformances are identified proactively and corrective actions implemented quickly and effectively. Much like any other organizational quality system, the project quality and compliance activities are intended to ensure that the controls are in place to guarantee the generation of results that meet or exceed stakeholder expectations.

WHAT IS QUALITY?

Quality is established by the project sponsor, customer, and/or stakeholders, and is generally defined as compliance to agreed-upon expectations. While a relatively straightforward definition, there are shades of grey intertwined that can and, often do, create difficulties for the project team unless identified early in the project planning stages. For example, Joseph Juran defined quality not as conformance to specifications, but rather fitness for use. In other words, the project deliverables (under this definition) are not required to comply with a comprehensive set of detailed specifications but rather must simply satisfy a specific use, outcome, or set of requirements for the customer.

A statement of work (SOW) defines expected outcomes for a project utilizing either detailed-based or performance-based specifications. *Detail-based specifications* dictate that the project team follows a specific set of guidelines, procedures, methods, protocols, specifications, etc., without variance or deviation. Under this approach, it is assumed that the end result will conform to expected norms or performance criteria. It is a rigid approach that places the risk of project failure solely on the customer or project sponsor. Conversely, *performance-based specifications* define a specific outcome and the terms under which its compliance to those expectations will be measured. The methods or approaches used to generate those outcomes are discretionary, thus placing the risk of project failure squarely on the shoulders of the project manager and his team (Juran's fitness for use methodology). It is, therefore, critical that the project manager and his team clearly understand that quality planning and risk planning are linked together from the project planning process to closeout of the project.

PROJECT QUALITY MANAGEMENT

Total quality management (TQM) is based upon the premise that prevention is always less costly than failure. The same holds true for project quality management. As illustrated in Figure 13-1, integration of quality planning with strategic project planning, budget planning, procurement planning, and risk management planning ensures that potential downstream issues and failures are identified early in the planning stages before the tactical implementation of the project (and its associated costs) begin. This proactive approach ensures the maximum potential for prevention while minimizing the potential for eleventh-hour surprises during the most costly phase of the project.

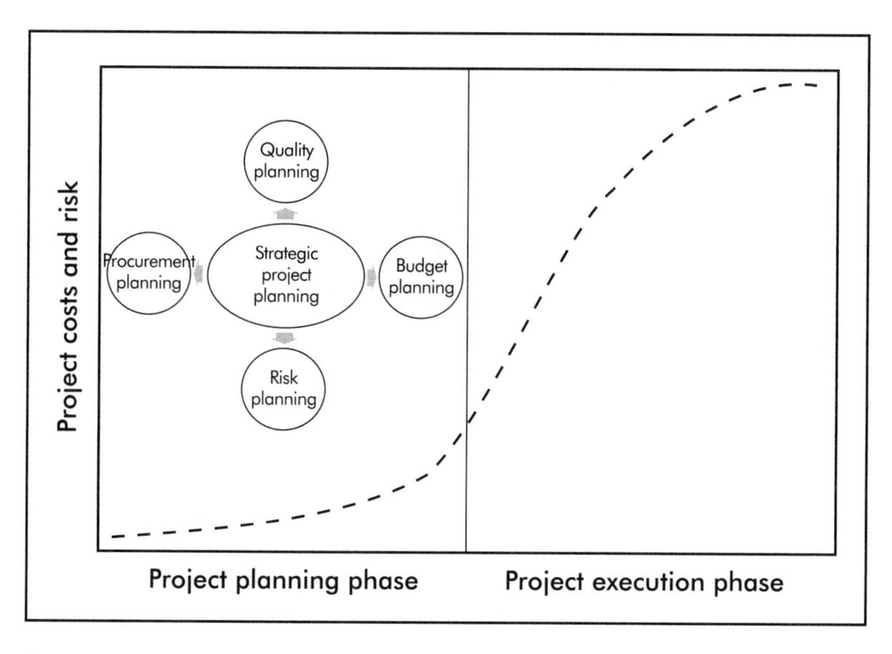

Figure 13-1. Integration of planning processes.

Various tools are used in the process of quality planning, the majority of which have their basis in statistical analysis. These quantitative tools include:

- supplier certification and development;
- supplier/contractor audits;
- quality planning (advanced product quality planning [APQP]);
- process problem solving;
- process and product benchmarking;
- product and process failure modes and effects analysis;
- design of experiments (Taguchi, Shannin, and other methodologies);
- $CP_{(k)}$ analysis;
- process control, capability, and capacity analyses;
- product and process validation systems;

- lean or six sigma processes;
- statistical process control (SPC) processes (control charts, Pareto analysis, statistical sampling, etc.);
- rapid product or process development techniques;
- concurrent development or integrated product development techniques; and
- value analysis and value engineering methodologies.

For product development projects, APQP incorporates supply-base input and involvement during the initial concept stages of the project. The supply-base capabilities and technologies are then integrated into the design phase of the project to ensure a seamless transition from design to production. This collaborative/concurrent approach ensures that the design not only complies with the customer's expectations and requirements, but also includes the inputs of the supply base to identify the most performance and cost-effective approach to the design of the product and its supporting processes (Termini 1997). The three basic questions addressed during the APQP process are:

1. Can the product and/or processes be error-proofed or variances minimized to acceptable levels?
2. Can the product or processes achieve an improved level of performance, capability, or cost reduction through any of the internally available statistical process control techniques?
3. What project controls will be developed and implemented to ensure compliance with all customer requirements and expectations on an ongoing basis throughout the project?

Quality Evaluation

For most projects, quality is evaluated from two perspectives: business requirements and technical requirements. From the perspective of the business, the project is evaluated against the schedule, budget, and performance/deliverables that are generated. From the technical perspective, the project is evaluated against its compliance with established corporate, industry, regulatory, or customer standards; the stability of the product or business process; and the level of robustness the product or process possesses against baselines of use, cost, and life-cycle reliability. In many cases, quality is based upon a fitness-for-use criterion that measures whether or not the project deliverables perform as expected. In other words, do they work?

It is important for the project team to clearly understand that there are differences between project quality and deliverable quality. As such, in his quality planning, the project manager prioritizes each during the project planning phase to ensure that project outcomes are maximized in the eyes of the project sponsor/customer, and that the project team members clearly understand the priorities. This is critical as a project may deliver less-than-expected quality. The opposite situation is also true. Therefore, effective quality planning addresses all possible issues, expectations, and sources of variation to be as comprehensive as possible.

Table 13-1 outlines the typical quality planning process. While it will differ from industry to industry, and from project to project, the fundamentals are essentially the same.

Contingency and Corrective Action Planning

As mentioned previously, quality planning and risk planning are companion processes. This is because, while every project is unique, there are always common failure modes that are foreseeable and predictable within every industry and every organization. Consequently, effective quality planning considers the lessons learned from prior projects. The lessons-learned database, developed from prior projects of a similar scope and nature, provides the project manager with a degree of insight into what possible problems or failure modes are likely so that they can be considered and addressed during the planning phases of the project. It is simply foolhardy to ignore those things that will likely impair the project quality once they have been identified. Other sources of good information include: internal and external experts; published data or business models; former project managers; senior management; vendors, contractors, and service providers; competitors; regulators or agency personnel; benchmark studies; and quantitative business analysis tools like process maps, gap analyses, preliminary

Table 13-1. The quality planning process.

Quality Planning Elements	Definitions
What will require quality checking?	Any significant deliverable or phase-gate requirement will require checking, which may include specific outcomes, communications, or reporting requirements, risk management plans, data or information gathered, scope, budget, and/or schedule control methods, etc.
What methods will be utilized?	The baselines of quality conformance or compliance checking are the standards utilized by the customer, company, industry, or regulatory bodies governing the business (domestic and international).
When will it be performed?	Quality checks will be performed dynamically throughout each phase of the project, but most commonly just prior to completion of the deliverable. In high-risk projects, checking is conducted more frequently to ensure that proactive corrective actions can be taken before failures occur.
Who will be involved?	The project team members, customer representatives, suppliers/contractors/providers of products and services, internal experts, red team representatives, members of management where appropriate, and representatives from external regulatory bodies will be involved.
What techniques/materials/systems will be used?	Established quality standards, check sheets, control charts, certification systems and criteria, templates, policies and procedures, protocols, quality processes, customer requirements, quality measurement tools, validation systems, published compliance guidelines or criteria, etc., will be used.

failure analyses, failure modes and effects analyses, fault tree analyses, fault failure analyses, etc.

Quality planning, therefore, incorporates contingency planning for those foreseeable failure modes likely to occur during the life cycle of the project. It also involves creating and documenting corrective actions that the team will use to execute those contingency plans.

SUMMARY

While this chapter covers project quality management in only a cursory manner, there are excellent sources of information that the project manager can reference for more detailed information (Ross 1996). In short, while the creation of a project quality plan is not complex, it is an essential element in the project planning phases. It involves identification of all project deliverables and expectations (implicit and explicit) coupled with an action plan that addresses how to quantifiably validate their compliance to established quality and business standards. Those things that can or will impact project quality are also identified. Preventive measures are then integrated into the quality plan to ensure that those failure modes are either eliminated or minimized to the greatest extent possible.

Remember, failure is always more costly than prevention . . . to the project and the project manager.

REFERENCE

Ross, Phillip J. 1996. *Taguchi Techniques for Quality Engineering*. New York: McGraw Hill.

Termini, Michael J. 1997. *The New Manufacturing Engineer . . . Coming of Age in an Agile Environment*. Dearborn, MI: Society of Manufacturing Engineers.

14
Tactical Project Management Planning Tools

OVERVIEW

With the strategic planning phases of the project completed, the project manager and his team have a concise definition of the expected project deliverables, the scope of the project, the methodology to be used in achieving the expected project deliverables, and the risks that will likely occur throughout the duration of the project's life cycle. It is now time to develop the tactical plans and project controls necessary to ensure successful implementation of the project. Successful project implementation requires a blend of the right decision, the right tactical plan, and the involvement and support of the right stakeholders (see Figure 14-1).

The common practice, and fallacy, at this stage of the project is that many times the project manager and his team immediately develop a Gantt chart with which to track project performance and progress. Unfortunately, by moving too quickly into the details of the tactical plan without a work breakdown structure (WBS) to guide the development process, the project manager will often overlook one or more key groupings of activities. The absence of these tasks in the final project plan will go unnoticed until it is too late to address them without creating a significant impact on the project budget or schedule. When that occurs, the project is in real trouble. The reason for this common mistake is simple. Without the WBS to provide the overall guidance in the detail development, there is no road map to guide the project team through the tactical development processes in a logical, orderly manner.

An experienced project manager recognizes the need to first develop a work breakdown structure for the project before moving

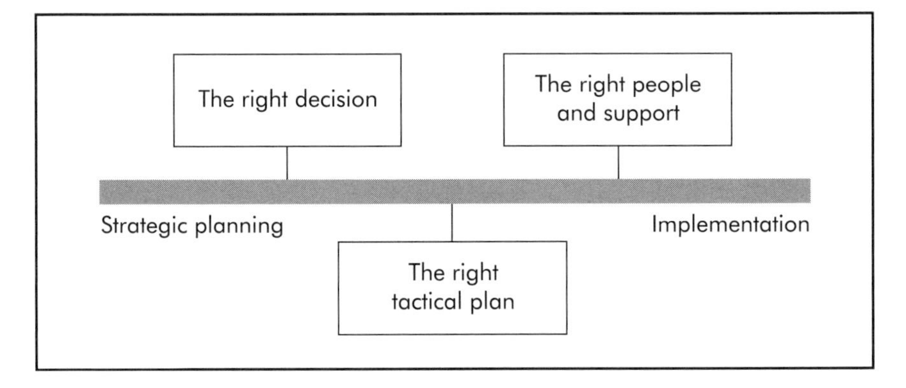

Figure 14-1. The elements of successful project implementation.

forward with the details of the tactical implementation plan. This will avoid the trap of overlooking one or more of the essential activities required to complete the project successfully.

THE WORK BREAKDOWN STRUCTURE

The WBS, much like a bill of material, decomposes the project definition into the successively smaller sublevel or sub-tier activities required to complete each parent (higher-level) activity. This approach provides an accurate overview of the entire project, while at the same time defining each of the major tier activities to be completed to achieve the project objectives. This, in subsequent planning stages, provides the basis for creating the detailed activities required to complete each element of the project along with their associated interdependencies. (See Figure 14-2.)

Tier Activities

The first step in creating the WBS, as illustrated in Figure 14-2, is to define the project objective, as well as all major activities or categories of activities required to accomplish it. These become the Tier-1 activities—the major milestones of the project (and the basis of the lessons-learned database). Next, the Tier-2 activities are defined.

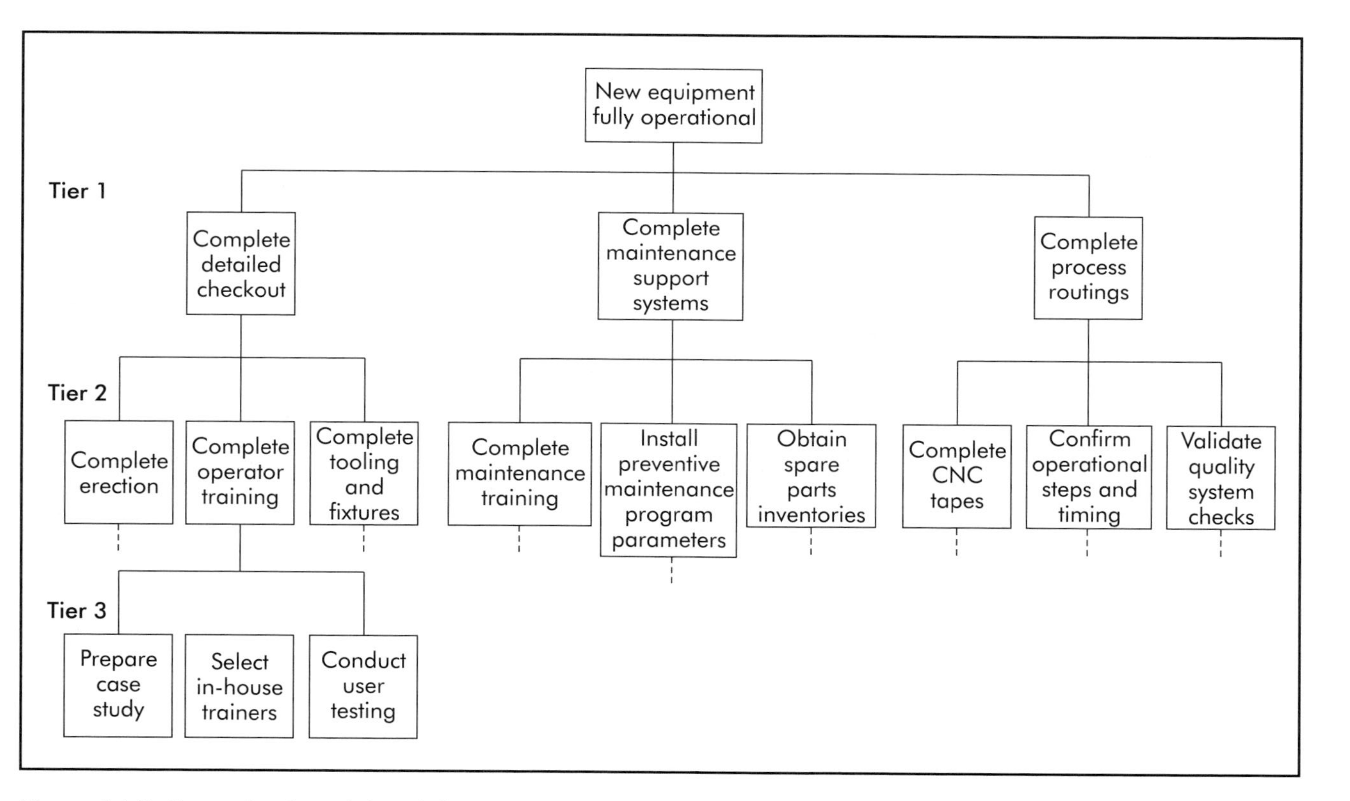

Figure 14-2. Example of work breakdown structure.

The WBS is the tool used by project managers to answer the question, "Can the project be done as budgeted and scheduled?"

Just as the Tier-1 activities represent child-parent relationships with the project objective, the Tier-2 activities represent child-parent relationships with the Tier-1 activities. Each subsequent sub-tier of activities represents the requirements for completing the next higher tier of activities, until sufficient detail is available with which to accurately describe the project in the aggregate. Then, like a bill-of-material cost rollup, the total project cycle time, resource consumption, and projected project costs can be forecasted in the aggregate as illustrated in the house-building example in Figure 14-3. While the accuracy of these forecasts will be dependent upon the data in the lessons-learned database from which they came, this first pass at the rough-cut numbers gives the project team an idea of how close they are to the targeted objectives established for the project. As the detailed plan is developed, these forecasted numbers will be refined into the final schedule and budget from which the project will be ultimately driven.

In most cases, typical business process improvement or product development projects require no more that four to six tiers. Again, this is a macro view of the project. It is not intended to be a detailed analysis. For construction or large, complex product development projects, typically no more that 10 to 12 tiers will be required.

Use of the WBS in the early planning stages of the project prevents the omission of critical project activities because it pictorially displays each of the major activities that must be addressed to complete the next higher tier activity, along with all associated interdependencies. It is much like creating an outline prior to writing a paper or report. It defines the scope and content of the project for subsequent refinement.

WBS Benefits

Benefits of the WBS are numerous:

1. It reduces the risks associated with missing critical project activities or groupings of activities.

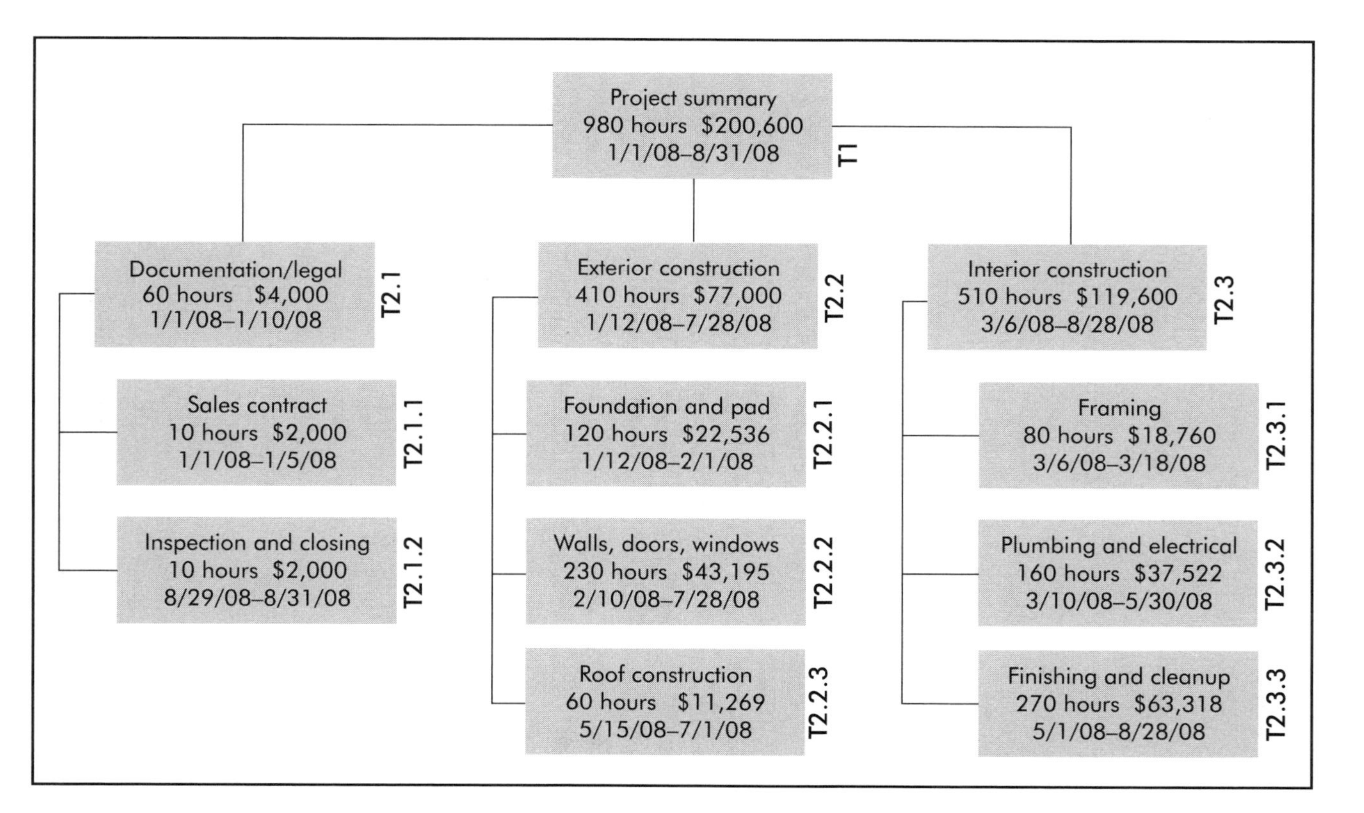

Figure 14-3. Typical WBS cost and resource rollup for a custom-built house.

2. As a visual tool, it provides an excellent overview of the entire project, and its structure, which can be used to explain to the customer or management how the project is planned and how it will be tracked.
3. It defines and illustrates the general existing dependencies and how they will be addressed.
4. It provides the basis for determining the resources, costs, and timing of the project.

Early Determination

As already emphasized, it is crucial to convey as early as possible to management whether or not the project can be completed on schedule and on budget with the allocated resources. Should the WBS indicate a problem in achieving the desired project performance or outcome, it is communicated back to management early in the planning stages so that options and alternatives can be explored. Once the project implementation is underway, those options and alternatives are largely eliminated, leaving management with little choice but to take the hit resulting from the project's failure. As indicated in the discussion on portfolio management, the impact of a single project failure within the strategic portfolio will likely result in additional impacts to other projects, reprioritization of the projects within the pipeline, or failure of the organization to achieve its strategic objectives. So, once again, it must be emphasized that failure is not an option.

The WBS is the definitive tool used to make an early determination about the viability of the project.

1. Beginning at the lowest tier in the WBS, the project manager calculates the costs, timing, and resource consumption associated with each activity block. All costs, resources, and timing are then summed and rolled up to the next tier.
2. Once the calculations for a given tier are completed, the project manager then performs the same calculation for the activities listed on the next upper tier, and so on, until all tiers have been calculated and totaled.

3. The summation of all of the Tier-1 activities provides the project manager with the total costs, resource requirements, and timing for the project in the aggregate. While not exact—because of certain resource dependencies that will be discussed later—it is close enough to provide the project manager with a realistic estimate of whether or not the project can be completed as requested by the customer or management.

Easily Understandable

Another benefit of the WBS format is that it is easily understandable by management. The logic behind the planning is readily apparent, and the cost and timing rollups are easily confirmed. Using a Gantt chart for this purpose often meets with less than acceptable results because it is too complex, too large, and the logic behind its creation is largely invisible. Management simply will not take the time to thoroughly study and analyze it. The WBS, however, is simple, logical, and can stand on its own merit.

ACTIVITY LISTING

The next step in the tactical project planning cycle is the creation of a detailed activity listing for each tier of the WBS. The topic-matter or discipline experts on the project team are assigned the responsibility for developing the detailed activities required for each tier of the WBS. Each expert on the team creates a separate activity listing to ensure that all critical issues are adequately addressed. Each activity is described in enough detail to ensure clarity, and then assigned a unique identifier so that it can be monitored against the project schedule. The duration of each activity is calculated (using one of the techniques that will be explained later in this section), along with its expected start or completion dates, as illustrated in Figure 14-4.

The project manager does not attempt to create the detailed activity listing alone. This is where the value of the project team is greatest. The project manager utilizes the expertise of the individual team members to build each element of the activity

Project number: 2009-1 Project description: Win the Super Bowl Project manager: The Big Tuna Project team: Miami Dolphins Tier-1 code: 1A					
Task No.	Description	Estimated		Actual	
		Time	Completion	Time	Completion
1A1	Draft rookies	90 d	2/08	85 d	1/08
1A2	Sign veterans	180 d	3/08	270 d	4/08
1A3	Sign free agents	60 d	5/08	60 d	7/08

Figure 14-4. Example of an activity listing.

listing within their respective disciplines. For example, if the project objective is to implement a new fully integrated business system, the systems engineers and systems analysts are assigned to develop the details for the activities associated with the systems integration, database conversions, and database cutover. Conversely, the IT network professionals are assigned the task of addressing the activities associated with system hardware and local area network (LAN) selection, installation, and prove-out. The maintenance professionals detail the activities associated with facility preparations, power quality reviews, fiber optics, and backbone installation. Human Relations personnel are involved in detailing the user training and testing activities. Purchasing personnel are involved in detailing the system software specifications and RFP processes. These are the experts within each discipline. Consequently, it makes good sense to assign them the task of developing the details for their areas of expertise rather than for the project manager to attempt to perform those detailed tasks on her own.

Once the experts have completed their individual tasks, the project manager and his team consolidates all activities into a master network diagram, making any necessary adjustments. The loop is closed with an overall review of the activity listing by the entire project team to ensure that nothing has been overlooked and that the appropriate dependencies have been identified and addressed.

As a general rule, the project manager assigns each of the various Tier-1 activities of the WBS to a member of the project management team. The specific Tier-1 activities then become the team member's responsibility throughout the entire project, including the coordination of dependencies with those responsible for the other Tier 1 activities of the WBS. This ensures ownership among the team members.

Milestones

The activities shown in the various tiers of Figures 14-2 and 14-3 in effect represent the primary project milestones—benchmarks within the project that signify the accomplishment of key project deliverables (for many project teams, the phase-gate requirements). Milestones for Tier-1 activities are (by definition) assigned in Tier 2; for Tier 2 in Tier 3; and so forth. The milestones are not planned management reviews arbitrarily assigned by the project manager. Management reviews can coincide with the milestone dates, but reviews are activities rather than milestones. *Milestones are the key deliverables within each phase of the project* and are defined by the way the project manager plans his project.

Milestones are typically used for planning and evaluating purposes throughout the project as a means of monitoring performance against established phase-gate targets. A good tool to consider for this purpose is a milestone listing (see Figure 14-5). It provides the visibility to keep the project manager apprised of the key project milestone dates along with who has been assigned the responsibility for that milestone. By assigning milestones to different members of the team, the project manager ensures ownership in the project and cooperation among members. It forces the various team members to work together to accomplish upstream and downstream activities.

Another variation of the milestone chart provides an excellent visual reporting tool for more senior managers or customers. By color-coding each milestone, the project manager can quickly and

Milestone	Target Completion	Assigned	Status
Complete project plan	3/1/09	Johnson	Completed 3/1/09
Select and train project team	5/15/09	Smith	Completed 5/3/09
Assess problem condition	8/9/09	Nelson	Completed 8/4/09
Develop alternatives	11/20/09	White	60% complete
Complete problem-solving	2/12/10	Edwards	
Identify root cause	3/1/10	Thompson	
Select final solution	4/15/10	Jones	
Quantity expected/return on investment	5/1/10	Johanson	
Prepare presentation	5/9/10	Shanks	

Figure 14-5. Milestone listing example.

easily denote its current status. Using the universal color code of red, yellow, and green, the colors illustrate current performance status, as well as where emphasis is required. Green signifies that the milestone was completed on schedule. Yellow indicates that the milestone is scheduled for completion within 10 days. However, based upon the current percentage completion calculation, it is not likely to be completed as scheduled. Red indicates that the milestone was not completed on schedule or is currently behind schedule.

PROJECT DEPENDENCIES

The next task for the project manager and his team in building their tactical project plan is to identify the dependencies that will exist between various activities within the plan. Recognizing and integrating these dependencies between activities into the project plan is critical, requiring careful consideration during the calculation of various cycle times and their ultimate conversion to calendar time. Dependencies are categorized as either serial, resource, discretionary, or external.

Serial Dependencies

A *serial dependency* is placed on an activity that cannot be initiated until its predecessor(s) is complete. In other words, these activities must be performed sequentially ("finish-to-start" logic). There is no opportunity for overlapping these activities or running them in parallel with others. They are purely sequential in nature.

Resource Dependencies

Activities with resource dependencies are somewhat different. They are constrained by the availability of a critical resource, such as personnel, funding, information, data, or materials. They simply cannot start until those limited resources are available ("start no earlier than xxx" logic). For example, assume that as part of the project, a systems analyst is required to write an accounts payable module for a new business system. She assesses the task and estimates that the total cycle time for the activity will not exceed 90 days. Should the project manager plug 90 days into the project plan? That depends. If the systems analyst can get right onto the activity, perhaps 90 days is correct. But what if there are four to five additional activities ahead of this assignment that must be completed before she can begin to program the new accounts payable module? If those activities will collectively take 12 months to complete, and if there is a singular resource available to perform those tasks, then the project plan will reflect 15 months to complete the task (12 months queue time plus 3 months work time). While this may seem ridiculous, it is real. In this case, the project manager has options: reprioritize the backlog of the systems analyst to pull the task forward to the front of her work queue, hire more systems analysts to redistribute the backlog or to complete the desired task, or outsource some or all of the development work. Should the project manager elect not to employ one of those options, then the desired task will not begin for 12 months.

Discretionary Dependencies

In each project, there are certain activities that are not linked, or dependent, upon other activities. These activities (often referred to as slack time activities) can, therefore, be planned for completion by the project team at any point in time in the project's life cycle. As a result, they are typically planned to accommodate the needs of the project or the team: for example, to level load the resources or to meet certain cash flow requirements. For instance, if the team's project is to create the next generation of Microsoft Windows 7® or Microsoft Office® 2010, one of the requirements of those projects is to design the box that will ultimately house and display the software and manual at the point of sale. Because the box is not tied to any other aspect of the project, it can be designed early in the project or late, as long as it is ready once production and final assembly begins on the software discs and manuals.

External Dependencies

External dependencies are those that link project activities to outside sources that are beyond the control of the project team. A good example is activities that require a federal regulatory agency's approval before the activity can be formally completed. The federal agency will work on its own time frame, completing the inspection or certification as its internal resources allow. The project team is simply at the mercy of the entity to complete those compliance tasks as quickly as possible.

When the project manager and his team begin sequencing these activities in their network diagram, care is taken to ensure that all such dependencies are identified and accounted for.

CALCULATING CYCLE TIME

When building the activity listing and subsequent network diagram for the project, the project team accurately calculates the cycle time for each activity within the project using one of several available methodologies. The subsequent rollup of the cycle times of all activities along the critical path is used to determine the project's total cycle time. As in most reengineering activities, *cycle time* is defined as the total consumed time from the beginning of an activity to its completion, including all value- and non-value-added time. Several issues deserve consideration when calculating the cycle time of an activity:

1. The complexity of an activity can add greatly to the time required to complete it. Simpler activities can be completed quicker.
2. The productivity level of the people performing the activity is never assumed to be 100%. Where available, actual productivity measurements are factored into the cycle time calculations. Where productivity figures are not available, a conservative productivity estimate of 70–75% is used. Often, personnel in many direct, administrative, and clerical jobs work at productivity levels well below the 70% mark.
3. Another factor in cycle time calculation is the degree of concurrency that can be employed, as identified in the serial and resource dependency analyses. Typically, the more activities that can be done in parallel, the shorter the total cycle time.
4. Accuracy of the activity description, workflow, or process specifications will help greatly in performing the activity in the shortest possible cycle time. Conversely, the lower the accuracy level, the longer the activity will take. Poorly defined activities require interpretation, which introduces an element of variability that will impact their actual cycle time.
5. The number of personnel trained and available to perform any given activity will also impact cycle time.

There are a number of ways to determine the cycle time of an activity. For simple, non-complex activities, standard industrial engineering time and motion studies are appropriate. Another alternative in calculating the cycle time for an activity is to use the PERT mathematical model:

$$C_T = \frac{O_T + (4 \times L_T) + P_T}{6} \quad \text{(eq. 14-1)}$$

where:

C_T = cycle time
O_T = optimistic time
L_T = likely time
P_T = pessimistic time

Interviews with the personnel normally performing the activity are also appropriate. But when using this methodology, the project manager always obtains a second opinion. Most people are optimists; they will give the best possible times or those that correspond to established business standards. The project manager is not interested in the time it *should* take, but rather the time it *actually* takes to complete the task or activity. The actual times are what drive the project.

For complex tasks, a good methodology is to videotape the activity. This provides two distinct advantages over the other methods:

1. The videotape does not exaggerate, misstate, or underestimate the time it takes to complete a given task. It tells it like it is—for better or worse. It documents the total consumed time for the activity. In many cases, employees performing a particular activity do certain tasks or sub-tasks that they are unaware of or which may add to the total cycle time. For example, the basis of single-minute exchange of dies (SMED) techniques is to eliminate those sub-tasks that do not add value within a given activity or process, and to realign those sub-tasks that do add value but are not done in the correct sequence.

   As an example, a painter is hired to paint a house. Logic would indicate that he would purchase the paint and supplies, accumulate all the required tools, and prepare the areas that are not to be painted *before* he begins. Unfortunately, what often happens is that he arrives on site without all of the needed materials and supplies, thus delaying the project while he retrieves those items. While not exactly the most expedient way to perform the assigned project, the cycle time calculated for the project must reflect those inefficiencies.

2. The videotape can be stored for future use should the project schedule start to slip. In such cases, the tapes can be pulled from the shelf and used as the basis for reengineering a given critical path activity to reduce its cycle time and, thus, the cycle time of the project.

Whichever methodology the project manager employs, he is always as conservative and as accurate as possible within the constraints of the project.

Example

One example involves a large West Coast bank that was conducting a business process reengineering project to improve customer service by better utilization of branch personnel. The intent was to free up time from routine activities performed by the branch tellers so they could spend more time with customers on a face-to-face basis as part of a customer relationship management initiative.

An initial situational assessment revealed that significant time was spent each afternoon (one of the busiest times of day for walk-in traffic at the branches) reconciling the automatic teller machines (ATMs). When one teller was asked to explain what she did and how she did it, she went into detail about the ATM reconciliation process. The total cycle time, she concluded, was about 25 minutes. After she was watched for a few days, it was determined that the cycle time always exceeded her estimate by a factor of two to three. The team decided to videotape her activities.

The results of the videotaping revealed that the actual cycle time was almost four times her estimate. Why? Many activities were found to overlap the reconciliation process, which caused the teller to stop and start several times. There were things that she had simply forgotten to mention or consider. In short, there were numerous factors that influenced the process cycle time. To make things even worse, the tellers at each branch were performing the ATM reconciliation differently, even though there was a written procedure.

The videotape provided the information needed to accurately assess the cycle time for the project, as well as the information that was ultimately required to reengineer the process.

Calendar Time Conversion

Projects are not planned on cycle time, but rather on the calendar time they consume. As a consequence, it is necessary for the project team to accumulate the individual activity cycle times and convert them into actual calendar time. In so doing, the project manager factors in various real-world constraints and realities, such as: scheduled down periods, vacations, and weekends. If unscheduled downtimes are common due to equipment breakdowns, supplier delivery problems, or any similar factor, a realistic estimate of the projected lost time is included in the calculations. Other factors are also considered:

- absenteeism,
- training requirements,
- available resources,
- organizational priorities,
- employee learning curves,
- availability of critical equipment,
- administrative cycle and approval times,
- labor contract expirations,
- customs or international processing times,
- international holidays,
- customer and supplier issues,
- turnover,
- employee skill sets,
- work backlogs,
- functional priorities, and
- queue times.

Believe it or not, even things like deer hunting season or international holidays will often throw the project behind if not appropriately considered. The rule of thumb is to make the conversion as accurate as possible. It is always better to err on the part of conservatism.

NETWORK DIAGRAMMING TECHNIQUES

For tactical planning, many project managers employ network diagramming techniques like the program evaluation and review technique (PERT) and critical path method (CPM). These visual tools help to build the logical activity flow, which will focus on minimizing project cycle times by identifying the degree of flexibility within the various network paths possible.

While the two techniques are similar, there are some differences. For example, CPM calculates both a single early and late start date, and similarly a single early and late finish date using sequential network logic and single duration estimates. From them, CPM calculates the activity float through the various networks to isolate which activities have the least degree of flexibility, setting the project schedule accordingly. PERT, on the other hand, combines activities, cycle times, and dependencies to develop a network diagram using sequential logic (as illustrated in Figure 14-6) but utilizing a weighted average duration. So in summary, the primary difference is that PERT uses the expected value of the distribution's mean while CPM uses the most likely estimate of probability. In most cases, the differences are minimal. However, on longer duration projects, the differences can be significant as illustrated in Figure 14-7. The project manager can use these differences to advantage in managing the project. For example, commitments can be made utilizing the PERT calculations, and the project can be managed utilizing the CPM calculations. So doing provides a cushion for the project team in the event of unanticipated slippages. Still another option is to make a commitment on the project's completion using a best case (CPM)/worst case (PERT) range of possibilities.

Critical Path

Another important project management tool is the critical path, which is derived from the computer models discussed in this chapter. The *critical path* is the optimum network path (series of activities) within the project plan. It is found by summing all individual activity cycle times in every conceivable path throughout the network of

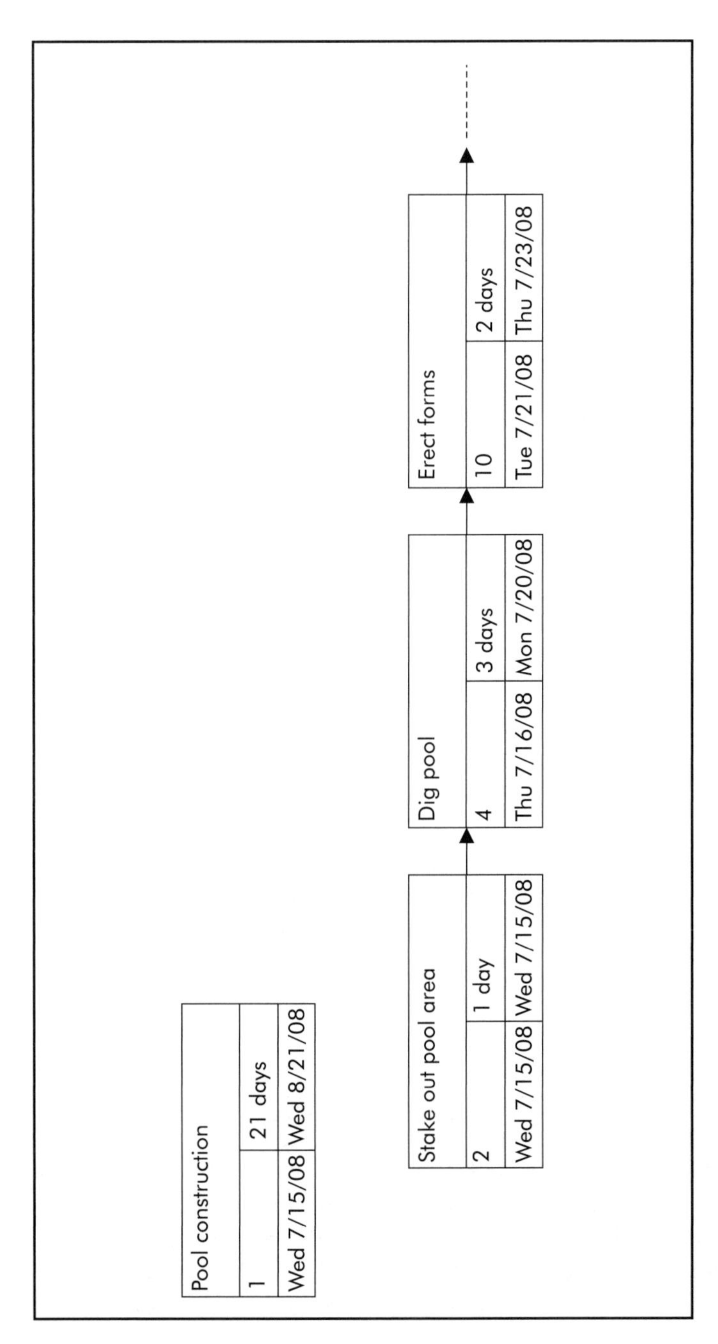

Figure 14-6. Example of a PERT chart.

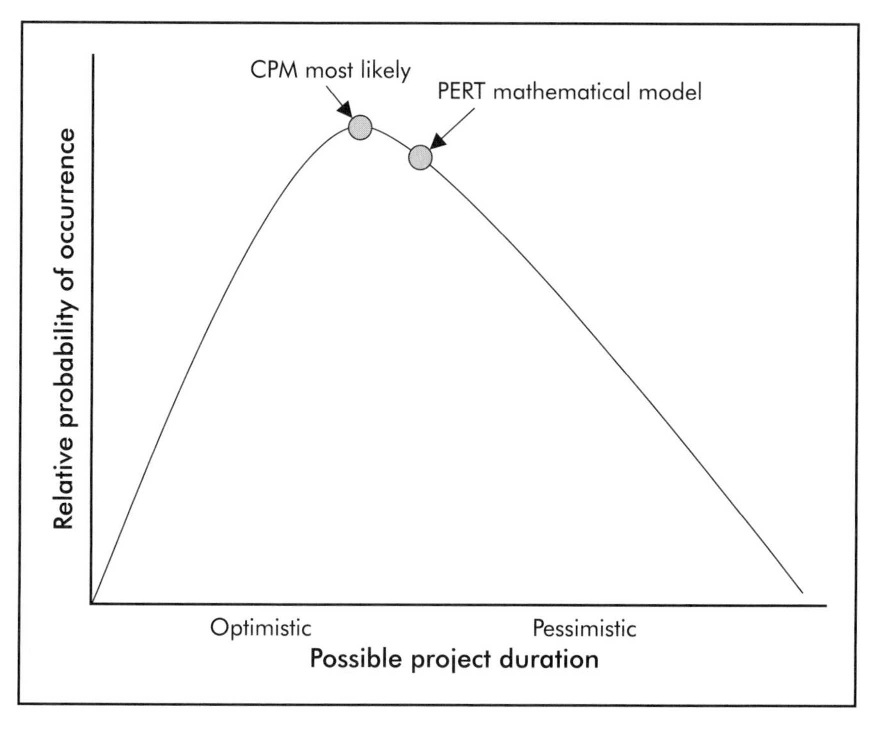

Figure 14-7. Comparison of PERT and CPM methodologies.

activities to determine the path with the least flexibility. One of the most important aspects of this calculation for the project manager to remember is that the critical path is dynamic in that it is dependent upon the cycle times of the activities that collectively comprise it. As individual activity cycle times that comprise the critical path slip or compress, the critical path will be impacted accordingly. Thus, as the critical path goes, so goes the project schedule, making this one of the most important monitoring tools available to the project manager. Experienced project managers monitor the critical path of their projects daily, even on large, time-consuming projects. Every day a slippage along the critical path goes unnoticed is a day of increased

The critical path should be monitored every day, even on large, time-consuming projects.

risk and cost to the project. The longer the slippage is allowed to continue unchecked, the higher the probability that the project schedule loss will be unrecoverable.

Slack Time

Slack time is yet another valuable management tool for the project manager. Every path through the network of activities, except the critical path, contains some degree of slack or flex time (see Figure 14-8). *Slack time* is the time difference between when an activity is planned and when it becomes a critical path activity. By identifying slack time (where it exists and to what degree), the project manager can better manage the project by reallocating limited resources from non-critical path activities to critical path activities as necessary to maintain critical path timing. In this way, the project manager is able to compress the project schedule should an unavoidable slip in one or more of the critical path activities occur. In essence, it gives the project manager a tool to better manage resources throughout the entire life cycle of the project.

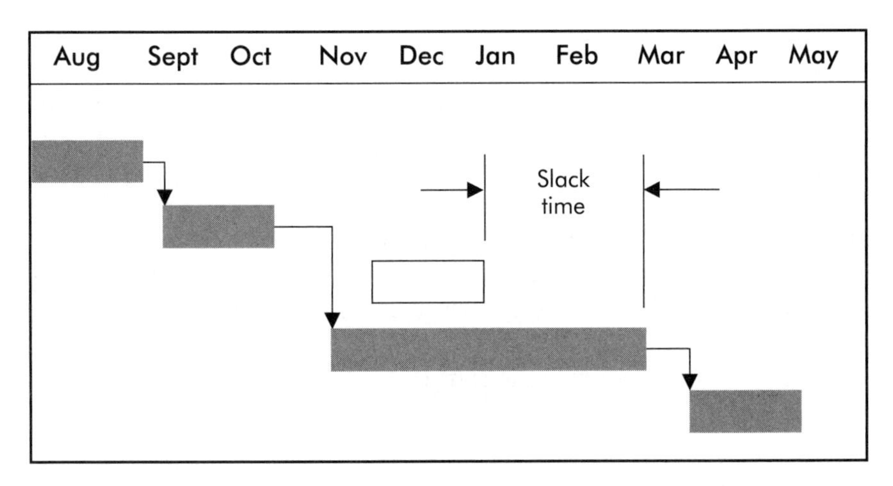

Figure 14-8. A chart used to estimate slack time.

GANTT CHART

The final and most widely used of the project management tools is the Gantt chart (see Figure 14-9), which illustrates the timelines of all the project activities, their dependencies, critical path, slack time, personnel assignments, as well as the total project cycle time.

In addition, with the most current versions of project management software, it is possible to add notes to document critical project decisions or actions. Macros like the color-coded stop-light technique can be used to illustrate visually how activities are progressing (green = completed, yellow = scheduled for completion within a given period but not tracking on schedule, and red = past due), and to track resource consumption or utilization, resource costs or expenses, and project phase gates. In short, the Gantt chart is the compilation of all of the project management planning tools and techniques that have been discussed to this point, making it a great planning and tracking tool.

A word of caution is necessary. The Gantt chart is a professional project management tool that contains a significant amount of valuable information. Its value, however, is predicated upon the accuracy of the data and planning that have been put into it. Like all software, the accuracy of the output depends on the accuracy of the input. Without comprehensive planning and detailed analyses prior to the creation of the Gantt chart, the document will contain misleading information. Further, the inaccuracy will not be evident until significant problems have arisen.

PROJECT MANAGEMENT SOFTWARE

With most project management software on the market, information entered by the project manager (activities, interdependencies, dates, durations, resources, etc.) is easily converted into Gantt or PERT charts with the critical path calculated and identified. User friendliness and flexibility are the two key elements differentiating most software products. In most cases, users will find it difficult at first to comfortably utilize most of these packages due to their complexity. But with practice, the tools prove invaluable.

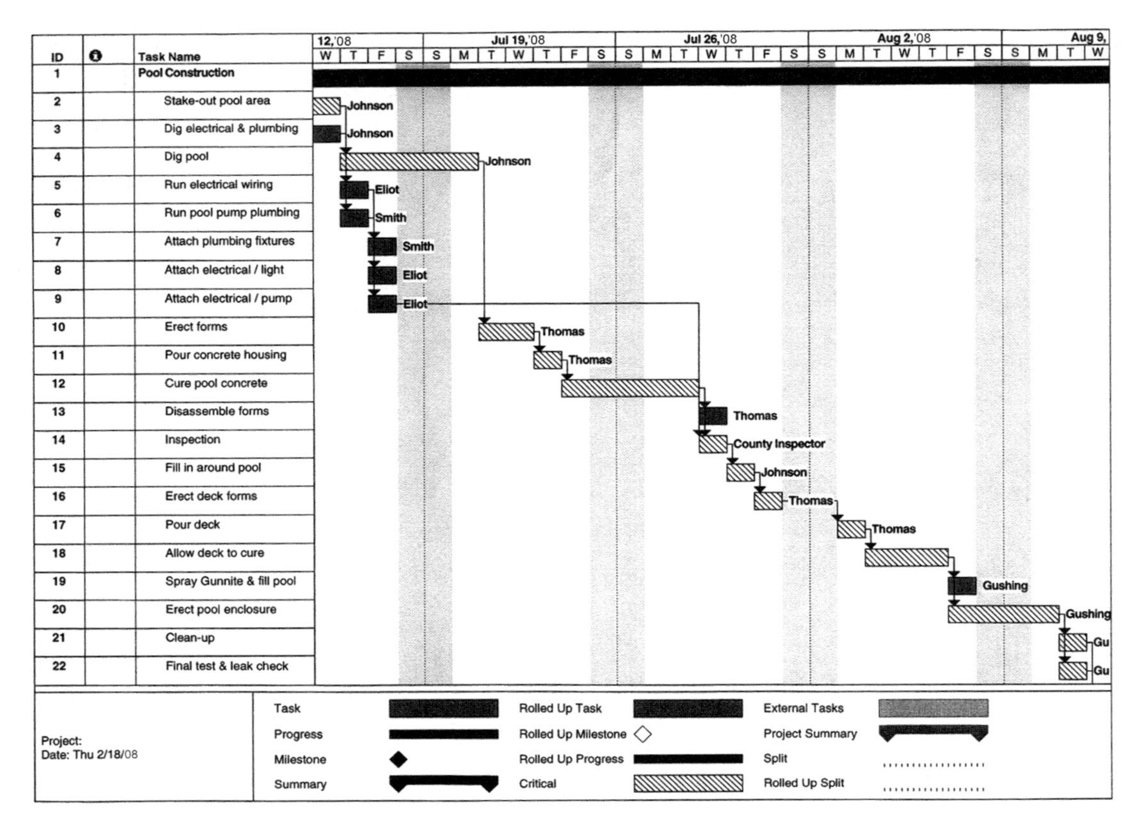

Figure 14-9. Example of a Gantt chart.

Costs, depending on the platform to be used and the functionality required, typically range from less than $250 per user license to well over $7,000 per user.

Which project management software is best? There is no single answer to that question. There are numerous good products on the market, each with its own set of advantages, depending on the nature and size of the project. Whichever software is chosen, consideration should be given to the following factors.

1. On which platform (equipment) will the software operate? What type of environment (stand-alone, file server, client-server, local area network [LAN], virtual network, internet network, etc.) will be used? Using what operating system?
2. How much memory will be required to support the software and ensure its responsiveness?
3. What type(s) of printer(s), back-up drive(s), or other peripheral equipment will the software support?
4. In selecting the software, the project manager always gives consideration to the number of activities the project will likely include, as this differentiates many of the available programs from their competitors. The larger the project plan, the more robust the software requirements.
5. What capabilities and features will make the selected software work effectively? Consider things like:

   - multiple currency and currency conversion functionality for projects that cross international boundaries;
   - availability of, or compatibility with, the basic project planning tools discussed earlier in this chapter (graphical WBS, PERT, CPM, resource leveling, compression techniques, etc.);
   - project cost management capabilities (progress payments, budgeting, multiple billing rates, multiple currency rates, etc.);
   - ease of use;
   - resource tracking and loading capabilities;
   - tie-ins to other software programs in the business systems;

- on-line technical support;
- on-screen tutorials; and
- reputation, user groups, and installed sites.

In general, most project management software products on the market are sound, proven products. The key is to select one that fits the size of the project and is compatible with internal business systems. With the comprehensive capabilities designed into the current off-the-shelf products, only in rare circumstances is it necessary to develop customized programs.

Resource Leveling

During the life cycle of many projects, there comes a time when operational, business, resource, or budgetary constraints require the project manager to realign the project schedule or budget to balance available resources with either business or organizational requirements. Resource leveling is the technique used by experienced project managers to spread project costs or allocate limited resources (like technical support or skilled labor) to coincide with the actual or budgeted consumption rate of those resources.

In essence, resource leveling involves a reallocation or shifting of project activities to comply with available project funding or other limited resources. For example, tight or unexpected financial constraints on the organization may force an extension of the project schedule to ensure that the project budget meets certain cash flow restrictions. Or, project costs may be held to a fixed level of spending for a specified time period.

As illustrated in Figure 14-10, the available funding for the project is $50,000 per month, but the actual planned expenditures vary according to the planned project resource consumption. The astute project manager realizes that some activities must be realigned to keep the project spending in line with available funds. As the project is currently planned, in the first 2 months the project team will under-spend the budget and look like pros. Then, in the third month, the project team will over-spend the available budget and all hell will break loose. In cases like this, the project

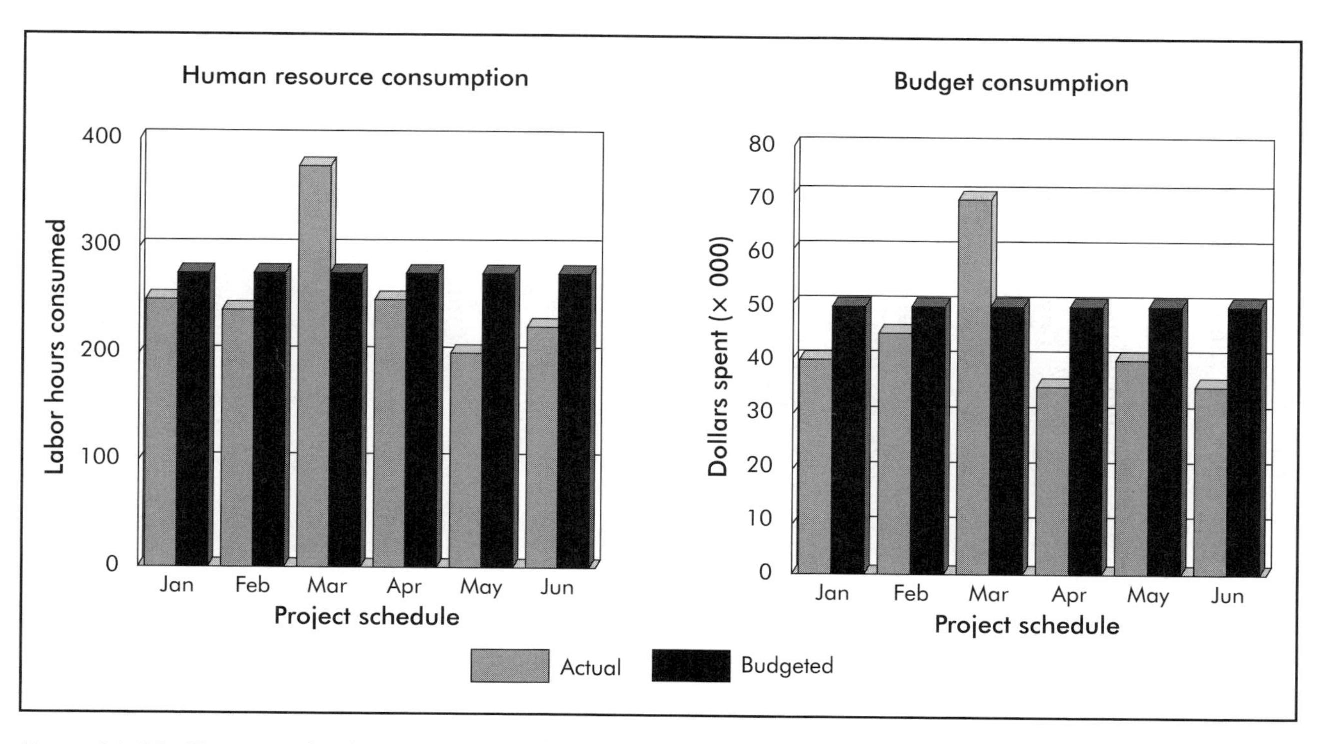

Figure 14-10. Charts used in budget leveling, a technique for allocating various project resources so they coincide with their actual rate of consumption.

team often mistakenly thinks that the carryover from the first 2 months will be used to offset the overage in month three. The reality is, however, that surpluses like these will be allocated by Accounting to other expense categories, leaving the project team exposed to budgetary noncompliance.

Whenever planned consumption (financial or human resources) differs from available resources, one of the two must be changed. In the example used, if cash flow constraints dictate the requirement for level budgeting of project expenses, then the project must be re-planned to coincide with available funds. In this case, the project duration will be extended.

The human resource chart in Figure 14-10 provides another example. It illustrates a planned rate of consumption of approximately 280 labor hours per month for the project. Again, in this example, actual availability of resources differs from that planned for the project. In the first 2 months, project labor is underutilized. In the third month, there is more work planned than there are resources available to complete it. Unfortunately, the work originally scheduled for the third month cannot be pulled forward into the first 2 months to offset the impact in the third month because of the serial and resource dependencies that have been defined in the project planning cycle. So, either the project must be re-planned to meet the capacity of the available human resources, or it falls behind schedule in the third month.

By effectively balancing the project up front against established project and organizational constraints, the project manager can effectively control their impacts.

The key is foresight. By effectively balancing the planned consumption rates up front against established project and organizational constraints, the project manager effectively controls the conflicts. As pointed out before, "prevention is always less costly than failure." Experienced project managers never set themselves up for a problem by overlooking the fundamental business or financial constraints of the organization.

A TIME FOR INTROSPECTION

Throughout the project planning and implementation phases, the project manager and his team frequently reassess the project objectives and status to ensure that the project remains correctly focused. Unplanned or unforeseen changes in business conditions, baseline planning assumptions, or project scope will often lead the project to be completed without the expected deliverables being achieved. Unplanned outside influences can make the original project objectives unachievable. Inadequate or untimely allocation of critical resources can push the project schedule beyond the expected completion date. Ineffective cost controls can cause budget overruns. In short, numerous internal and external factors can negatively impact the project performance, timing, or costs. It is, therefore, incumbent upon the project manager to constantly monitor every possible variable to ensure continued compliance with the project plan. One approach used by successful project managers is to maintain a running project checklist like that shown in Figure 14-11. Constant critical assessments, like these, will ensure that no eleventh-hour surprises occur to derail the project.

SUMMARY

This chapter discusses the basic tactical planning tools for project management. As with the strategic planning tools, there must be structure in the tactical planning. Everything discussed to this point builds upon the prior strategic or tactical element. There are no shortcuts. While it may seem cumbersome, each step in the process is critical to ensuring that the project is planned and implemented correctly—in essence, reducing the risk to the project and its manager.

Project Management Checklist	Yes	No	Corrective Action
Have all activities been identified and listed?	☐	☐	
Has the cycle time of each activity been calculated?	☐	☐	
Have the necessary team skills been identified?	☐	☐	
Have the correct team members been selected?	☐	☐	
Is the team working well as a unit?	☐	☐	
Are assignments being completed on schedule?	☐	☐	
Is the team's problem-solving approach effective?	☐	☐	
Are critical decisions being made on a timely basis?	☐	☐	
Are any hidden agendas arising?	☐	☐	
Is the team maintaining focus?	☐	☐	
Has the team's time been properly allocated to the project?	☐	☐	
Has the critical path been identified?	☐	☐	
Have all project planning tools been employed?	☐	☐	
Has all slack time been identified and reallocated properly?	☐	☐	
Have critical milestones been identified?	☐	☐	
Have management review schedules been set?			
Have all support systems been confirmed?	☐	☐	
Are the conditions the same as when the project was launched?	☐	☐	
Are the initial objectives still valid? Are they attainable?	☐	☐	
Have all assumptions been reviewed and validated?	☐	☐	
Has the scope of the project changed?	☐	☐	
Has the project been impacted by any outside influences that could negatively alter the schedule, costs, or performance?	☐	☐	
Has management altered the original priority assigned to the project?	☐	☐	
Have project expectations changed since the project was started?	☐	☐	

Figure 14-11. Using a checklist like this helps a project manager constantly monitor all aspects of the project to ensure that unexpected variances do not negatively impact progress.

15
Assessing Project Alternatives through Trade-off Analyses

OVERVIEW

No project manager is immune to unwelcome surprises. Risk, which exists in every project, must always be managed effectively to be kept within acceptable levels. But sometimes, even with professionally managed projects, an unforeseen problem arises that impacts the expected project deliverables, throwing the project off schedule or creating an over-budget condition. In such cases, the project manager immediately assesses the various alternatives available to bring the project back under control to ensure that the customer receives those deliverables that are of the highest priority.

The focus of any trade-off decision alternative must always be the customer and the customer's expectations. This is where trade-off analyses come into play. In many situations, one or more of the project variables must be compromised or renegotiated with the customer to bring the remaining variables in as planned. The business, financial, and performance constraints that confront the project manager when faced with a trade-off decision are balanced with those priorities defined by the customer early in the project planning cycle to guarantee the best possible compromise for the project.

Every project begins with one or more variables fixed, as seen in Table 15-1. Typically, all three variables are considered to be fixed once the project scope is defined: the expected deliverable or performance, the schedule, and the project budget. In reality, however, every project has some latitude for compromises to be made without sacrificing the success of the project in the eyes of the customer. To effectively conduct a trade-off analysis, the

Table 15-1. Assessing project trade-off options.

Project Deliverable	Project Schedule	Project Budget/Cost
Fixed	Fixed	Fixed
Variable	Variable	Variable
Fixed	Variable	Variable
Variable	Fixed	Variable
Variable	Variable	Fixed
Fixed	Fixed	Variable
Fixed	Variable	Fixed
Variable	Fixed	Fixed

project manager isolates where that latitude is—the extent of tolerance that exists from the customer's perspective, and then executes the trade-off actions in strict accordance with those priorities.

To begin, the project manager explores the internal issues like, "Can the project scope be redefined without compromising performance, cost, or schedule?" Next, other internal issues are explored. If, for example, the schedule is the customer's first priority, the project will not be successful unless it is brought in on time. While not happy that any other variables may be compromised, the customer will at least consider a compromise as long as the schedule is met.

TRADE-OFF OPTIONS

Schedule as #1 Priority

The project manager begins by giving consideration to reallocating resources from activities not on the critical path (slack-time activities) to activities on the critical path that have shown some degree of slippage. The intent in doing so is to bring the project schedule back into the expected range. Once the critical path activities have been brought back under control, the project manager then redirects project resources back to those non-critical path activities to complete them in a timely manner. In so doing, the project manager carefully monitors those slack time activities to ensure that their slippage does not drive them to a point where they become critical.

Figure 15-1 illustrates the timeline for the fabrication of an enclosed backyard pool. The tasks associated with the fabrication of the pool and enclosure, along with their associated times and dependencies, were defined by the project manager. The resource loading and critical path are shown for planning and tracking purposes.

As an example, assume that the schedule has begun to slip in early July due to heavier than anticipated rains, which have delayed excavation by one day. As this is a critical path item, by definition, the project will slip unless something is done to make up the time. In this case, the project manager can pull Eliot in to assist Johnson on the digging of the pool and delay the start of the electrical wiring by one day. This would bring the critical path back on schedule without impacting the project budget or deliverable. This, of course, assumes that Eliot can handle a shovel. This approach would cause Eliot's activities 8 and 9 to become critical as their available slack time would be consumed. So, any additional slippage here would be problematic, requiring other actions on the part of the project manager downstream. But assuming there are no other problems, the project is now back on schedule.

A second, or alternative approach, is to either reprioritize or eliminate one or more of the non-critical path activities to free up critical project resources. In doing so, care is taken by the project manager so as not to compromise either internal control or other important issues that may further impede the project. In many cases, there are a few activities that can be eliminated without sacrificing the customer's perception of successful project completion. For example, assume that contingency planning was done to address an anticipated risk. If that failure did not occur, the actions and resources that had been set aside for that purpose can now be eliminated.

Another approach is to apply additional resources to the project to ensure that the scheduled completion date is achieved. Is

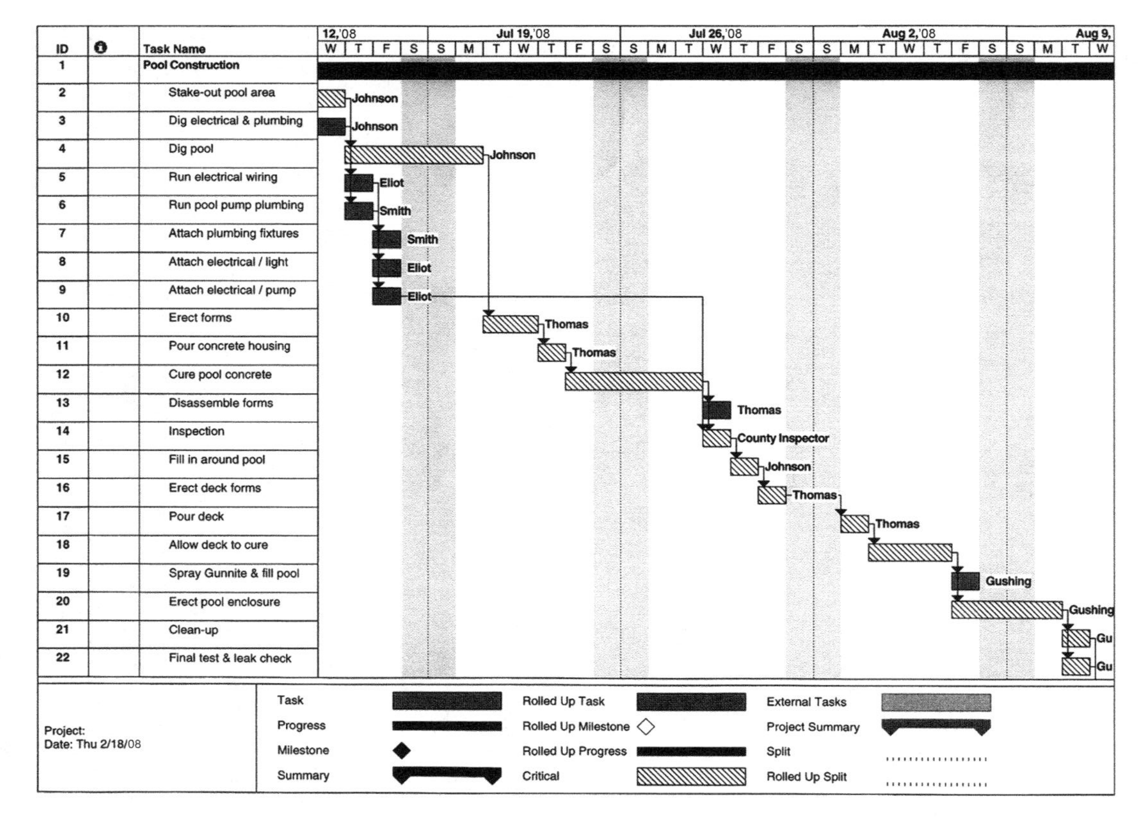

Figure 15-1. Time line for the construction of a swimming pool.

there a cost to this option? Yes, there most certainly is. But, the customer's top priority in this scenario is schedule, so cost is of secondary importance. However, the project manager should not get carried away. The company will end up eating those cost overruns.

Still another option is to employ other compression techniques like concurrency, reengineering, or crashing to reduce the total project cycle time as much as possible along the critical path. Questions that the project manager always considers with these options are: "What remaining activities can be done in parallel instead of in sequence?" "What are the risks?" "Can those risks be minimized and controlled?"

Overtime is another option. Again there is a cost, but the priority is schedule.

Another possibility is to assign some or all of the remaining non-critical path project activities to either administrative or clerical personnel. This approach will free project team members with critical skills or other specialty skilled project resources to take on other, more critical project assignments along the critical path. This approach focuses resources with the most specialized skill sets on those critical path activities that require the most attention. It not only has a lower cost but also is much safer than other alternatives available to the project manager.

If it is technically and economically feasible, subcontracting or outsourcing some of the remaining project activities is an option. Activities selected for outsourcing must be effectively controlled to minimize the exposure to the project relative to failure or delay.

Reengineering is also an option at this juncture. Using the videos from the activity cycle time assessments, the project team assesses the critical path activities in descending cycle time sequence to determine which ones can be reengineered to:

- minimize their total cycle time;
- incorporate concurrent methodologies;
- eliminate all waste and redundancies; or
- identify and address all process, material, and information bottlenecks and queues.

When included as part of the project team's contingency planning processes, reengineering is an especially powerful tool for the project manager. By knowing in advance what actions need to be taken relative to reengineering, the project manager can quickly move the project team into action with little wasted time and effort.

Consideration is also given to automating material and information processing activities where possible to minimize critical path activity cycle times and costs. Automation is *not* always the answer, but in certain cases it is a feasible approach to reducing the cycle time along the critical path.

Seasoned project managers never overlook the resources available through the supply base. Most key suppliers will have a wealth of knowledge and experience that can be drawn upon to assist the project team in meeting the schedule. Suppliers will often provide assistance at no or little cost, just to enhance their standing with the organization. Benefits are there for both sides—the project manager gets the help needed for the project and the supplier is involved in the ultimate solution or design. It is a win-win situation.

Multiple approvals within the project cycle associated with customer or senior management buy-off often take more time and money than necessary to ensure the intended degree of internal control. When the project schedule is in jeopardy, the project manager seeks ways to avoid all unnecessary approvals to further improve the critical path cycle time.

In cases where none of the alternatives discussed here are plausible, the project manager explores ways to make the schedule extension valuable to the customer or senior management. Will the extension allow the project team to offer any free additional features, quality, or functionality to the customer? With a reasonable delay, can reliability or market differentiation be expanded at no or little cost to the customer? Will the value to the customer outweigh the inconvenience of the delay?

Project Cost as #1 Priority

If the variable of most importance to the customer is cost rather than project schedule or performance, then the aforementioned options are of little use to the project manager. Instead, options that focus on project cost or budget reduction take the forefront.

The project manager first identifies where the project cost or budget overruns have occurred and why, and then determines if excess or unused funds can be allocated from other elements or activities within the project to offset the current or projected overruns. Next to be determined are activities that can be allocated to lower cost personnel, especially where the risk of failure is minimal or can be controlled. Another possibility is to outsource where control and risk management dictate a low probability of failure. Many project managers shun this option, believing that they do not have the time needed for outside resources to be brought up to speed. However, in many cases, outside resources have more capabilities and capacities than the project team, along with a lower overhead cost structure.

There are still other cost-related options recommended for the project manager. Reengineering is considered once again. In most cases, a reduction in activity or process cycle time brings with it a corresponding reduction in process costs or overall overhead costs. Some activities may be eliminated altogether, thus saving their costs for reallocation to the project overages. However, the integrity of the project cannot be compromised. That just moves the problem further downstream.

Still another approach, as discussed previously, is the application of value analysis or value engineering techniques to identify ways to generate the same results using lower cost methods, materials, or technologies.

The project manager may also decide to simply absorb the cost overrun rather than pass it along to the customer. This decision should be weighed carefully, especially if it offsets the initial project cost variances by bringing in additional business or downstream revenues in the longer term.

Project Performance or Deliverable as #1 Priority

If the critical priority for the customer is the project deliverable(s), then the project manager has a number of options for the trade-off actions:

1. Apply additional resources or capital to the project to ensure that the original performance targets are met. There is an impact on project costs, but the prime focus is on delivering what has been committed. Cost, again in this case, is secondary.
2. Apply other technologies, processes, or methodologies available to the project team to meet the original performance targets or deliverables. There are often lower-cost or cost-equivalent alternatives available to accomplish the same end. Bias or internal agendas should not keep the project team from exploring them all. Value analysis or value engineering techniques at this juncture are excellent tools to identify the most attractive value/cost alternatives to any business process, product, or service.
3. It is common for a designer of a product or service to build additional robustness or capability into a design with the intent of exciting the customer, expanding market competitiveness, or for other noble reasons. If the original internal performance targets or deliverables for the project exceed the expectations of the customer, it may be prudent to back off to the intended (and expected) level of product or service robustness and then come back at a later time with the additional features or capabilities.

If all avenues have been exhausted internally by the project team, then the project manager addresses other options with the customer or management. Before doing so, however, it is wise to determine if the customer was responsible for the project delays, cost overruns, or changes in deliverables or performance criteria. In many cases, if the project manager has done an effective job of getting customer approval for changes to the original project scope and priorities up front, then the customer will likely accept responsibility for their impacts.

MANAGING DOWNSIDE RISK

When selecting alternatives, the experienced project manager assesses all possible liabilities resulting from the project team's failure to comply with the project requirements. Consideration is given to whether the project team's failure to comply will likely impair the organization's ability to obtain additional business from this, or any other, customer within the industry. Consideration is also given to whether a failure exposes the organization to direct financial liabilities, penalties, or contingent liabilities that may not be evident at the present time. The project manager also considers the potential for product liability or personal injury litigation where financial impact can be unimaginable.

The following example illustrates a common scenario. The project team was retained to resolve a long-running system integration problem that had been plaguing a major financial institution for more than a year. The team failed to complete the project on time for a number of reasons. As a result, the financial institution was forced by federal regulators to discontinue business operations until the project could be completed. Who absorbed the costs associated with the financial institution's actual lost business, actual business costs, and/or opportunity losses? The penalties and contingent liabilities associated with these issues often well exceed any cost overruns that the project team had considered.

TRADE-OFF ALTERNATIVES MATRIX

Comprehensive, quantitative techniques are used by project managers to aid the project team in making a trade-off decision. Such an approach ensures an objective, customer-sensitive solution. The project manager begins by developing a listing of all alternatives and objectives available to the project team. The list can be lengthy, or rather short, depending upon the business and the project's customers. The project team identifies as many plausible alternatives as possible, and then assesses each to determine which alternatives represent the best

A project manager should plan, anticipate, assess, then act quickly with vision and determination. When trade-offs are necessary, they should be conducted with great care.

possible outcome for the customer. To assist his team in doing so, the project manager prepares a decision matrix similar to the one discussed in Chapter 9. Table 15-2 shows a typical example.

Next, the project manager assigns a weighting factor to each objective consistent with those customer priorities established early in the project. Note in Table 15-2 that 95% of the total weighting goes to customer-focused objectives, with only 5% to project team objectives. This is always the case. The customer's needs always receive first consideration, with the project team's secondary. Finally, the project manager assigns a probability of success to each alternative in meeting each of the respective objectives. The probabilities are multiplied by the weighting factor and then summed for a total score for each alternative. The numbers will lead to the singular alternative that provides the highest probability of success in meeting the objectives established relative to the customer's priorities.

As illustrated in Figure 15-2, the numbers in the trade-off analysis will produce a Pareto distribution, which yields a statistically supportable conclusion.

The corrective action selected by the project manager must address the root cause of the project problem. And, it must be measurable in time and/or dollars, as well as capable of being implemented within an acceptable time frame based upon the remaining project schedule. The longer it takes to implement the selected corrective action, the higher the probability that the project objectives will not be met or, at the very least, compromised significantly. The alternative that best addresses the customer's requirements and respective priorities is chosen.

Once the final alternative is selected, the customer is immediately advised of the intended course of action. Like elephants, customers who receive last-minute surprises regarding project delays, cost overruns, or performance deficiencies have a tendency *never* to forget.

All assumptions, corrective actions, and their results are documented clearly and comprehensively by the project manager and his team. The alternative selected to address the project performance, budget, or schedule problems must be supported by the

Table 15-2. Decision matrix example.

	Objective					
	Meet Deliverable	Meet Cost Schedule	Increase Requirements	Maximize Business	Profits	Total
Applied Weights	0.20	0.50	0.25	0.025	0.025	1.00
Alternative						
Request extension	100%	0%	95%	50%	100%	48
Absorb added cost	90%	85%	100%	75%	0%	87
Miss delivery	95%	0%	80%	10%	90%	42
Add resources	95%	95%	50%	90%	0%	81
Reduce quality	0%	85%	85%	15%	90%	66

data used in its selection, along with its associated implementation plan. This is cumbersome, but necessary. If the project team has done an exhaustive job of analyzing, prioritizing, assessing, and selecting all feasible alternatives to correct the project problem, the customer will be assured that everything possible has been done to conform to the agreed upon requirements. A customer may even think more of the team for its efforts.

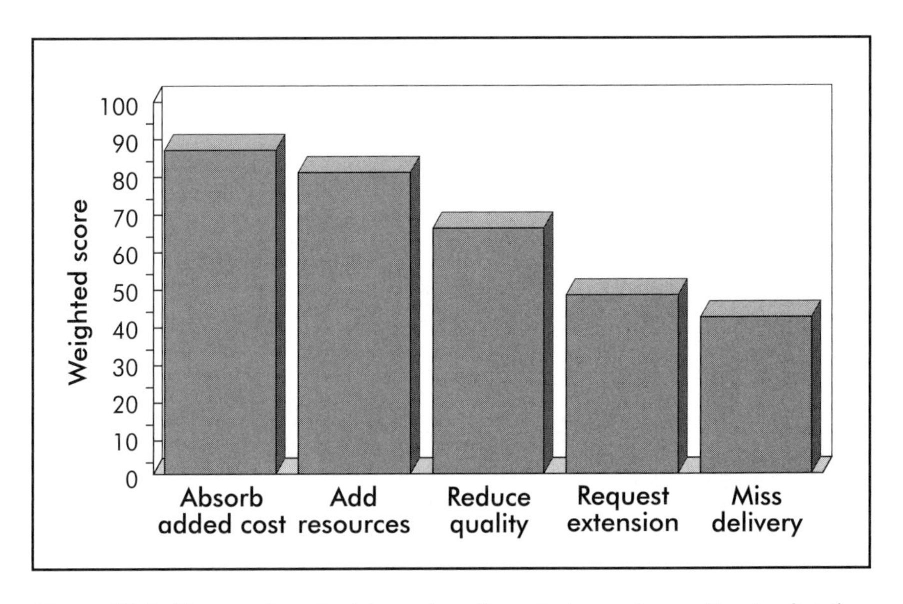

Figure 15-2. The numbers in this trade-off analysis produce a Pareto distribution, which yields a statistically supportable conclusion.

16

Case Study: Florida Southeast Developers

INTRODUCTION

The following case study illustrates the application of the tools and techniques covered in this book. As with all of the case studies contained herein, it was derived from an actual project assignment. To ensure confidentiality, the name of the company, actual location, and several details surrounding the project have been altered.

SITUATIONAL ASSESSMENT

Florida Southeast Developers (FSD) owns approximately 5,000 acres in southeast Florida. Known as Wellington, the total area is a tract of land of approximately 10,000 acres (40.5 km^2), surrounding two large inland freshwater lakes, nestled comfortably in the Florida Everglades National Park Reserve. Adjacent to the famous Palm Beach Polo Grounds, with easy access to main shopping districts like Worth Avenue, Wellington Greene, and the Palm Beach Gardens Mall, direct tie-in to the primary business districts of West Palm Beach, as well as the Palm Beach International Airport, Wellington has been a mecca for developers over the last 10 years.

Florida Southeast Developers, one of the original custom housing developers in the West Palm Beach area, was instrumental in the initial development projects in Wellington, giving the company an early competitive edge against other developers. Brisk sales have kept crews busy, even through the recession of 2007, 2008, and early 2009. Profits have consistently ranged in the 25–28% pretax range on average annual revenues of $14.5 million, while the backlog of sold home sites awaiting construction has averaged between 12–15 throughout the last 10 years. The company's quality has remained consistently high, resulting in a significant number of "word-of-mouth" inquiries, many leading to actual sales. The company's advertising costs, as a result, have remained relatively low, approximately 4% of gross sales.

Since early 2008, there has been a noticeable change in the market, driven primarily by builders who have demonstrated the ability to build quality custom homes in less time than that available through FSD. The company's management tried using rudimentary project scheduling techniques to improve cycle times and reduce costs but, due to the number of unexpected changes that occurred on a regular basis, did not find them useful. Sensing a pending business crisis, FSD decided to retain the services of a professional project manager to improve its delivery performance.

Management's comments were: "We are willing to try anything that will improve our ability to meet customer expectations. Our objective is to compete directly with our competitors without sacrificing either quality or profitability, if that's possible. And time is of the essence, because we are losing business rapidly. Our close rate has dropped from 84% to under 40% in the last 18 months. We need help!"

That is how this project was launched.

Phase I: Fact Finding

In the project manager's initial fact-finding discussions with the management of FSD, he was advised that FSD's average time from contract signing to close was approximately 6.5 months. An initial market assessment indicated that the competition was averaging 4.25 months, with no apparent reduction in quality, making the performance gap approximately 2.25 months.

The project manager's preliminary competitive benchmarking also revealed that the competition had lowered the price of a comparable home (2,850 ft^2 [265 m^2], central heating and air, two-car garage, living room, formal dining room, great room, dinette, four bedrooms, three full baths, double-door walk-in closets, fully equipped kitchen and utility room, quality tile and carpeting throughout, intercom and security systems, enclosed in-ground 15 × 30 ft [4.6 × 9.1 m] heated pool and deck, automatic sprinkler system, and full landscaping) to $311,500 complete with waterfront lot. Florida Southeast Developer's price was $327,500 for a comparable custom-built house.

FSD's senior management initially assumed that pricing was the critical factor behind the loss in market share. The project manager realized that the risk behind that assumption could be significant. If FSD simply lowered the price of its homes without clearly understanding all factors behind the market, it could conceivably go out of business.

Based upon findings from his preliminary situational and risk assessments, the project manager concluded that additional information was required before the project scope and deliverables could be defined. From discussions with previous, past, and potential customers of Florida Southeast Developers, the project manager found that it was not the differential in pricing or any perceived difference in quality that influenced the final buying decision, but rather the quoted time it would take to complete the home. In addition, the project manager concluded from the data collected from past customers that the company universally failed to hit its targeted completion dates. That angered customers because it delayed their move-in, creating or prolonging costs for furniture storage and interim apartment rental.

Penalties for failing to comply with the contracted completion dates had been infrequent in the past, but demands for compensation from buyers had started to increase within the last several months. Competitors had gotten wind of FSD's delays and were now using it to attract potential FSD customers.

Phase II: Problem Analysis

To gain a better understanding of the company's operating processes along with its actual cycle times, the project manager began a situational assessment by analyzing the steps Florida Southeast Developers undertook to build homes, along with the associated cycle time for each step. In addition to quickly identifying several process issues, the project manager learned that the cycle time/calendar time conversions had to consider the fact that the company's employees did not normally work either weekends or holidays. Further, if such a work schedule was necessary, subcontractors would usually charge double their normal rates for weekend work and triple time for holidays. He also found that the county inspectors, to a large extent, governed the pace of each project, as well as the quality pursuant to county building codes.

Phase III: Process Analysis

The process begins with the signing of a construction contract with the buyer. FSD requires a 20% down payment at the time of signing, with the balance due at closing. This is generally a 1-day activity, but it occasionally takes from 5–10 days for the buyer's check to clear, especially for out-of-state checks. And, the project manager found that FSD made it a policy *never* to begin until it had money in hand.

Once the company has the cash, the in-house survey team conducts a site survey. This is normally completed within 1 week from the date of order due to a backlog, along with the time needed to get staff organized and onto the site. The survey is then reviewed against the county's plot plans to be sure of the easement locations, power and sewer line locations and tie-ins, and any possible interference with existing homes adjacent to the property. Once this is completed (approximately 1–2 days), FSD applies for a building permit from the county. The county requires the company to show proof of its builder's bond, the deed to the property along with any associated liens or encumbrances, its site survey, and the results of the site assessment. The company can receive its permits in as little as 2 days or as long as 2 weeks. It depends upon when the county gets to it. Since there is no way to start without that permit, FSD just waits.

Once the permit is in hand, FSD personnel prepare the site. This 1–2-week project includes removing trash from the site, cutting and removing brush, and cutting and removing trees. The company must be careful because removing cypress trees from the site is restricted by code to only that area where the house will actually sit. Because they are an endangered species, all other cypress trees on the lot must be maintained, even if the buyer requests the builder to remove them.

Once the site preparation is concluded, company personnel begin grading the site for placement of the pad upon which the house will be built. In addition, FSD personnel dig trenches for electrical lines, telephone lines, and water lines. Florida code dictates the compression ratio of the soil (to ensure it is rigid enough to prevent cracking of the pad once poured). So, company personnel spend approximately 2–3 weeks leveling the lot, compressing the sand/soil combination, adding materials as necessary, and then checking grade to ensure the proper runoff.

After the desired grade and compression are achieved, company personnel take a soil sample for analysis by the Florida State labs to ensure there are no hazardous waste materials present. If there is any trace of hazardous materials, the company must turn over the entire lot to a depth of 5–8 ft (1.5–2.4 m) for a second sample. If it too proves to contain hazardous waste, the Florida and federal Environmental Protection Agency (EPA) inspectors are called in to decide what actions to take. If no problems arise, as is the case 90% of the time, the soil sample is turned around in 1–2 weeks. If a second sample is required, which occurs maybe 1 in 100 times, it will take at least 1 month to get things resolved and back underway. If the state and federal EPA inspectors are called in, company personnel simply pack up and move to another job until the problem is resolved, typically away for anywhere from 6–12 months.

Once the company gets the go ahead, it contacts the exterminators to spray the soil for termites and fire ants. The exterminators spray the soil 2–3 times to ensure that there is good penetration, usually to a depth of 18–24 in. (46–61 cm). This kills the fire ants and termites for approximately 18 months, enough time for the company to get the house built, closed, and the buyers to set a plan with their own exterminators. It is a 3–5-day process, depending on when the exterminators get started. Normally the company is forced to wait anywhere from 1–3 weeks for the exterminators to get on site because of the exterminator's backlog.

At this point, it is time to call the building inspectors to review the site, along with the building permits and associated papers. After company personnel call the county inspection office, the inspectors arrive within 5–7 days, and finish the required inspections within 1 hour.

At this point, things really get rolling. The subcontractors lay the forms for the pad, based upon the exterior dimensions of the house as defined by the architect. Placement on the lot is given due consideration to ensure that the house does not get too close to easements and to be sure the house is well situated. For example, if the buyer wants a circular driveway, the company places the house about 10–20 ft (3–6 m) further back on the lot. This gives the appearance of more depth to the yard and prevents the driveway from consuming the entire front view, thus overpowering the front elevation of the house. As a rule, the subcontractors get it right the first time. It is a 5–7-day job, but they can push it through in 3 days if they work at it. Lead time for the framers (subcontractors who put in the forms for the pad) is usually 1 week or less.

The company next calls in the plumbers to lay the plumbing mains and drains for the bathrooms, kitchen, hot water heater, and outside faucets. It is like a jigsaw puzzle. The plumbers cut and piece together hundreds of pieces to get the pipes in the right spots, then cap them to be sure the other subcontractors do not get concrete and dirt into them. They then run a trunk line outside the perimeter of the pad for connection to the main sewer and water lines after the pad is poured. This whole process consumes from 2–3 weeks. In its planning, the company normally allows an additional 2 weeks for the plumbers to show up because of the plumbing company's backlog.

The concrete subcontractors are then called in to lay the rebar (reinforcing bars) before the concrete can be poured for the pad. This adds torsion and shear strength to the pad, thereby keeping the overall depth of the pad to about 10 in. (25 cm) or less. This is a 3-day job at most. Company personnel normally plan on 3 days on site for the concrete subcontractors, but in reality they usually get the job done in 1–2 days. Because FSD uses one of the best concrete subcontractors in the area, its wait time for them to get to the site is generally 3 days.

It is now time for the building inspectors again. Normal lead time is 2–3 weeks. In most cases, company personnel get the inspection completed, the usual required fixes done, and the reinspection completed within about 2 weeks.

When the concrete subcontractors pour the pad, company personnel begin each pour with what is known as a slump test to measure the consistency of the concrete. This ensures that FSD receives acceptable concrete with each pour. Once the concrete subcontractors begin the pour, they must get it done quickly, so FSD personnel plan ahead about 1–2 weeks by setting the pour date with the subcontractors. Unless delayed by weather, the subcontractor begins pouring around 6:00 a.m. The subcontractor keeps the trucks coming throughout the morning to ensure an uninterrupted flow of concrete. The mudders (guys who spread and smooth the concrete while it is being poured) work feverishly throughout the day, making sure that the concrete is pushed into every corner of the forms, around every pipe, and that it flows evenly around the rebar. Surfacing is completed by mid-afternoon to guarantee that the top surface of the pad is as flat as possible. In Florida, builders use ceramic floor tile extensively in custom homes. If the floor is not even, the tile will not lay evenly, making it very visible to the naked eye. In the rare case when the company is forced to grind down high spots, FSD loses 2–3 days and about $10,000. By the end of the day, the job is done and the pad is covered with tarps to protect the green concrete from damage by rain or dirt. The pad is allowed to cure for approximately 2 weeks before FSD begins erecting the walls.

It is now time for the next required building inspection. After another 1–2-week wait to complete the inspection, the erection of the walls begins. The masons, subcontractors who erect the walls of the house using concrete blocks, are called to begin work. They typically complete the job in 5–7 days. The wait for them to start, 2–3 weeks, is generally longer than their actual work time. The walls are allowed to cure for another 5 days before the roofers begin erecting the roof trusses. FSD generally allows 1 week for the roofers to schedule the project into their work queue.

Trusses are secured to the walls with the reinforcing straps that were installed by the masons and then reinforced with ceiling beams around the perimeter of the inner walls. Plywood is then nailed to the trusses to provide the inner shell of the roof. Black tar paper is then nailed down over the plywood to provide a moisture barrier. Then, the seams are tarred to ensure a tight seal. At that point, the roofers have completed their initial work. The whole sub-roofing job is completed within 7–10 working days.

The building inspector is called once again for a review of the walls and roof. This typically takes 1–2-hours, with the wait time for the inspector anywhere from 1–2 weeks. Once the inspection is completed and buyoff is received, the company begins the work on the interior walls (called the rough-in). Before personnel can begin, however, they must place the tubs and shower stalls in approximately their correct places. This is required because, once the walls are in place, these units are too large to pass through the door openings. This is normally a 1-day job. They then begin erecting the walls. The rough-in crews are typically available within 5–6 days from the time company personnel call them. In Florida, because of the termite and carpenter ant problems, builders generally use a combination of wooden studs and steel. The ceiling studs and the interior garage walls are wood, the interior wall studs, steel. The outer door frames are steel, but the door trim is wood. The rough-in is a 3-week job from start to finish.

Once the walls are up, the electricians begin running wire and placing the electrical boxes for the mains, switches, and plugs, along with all major appliances. This includes both the interior and exterior electrical circuits. The conduits, placed in the ground before the pad was poured, are used to feed the wiring into the various rooms in the house. Everything ties back into the location selected for the main circuit box. The feeders are then run from the main circuit box under the pad to the location where the Florida Power & Light (FPL) crew designates placement of the electrical meter. This is a 5-day process, but the wait for the electricians can be up to 3 weeks.

Next, the company contacts the heating and air conditioning subcontractors. Within a week they show up to place the ducts for the heating, ventilation, and air conditioning (HVAC) units, pour the pad(s) for the heat pumps, and look over the wiring. When the pads are dry (in about 2 days), they locate the heat pump(s) and connect them to the main circuits. A continuity test is conducted to ensure the wiring is sound. The whole HVAC job is completed in 2–3 days.

Once the HVAC subcontractors are finished, company personnel call the finishing contractor to install the windows and doors. This is the first time the house can be truly secured. Within 2–3 days the subs are on site and within another 3–4 days, the job is completed. The rockers, people who install the wallboard, are then ready to begin. They are usually on site within 1–2 weeks to install the ceiling and wallboard, tape and finish the seams, and smooth the joints. Ceiling texturing comes next. Walls and ceilings are completed within 2–3 weeks. Carpenters are then called to install the cabinets and interior trim molding (baseboards, door frames, etc.). Any custom woodwork is completed at this point—things like special cabinets, ceiling trim, and paneled walls. Staining and varnishing are also completed at this stage. The carpenters require a 2-week notice and complete their work within 4–5 days.

With the carpentry work complete, the plumbers can complete the final installation of the fixtures, showers, basins, toilets, and exterior faucets. They also install the hot water heater and dishwasher, and then check for leaks. This is a 3–4-day process. And because the plumbers generally estimate when FSD will be ready for them, they are normally available within 2–3 days from the time company personnel call them.

The building inspectors are called to inspect the plumbing and electrical wiring, as well as the windows and doors. As before, it takes only a few hours for the inspection and buyoff of the completed work, but it usually requires 1 week to get the inspectors on site. They usually find one or two small building code infractions. Every effort is made to fix them while the inspectors are on site. If not, it could be another 1–2 weeks before FSD can get the inspectors back for a reinspection.

The electricians are then called to complete the electrical work, install the major appliances, intercom, and security systems. While they are on site, company personnel call FPL to tie in the electrical meter to the main FPL trunk lines to provide power for the house. The electricians, in concert with FPL, conduct a final circuit test and turn on power to the main fuse box. Any problems are diagnosed and fixed while the electricians are on site. The company also contacts Southern Bell Telephone to connect the telephone lines to the main trunk lines. It normally takes from 2–3 weeks for the workers to get on site, but their work is usually completed in 1 day or less. FSD personnel try to get the phone installers in while the electricians are on site, if possible, in case of a wiring problem. They are not normally successful, however.

It is now time for a quick walk-through by the county inspectors.

So within a week after the plumbers, electricians, FPL, and Southern Bell are through, FSD personnel have the house plumbed and powered. They then contact the contractors to lay the bathroom, kitchen, counter, and floor tiles. It normally takes the subcontractors 2 weeks to get on site and 2 weeks to complete the work. While this is being done, company personnel bring in a cleanup crew to clean the interior floors of debris, sweep, and pick up around the exterior of the house, a 2-day job at most.

The roofers are then called to tile the roof. In most cases, their work is completed in 5–6 days, including cleanup. It is generally a different crew than the one that did the base work. However, it can take up to 3 weeks to get them on site. The style of tile is also a factor. Because of the ridging, the barrel tiles usually take 2–3 days longer to install. Corners and ends require careful cutting, and the sealing is a little trickier. Once the work is completed, FSD personnel call the building inspector for a final roof approval. Once again, the inspector spends a few hours on the site, but it takes up to a week to get him there.

The painters are then called in to paint the interior of the house. They usually spray the ceilings first, after covering any tiled countertops or special woodwork. Then they spray the walls with one coat of sealer, then a second coat of interior flat. The interior doors are painted prior to being hung to guarantee that both sides and all four edges are adequately covered. Painting goes relatively quickly, requiring only 3–4 days for completion. And, once they are called, the painters are generally available within just 2–3 days.

The stucco subcontractors are next in line. Within 2–3 days from the time company personnel call, the subcontractors show up to install the base mat and begin the stucco application. These guys are quick—it takes 2–3 days tops, and the whole house is done—including cleanup.

FSD personnel next lay the forms for the driveway and sidewalks around the house. The company does this with its own rough-in crews for expediency. They are available within 1–2 days and can lay the forms and place the rebar in 1 day. FSD then calls for the concrete. It typically takes just 1–2 days for the trucks to roll in, and within 1 day the concrete is poured, smoothed, and covered for curing. It sets for about a week before any other work is done to be sure it cures adequately.

The painters are again called, this time to paint the exterior of the house. As before, they spray paint a sealing coat, then a finishing coat. The trim is done by hand to the buyer's specifications. This is a 2–3-day job, with a 1-week wait for the painters to get on site. Once completed, though, the company can call in the electricians for the final hookups. They install the interior lights, fans, switches, and outlets. They also install the exterior lights and fans. Everything is tested before they leave. This is a 3-day job, unless they have to wait for the buyer's fixtures. If so, they simply move on to their next job and reschedule when the fixtures arrive. As before, wait time is 7–10 days.

The cleanup crews are then called in to clean the interior of the house thoroughly, including washing the windows, cleaning off the paint over-spray, cleaning the appliances, and washing down the tiles. The crews are always available within 1–2 days after FSD personnel call them, and can complete their work in about 5 days. The carpet layers, then, are cleared to lay the carpets. Company personnel always have to remind them not to bang up the walls and woodwork. If they do, FSD is forced to call the painters back in to repaint. The carpet layers are generally in and out within 2 days, including hauling off the remnants. With the carpets in, company personnel hang the interior doors and trim them to clear the carpets. Because they are FSD personnel, they are on the site the same day, and finish within the day. The interior of the house is now complete.

FSD personnel next focus on completing the outside of the house. The gutter subcontractors are called in to hang the gutters around the perimeter of the roof. Downspouts are placed so they are as inconspicuous as possible on each side. The gutter subcontractors can hang the entire house in less than 5 hours with little, if any, scrap. Their workload is so heavy, however, that FSD may have to wait as long as 3 weeks for them to get to the site. But normally, they show up in a little less than two. General cleanup then begins outside. Picking up wood and metal scraps, concrete blocks, leftover forms, etc. takes about a day for the crew to complete.

It is now time for another inspection. Again, it takes approximately 1 week to get the inspectors on site and less than 2 hours to complete the required inspection. If FSD personnel (and subcontractors) have done their jobs, there are no problems. If there are problems, it is normally a 3-week cycle to get the appropriate subcontractors back on site to make corrections, and then to get the building inspector back to confirm that the infractions have been resolved. Most often, the subcontractors get it right the first time.

The house itself is now complete. It is time to call in the pool subcontractors to build the pool. Within 10–12 days from the call, the pool subcontractors begin to dig the pool foundation. During the wait period, FSD gets the building permits for the pool (they are separate from the house). The foundation is ready within 2 days, including the trenches for connecting the electrical and water lines. The forms are then set in and secured within 3 days. Electrical and water lines are then run to the pump site the following day. A pad is set and poured for placement of the pool pump and filter. Pour and cure time is about 1 week. Once the pad is ready, the filter and pump unit is installed within 1–2 days. The pool and patio are poured in 1 day and allowed to cure for about 1 week. Before the Gunite® is sprayed, however, the building inspector is called to inspect the water and electrical lines, hookups, and foundation. As before, the inspector spends a few hours on site after 1–2 weeks of waiting on the part of FSD. After that, however, the pool is ready for finishing.

The Gunite spraying and pool filling happen simultaneously, as the pool water is a catalyst in hardening the Gunite. But the water from the house lines does not flow fast enough to keep up. So, the pool subcontractor hires a local trucking firm to haul in 15,000 gal (56,775 L) of water. Queue time is only about 2 days, so there is not much delay by waiting on the water. Once the spray begins, the water is pumped in immediately behind it. This phase of the job is completed in a single day. Curing is done in 4–5 days. When the curing is completed, the pool light is connected and the entire electrical and pump system is tested. This is a 1-day operation.

The pool subcontractor then begins the process of building the pool enclosure. Although the pool is of a standard size and configuration, allowing the majority of the enclosure to be specified and configured in advance to speed erection, the final tie-in to the house is always a custom fit. The beams are set first and then the doors are hung. Cutting and installation of the screens is then completed. The enclosure takes anywhere from 1–2 days, including cleanup. When complete, the building inspector is called for a final review.

The company now calls the sprinkler system subcontractors to lay in the pipe and sprinkler heads. Within a week they are on site. They locate the site for the sprinkler pump and electrical box first, and pour a pad (1 day). After the pad is cured in 2–3 days, the main sprinkler pump is set and connected to the electrical control box, which was installed while the pad was curing. This is about a 4-hour job. The main lines are then run, followed by the feeder lines. The main feed line from the pump to the canal or main city water lines is then set in and plumbed. This is a 2-day process. The next day, after connecting all of the sprinkler heads and testing them for leaks and direction, the subcontractors clean up and leave.

Next, the landscapers come in. They bring fill dirt because there is not much of it naturally in Florida. They begin by laying out the placement of the trees, shrubs, and flowers. The trees go in first, followed by the shrubs. Then the flowers are placed in the beds. Bedding mulch goes in last. After that, the sod is laid, making sure not to cover the sprinkler heads. Invariably, they cut one or two sprinkler lines. The landscaping is done in 3–4 days; the sprinkler line repairs in another 2 days, including queue time. FSD personnel then dig a hole for the mailbox and cement the post in place. The following day, the mailbox is attached.

The house is now done! FSD calls the building inspector out for a final inspection. There is rarely a problem at this point. Once the final papers have been cleared, the buyer is contacted for a final walk-through. The buyers usually come by themselves, but occasionally will bring out their own mechanical or electrical inspectors for a final look. The final inspection and walk-through are completed within 2–3 weeks. FSD and the buyers are now ready for closing. The bankers and lawyers are generally available within 7–10 days at the maximum. Then it is done. FSD hands over the keys and wishes the buyers well.

Results of Initial Process Analysis

The project manager, now armed with the data from his initial situational assessment and process analysis, began a problem analysis. Using the process data, he created an activity listing, including dependencies, along with a resource loading chart to determine where the majority of the cycle time was being consumed. As illustrated in Figure 16-1, the largest element of cycle time was in queue time, consuming 353 days.

From his resource loading analysis (see Figure 16-2), he then calculated the costs for each major project element using a cost analysis worksheet (Figure 16-3). His intent was to identify all relevant cost, resource, and cycle time issues before setting out with his alternative analysis. In this example, the actual costs have been left off for proprietary reasons. The format used, however, is as illustrated.

The project manager next created a Gantt chart (see Figure 16-4) to determine the total cycle time FSD actually consumed in the building process. The project manager immediately concluded

ID	Task Name	Duration	Start	Finish	Predecessors	Resource Names
1	**Build Custom House - FSD**	**613d**	**9/11/98**	**1/16/01**		
2	Sign contract w/ buyer	10d	9/11/98	9/24/98		FSD
3	Site survey	5d	9/25/98	10/1/98	2	FSD
4	Review survey	2d	10/2/98	10/5/98	3	FSD
5	Apply for permit	10d	10/6/98	10/19/98	4	FSD
6	Prepare site	10d	10/20/98	11/2/98	5	FSD
7	Grade site	15d	11/3/98	11/23/98	6	FSD
8	Dig utility trenches	1d	11/3/98	11/3/98	6	FSD
9	Soil sample submitted	10d	11/24/98	12/7/98	7	Florida State
10	Exterminator queue	15d	12/8/98	12/28/98	9	Queue
11	Spray soil for insects	5d	12/29/98	1/4/99	10	Exterminator
12	Building Inspector queu	7d	1/5/99	1/13/99	11	Queue
13	Inspection	1d	1/14/99	1/14/99	12	County Inspector
14	Forms sub queue	5d	1/15/99	1/21/99	13	Queue
15	Lay forms for pad	7d	1/22/99	2/1/99	14	Forms sub
16	Plumber queue	10d	2/2/99	2/15/99	15	Queue
17	Plumbing mains & drain	14d	2/16/99	3/5/99	16	Plumber
18	Trunk lines	1d	3/8/99	3/8/99	17	Plumber
19	Concrete sub queue	3d	3/9/99	3/11/99	18	Queue
20	Lay rebar for pad	3d	3/12/99	3/16/99	19	Concrete sub
21	Building inspector queu	10d	3/17/99	3/30/99	20	Queue
22	Inspection	1d	3/31/99	3/31/99	21	County Inspector
23	Rework & re-inspection	10d	4/1/99	4/14/99	22	Concrete sub
24	Pour pad	1d	4/15/99	4/15/99	23	Concrete sub
25	Slump tests	1d	4/15/99	4/15/99	23	FSD
26	Pad cure time	10d	4/16/99	4/29/99	24	Queue

Figure 16-1. Activity listing used to determine where FSD spent the most time in the construction process.

that the management of Florida Southeast Developers had dramatically underestimated their current process cycle time. Rather than the 6–7 months they had assumed it took them to build a

ID	Task Name	Duration	Start	Finish	Predecessors	Resource Names
27	Building Inspector queu	10d	4/30/99	5/13/99	26	Queue
28	Inspection	1d	5/14/99	5/14/99	27	County Inspector
29	Mason queue	15d	5/17/99	6/4/99	28	Queue
30	Erect exterior walls	7d	6/7/99	6/15/99	29	Masons
31	Wall cure	5d	6/16/99	6/22/99	30	Queue
32	Roofer queue	5d	6/23/99	6/29/99	31	Queue
33	Erect roof trusses	7d	6/30/99	7/8/99	32	Roofers
34	Subroof applied	2d	7/9/99	7/12/99	33	Roofers
35	Paper & seal roof	1d	7/13/99	7/13/99	34	Roofers
36	Building Inspector queu	10d	7/14/99	7/27/99	35	Queue
37	Inspection	1d	7/28/99	7/28/99	36	County Inspector
38	Place tubs & showers	1d	7/29/99	7/29/99	37	FSD
39	Rough-in sub queue	6d	7/30/99	8/6/99	38	Queue
40	Rough-in interior walls	15d	8/9/99	8/27/99	39	Rough-in subs
41	Electrician queue	15d	8/30/99	9/17/99	40	Queue
42	Wiring	5d	9/20/99	9/24/99	41	Electricians
43	HVAC sub queue	5d	9/27/99	10/1/99	42	Queue
44	HVAC install	1d	10/4/99	10/4/99	43	HVAC sub
45	Pour pads	1d	10/4/99	10/4/99	43	HVAC sub
46	Pad cure	2d	10/5/99	10/6/99	45	Queue
47	Install heat pumps	1d	10/7/99	10/7/99	46	HVAC sub
48	Finishing sub queue	3d	10/8/99	10/12/99	47	Queue
49	Install windows & doors	4d	10/13/99	10/18/99	48	Finishers
50	Rocker sub queue	10d	10/19/99	11/1/99	49	Queue
51	Install interior wall boar	12d	11/2/99	11/17/99	50	Rockers
52	Ceiling texturing	3d	11/18/99	11/22/99	51	Rockers

Figure 16-1. (continued)

house, it actually took around 2 years. Thus, the project manager pinpointed the reason for the drop in business and profitability.

The project manager had discussions with FSD's senior management staff regarding the gap between their expected and actual

ID	Task Name	Duration	Start	Finish	Predecessors	Resource Names
53	Carpenter queue	10d	11/23/99	12/6/99	52	Queue
54	Install cabinets & trim	5d	12/7/99	12/13/99	53	Carpenters
55	Plumber queue	3d	12/14/99	12/16/99	54	Queue
56	Final plumbing install	4d	12/17/99	12/22/99	55	Plumbers
57	Building Inspector queu	5d	12/23/99	12/29/99	56	Queue
58	Inspection	1d	12/30/99	12/30/99	57	County Inspector
59	Electrician queue	5d	12/31/99	1/6/00	58	Queue
60	Complete electrical inst	3d	1/7/00	1/11/00	59	Electricians
61	FPL electrical meter	1d	1/7/00	1/7/00	59	FPL
62	Check & power-up	1d	1/12/00	1/12/00	60	Electrician & FPL
63	Southern Bell queue	15d	1/13/00	2/2/00	62	Queue
64	Connect telephone lines	1d	2/3/00	2/3/00	63	Southern Bell
65	Building Inspector queu	5d	2/4/00	2/10/00	64	Queue
66	Inspection	1d	2/11/00	2/11/00	65	County Inspector
67	Tile sub queue	10d	2/14/00	2/25/00	66	Queue
68	Lay floor & wall tile	10d	2/28/00	3/10/00	67	Tile sub
69	Clean-up	2d	2/28/00	2/29/00	67	FSD
70	Roofer queue	15d	3/13/00	3/31/00	68	Queue
71	Tile roof	6d	4/3/00	4/10/00	70	Roofers
72	Building Inspector queu	5d	4/11/00	4/17/00	71	Queue
73	Inspection	1d	4/18/00	4/18/00	72	County Inspectors
74	Painter queue	3d	4/19/00	4/21/00	73	Queue
75	Paint interior	4d	4/24/00	4/27/00	74	Paint Sub
76	Stucco sub queue	3d	4/28/00	5/2/00	75	Queue
77	Stucco exterior	3d	5/3/00	5/5/00	76	Stucco sub
78	Lay driveway forms	3d	5/8/00	5/10/00	77	FSD

Figure 16-1. (continued)

cycle time performance and shared his conclusions regarding the tie-in of that cycle time performance to lost market share. Then the project manager set out to develop a project planning and execution model for use in reducing FSD's process cycle time to competitive

ID	Task Name	Duration	Start	Finish	Predecessors	Resource Names
79	Queue for concrete	2d	5/11/00	5/12/00	78	Queue
80	Pour driveway & walks	1d	5/15/00	5/15/00	79	FSD
81	Concrete cure	5d	5/16/00	5/22/00	80	Queue
82	Painter queue	5d	5/23/00	5/29/00	81	Queue
83	Paint exterior	3d	5/30/00	6/1/00	82	Paint Sub
84	Electrician queue	10d	6/2/00	6/15/00	83	Queue
85	Final hook-ups/applianc	3d	6/16/00	6/20/00	84	Electrician
86	Clean-up sub queue	2d	6/21/00	6/22/00	85	Queue
87	Interior clean-up & prep	5d	6/23/00	6/29/00	86	Clean-up sub
88	Carpet layer queue	1d	6/30/00	6/30/00	87	Queue
89	Lay carpets	2d	7/3/00	7/4/00	88	Carpet layers
90	Hang interior doors & tri	1d	7/5/00	7/5/00	89	FSD
91	Gutter sub queue	15d	7/6/00	7/26/00	90	Queue
92	Hang gutters	5d	7/27/00	8/2/00	91	Gutter sub
93	Exterior clean-up	1d	8/3/00	8/3/00	92	FSD
94	Building Inspector queu	5d	8/4/00	8/10/00	93	Queue
95	Inspection	1d	8/11/00	8/11/00	94	County Inspector
96	Pool sub queue	12d	8/14/00	8/29/00	95	Queue
97	Pool permits	1d	8/14/00	8/14/00	95	FSD
98	Dig pool & foundation	2d	8/30/00	8/31/00	96	Pool sub
99	Set pool forms	3d	9/1/00	9/5/00	98	Pool sub
100	Electrical & water lines	1d	9/6/00	9/6/00	99	Pool sub
101	Pool pump pad pour	5d	9/7/00	9/13/00	100	Pool sub
102	Install filter & pump	2d	9/14/00	9/15/00	101	Pool sub
103	Pour pool & patio	1d	9/18/00	9/18/00	102	Pool sub
104	Concrete cure time	5d	9/19/00	9/25/00	103	Queue

Figure 16-1. (continued)

levels. Doing so required a completely new way of approaching FSD's business, as well as some "out-of-the-box" thinking. To start with, the project manager developed an alternative analysis. Then, using a revised work breakdown structure (WBS) to guide the

ID	Task Name	Duration	Start	Finish	Predecessors	Resource Names
105	Building Inspector queu	10d	9/26/00	10/9/00	104	Queue
106	Inspection	1d	10/10/00	10/10/00	105	County Inspector
107	Water queue time	2d	10/11/00	10/12/00	106	Queue
108	Spray Gunite & fill pool	1d	10/13/00	10/13/00	107	Pool sub
109	Cure time	5d	10/16/00	10/20/00	108	Queue
110	Connect pool light	1d	10/23/00	10/23/00	109	Pool sub
111	Test electrical wiring	1d	10/23/00	10/23/00	109	Pool sub
112	Build pool enclosure	2d	10/24/00	10/25/00	111	Pool sub
113	Building Inspector queu	1d	10/26/00	10/26/00	112	Queue
114	Pool inspection	1d	10/27/00	10/27/00	113	County Inspector
115	Sprinkler sub queue	5d	10/30/00	11/3/00	114	Queue
116	Install sprinkler pipes	1d	11/6/00	11/6/00	115	Sprinkler sub
117	Lay forms & pour pad	1d	11/7/00	11/7/00	116	Sprinkler sub
118	Pad cure	3d	11/8/00	11/10/00	117	Sprinkler sub
119	Install control box	1d	11/8/00	11/8/00	117	Sprinkler sub
120	Run main water feed lin	1d	11/9/00	11/9/00	119	Sprinkler sub
121	Run water feeder lines	1d	11/9/00	11/9/00	119	Sprinkler sub
122	Connect sprinkler heads	1d	11/10/00	11/10/00	121	Sprinkler sub
123	Landscaper queue	1d	11/13/00	11/13/00	122	Queue
124	Landscaping	4d	11/14/00	11/17/00	123	Landscaper
125	Sprinkler repairs	2d	11/20/00	11/21/00	124	Sprinkler sub
126	Dig mailbox & cement	1d	11/22/00	11/22/00	125	FSD
127	Attach mailbox	1d	11/23/00	11/23/00	126	FSD
128	Building Inspector queu	10d	11/24/00	12/7/00	127	Queue
129	Final inspection	1d	12/8/00	12/8/00	128	County Inspector
130	Buyer queue	15d	12/11/00	12/29/00	129	Queue
131	Buyer walk-through	1d	1/1/01	1/1/01	130	FSD
132	Closing queue	10d	1/2/01	1/15/01	131	Queue
133	Closing	1d	1/16/01	1/16/01	132	FSD

Figure 16-1. (continued)

project team's thinking, he created a new Gantt chart planning model to guide the implementation.

ID	Resource Name	Work	'98	Sep 20, '98		Dec 13, '98		Mar 7, '99		May 30, '99	
			T	S	W	S	T	M	F	T	S
1	**FSD**	**544h**	88h	**224h**	112h				8h		8h
2	Florida State	80h			80h						
3	Exterminator	40h				40h					
4	Queue	2768h			32h	176h	88h	104h	168h	176h	120h
5	County Inspector	80h				8h		8h	8h		8h
6	Forms sub	56h					56h				
7	Plumber	120h					72h	48h			
8	Concrete sub	112h						72h	40h		
9	Masons	56h								56h	
10	Roofers	128h									80h
11	Rough-in subs	120h									
12	Electricians	64h									
13	**HVAC sub**	**24h**									
14	Finishers	32h									
15	Rockers	120h									
16	Carpenters	40h									
17	Plumbers	32h									
18	FPL	8h									
19	Electrician & FPL	8h									
20	Southern Bell	8h									
21	Tile sub	80h									
22	County Inspectors	8h									
23	Paint Sub	56h									
24	Stucco sub	24h									
25	Electrician	24h									
26	Cleanup sub	40h									
27	Carpet layers	16h									
28	Gutter sub	40h									
29	**Pool sub**	**152h**									
30	**Sprinkler sub**	**88h**									
31	Landscaper	32h									

Figure 16-2. Resource loading analysis.

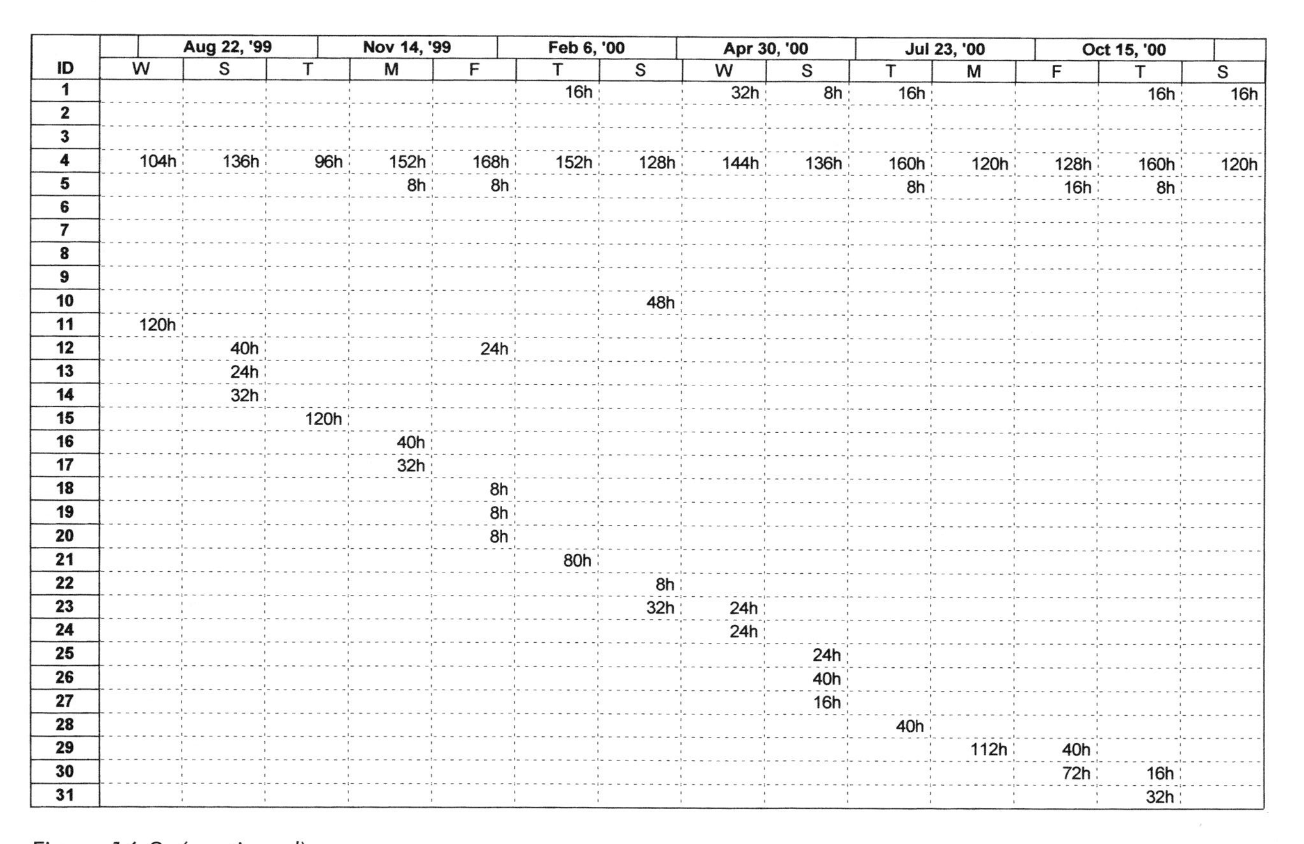

ID		Aug 22, '99		Nov 14, '99		Feb 6, '00		Apr 30, '00			Jul 23, '00		Oct 15, '00	
	W	S	T	M	F	T	S	W	S	T	M	F	T	S
1						16h		32h	8h	16h			16h	16h
2														
3														
4	104h	136h	96h	152h	168h	152h	128h	144h	136h	160h	120h	128h	160h	120h
5				8h	8h					8h		16h	8h	
6														
7														
8														
9														
10							48h							
11	120h													
12		40h			24h									
13		24h												
14		32h												
15			120h											
16				40h										
17				32h										
18					8h									
19					8h									
20					8h									
21						80h								
22							8h							
23							32h	24h						
24								24h						
25									24h					
26									40h					
27									16h					
28										40h				
29											112h	40h		
30												72h	16h	
31													32h	

Figure 16-2. (continued)

ID	Resource Name	Initials	Group	Max. Units	Std. Rate	Ovt. Rate	Cost/Use	Accrue At
1	FSD	F		5	$0.00/h	$0.00/h	$0.00	Prorated
2	Florida State	F		1	$0.00/h	$0.00/h	$0.00	End
3	Exterminator	E		1	$0.00/h	$0.00/h	$0.00	End
4	Queue	Q		1	$0.00/h	$0.00/h	$0.00	Prorated
5	County Inspector	C		1	$0.00/h	$0.00/h	$0.00	End
6	Forms sub	F		4	$0.00/h	$0.00/h	$0.00	Prorated
7	Plumber	P		2	$0.00/h	$0.00/h	$0.00	Prorated
8	Concrete sub	C		4	$0.00/h	$0.00/h	$0.00	Prorated
9	Masons	M		8	$0.00/h	$0.00/h	$0.00	Prorated
10	Roofers	R		6	$0.00/h	$0.00/h	$0.00	Prorated
11	Rough-in subs	R		4	$0.00/h	$0.00/h	$0.00	Prorated
12	Electricians	E		2	$0.00/h	$0.00/h	$0.00	Prorated
13	HVAC sub	H		2	$0.00/h	$0.00/h	$0.00	Prorated
14	Finishers	F		4	$0.00/h	$0.00/h	$0.00	Prorated
15	Rockers	R		4	$0.00/h	$0.00/h	$0.00	Prorated
16	Carpenters	C		3	$0.00/h	$0.00/h	$0.00	Prorated
17	Plumbers	P		2	$0.00/h	$0.00/h	$0.00	Prorated
18	FPL	F		1	$0.00/h	$0.00/h	$0.00	End
19	Electrician & FPL	E		1	$0.00/h	$0.00/h	$0.00	Prorated
20	Southern Bell	S		1	$0.00/h	$0.00/h	$0.00	End
21	Tile sub	T		3	$0.00/h	$0.00/h	$0.00	Prorated
22	County Inspectors	C		1	$0.00/h	$0.00/h	$0.00	End
23	Paint Sub	P		6	$0.00/h	$0.00/h	$0.00	Prorated
24	Stucco sub	S		8	$0.00/h	$0.00/h	$0.00	Prorated
25	Electrician	E		2	$0.00/h	$0.00/h	$0.00	Prorated
26	Cleanup sub	C		5	$0.00/h	$0.00/h	$0.00	End
27	Carpet layers	C		2	$0.00/h	$0.00/h	$0.00	End
28	Gutter sub	G		4	$0.00/h	$0.00/h	$0.00	End
29	Pool sub	P		3	$0.00/h	$0.00/h	$0.00	Prorated
30	**Sprinkler sub**	**S**		**1**	**$0.00/h**	**$0.00/h**	**$0.00**	**Prorated**
31	Landscaper	L		6	$0.00/h	$0.00/h	$0.00	End

Figure 16-3. Cost analysis worksheet.

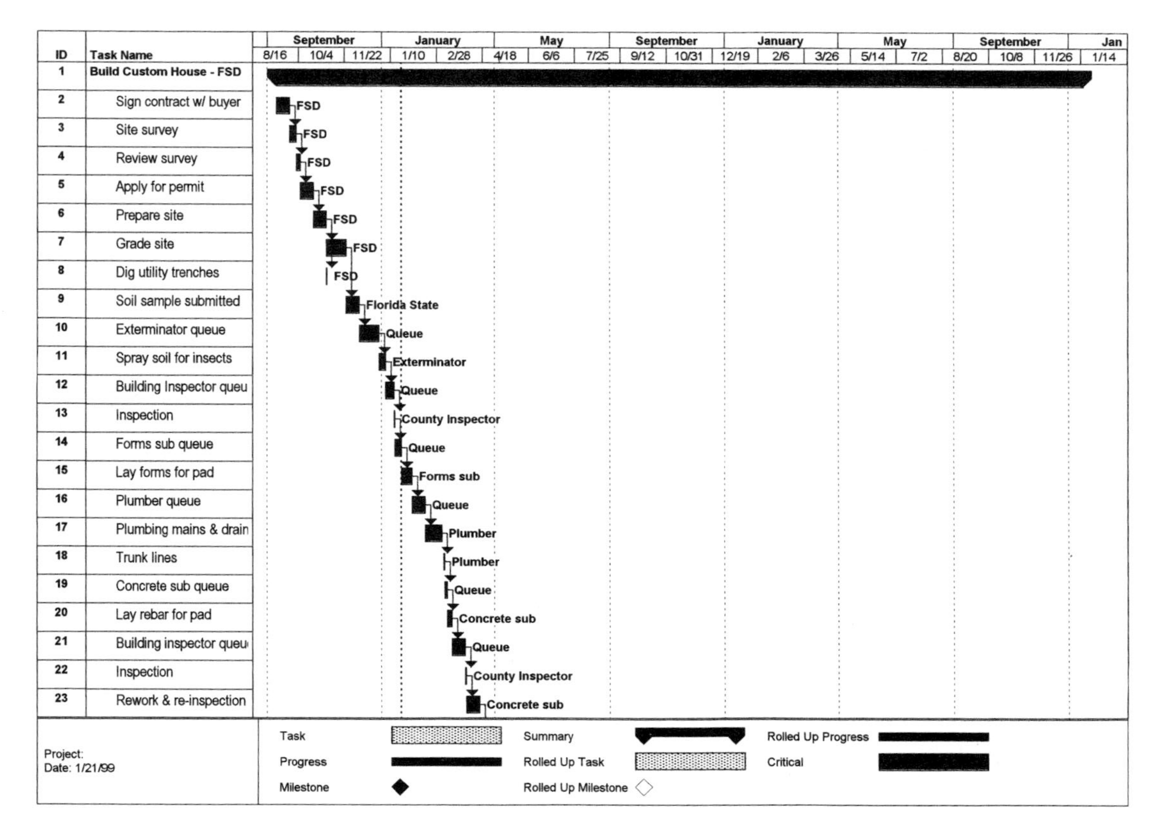

Figure 16-4. Gantt chart developed to determine actual time of construction process.

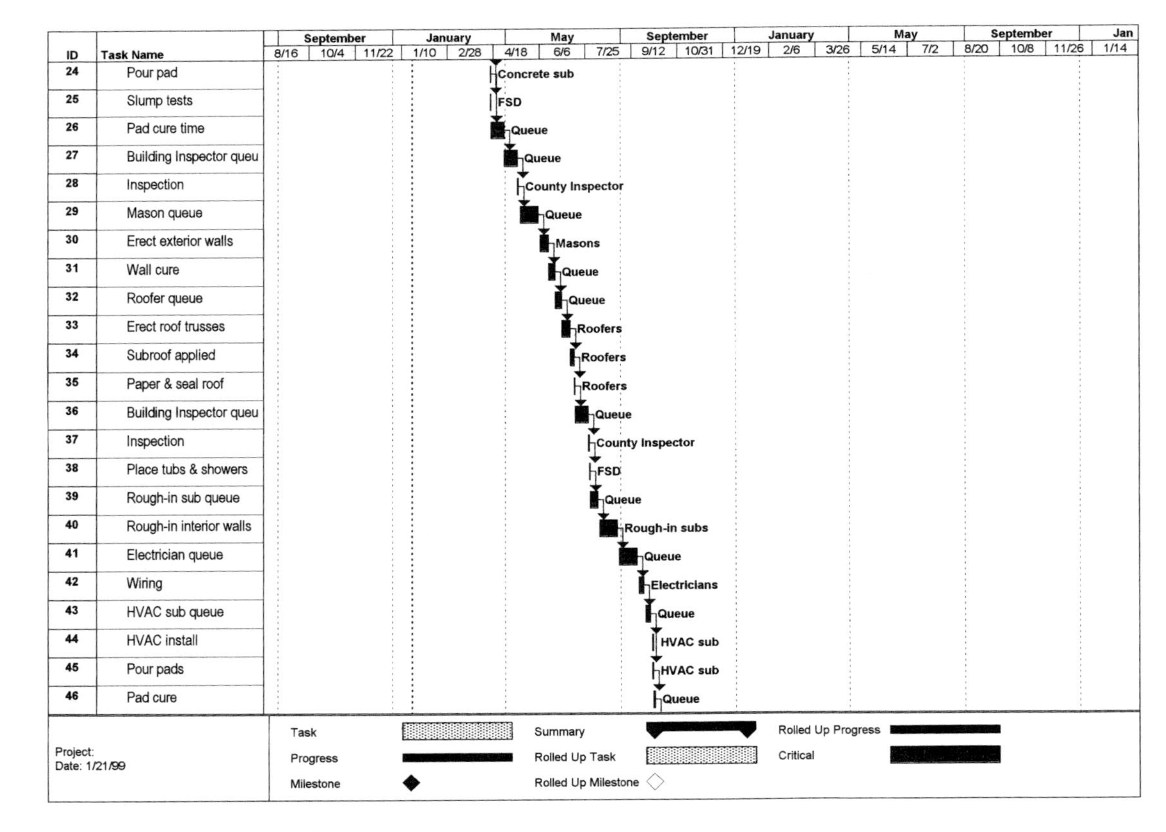

Figure 16-4. (continued)

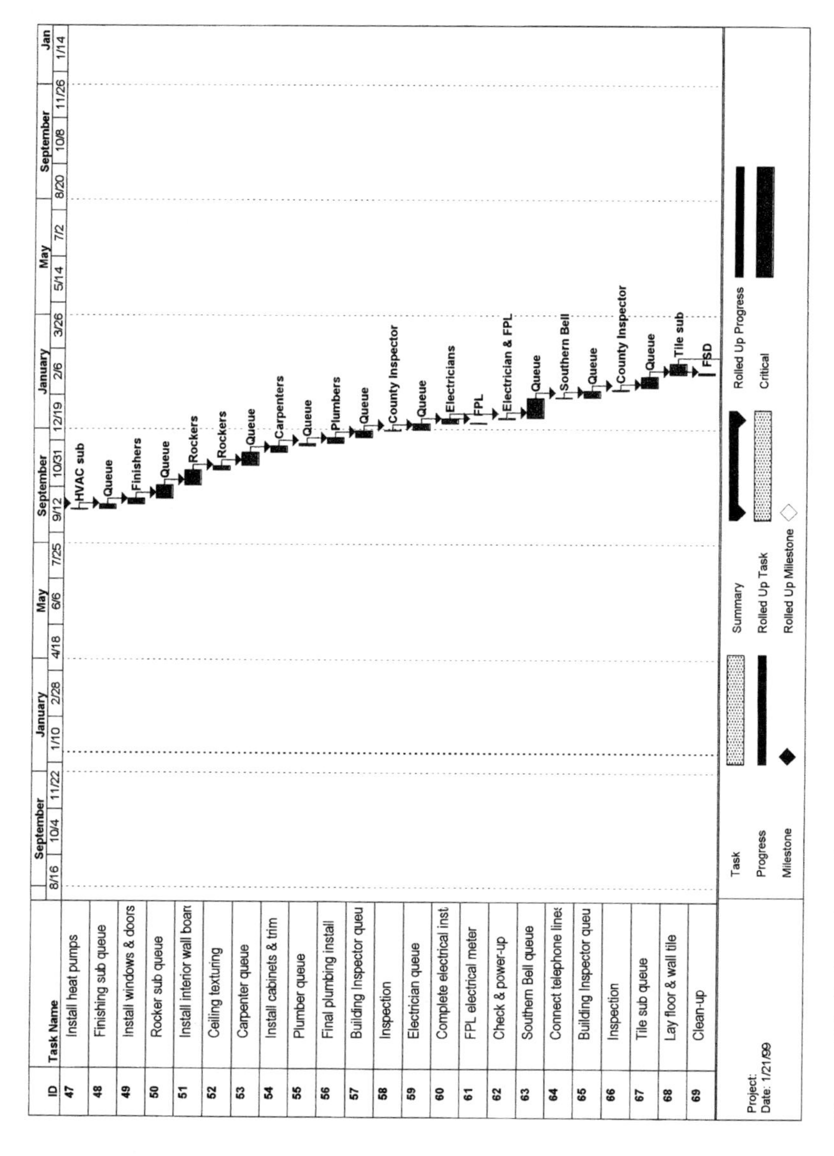

Figure 16-4. (continued)

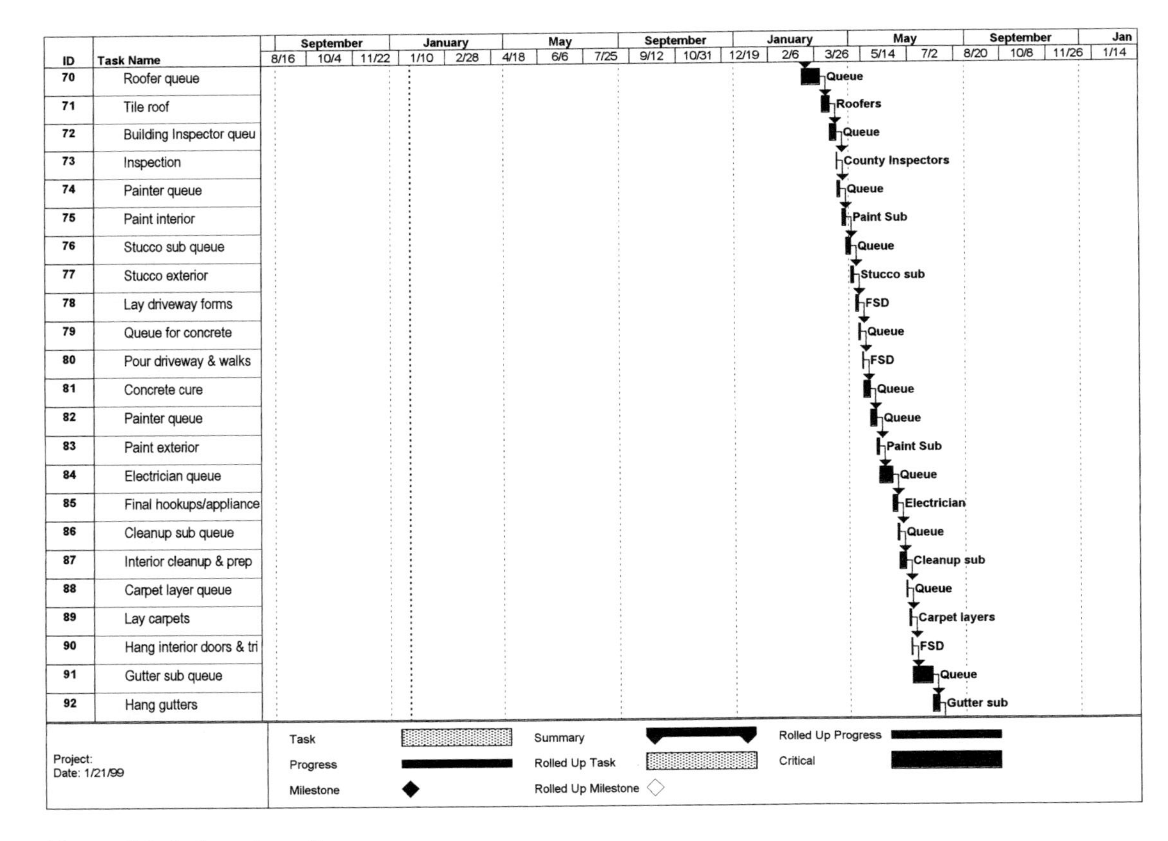

Figure 16-4. (continued)

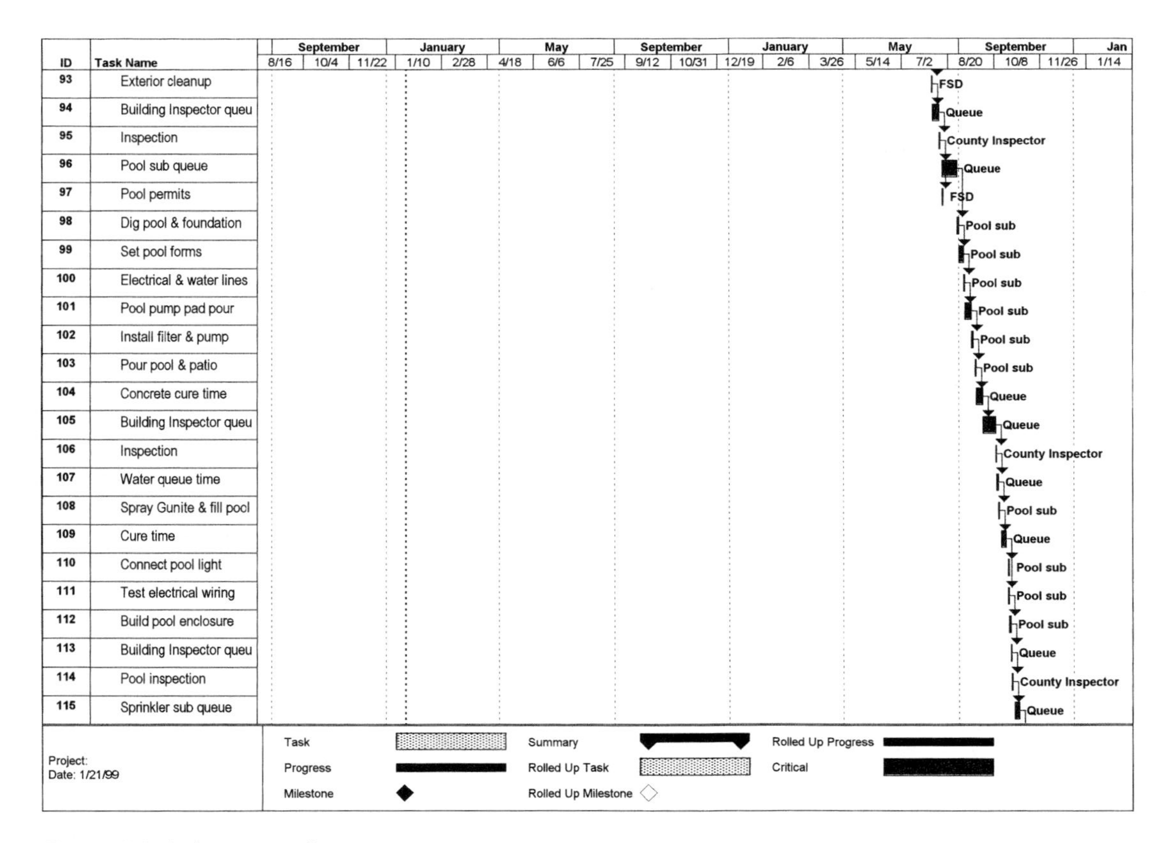

Figure 16-4. (continued)

ID	Task Name	Resource
116	Install sprinkler pipes	Sprinkler sub
117	Lay forms & pour pad	Sprinkler sub
118	Pad cure	Sprinkler sub
119	Install control box	Sprinkler sub
120	Run main water feed lin	Sprinkler sub
121	Run water feeder lines	Sprinkler sub
122	Connect sprinkler heads	Sprinkler sub
123	Landscaper queue	Queue
124	Landscaping	Landscaper
125	Sprinkler repairs	Sprinkler sub
126	Dig mailbox & cement	FSD
127	Attach mailbox	FSD
128	Building Inspector queu	Queue
129	Final inspection	County Insp
130	Buyer queue	Queue
131	Buyer walk-through	FSD
132	Closing queue	Queue
133	Closing	FSD

Timeline: September (8/16, 10/4, 11/22), January (1/10, 2/28), May (4/18, 6/6, 7/25), September (9/12, 10/31, 12/19), January (2/6, 3/26), May (5/14, 7/2), September (8/20, 10/8, 11/26), Jan (1/14)

Project:
Date: 1/21/99

Legend: Task, Progress, Milestone, Summary, Rolled Up Task, Rolled Up Milestone, Rolled Up Progress, Critical

Figure 16-4. (continued)

Alternative Analysis

The situational assessment and problem analyses clearly demonstrated that the cycle time of Florida Southeast Developer's projects was the driver behind its loss in market share. A remedy required a different set of alternatives and, along with them, a new set of assumptions requiring validation so that additional risk would not be introduced into the business. Table 16-1 illustrates the project manager's approach to developing and assessing the possible alternatives.

Table 16-1. Project manager's approach for determining alternatives for FSD.

Assumptions	Risk	Confirmation
Inspections can be prescheduled	High	Yes
Inspections can be grouped	High	Yes
Inspectors are multi-disciplined and can inspect multiple things during one visit	High	Yes
Subcontractors can be prescheduled	High	Yes
Subcontractors can be on site at the same time	High	Yes
All concrete can be poured at once	High	Yes
Much of the site preparation and permit work can be done in advance	Medium	Yes
The pool can be done in conjunction with the house versus separately	Medium	Yes
Pre-layouts of house footprints can be used for permits before contract signing	Medium	Yes
Dirt from the pool can be used for the pad saving $65 per load in and out	Low	Yes
Internal and external tasks can be overlapped	Low	Yes
All painting can be done at one time	Low	Yes
Subcontractors can be paid by the job versus time	Low	Yes
Certified funds can be required from buyers for contract signing	Low	Yes

The revised WBS was then created, based upon the results of the team's assumptions analysis, coupled with several commonsense concepts that were developed in conjunction with several of the subcontractors. The primary focus in the development of the new WBS was to eliminate the huge queue time element in the original project model, and to incorporate as much concurrency as possible into the new approach.

As Figure 16-5 shows, the project team created a WBS with 10 levels. Within each level or tier, all activities that could be performed simultaneously were identified. As the team rolled down consecutive levels, additional refinement was added until the team felt comfortable that all elements of the construction process had been adequately identified.

From the WBS, the project manager and his team began to create the activity listing shown in Figure 16-6 and Gantt chart (see Figure 16-7), being careful to include all activities, dependencies, and time elements. The results of their work yielded a significant reduction in project cycle time from over 2 years to under 4 months—with no additional risk factors. And, as can be seen from the final resource loading (Figure 16-8), the queue time was reduced from 353 days to just 20 days. While there was still room for improvement, the performance gap was addressed effectively and the project model was adopted by FSD. At the time of this writing, the project manager and his team have reduced the total cycle time to 3 months and four days.

CONCLUSION

The situational assessment and problem and process analyses all come together, resulting in a greatly reduced project cycle time. It seems straightforward enough, and it really is for the project manager and his team. When the project manager knows the situation and the associated business and/or process problems creating that situation, then he or she will make good decisions to guide the project successfully. That is the secret. And, it will never fail.

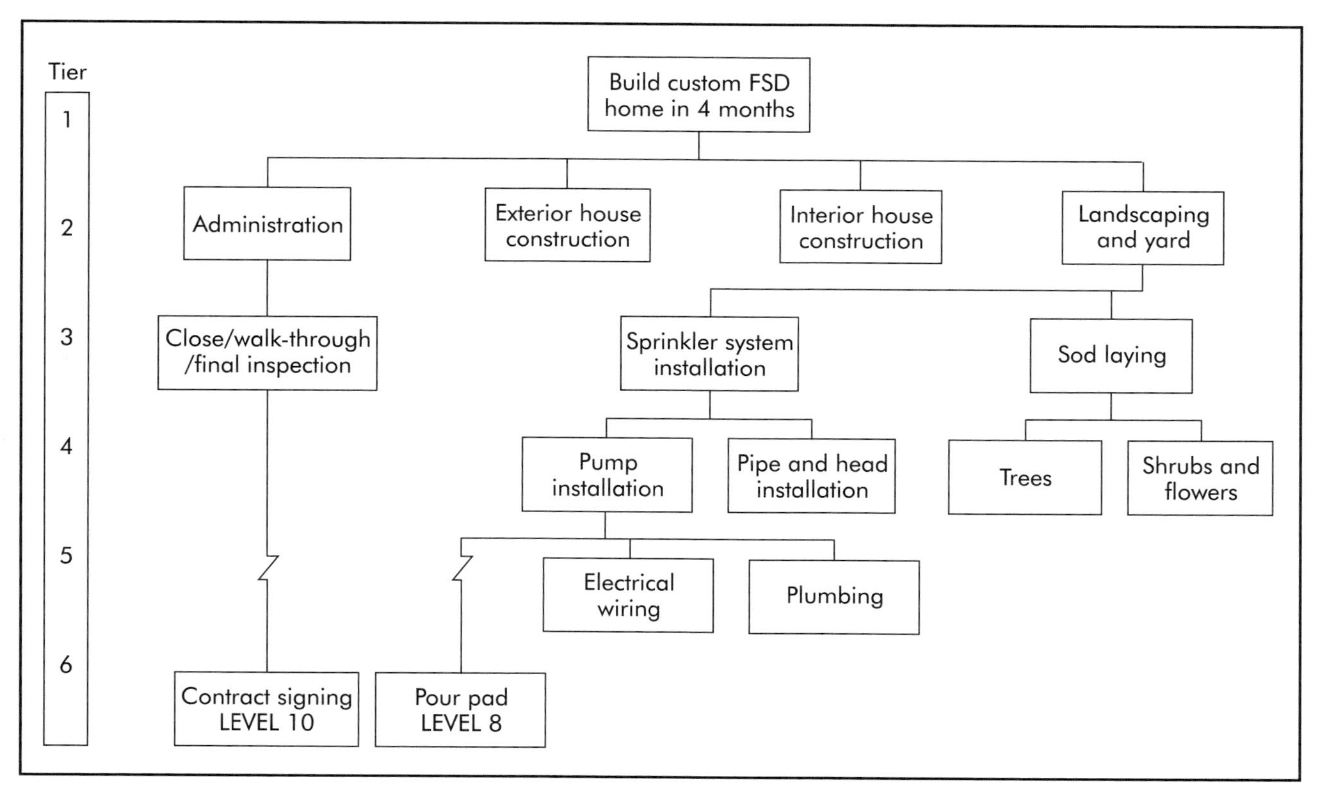

Figure 16-5. WBS created to study FSD construction process.

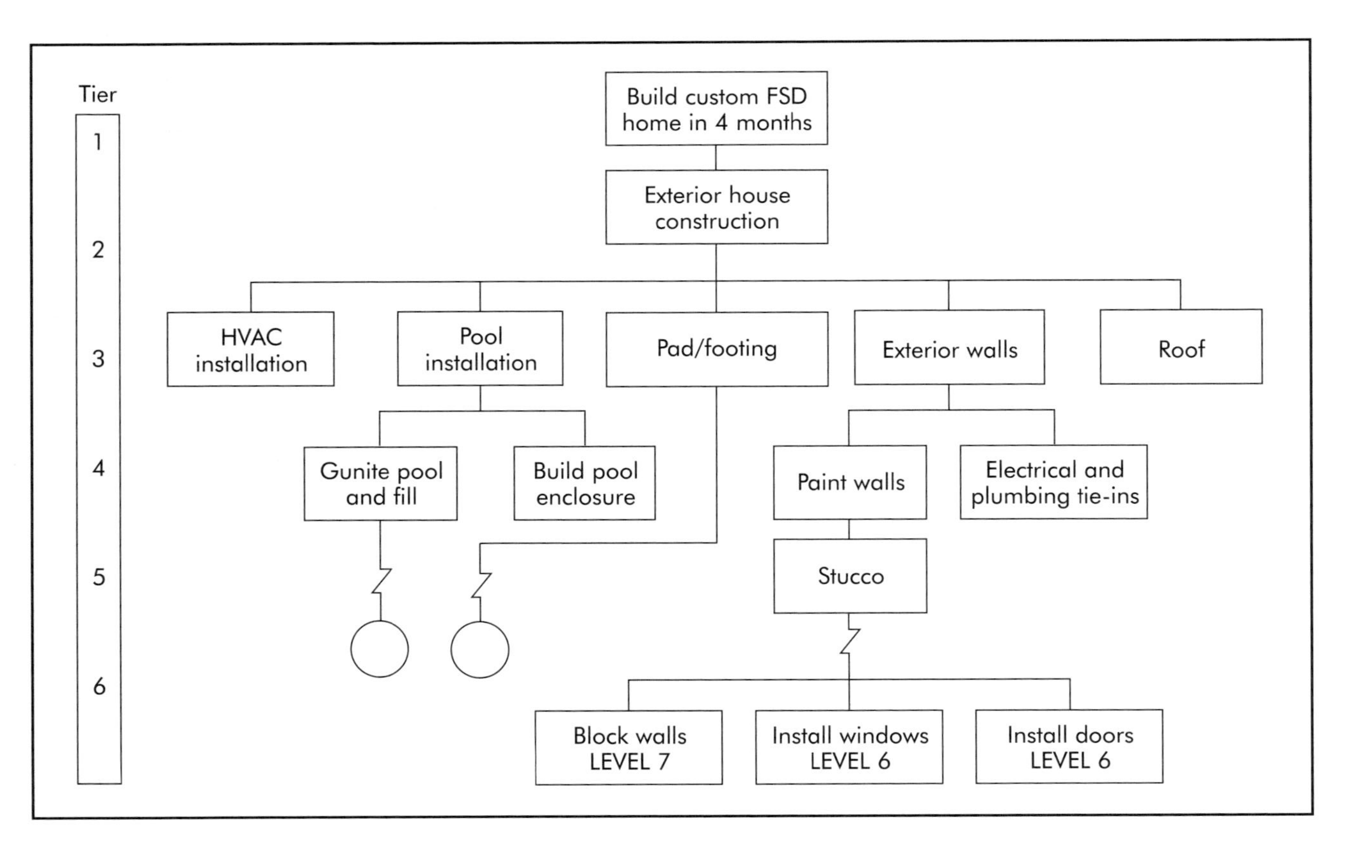

Figure 16-5. (continued)

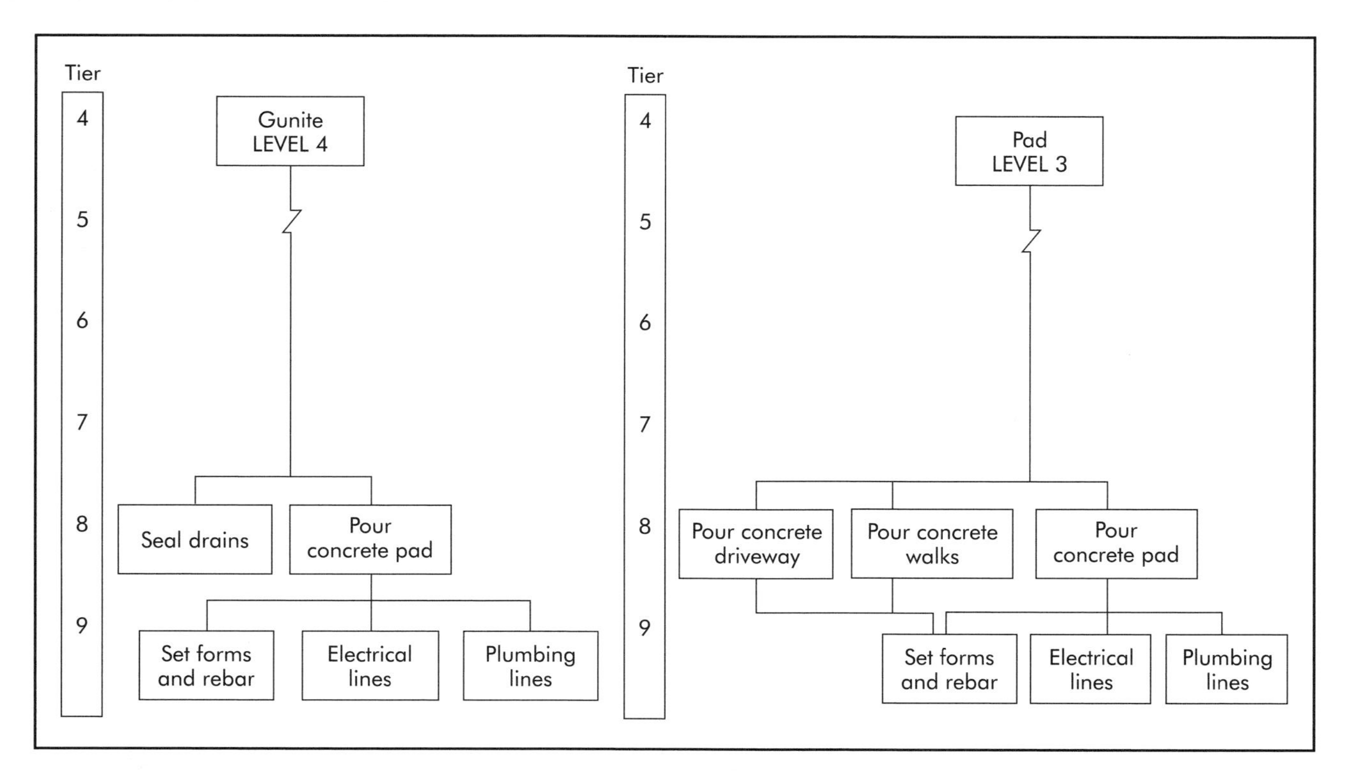

Figure 16-5. (continued)

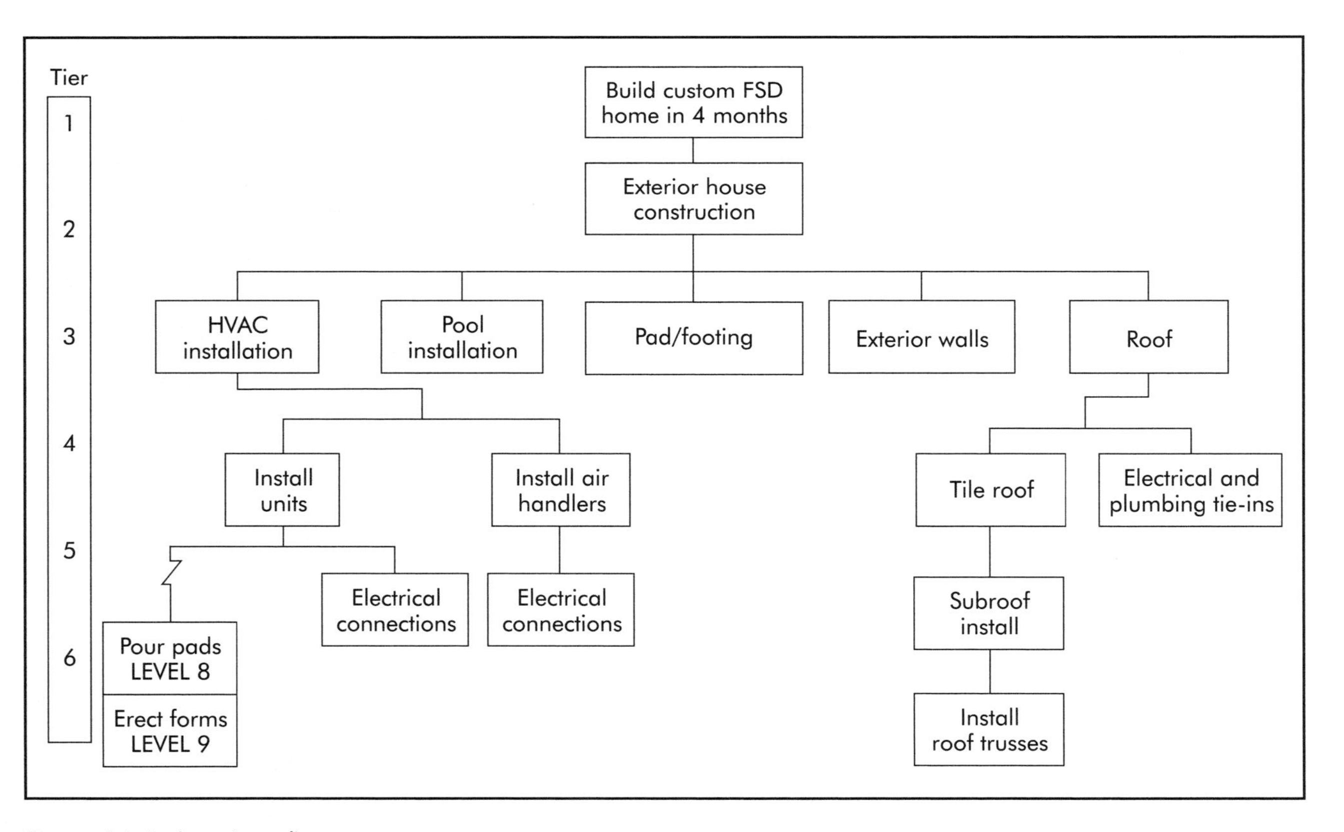

Figure 16-5. (continued)

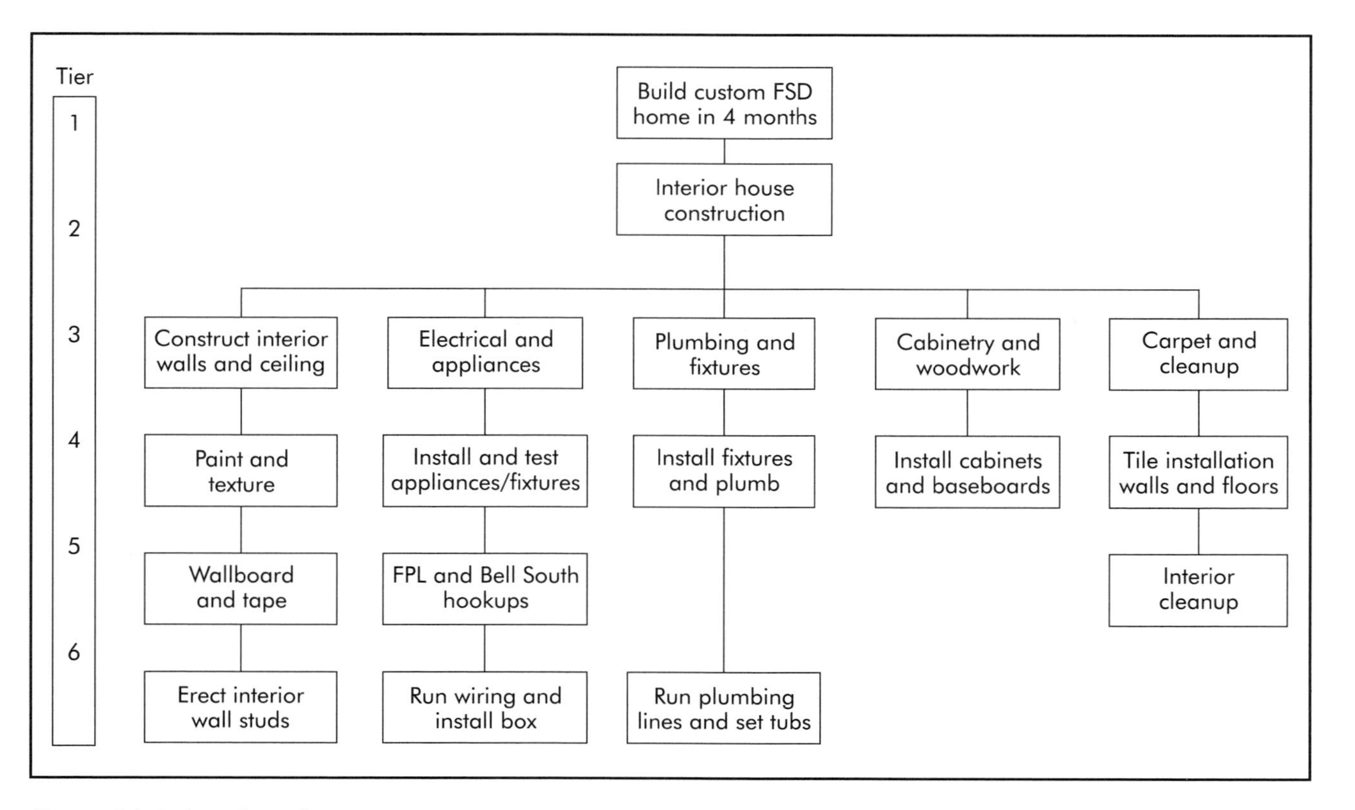

Figure 16-5. (continued)

ID	Task Name	Duration	Start	Finish	Predecessors	Resource Names
1	**Build Custom House-FSD**	**115d**	**9/21/98**	**2/26/99**		
2	Sign contract w/buyer	1d	9/21/98	9/21/98		FSD
3	Final building permit	1d	9/22/98	9/22/98	2	FSD
4	Dig utility trenches	1d	9/23/98	9/23/98	3	FSD
5	Dig Pool	2d	9/23/98	9/24/98	3	FSD
6	Pad grade & prep	5d	9/23/98	9/29/98	3	FSD
7	Lay forms for pad	5d	9/30/98	10/6/98	6	Forms sub
8	Lay forms for driveway	1d	10/5/98	10/5/98	6	Forms sub
9	Lay forms for utility pad	1d	10/6/98	10/6/98	6	Forms sub
10	Lay forms for sidewalks	1d	10/5/98	10/5/98	6	Forms sub
11	Lay forms for pool	3d	9/30/98	10/2/98	6	Pool sub
12	Plumb mains & drains	10d	10/7/98	10/20/98	7	Plumber
13	Plumb pool	1d	10/7/98	10/7/98	7	Pool sub
14	Electrical conduit-house	1d	10/7/98	10/7/98	7	Plumber
15	Electrical conduit-pool	1d	10/7/98	10/7/98	7	Pool sub
16	Trunk lines	1d	10/21/98	10/21/98	12	Plumber
17	Lay rebar for pad	3d	10/22/98	10/26/98	16	Concrete sub
18	Lay rebar for drive & w	1d	10/22/98	10/22/98	16	Concrete sub
19	Lay rebar for pool	2d	10/8/98	10/9/98	15	Pool sub
20	Inspection	1d	10/27/98	10/27/98	17,18,19	County Inspector
21	Place building materials	1d	10/26/98	10/26/98		FSD
22	Pour pool & patio	1d	10/28/98	10/28/98	20	Concrete sub
23	Pour pads	1d	10/28/98	10/28/98	20	Concrete sub
24	Pour drive & walks	1d	10/28/98	10/28/98	20	Concrete sub
25	Concrete cure time	10d	10/29/98	11/11/98	22,23,24	Queue
26	Inspection	1d	11/12/98	11/12/98	25	County Inspector

Figure 16-6. Revised activity listing.

ID	Task Name	Duration	Start	Finish	Predecessors	Resource Names
27	Erect exterior walls	7d	11/13/98	11/23/98	26	Masons
28	Wall cure	5d	11/24/98	11/30/98	27	Queue
29	Place tub & showers	1d	11/24/98	11/24/98	27	FSD
30	Set windows & doors	4d	11/24/98	11/27/98	27	Finishers
31	Erect roof trusses	7d	12/1/98	12/9/98	28	Roofers
32	Subroof applied	2d	12/9/98	12/10/98	31FS-1d	Roofers
33	Paper & seal roof	1d	12/11/98	12/11/98	32	Roofers
34	HVAC air handlers	1d	12/11/98	12/11/98	32	HVAC sub
35	Heat pumps placed	1d	12/11/98	12/11/98	32	HVAC sub
36	Rough-in interior walls	15d	12/10/98	12/30/98	32FS-1d	Rough-in subs
37	Electrical wiring	5d	12/28/98	1/1/99	36FS-3d	Electricians
38	Inspection	1d	1/4/99	1/4/99	28,33,36,37	County Inspector
39	FPL electrical meter	1d	1/5/99	1/5/99	38	FPL
40	Install telephone lines	1d	1/5/99	1/5/99	38	BellSouth
41	Tile roof	6d	1/5/99	1/12/99	38	Roofers
42	Hang gutters	3d	1/13/99	1/15/99	41	Gutter sub
43	Stucco exterior	3d	1/5/99	1/7/99	38	Stucco sub
44	Install wall board	12d	1/5/99	1/20/99	38	Rockers
45	Ceiling texture	3d	1/19/99	1/21/99	44FS-2d	Rockers
46	Paint interior	4d	1/22/99	1/27/99	45	Paint sub
47	Paint exterior	3d	1/22/99	1/26/99	45	Paint sub
48	Install cabinets & trim	5d	1/27/99	2/2/99	46FS-1d	Carpenter
49	Final plumbing hookups	4d	2/2/99	2/5/99	48FS-1d	Plumbers
50	Final electrical install	3d	2/2/99	2/4/99	48FS-1d	Electricians
51	Check & power-up	1d	2/5/99	2/5/99	50	Electricians
52	Appliance install	3d	2/8/99	2/10/99	51	Electrician

Figure 16-6. (continued)

ID	Task Name	Duration	Start	Finish	Predecessors	Resource Names
53	Lay floor & wall tile	10d	1/28/99	2/10/99	46	Tile sub
54	Interior cleanup & prep	5d	2/9/99	2/15/99	53FS-2d	Cleanup sub
55	Lay carpets	2d	2/16/99	2/17/99	54	Carpet layers
56	Install pool pump	2d	2/8/99	2/9/99	51	Pool sub
57	Final pool hookups	2d	2/8/99	2/9/99	51	Pool sub
58	Spray Gunite & fill pool	1d	2/10/99	2/10/99	57	Pool sub
59	Cure time	5d	2/11/99	2/17/99	58	Queue
60	Build pool enclosure	2d	2/11/99	2/12/99	58	Pool sub
61	Install sprinkler pump	1d	2/8/99	2/8/99	51	Sprinkler sub
62	Install sprinkler water lir	1d	2/9/99	2/9/99	61	Sprinkler sub
63	Install pipe & heads	1d	2/9/99	2/9/99	61	Sprinkler sub
64	Test	1d	2/10/99	2/10/99	63	Sprinkler sub
65	Landscaping - trees & s	2d	1/27/99	1/28/99	47	Landscapers
66	Landscaping-sod	2d	2/11/99	2/12/99	64	Landscapers
67	Sprinkler repairs	1d	2/12/99	2/12/99	66FS-1d	Sprinkler sub
68	Dig & cement mailbox p	1d	1/27/99	1/27/99	47	FSD
69	Attach mailbox	1d	1/28/99	1/28/99	68	FSD
70	Final inspection	1d	2/18/99	2/18/99	55,60,64,67	County Inspector
71	Buyer walk-through	1d	2/19/99	2/19/99	70	FSD
72	Closing	5d	2/22/99	2/26/99	71	FSD

Figure 16-6. (continued)

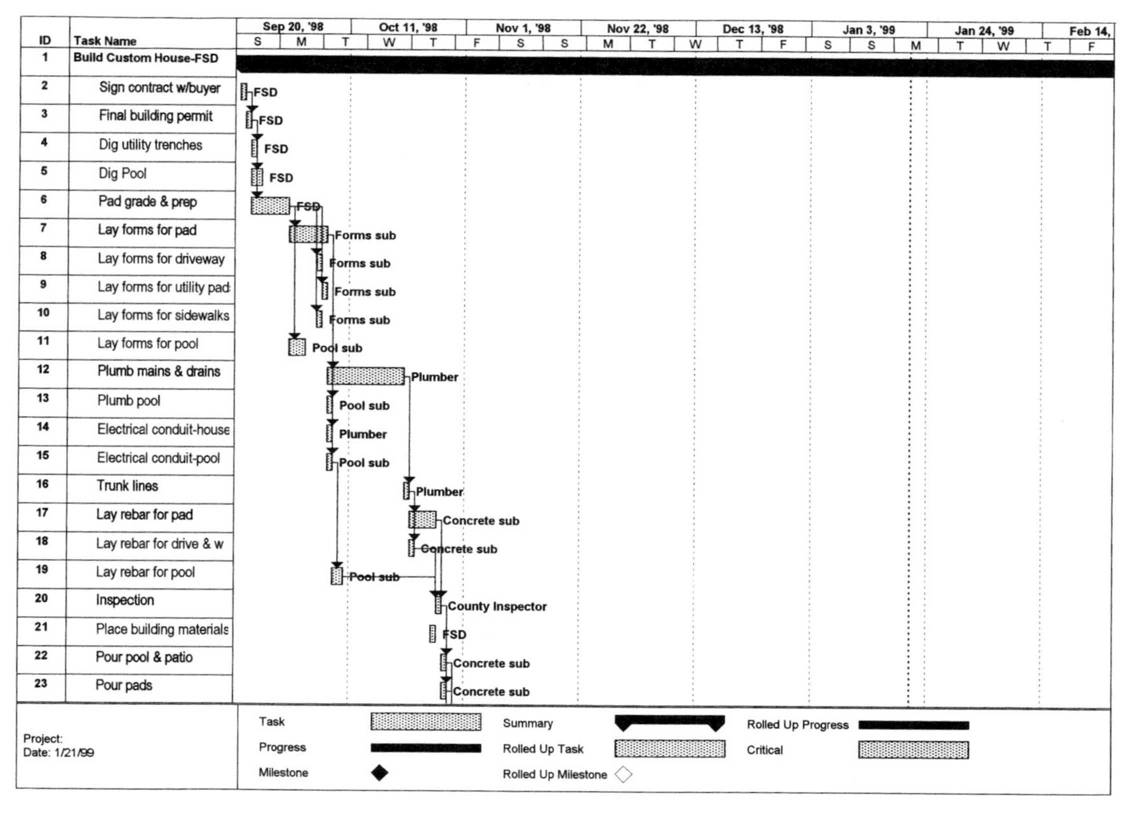

Figure 16-7. Gantt chart showing reduction in cycle time.

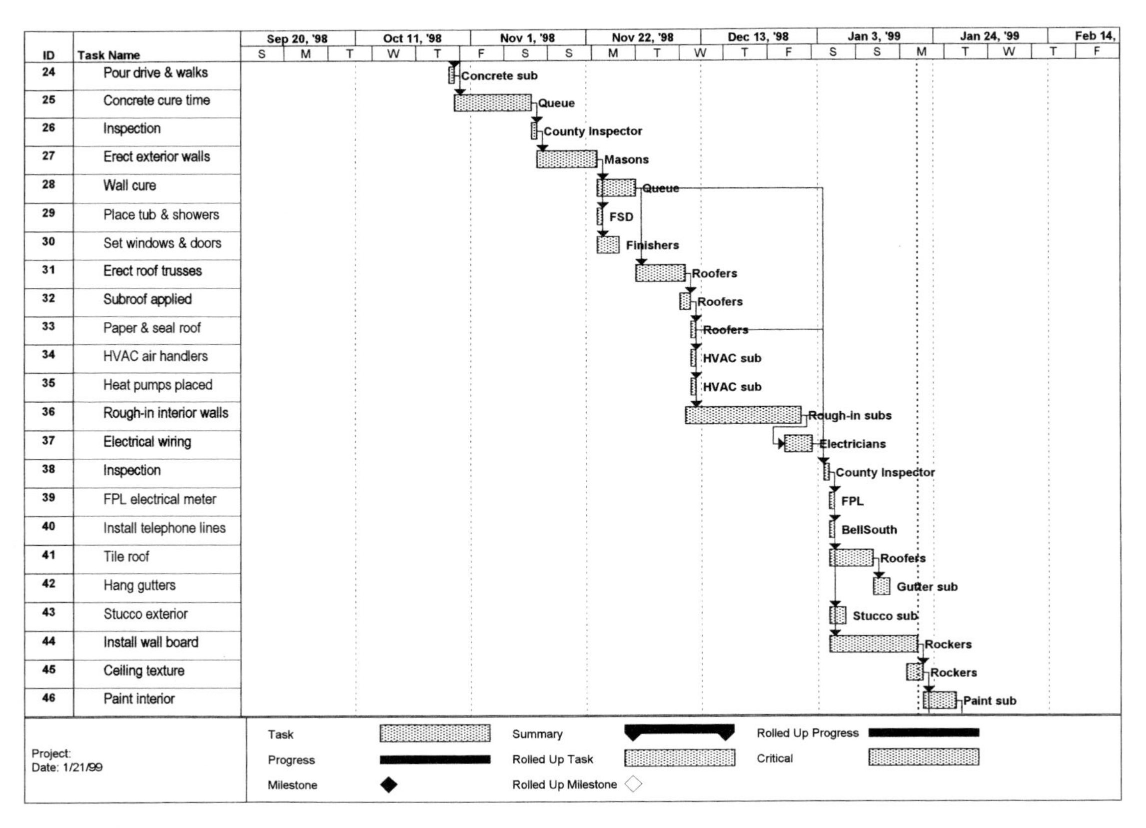

Figure 16-7. (continued)

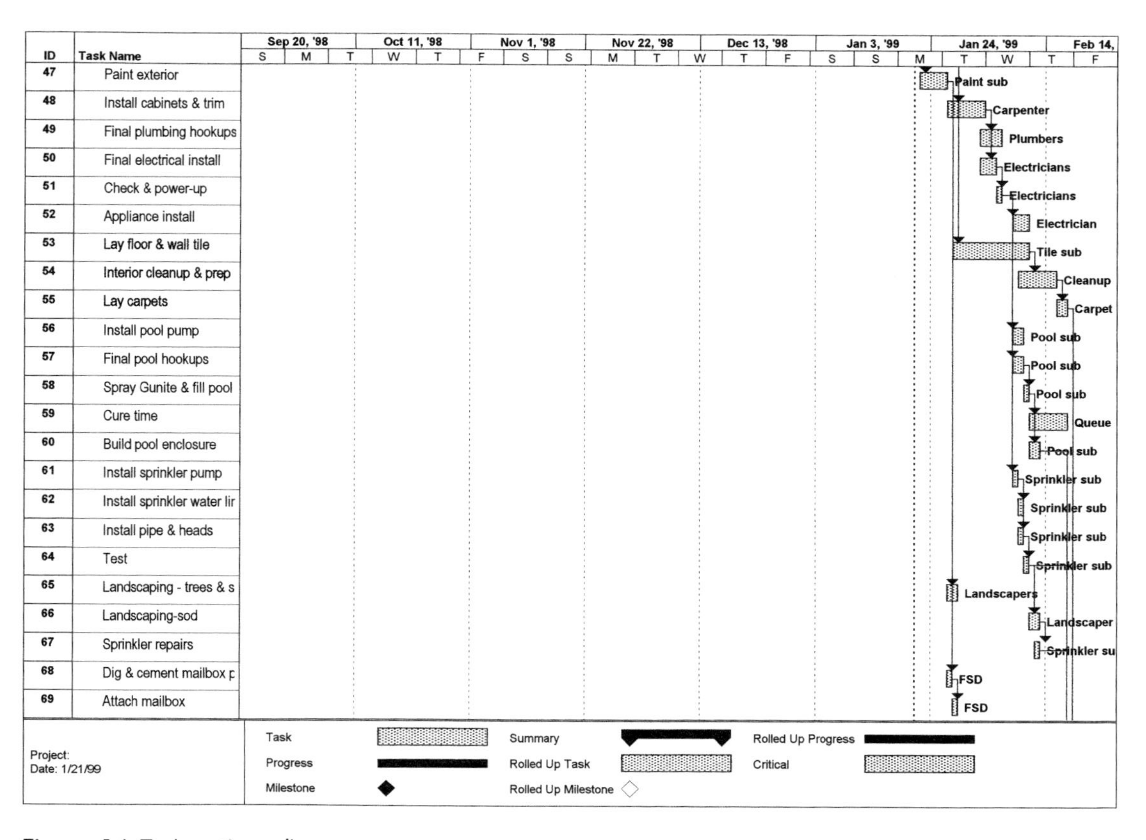

Figure 16-7. (continued)

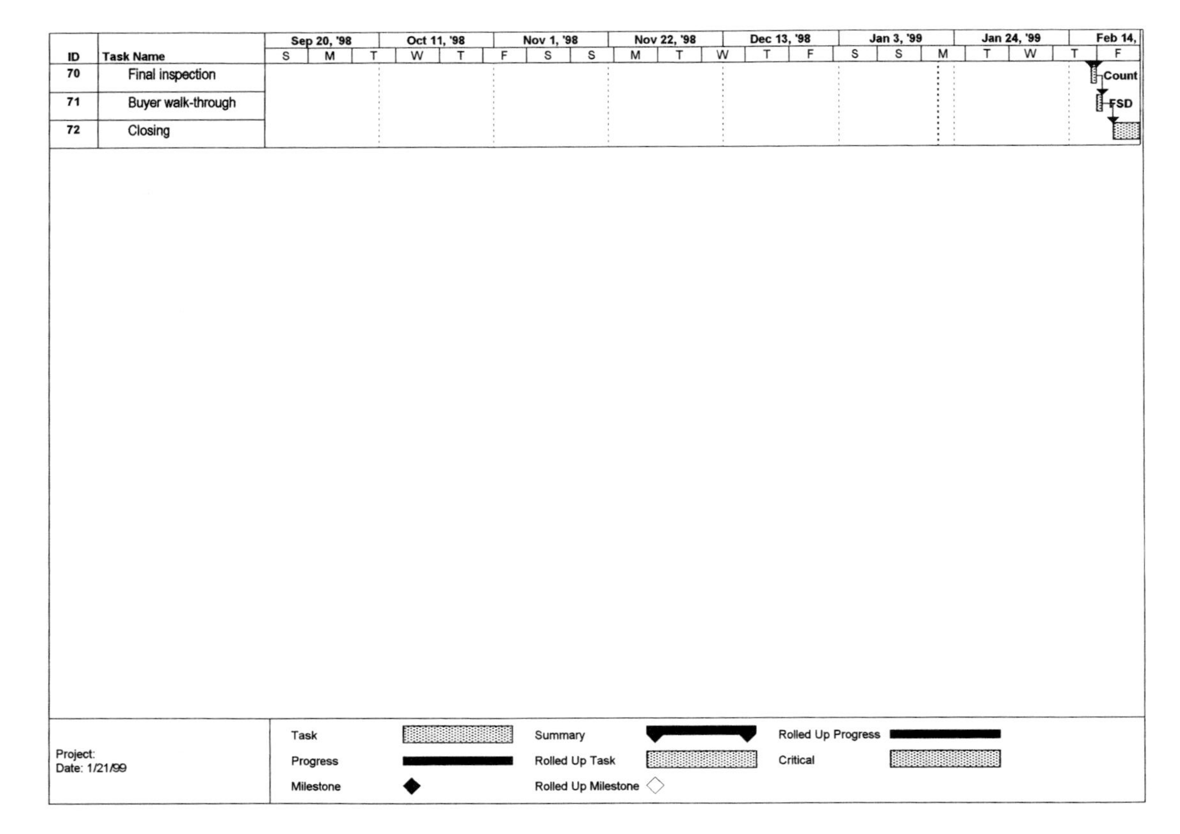

Figure 16-7. (continued)

ID	Resource Name	Work	Sep 20, '98		Oct 11, '98			Nov 1, '98		
			S	M	T	W	T	F	S	S
1	**FSD**	**160h**	**64h**	16h			8h			
2	**Forms sub**	**64h**		48h	16h					
3	**Pool sub**	**112h**		24h	32h					
4	**Plumber**	**96h**			48h	48h				
5	**Concrete sub**	**56h**					**56h**			
6	County Inspector	32h					8h		8h	
7	Queue	160h					8h	48h	24h	
8	Masons	56h							8h	40h
9	Finishers	32h								
10	**Roofers**	**128h**								
11	**HVAC sub**	**16h**								
12	Rough-in subs	120h								
13	Electricians	72h								
14	Gutter sub	24h								
15	Stucco sub	24h								
16	**Rockers**	**120h**								
17	FPL	8h								
18	BellSouth	8h								
19	**Paint sub**	**56h**								
20	Carpenter	40h								
21	Plumbers	32h								
22	Tile sub	80h								
23	Electrician	24h								
24	Cleanup sub	40h								
25	Carpet layers	16h								
26	**Sprinkler sub**	**40h**								
27	Landscapers	32h								

Figure 16-8. Final resource loading analysis.

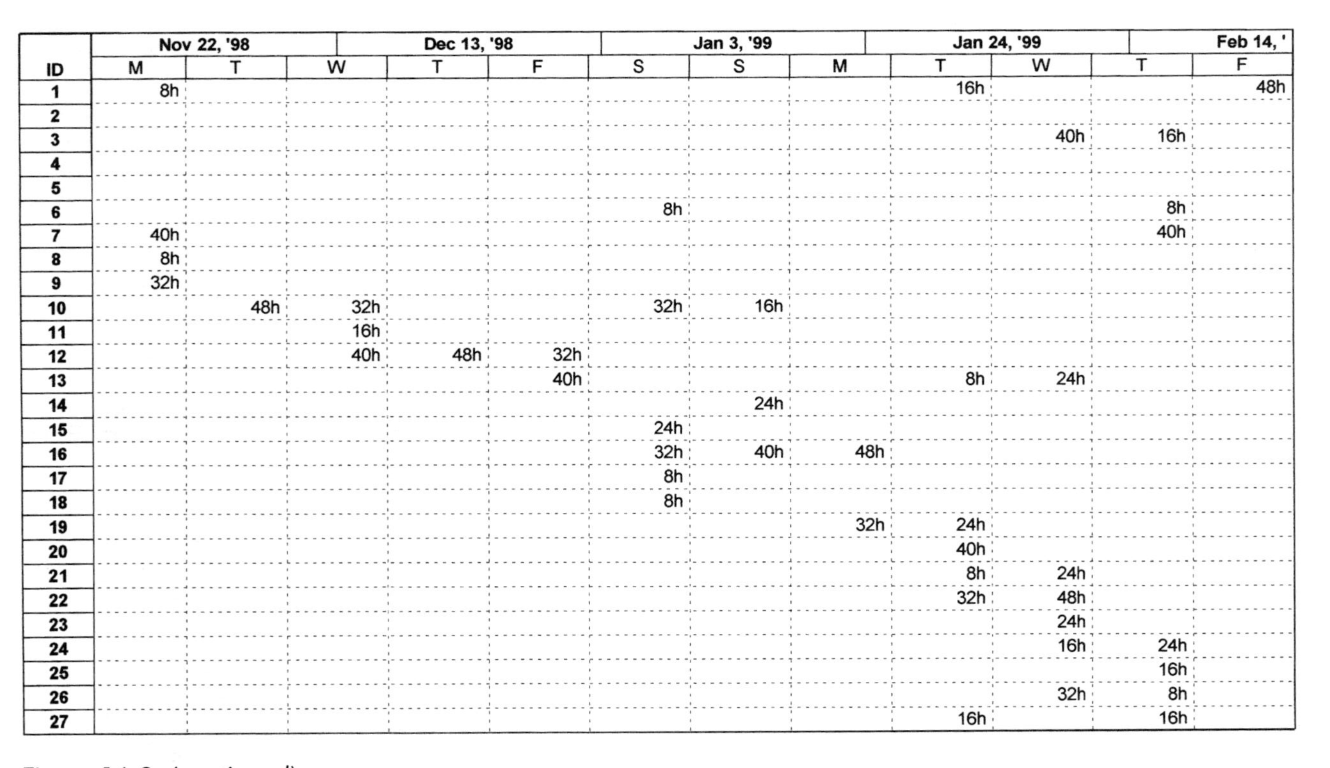

ID	Nov 22, '98			Dec 13, '98		Jan 3, '99			Jan 24, '99			Feb 14, '
	M	T	W	T	F	S	S	M	T	W	T	F
1	8h								16h			48h
2												
3										40h	16h	
4												
5												
6						8h					8h	
7	40h										40h	
8	8h											
9	32h											
10		48h	32h			32h	16h					
11			16h									
12			40h	48h	32h							
13					40h				8h	24h		
14							24h					
15						24h						
16						32h	40h	48h				
17						8h						
18						8h						
19								32h	24h			
20									40h			
21									8h	24h		
22									32h	48h		
23										24h		
24										16h	24h	
25											16h	
26										32h	8h	
27									16h		16h	

Figure 16-8. (continued)

17
Organizing and Launching the Project Management Office

As stated throughout this text, the alignment of strategic and tactical business strategies with the projects being planned and implemented throughout the organization is critical to the achievement of senior management's vision for the organization. As a consequence, every project within the portfolio and pipeline must be successfully implemented to:

- contribute to the organization's business and financial performance,
- generate an acceptable and predictable return on investment for the organization's funding of the project,
- ensure effective utilization of the organization's business, financial, and human capital, and
- maximize the organization's brand and market position.

The ability of an organization to execute projects in a mode of "better, faster, cheaper" is made possible by the use of proven, universally sanctioned project management methodologies, policies, and procedures across all business units. This commonality of approach provides balance and alignment by focusing key (and often limited) resources on those initiatives of critical importance to the organization's success. It is in this environment that the project management office (PMO) provides true value to an organization.

A PMO aids in eliminating miscommunication and resulting wasted assets that can result from disconnects between the direction established by senior management for the organization and the projects launched at the operating levels, which are often opposed to that intended direction. With a PMO in place, the organization's strategic business objectives are tied directly to the strategic projects launched within the various business operations. Thus, all corporate assets are deployed correctly and in alignment with what senior management wants accomplished.

OVERVIEW

It is the responsibility of the PMO staff to shepherd and direct all corporate assets toward the achievement of senior management's three to five year business plan. Thus, the PMO serves as a developer and a repository of project management standards, processes, and methodologies to ensure consistently acceptable performance across all organizational levels. Generally speaking, the PMO provides:

- project support,
- project management processes, methods, systems development, training, and enhancements,
- centralized oversight of all projects within the portfolio and pipeline,
- mentoring and development of the organization's project management professionals, and
- input into portfolio and pipeline planning at the senior levels.

Many organizations have implemented PMO strategies and structures with the expectation that easy and immediate resolutions to complex organizational, business, or cultural problems will be possible, or, in some cases, so that immediate and substantial financial returns will be realized. Instead, these organizations have found that the near-term results generated from the implementation of a PMO have fallen far short of these lofty expectations. Will, in the long run, the PMO systems and methodologies generate those expected results? Yes, but only with time, consistent organizational support, and the proper implementation strategies. In the short run, the PMO will deliver improved project success rates, which will in turn lead to increased organizational alignment and success. This phenomenon is illustrated in Figure 17-1. In most

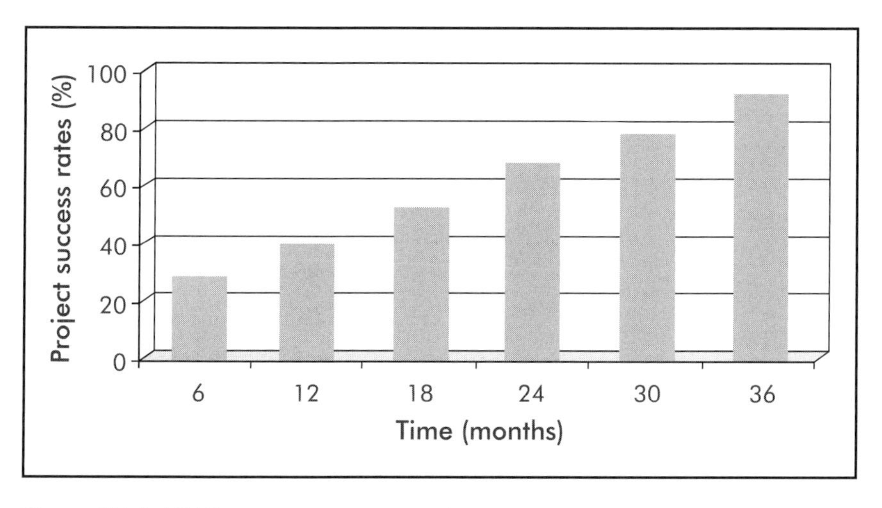

Figure 17-1. PMO success rates over time.

cases, project success rates will improve 20 to 40% within the first 6 to 12 months after the PMO is implemented and operational. The success rate will continue to grow as the PMO staff gains experience and successes, as well as acceptance and support from the organization. Over the span of 30 to 36 months, significant improvement in project success rates is typically realized.

PMO STRUCTURES

There are three basic types of PMO structures: consultancy, strategic, and enterprise. Each type provides benefits to an organization. However, the scope of each is dramatically different. In general, an organization is wise to "grow into" the PMO methodology over time as it gains acceptance throughout the organization and becomes integrated into organizational systems and policies. Organizations that attempt to launch an enterprise-level PMO out of the gates often meet with less than desirable results. In general, it is better to start slow and then expand the scope of the PMO at a pace the organization can comfortably support and readily accept.

Table 17-1 illustrates the differences in organizational structure, staffing, and responsibilities of each form of PMO. In general,

Table 17-1. Organizational structure, staffing, and responsibilities of each form of PMO.

Consultancy	Strategic	EPM
Solid project management knowledge	Strong project and risk management knowledge	Exceptional project management, risk, and business systems knowledge
Broad-based project experience	Strong business and industry knowledge	Exceptional business and organizational knowledge
Sound mentoring and coaching skills	Strategic and tactical management experience	Strategic, tactical, and systems management experience
Sound marketing, sales, and communication skills	Operational, financial, and general management expertise	Expertise in all functional and operational areas
Small staff of 1–3 professionals	Strong communication and presentation skills	Multi-faceted communication skills at all organizational levels
	Specific technical and operational expertise	Technical and operational skills from departments and functions
	Multi-faceted project experience	System-level program/ project implementation expertise
	Exceptional management and leadership skills	Exceptional management and leadership skills
	Mid-sized staff of 6–10 project professionals	PMO staff of 10–25 supported by 1–3 project managers in each department

the consultancy PMO is implemented first to establish a baseline of project management methodologies, processes, and controls. The consultancy PMO structure operates for approximately two years or 10 projects to ensure that all systems, methodologies, and controls are optimized. Thereafter, many organizations expand into the strategic PMO structure, optimizing and expanding project management skills and systems to manage larger, more organizationally critical projects. This structure is maintained for an additional three to five years over the span of up to 25 strategic projects. It is at this point that consideration of the enterprise PMO structure is feasible.

A key element to the success of the PMO is to seamlessly blend it into the fabric of the organization's culture. By so doing, resistance is eased because actual organizational constraints are considered as part of the integration process. An equally important element in the success is acceptance by the PMO staff of the requirement to focus on collaboration and soft selling versus being overly rigid or bureaucratic in approach. Attempting to force-feed any change process through an organization will always lead to resistance and rejection. As any successful sales professional will attest to, it is not possible to sell something to someone who is unwilling to accept it. Only by selling the benefits of the PMO to all affected parties will success be assured. Even then, it will take time, effort, and consistency in approach.

The secrets to sales planning of the strategic PMO and enterprise PMO structures include:

- *Never over-commit.* Project management professionals who have been part of a successful PMO launch recognize the importance of starting slow. Make commitments that are feasible given the constraints under which the PMO staff and the organizational managers and their employees operate each day. The ability to deliver on each promise is critical in building trust that the PMO approach provides true value throughout all levels of the organization.
- *Use story-telling.* Project professionals recognize the need to illustrate by comparison what has worked in other parts of the organization, corporation, or industry as well as what

has not. Through the use of story-telling, experienced project managers convey valuable lessons about past mistakes so that they will not be repeated in this PMO implementation process. And, through their leadership and planning, they relate the specific steps that have been taken to ensure success.

- *Use benefit selling*. Successful project professionals prepare a sales plan that illustrates how the PMO will benefit managers and employees alike (individually as well as collectively). These soft-selling techniques are designed to focus specifically on how the PMO will benefit departments, disciplines, and work groups, as well as how it will seamlessly integrate into their cultures and day-to-day operations without disruption or chaos. Illustrations like that shown in Figure 17-2 are used to demonstrate how the PMO enhances performance in multiple areas, departments, or disciplines.

Consultancy PMO

The consultancy PMO acts in an internal consulting or mentoring capacity. It provides training, guidance, and best-in-class project management methodologies to project managers working within the operating levels of the organization. With the consultancy PMO structure, hands-on control over and responsibility for projects rests solely at the operations or business unit levels. This form of PMO works well in organizations seeking small to modest gains in project efficiency, lower ongoing overhead costs, and minimal start-up risks.

Strategic PMO

With a strategic PMO structure, the PMO is staffed with project management professionals who manage the organization's strategic programs and projects in support of the operational and business units. In addition to providing the training and development duties of the consultancy PMO structure, the permanent strategic PMO staff also:

- actively supports senior management's portfolio management activities,

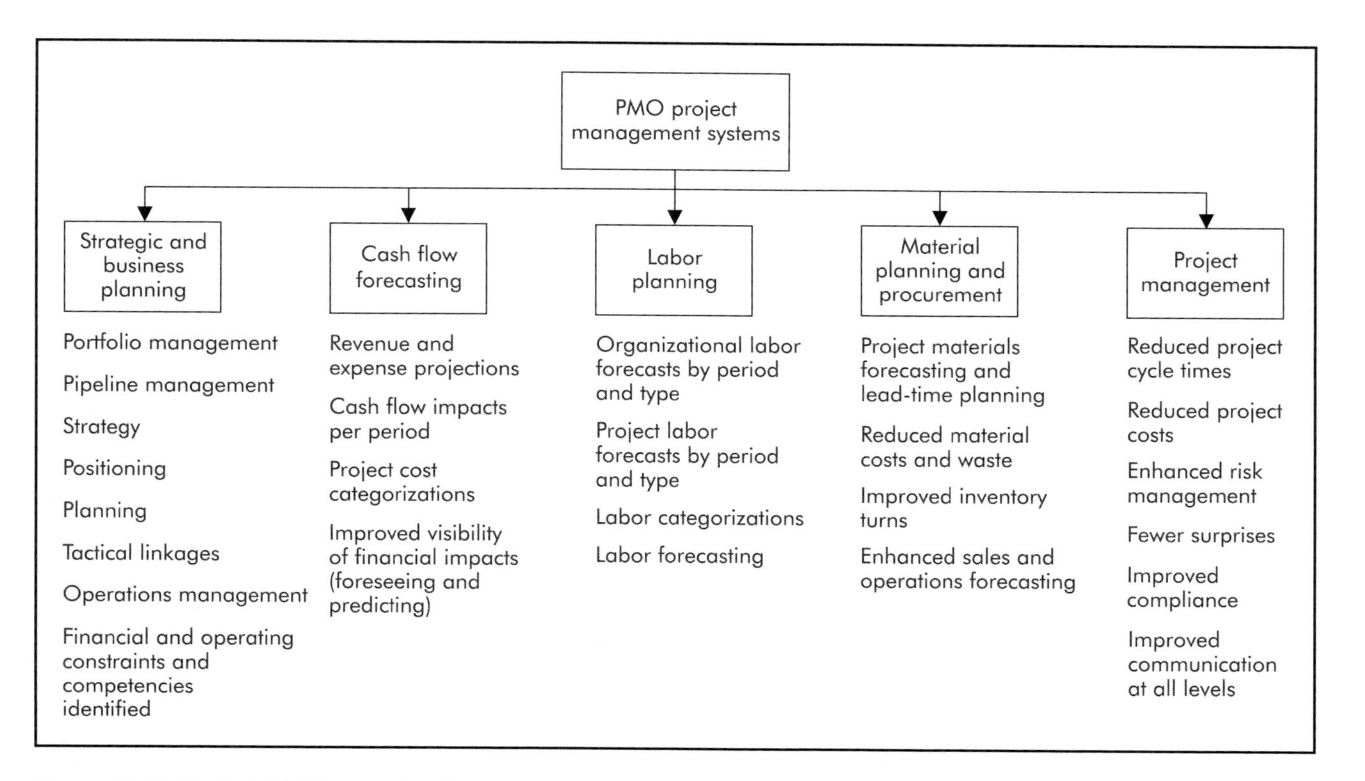

Figure 17-2. Typical PMO organizational impacts.

- oversees the pipeline management activities, and
- directs strategic projects to ensure compliance and alignment with senior management's organizational vision and mission.

Enterprise PMO

The enterprise PMO structure is feasible for organizations in which a more global approach is preferred, and one in which the PMO concepts are already firmly in place. The benefits of the enterprise PMO structure are more far-reaching and broadly cross-functional than the two structures previously mentioned.

- The enterprise PMO structure provides increased agility and flexibility within the organization in addressing critical business unit or strategic issues. It formally links the day-to-day project activities to the senior management staff through formal reporting and scorecarding techniques for increased visibility and control.
- Core competencies within the organization are enhanced because of an increased focus on the use of a structured project management methodology, which is followed by all employees at all levels within the organization. Expectations become universal as core business processes are optimized to provide maximum performance at both lower cost and lower risk levels.
- Trends within the portfolio that will have an adverse impact on the organization's ability to meet short- and longer-term objectives are quickly identified through the oversight of the PMO staff. As a result, corrective actions are implemented earlier where costs and risks are more manageable.
- The PMO staff constantly adjusts priorities within the pipeline using trade-off techniques based upon the actual performance of all projects versus a single project, thus providing better organizational balance and portfolio performance.
- Because of their proximity to all projects, the PMO staff is able to quickly and accurately collect project needs information and disseminate it to the appropriate levels for immediate

action. By so doing, critical or limited resources are deployed more efficiently and expeditiously. In addition, proximity to the projects provides enhanced governance and control at all levels, thus improving overall portfolio performance.

With the enterprise PMO structure, the PMO staff actively manages all organizational projects as a collective portfolio for optimum organizational alignment, resource utilization, and risk mitigation. The enterprise PMO staff, in essence, provides the direct linkage between the business strategies and the capabilities of the organizational elements chartered to execute them. Underperforming projects and project teams are quickly identified. Corrective actions are implemented by the PMO staff professionals to ensure that slippage within the pipeline, and the associated impact to the entire portfolio, is minimized. Organizational resources are directed and used for only the projects deemed most important in achieving organizational success, and controls are employed at every level to reduce organizational exposure and risk.

ROLES AND RESPONSIBILITIES

Whichever form of PMO selected, it is important to have clearly defined roles and responsibilities. Every business unit, manager, and employee must clearly understand his or her unique role in the achievement of the organization's mission. As Figure 17-3 illustrates, the typical levels of responsibility are segmented into four categories. Executive or senior management (steering committee) establishes the vision, mission, and business plans designed to guide the organization in meeting its business objectives. The PMO staff then creates and manages the portfolio and pipeline using project and portfolio scorecarding techniques to monitor and report performance. In addition, the PMO staff assumes responsibility for the leadership of each project. At the business unit level, the management staff assumes responsibility for development of the project plan, budget, and phase-gate performance goals, as well as support for its execution. At the employee level, projects are executed and handed off to continuing operations personnel for ongoing oversight and continuous improvement.

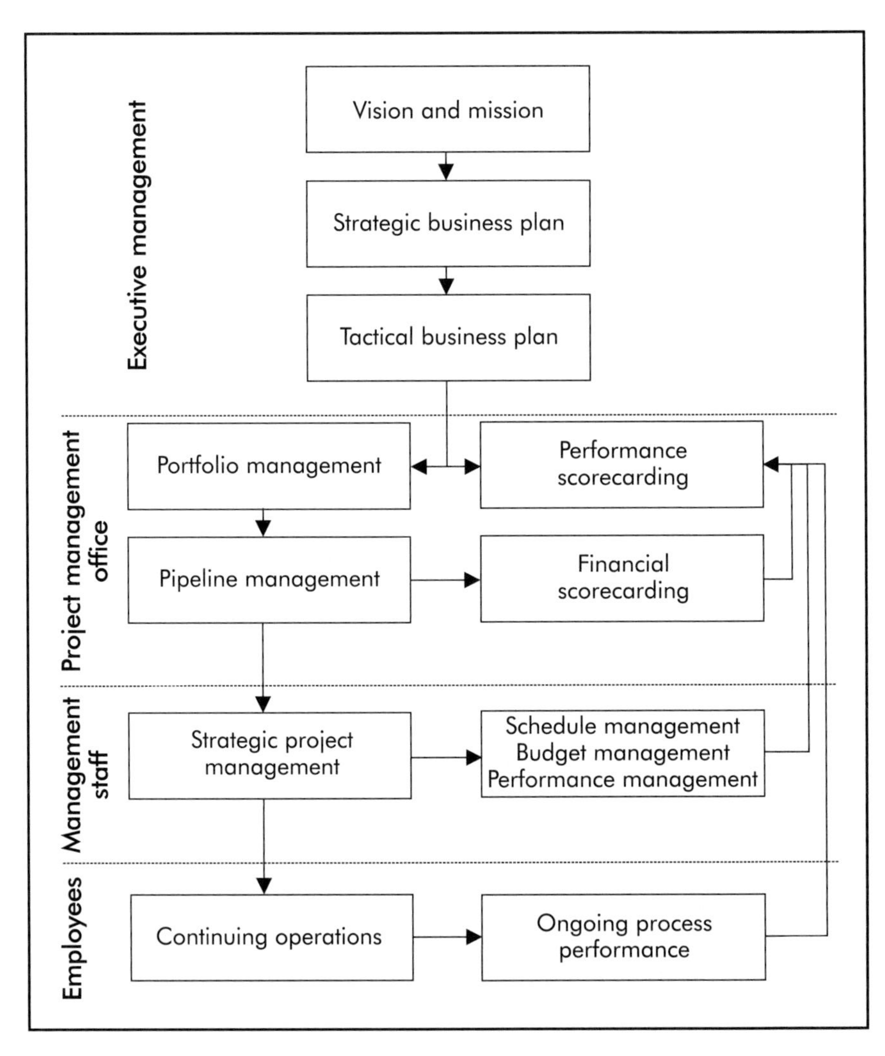

Figure 17-3. Roles and responsibilities.

IMPLEMENTATION

The approach used to implement the PMO requires a significant degree of planning, adequate resources, and sufficient time to complete successfully. The three phases, as illustrated in Figure 17-4, begin with a thorough assessment of the organization's needs and readiness. This is followed by the planning and structuring phase and, ultimately, a carefully controlled implementation phase.

Phase I: Assessment

The initial phase of the PMO launch process includes the chartering, funding, and executive acceptance of the proposed PMO structure, concepts, and methodologies. In this initial phase, the PMO project team also conducts a readiness assessment to isolate pockets of resistance that will be addressed as part of the project risk and contingency planning.

The first consideration during the assessment phase is whether a PMO is appropriate for the organization. Organizations that routinely plan and execute projects are ideal candidates for a PMO. Conversely, organizations that rarely plan and execute projects may be better served by either training a select number of internal project professionals to manage these "out-of-the-norm" assignments or contracting with a project management professional when the need arises.

The next step is to determine the most appropriate form of PMO for the organization: consultancy, strategic, or enterprise. In so doing, the project team is wise to consider the actual constraints and business culture existing within the organization, as well as the likely level of resistance to a PMO structure within the various levels of the organization. The experience levels of the organization's current project management professionals, efficacy of existing project management methods, policies, and control mechanisms, support systems, available funding, staffing levels and availability, and urgency in bringing the PMO to fruition are just a few of the many issues that must be considered. Before the PMO can be successfully implemented and managed, there must be agreement among all parties regarding its scope, management, and expectations. For example, is this project a singular event or is it intended to be an ongoing, disciplined business process?

The PMO launch team will be responsible for the initial implementation process. Thereafter, the responsibility to manage the PMO may be assigned to other permanent staff members. Or,

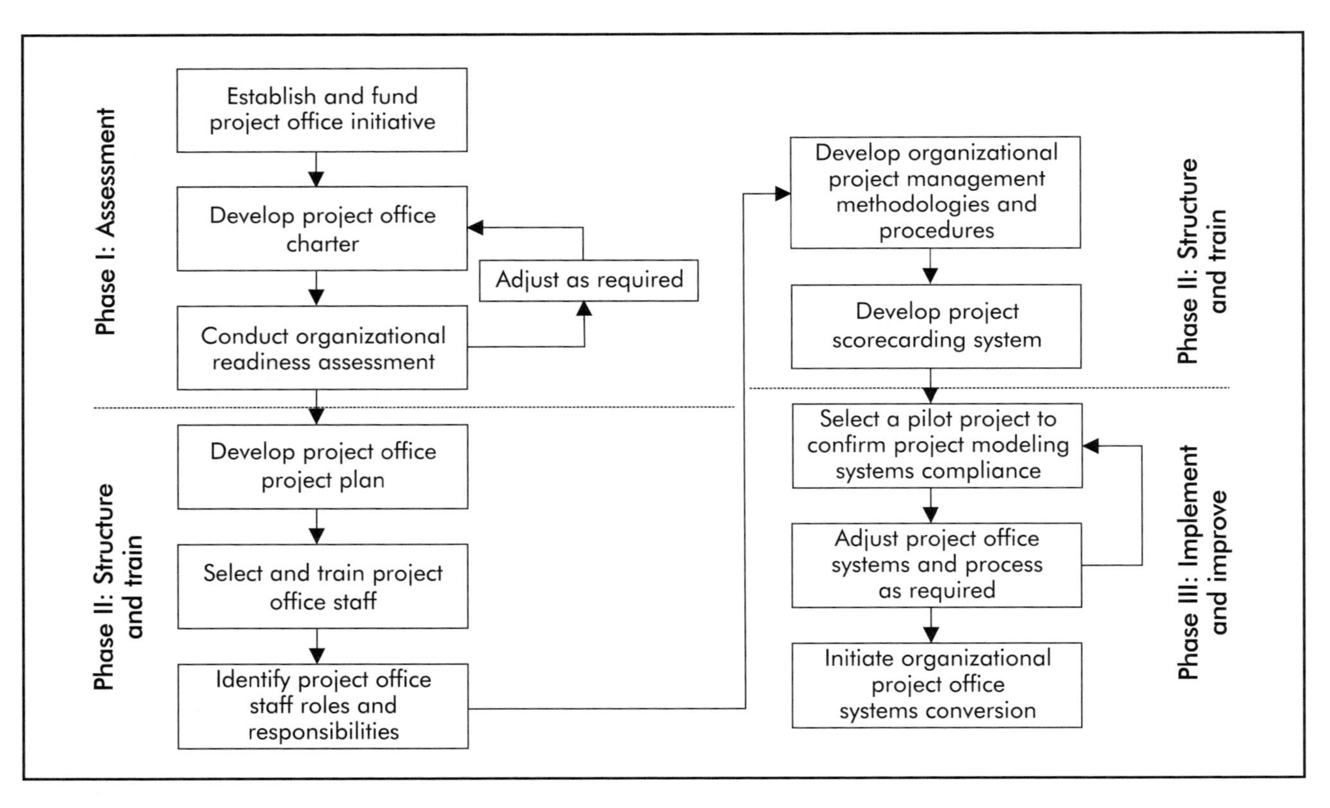

Figure 17-4. The PMO launch process.

conversely, the launch team may be assigned to manage the PMO they have created. Either way, one of the roles and responsibilities of the PMO staff will be to develop and implement a consistent set of project, organizational impact, risk management, phase-gate performance reporting, procurement, compliance tracking, budgeting, and corrective action processes, systems, and templates. All project managers will be required to use this same methodology consistently to ensure that all future projects are launched utilizing a common approach. Once approved, the PMO staff will be responsible for developing and implementing the training systems to build, test, and enhance the competencies of future project managers and project team members on those processes. Next, performance scorecarding systems will be developed for senior management, project managers, and project team members to monitor portfolio, project, and project team performance respectively. The focus of each of these processes and procedures is on proactive management and contingency planning to maximize the probability of success of each project launched, and ultimately the entire portfolio of projects. Each process or system developed for these purposes will employ quantifiable metrics, controls, and reporting methods to ensure consistently accurate results.

Other considerations, while routine, are equally as important in this early assessment phase. For example, what level of responsibility will be assigned to the PMO staff? What level of authority will be vested in the PMO staff? To who will the PMO staff report? What will the initial staffing levels be for the PMO organization? Are job descriptions, grades, and compensation levels developed? Where will the PMO be located? What support requirements will be necessary? Will the PMO budget be incorporated into the financial baselines of the portfolio or will a separate departmental budget be required? Just as required of any other project, early assessment and planning for these and numerous other factors will ensure a smooth launch of the PMO.

Once the form of PMO and associated staffing questions have been decided, the next step is to determine if the organization is ready for the change required of a PMO implementation. To accurately isolate the overall level of readiness of the organization, as well as individual areas of concern or resistance, the PMO project launch team conducts a readiness assessment using the analysis tool illustrated in Table 17-2. The scoring methodology used for the analysis is as follows:

- score of 1 indicates strong agreement,
- score of 2 indicates moderate agreement,
- score of 3 indicates neither agreement nor disagreement,
- score of 4 indicates moderate disagreement, and
- score of 5 indicates strong disagreement.

An aggregate score of 65 or greater indicates significant resistance to the PMO process. This level of resistance indicates a high level of risk in pursuing the project. The project team is wise to consider re-scoping the project when scores of this magnitude surface. For instance, it may make sense to scale down from a strategic or enterprise PMO structure to a consultancy PMO structure. The project launch team is also well served to look for common areas of concern across the organization. For example, if a common concern is whether the implementation timing is sufficient given the workloads of the existing staff members, or if there is insufficient staffing to effectively manage the project along with other day-to-day responsibilities, the launch team can factor these concerns into the schedule and budget planning for the project.

A moderate level of resistance to the PMO process is indicated by an aggregate score of between 31 and 64. This level of resistance (especially at the lower extremes) can usually be addressed through expanded soft selling of the PMO project with particular emphasis on those areas of common concern. It cannot, however, be ignored. Doing so usually results in a failed project implementation.

An aggregate score of 30 or less indicates an acceptance of or tolerance for the proposed adoption of the PMO methodology.

Phase II: Structure and Train

The structure and planning phase of the PMO launch project follows the processes described throughout this text, starting with

Table 17-2. Readiness assessment survey.

Statement	Yes	No
1. The purpose of and reasons for implementing a PMO are understood by all affected functions, functional managers, and employees.	☐	☐
2. In the eyes of the employees responsible for executing projects, adoption of a PMO is necessary to achieving organizational needs and performance requirements.	☐	☐
3. The appropriate personnel will be involved in or kept apprised of all aspects of the PMO planning and implementation.	☐	☐
4. Communication regarding the PMO process and management's objectives for it will be thorough and accurate.	☐	☐
5. I believe that the PMO implementation will have a low emotional and career impact on those responsible for its planning and implementation.	☐	☐
6. I believe there will be tangible rewards associated with the implementation of a PMO within this organization to me personally and to the organization as a whole.	☐	☐
7. I believe the adoption of a PMO methodology will support the vision and values of the entire organization.	☐	☐
8. I believe there is strong management commitment to the adoption of a PMO.		
9. I will actively support the adoption of a PMO.	☐	☐
10. I believe that the relationships between employees, project managers, functional managers, and department managers will be enhanced as a result of the implementation of a PMO methodology.	☐	☐
11. I believe the required resources to implement and maintain a PMO will be allocated and deployed as required by all levels of management.	☐	☐
12. I believe the organization will realize project performance gains and positive financial results from the implementation of a PMO methodology.	☐	☐

Table 17-2. (continued)

Statement	Yes	No
13. I believe that the appropriate amount of time, personnel, and capital will be provided for the implementation of the PMO processes.	☐	☐
14. I believe that the workload of the employees affected by the implementation of the PMO will be given due consideration by management.	☐	☐
15. I believe that my department will be positively impacted through the adoption of the PMO approach.	☐	☐
16. I believe employees involved in the implementation of the PMO will not be harshly treated for making an error during the implementation process.	☐	☐
17. I believe that my abilities and skills are sufficient to support the PMO approach both during and after its implementation.	☐	☐
18. I trust those responsible for the implementation of the PMO methodology in this organization.	☐	☐
19. I believe that the management staff responsible for implementing the PMO has the needed skills and position with which to successfully implement the initiative in all areas of the company.	☐	☐
20. I believe that management will follow through with the implementation of the PMO approach even if difficulties, cost overruns, or delays arise.	☐	☐

the strategic planning model and followed by the tactical planning model. Running in parallel is the development of the project budget and financial control systems, acquisition planning, quality and compliance planning, and risk management and contingency planning. As with all other projects, the PMO launch team is advised to remain detailed, conservative, and fact based throughout these phases. A heavy dose of reality goes along with the planning phase as organizational change projects require more time and contain more risk than almost any other type of project.

Training requirements for the PMO staff and the organization's other project management professionals are incorporated into the project launch schedule and budget. In so doing, consideration is given to the use of internal and/or external resources, availability of the needed training resources, certification requirements, costs, extended term training requirements, logistics, and training system requirements to name only a few of the possible cost and schedule drivers. The experienced project manager recognizes that skill set requirements are radically different for the various PMO structures, as are staffing levels and required expertise. It is therefore wise for the project launch team to match the required skill sets for the PMO structure selected to the training needs for all PMO and project personnel to ensure that all skills needed for a successful launch, as well as for the ongoing performance, are available.

As mentioned earlier, the PMO project launch team is responsible for developing the project management systems, methodologies, templates, standards, procedures, and policies that will be used by both the PMO staff and the organization's project managers. While structure is a requirement for any project management methodology, the tools developed by the PMO launch team must be flexible enough to be universally applicable to all projects within all disciplines, scalable for various size projects, comprehensive but not cumbersome, and must comply with all applicable internal and external regulatory, quality, and compliance requirements. The tools must be thoroughly documented and integrated into the existing organizational systems, processes, and procedures. In the preparation of these tools, the project team must be aware of possible conflicts with existing operational processes or procedures, employee job descriptions, business process definitions, financial controls, etc. Through critique and discussions with functional managers, operating level employees, and senior management, the launch team identifies these conflicts and resolves them before the project management tools are adopted.

Phase III: Implementation

The implementation phase of any project is critical. It is at this stage that costs and risks escalate, so detailed management of all aspects of the project is essential. The intent of this phase is to test all aspects of the selected PMO processes, systems, methodologies, and procedures, as well as the PMO staff's ability to manage them effectively and consistently. Typically, it is wise to select a singular project with which to test the efficacy and robustness of the PMO processes and methodologies. This is especially true for a consultancy type PMO. For the strategic type, a small portfolio of three to five projects is acceptable, whereas for an enterprise PMO, a comprehensive portfolio of projects is required to thoroughly test the systems and processes. In general, it is wise to be conservative. The experienced project manager selects a project or portfolio that provides broad utilization and testing of all PMO systems to ensure that all possible failure modes and risks are identified. In this way, final adjustments can be made before final rollout. The scope of the confirmation process must be consistent with the resources available, the intended and approved PMO project scope, and financial constraints of the organization.

Things will go wrong. Thus, the launch team members cannot become overly rigid in either their thinking or approach. Again, the purpose of the confirmation testing is to identify the weaknesses or deficiencies of the PMO systems considering the realities of the organization's capabilities, competencies, and capacities. So, a post-mortem is an integral part of the process. As mistakes or failures occur, they are thoroughly analyzed, corrected, and documented. Training materials, as well as PMO systems, are updated with the changes, and then tested once again to ensure the failure mode has been completely eliminated. The lessons-learned database becomes the repository for these changes along with the reasons behind them. It will become a living document thereafter, used and updated by the PMO staff on a regular basis and used to guide other projects and educate other project managers.

SUMMARY

The intent of a project management office is to provide consistency and direction throughout an organization in the planning and execution of its critical strategic projects. The benefits are numerous and certainly worthy of consideration when compared against the datum of cost and effort required for a successful

PMO implementation. The scope of the initial launch, however, must be considered carefully. It is always better to start small and grow the PMO processes over time. This will force problems to the surface so that they can be addressed more readily than is possible with a much broader, complex implementation project. Like any other project, taking the time to properly assess the business environment, isolate the drivers behind it, and effectively plan for the risks and likely failures will provide the framework for a successful launch. As with any other strategic project, failure is not an option.

18
Parting Thoughts

Project management can no longer be taken lightly, as it often was in the past. It requires a high level of commitment and effective oversight to be done successfully. So, before project managers embark on an assignment, they should take a minute to reflect upon their commitment and what must be done to make it successful.

If you are selected as a project manager, plan effectively. Control all possible variables. Select the right team members. Manage time and money with equal care. Make decisions based upon sound, quantitative techniques and good data. When problems occur, address them quickly and decisively. Manage the project as you would manage your own business.

Project management is not an easy assignment, but it can be personally and professionally rewarding if done correctly.

Bibliography

Anderson, Richard E. 1993. "HRD's Role in Concurrent Engineering." Training & Development, June.

Calvert, Gene. 1993. *Highwire Management*. San Francisco, CA: Jossey-Bass.

Chew, W. Bruce, Leonard-Barton, Dorothy, and Bohn, Roger E. 1991. "Beating Murphy's Law." Sloan Management Review.

Dubensky, Robert G. 1993. "Simultaneous Engineering." Automotive Engineering, June.

Langenbach, Cliff. 1993. "Using STEP: A Concept of Operations." CALS Journal, September.

Mowen, John C. 1993. *Judgement Calls*. New York: Simon & Shuster.

Nagel, Roger and Dove, Rick. 1991. *21st Century Manufacturing Enterprise Strategy*. Bethlehem, PA: Iacocca Institute, Lehigh University.

Parasuraman, A., Berry, Leonard L., and Zeithaml, Valerie A. 1992. "Understanding Customer Expectations of Service." Sloan Management Review.

Project Management Institute. 2004. *A Guide to the Project Management Body of Knowledge*, Third Edition. Newtown Square, PA: Project Management Institute, Inc.

Project Management Institute. 2005. *Q&As for the PMBOK Guide*, Third Edition. Newtown Square, PA: Project Management Institute, Inc.

Shechtman, Morris R. 1994. *Working Without a Net*. Englewood Cliffs, NJ: Prentice Hall.

Sheridan, John H. 1993. "Agile Manufacturing: Stepping Beyond Lean Production." Industry Week, April.

Termini, Michael J. 1997. *The New Manufacturing Engineer: Coming of Age in an Agile Environment*. Dearborn, MI: Society of Manufacturing Engineers.

Termini, Michael J. 1999. *Strategic Project Management: Tools and Techniques for Planning, Decision Making, and Implementation*. Dearborn, MI: Society of Manufacturing Engineers.

Termini, Michael J. 2007. *Walking the Talk: Moving into Leadership*. Dearborn, MI: Society of Manufacturing Engineers.

Walsh, James. 1996. *True Odds*. Santa Monica, CA: Merritt Publisher.

Waterman, Jr., Robert H. 1990. *Adhocracy: The Power to Change*. Knoxville, TN: Whittle Direct Books.

Wunnicke, Diane B. 1992. *Corporate Financial Risk Management*. New York: John Wiley and Sons.

Index

D

E

K

L

M

N

O

P

Q

R

S

T

U

V

W

Y

Z